Early Mādhyamika In India And China

EARLY MĀDHYAMIKA IN INDIA AND CHINA

by Richard H. Robinson

MADISON, MILWAUKEE, AND LONDON
1967

Published by
THE UNIVERSITY OF WISCONSIN PRESS
Madison, Milwaukee, and London

U.S.A.: Box 1379, Madison, Wisconsin 53701
U.K.: 26–28 Hallam Street, London, W. 1

Printed in the United States of America
by North Central Publishing Co., St. Paul, Minnesota

Library of Congress Catalog Card Number 66-22853

To Hannah

dīrgharātrasahayai sahacaryai

samarpitam

Acknowledgments

I wish to express my gratitude to Arthur Waley and David Friedman, who supervised and approved this work as a doctoral thesis in the University of London, and whose example and instruction have contributed materially to my formation as a scholar. Special thanks are due to my ***kalyāṇamitra***, Edward Conze, whose ***anubhāva*** has stimulated my Buddhological investigations. I record my warm appreciation to Mrs. Joan Theall and Mrs. Barbara Kennett for typing and re-typing the manuscript, and to Miss Catherine Huang for writing the Chinese characters that appear in this book. Mr. Douglas Daye prepared the Index, thus earning the author's gratitude and furnishing "a ford and bridge" (p. 213) for the intrepid.

Richard H. Robinson

Madison, Wisconsin
September, 1965

Contents

List of Abbreviations

Throughout this work the abbreviation 'T' is used to indicate the Taishō Shinshū Daizōkyō.

Correspondence	Ta-ch'eng-ta-i-chang, T, 1856
CST	Ch'u-san-tsang-chi-chi, T, 2145
GPWT	Great Perfection of Wisdom Treatise (Ta-chih-tu-lun), T, 1509
HKSC	Hsü-kao-seng-chuan, T, 2510
HMC	Hung-ming-chi, T, 2102
HT	Hundred Treatise (Pai-lun), T, 1569
KHMC	Kuang-hung-ming-chi, T, 2103
KSC	Kao-seng-chuan, T, 2509
LTSPC	Li-tai-san-pao-chi, T, 2034
MT	Middle Treatise (Chung-lun), T, 1564
TT	Twelve Topic Treatise (Shih-erh-men-lun), T, 1568

Early Mādhyamika In India And China

Chapter I
Questions And Method

It is customary to begin expositions of Mādhyamika with a statement that, despite the time that has elapsed since 1844 when Burnouf gave Europe its first notice of Candrakīrti's *Prasannapadā*,[1] and notwithstanding the admirable efforts of one's predecessors, we still do not really understand this school.[2] One then lists the philological and philosophical obstacles that have impeded the inquiry and pays tribute to the central position of Nāgārjuna in the history of Indian thought, perhaps adding that his homeopathic remedy for perplexity applies especially to the contemporary situation.

Having in a previous publication invoked Mañjuśrī in the time-honored way,[3] I do not need to do so again; and having in the meantime seen the publication of several more excellent works on the subject,[4] I can no longer say that we do not understand Mādhyamika, except perhaps in the way in which it can be said that, "We do not really understand Plato." However well the modern man reconstitutes the thought world of his ancient thinker, no matter how the investigator reasons and intuits his way into the intellectual skin of the other, the archaic mind abides like Schweitzer's Jesus in alien remoteness.

This book was conceived twelve years ago as two fairly concise introductory chapters in a history of the Chinese Sanlun School. At that time I supposed that it would be necessary merely to summarize existing works on early Indian Mādhyamika and to do a modest amount of further research on the Buddho-Taoists on whom Liebenthal had already published some of his studies.[5] But it soon became clear that the presuppositions, problems, and methods of previous writers were such that I could not extract from them what my purpose required. As Seng-chao says, "The different skein-ends were all tangled up" (Doc. 7.2; Doc. 8, n. 1), and there seemed little point for my purposes in attempting to gather up one by one the loose ends of the controversy between Stcherbatsky, La Vallée Poussin, and Schayer.[6]

None of these scholars began with the intention of describing Nāgārjuna's whole darśana and nothing else. La Vallée Poussin said in 1913: "Je compte publier un sommaire de la Madhyamakavṛtti, qui sera un exposé systématique du système de Nāgārjuna-Candrakīrti, . . ."[7] In 1915 he published the article "Madhyamaka" in Hastings'

Encyclopaedia of Religion and Ethics, which is too brief and not technical enough to qualify as a systematic exposition. Since then numerous brief summaries have appeared, many of them excellent in their way, but none of them going much beyond a summary-paraphrase of the texts with some judgments and opinions interspersed.[8] To do this sort of thing again would be ārambha-vaiyarthya.

Meanwhile, Stcherbatsky published his *Nirvāṇa* as a reply to La Vallée Poussin's *Nirvāṇa*, incidentally launching the Mādhyamika controversy as one strand in a complex problematic that comprised the nature of primitive versus later Buddhism, the nature of Nirvāṇa, how to translate Buddhist treatises, and the comparison of Buddhist philosophy with Kant and Hegel. He inaugurated the practice of dispersing important statements throughout footnotes, which subsequent translators of the *Prasannapadā* have followed with the result that there is a hiatus of induction between the footnotes and the articles and prefaces in which these translators have stated their generalizations.[9]

The dominant problem for the European discussants has remained the Mādhyamika ontology—whether this system acknowledges an absolute; whether it is Monism, Relativism, Nihilism, Scepticism, Absolutism; whether it has an ontology at all or confines itself to epistemology. On the whole, this concern has impeded progress towards a synoptic description of the Mādhyamika system, and has drawn attention away from problems such as the Mādhyamika logic on which Stcherbatsky and Schayer had made a good beginning.

To date there has been one full-scale book on Mādhyamika in a European language—T. R. V. Murti's *Central Philosophy of Buddhism*. To some degree, Murti shares the problematic of the Europeans—the nature of the absolute and whether the system applies to knowing, to being, or to both. Though fuller, more complete, and more sustained than the European works, Murti's book shares with Stcherbatsky a fascination with analogies between Kant and Mādhyamika. A comparison of Kantian and Nāgārjunian critical dialectic runs throughout the book and, despite the objections raised by May,[10] Murti's main point still seems quite cogent. This comparative theme, though, constitutes a digression from the description of Nāgārjuna's philosophy as it is in itself. Moreover, Murti's meta-philosophy is inextricable from the Kant-Hegel-Bradley side of his comparison, in addition to which much of his effort goes into expressing a distinctive and interesting personal philosophy. He manages to treat Mādhyamika as a contemporary philosophy, a remarkable tour de force, but in so doing he deprives it of its own archaic complexion.

My expectation that the Buddho-Taoists could be dealt with easily and briefly was disappointed as soon as I began to examine Liebenthal's work carefully and to probe the texts. I found that I disagreed with most of Liebenthal's philosophico-religious interpretations, as well as with his methods of translation. The appearance of *Jōron*

Kenkyū in 1955 assisted somewhat with philology; the articles both illuminated the subject and, by revealing some of the same methodological and interpretive problems as European work on Mādhyamika, rendered my emergent problematic more clear and more pressing.

My pivotal problem is the introduction of Mādhyamika to China by Kumārajīva between A.D. 401 and 409. My original theme, the influence in China of the first-introduced Indian systematic philosophy (other than Abhidharma), has survived the course of research and has been focused on a brief period which constitutes a turning point in Chinese intellectual history.

Among Chinese Buddhist intellectuals, the period for several decades before and after A.D. 400 was one of intense inquiry into philosophical problems. At this time there was already a large quantity of Buddhist scriptures in Chinese translation, and throughout the period this stock was increased both in quantity and in variety.[11] A high point of this age is Kumārajīva's translation of four Mādhyamika treatises between A.D. 401 and 409. Buddhist thinkers then saw Mahāyāna systematic philosophy for the first time, and Kumārajīva's students read these texts with excitement and a sense of discovery. As one of them said: "How fortunate it is that this land of China has suddenly had Mount Gṛdhrakūṭa moved to it to be its chief mountain and that biased minds in outlying areas receive the flowing light of its surplus of kindness" (Doc. 5.3).

Some information about the initial impact of Mādhyamika in China is afforded by the surviving essays, prefaces, letters, obituaries, and commentaries written by Kumārajīva's disciples and associates. Further fragments of their writings and much information about the history of this school are provided by the sixth-century biographies and catalogues. The Chinese Saṅgha preserved these documents because it valued them as religion and philosophy, which fact gives them a claim to be studied for their own intrinsic merit. But as evidence from a critical period in the introduction of Indian ideas into China they illuminate a number of questions that are currently topical in the field of intellectual history. Among these questions are: To what degree and in what way did fifth-century Chinese Buddhists understand the Mādhyamika teaching that Kumārajīva introduced? Did they accept it as a philosophical system or as a mystical teaching? In what respects was the Buddhism of Kumārajīva's disciples Indian, and in what respects was it Chinese?[12]

The first question concerns the transmission of a system of thought from one culture to another. It is currently topical because of the intrusion of Western culture into non-Western areas. In China's case, the introduction of Buddhism is the closest precedent. As Demiéville says:

In recapitulating some traits of that first penetration of Indian influence into the Chinese philosophical tradition, one cannot help noting certain coincidences with

China's reactions since its first contacts with European civilization. In one case as in the other, the essential fact is that that tradition maintained itself and that there was no going under comparable to that of our paganism under the impact of Christianity, or in India to that of Buddhism since the Muslim invasions conjoined with the resurgence of Brahmanism or Hinduism.... Buddhism required an incubation period of two or three centuries before it finally made its way into literate circles and made its first mark on the philosophical tradition; and still, as we have seen, the attention of Chinese philosophers, by an instinctive choice, only focused on certain Buddhist doctrines which awoke an echo in their own problematic. In the contemporary period, when Chinese was finally confronted with Occidental philosophy in the strict sense, a no less severe selection kept only eclectic and fragmentary aspects....The rest of our philosophy has exercised practically no influence in China, just as the latter did not assimilate all in Buddhism that did not respond to Chinese harmonics ("Pénétration," p. 36).

It is evident that the third question is involved to a great degree in the first; the study of cultural transmissions includes the attempt to isolate factors in the result which have their parentage in the invaded culture from those whose parentage is in the invader. In the present state of our knowledge about the penetration of Buddhism into Chinese civilization, all conclusions are valuable more as hypotheses for further investigation than as factual judgments. The several models that have been posited to describe the interaction of Buddhism and the Chinese tradition thus serve as orientation to studies such as the present one, but are not completely confirmed or refuted by them.

The dominant model for some time has been that offered by Hu Shih, himself a major figure in the intellectual Westernization of modern China:

But great waves of religious fanaticism have been the usual historical occasions of large-scale cultural borrowing. During such periods of powerful mass conversions to a new religion, people easily lose their sense of calm evaluation and embrace everything that may accompany the new faith. Sometimes such conversion requires a long period of slow penetration; sometimes it requires great leaders of magnetic force; but when it becomes a mass movement of vast numbers, the momentum is so great that kings and queens, emperors and empresses, princes and princesses, the noble and the lowly, are swept along with it, and the new faith, together with all its vast paraphernalia, good or bad, useful or useless, desirable or undesirable, digested or indigestible, is accepted in toto with eagerness and enthusiasm.... With the return of calm judgment, and, what is more important, with the natural re-assertion of the inertia and resistance of the native culture, the borrowed culture necessarily undergoes all forms of change, modification, adaptation, domestication and elimination.... But Buddhism could not so easily be uprooted by persecution. For two thousand years it continued to be the greatest religion of China, continuing to Indianize Chinese life, thought, and institutions. It constituted the only important source of China's cultural borrowing prior to her contact with the European civilization. It continued to flourish in China, and, through China, in Korea and Japan, even long after it had disappeared in its mother country, India. It continued to Indianize China long after it had ceased to be a vital and powerful religion in China. Indeed, as we now begin to understand, Indianization became more powerful and effective throughout those centuries when

Chinese thinkers began to rejoice that they had killed Buddhism or at least made it innocuous. Buddhism is dead in China—long live Buddhism! ("The Indianization of China," pp. 221–23).

This is the organic model. A culture is an organism that ingests extraneous materials, digests some, and eliminates others. The structure is that of the organism and the ingested materials are first destructured and then, being incorporated into the organism, are restructured. This model implies a holistic view of societies such as underlies Hegel's, Spengler's, and Toynbee's theories of history.

Another model has been proposed by Walter Liebenthal: "Under the impact of Indian Buddhism they were able to create a new religion the theoretical aspect of which was fundamentally Chinese" ("Hui-yüan," p. 244b). This is the model of stimulus diffusion. Liebenthal presents it parenthetically in the course of explaining his version of the organic model, and does not develop it. Without excluding its claim to consideration, I doubt that stimulus diffusion really describes what took place in the monastic schools of China, though it probably operated in the formation of popular cults. In the verified cases, such as Sequoiah's Cherokee script, stimulus diffusion seems to have operated when the stimulant system was known in a very external and imperfect way. Still, the possibility remains to be considered in any case under examination.

Another model has been suggested by Arthur Link: "To comprehend Chinese Buddhism we must understand it not just as Indian Buddhism in China but rather as a cultural amalgam, a synthesis of Indian thought and Sinic concepts and ideals" ("Daw-an," p. 1b). This simile of the amalgam has several advantages. It avoids the thesis that Indic and Sinic each retain their intrinsic individuality forever. It emphasizes the synthetic nature of the process, while likening the affinity of imported features for domestic ones to the affinity of chemicals for one another, thus preserving the primacy of selection and rejection as factors in cultural assimilation.

I make a number of assumptions about cultural transmissions in general which delimit my study of the transmission of Mādhyamika ideas. In the first place, I assume that no smallest and no largest unit of culture need be posited, that neither a holistic view of culture nor an atomistic conception of the individual's world-view is necessary to the inquiry. Consistency and homogeneity within the cultural behavior of individuals and groups may of course be discovered, but should not be presupposed.

Secondly, the degree and manner in which different individuals participate in one culture differ greatly. From the individual point of view, any cultural behavior must be learned in order to be inherited, and this learning process proceeds gradually, piecemeal, and imperfectly, whether one is learning an ancient property of one's own society or a recent import from abroad. Usually any one individual masters only part of a tradition, and forgets parts that he has learned and no longer uses. Generally, only a part of a historic tradition is in vogue at any time. Consequently, it is dangerous to predict a priori that anyone will actually possess any universal trait that has been posited for his culture. As Sapir says:

Anthropology has allowed itself to be victimized by a convenient but dangerous metaphor. This metaphor is always persuading us that culture is a neatly packed up assemblage of forms of behavior handed over piecemeal, but without serious breakage, to the passively inquiring child. I have come to feel that it is precisely the supposed "givenness" of culture that is the most serious obstacle to our real understanding of the nature of culture and cultural change. . . . As soon as we set ourselves at the vantage point of the culture-acquiring child, . . . everything changes. Culture is then not something given but something to be gradually and gropingly discovered (*Culture, Language and Personality*, pp. 204–5).

Thirdly, the persisting biases of a cultural community are transmitted chiefly through its institutions of learning. People usually learn first and most from immediate associates and approach the remote through the interpretation of familiar spokesmen. The infants who grew up to be Chinese dharma-masters were born ignorant of everything Chinese or Indian. They acquired native and imported ways alike by a process of gradual and groping discovery, conditioned by their instruction in the family, by their tutors, and in the Saṅgha. The distinctive biases of certain kinds of families and tutors, and of different monastic schools, are sometimes discoverable in the biographies of eminent monks. To the extent that we understand these factors, we understand perhaps the major circumstances that promoted or inhibited assimilation of novel ideas and practices.

Though it is not an aim of this study to investigate the role of education in the history of Chinese Buddhism, the subject is both intrinsically interesting and pertinent to the manner in which the Indian Buddhist philosophy was received in China. The story of the education of Tao-an (A.D. 312–85), the great master who prepared the way and straightened the path for Kumārajīva, is typical of most monks of the period whose lives have been recorded:

His family for generations has been eminent literati. At an early age he lost the shelter and shade [of family and fortune] and was reared by his elder maternal cousin of the K'ung family. When he was seven years old he could read books; by twice looking at them he could recite them by heart and the country folk and neighbors sighed and thought him unusual.

When he turned twelve he went forth from his family [to become a Buddhist monk] (*pravrajita*). He was a genius, quick in understanding, yet in figure and feature he was extremely vulgar, and was not esteemed by his teacher. Forced to work as a menial in the fields and huts for three years, he came forward to labor with diligence, and never flushed in resentment. Sincere by nature, vigorous in

advance (*vīrya*), in his observance of abstention precepts there was nothing lacking.

After several years he began to beg the scriptures from his teacher. His teacher gave him the *Sūtra on the Discrimination of Meaning (pien-i-ching)* in one chapter of approximately five thousand words. An reverently carried the *sūtra* with him when he entered the fields and utilized his rest period for reading. At sunset he returned and gave the *sūtra* back to his teacher and once more begged for another. His teacher said, "You still haven't read the *sūtra* of yesterday and again you beg for one, eh?" He replied, "I have already memorized it." Although his teacher thought this odd and did not believe it, he gave him the *Ch'eng-chü kuang-ming ching*[13] in one chapter of less than ten thousand words. He carried it with him as he did on the first occasion, and at sundown again returned it to his teacher. When his teacher, holding the *sūtra*, made him repeat it, he did not miss a single word! Vastly astonished, his teacher exclaimed and marveled at him. Afterwards he had him receive all the prohibitions [entailed by full ordination], and permitted his traveling for study (Link, "Shih Tao-an," pp. 4–7).

Here is a typical pattern. The boy from a gentry family which has fallen on hard times studies the secular classics in his childhood, and then enters the Saṅgha in his teens. There is discrimination in the treatment of novices, and while those who find favor with the master pursue their studies, the others work as laborers on the monastic estates. It was evidently remarkable for Tao-an to have received any sort of Buddhist education at all after he had been classed as a laborer. There is also the fact that scriptures were carefully guarded by the dharma-master and issued on brief loan and rather unforthcomingly to students. Then it appears that memorization of the text was a recognized goal of study. It is also significant that one of the texts lent to Tao-an is a brief Śūnyavādin sūtra, comparable to the *Anavatapta-nāgarāja-paripṛcchā* (T 635), the *Vimalakīrti-nirdeśa* (T 475), and to the *Vajracchedikā* (T 235), which was not yet known in China. These texts were quite commonly given to teen-age novices as a sort of primer.[14] Lastly, a novice could not travel as he pleased, but must first receive full ordination and the permission of his master.

Perhaps the history of Chinese Buddhism would have been quite different if the Saṅgha had gone into the business of providing elementary education for the children of the laity and had cut at the roots of the secular tradition in the schools. The spokesmen for imported novelties and for domestic discoveries share the problem of teaching the new things to their contemporaries, and both are hindered and helped by what their hearers have learned already and by the institutions through which they communicate their novelties. Their problems differ chiefly in that people usually regard novelty from abroad otherwise than novelty discovered at home. Sometimes they are more receptive to one, and sometimes to another. According to the evidence, the intellectual pathfinders of China in the fourth and fifth centuries were very receptive to both, and they both assimilated and invented. However, their minds were preconditioned by early education in the literature of a highly conservative and mundane school which failed to prepare them for systematic thinking about abstract subjects.

Selection and rejection, operating in individual and collective choices, are major factors in modifying traditions. This affects both native and imported elements. For Chinese Buddhist intellectuals in the period under consideration, some of these factors can be identified, but it is not possible to establish a determinist explanation of the observable patterns of selection and rejection. The biographies are not informative enough, and they are written by men who were themselves the product of the educational system of the times, with the characteristic biases and limitations. However, even if we knew everything, we could not wholly reduce the lives and thoughts of these men to typological generalities. We must allow for the qualitative uniqueness, and value the intrinsic worth of the outstanding men whose biographies happen to have been recorded.

The second question to be considered—the relation between the mystical and the rational aspects of early Chinese Mādhyamika—is topical now for many reasons: because the general problem is perennial in Western philosophy, because it bears on the controversial question of the connection between philosophy and religion, and because Oriental philosophies have been called to witness in the modern dispute between the advocates of intuition and those of the intellect.[15]

D. T. Suzuki presents the viewpoint of anti-rational intuitionalism:

> Philosophers will naturally try to solve these questions in some logically methodical manner worthy of their profession and may pronounce them absurd because they do not yield to intellectual treatment. Or, they might say that they would have to write a book to give the subject an intelligent solution, if there were any. But the *prajñā* method is different. If the demand is to see the flower before it blooms, *prajñā* will respond without a moment of delay, saying, "What a beautiful flower it is!" If it is about God prior to the creation of the world, *prajñā* will, as it were, violently shake you by taking hold of your collar and perhaps remark, "This stupid, good-for-nothing fellow!" . . . *Prajñā*-intuition settled such grave questions instantly, while philosophers or dialecticians spend hours, nay, years, searching for "objective evidence" or "experimental demonstration" . . . . Paradoxical statements are therefore characteristic of *prajñā*-intuition. As it transcends *vijñāna* or logic it does not mind contradicting itself; it knows that a contradiction is the outcome of differentiation, which is the work of *vijñāna* ("Reason and Intuition," pp. 22, 24).

Bertrand Russell has stated the opposite viewpoint:

> The logic of mysticism shows, as is natural, the defects which are inherent in anything malicious. The impulse to logic, not felt while the mystic mood is dominant, reasserts itself as the mood fades, but with a desire to retain the vanishing insight, or at least to prove that it *was* insight, and that what seems to contradict it is illusion. The logic which thus arises is not quite disinterested or candid, and is inspired by a certain hatred of the daily world to which it is to be applied (*Mysticism and Logic*, p. 26).

Both Russell and Suzuki hold that there is something peculiar about the logic of mysticism. Rudolph Otto agrees, and has stated his viewpoint in precise and explicit terms:

> This results in the peculiar logic of mysticism, which discounts the two fundamental laws of natural logic: the law of Contradiction, and of the Excluded Third. As non-Euclidian geometry sets aside the axiom of parallels so mystical logic disregards these two axioms; and thence the "coincidentia oppositorum," the "identity of opposites" and the "dialectic conceptions" arise (*Mysticism East and West*, p. 45).

The thesis that there is a necessary antagonism between reason and mystical intuition is repudiated by Cuthbert Butler:

> Sometimes it is said that a vigorous play of the intellect is an impediment to mystical contemplation. Yet who has been a greater intellectualist than Augustine, with his keen joy in philosophical speculation, and his ever-flowing output of intellectual writing, that to this day has influenced Western theological thought as none other since St. Paul?... Augustine is for me the Prince of Mystics, uniting in himself, in a manner I do not find in any other, the two elements of mystical experience, viz. the most penetrating intellectual vision into things divine, and a love of God that was a consuming passion. He shines as a sun in the firmament, shedding forth at once light and heat in the lustre of his intellect and the warmth of his religious emotion (*Western Mysticism*, pp. 24, 25).

Butler also delimited a problem with reference to Christian mysticism which incidentally points the way for inquiries into the mystical doctrines of China and India:

> What is needed is a more objective presentation of what the mystics themselves thought about their mysticism, to be determined by a systematic study and formulation of the ideas of a number of the principal mystics, such as is here attempted in the case of three of them. This seems to be the necessary basis for any scientific treatment of the subject (*Western Mysticism*, p. viii).

Otto's *Mysticism East and West* is in many ways a model application of such principles as Butler's to the study of an Indian mystical writer (Śaṅkara). However, Otto presupposes an opposition between the rational and the mystical which reflects the situation in twentieth-century Protestant theology rather than being deduced from the evidence that he presents. As he says elsewhere:

> Essentially Mysticism is the stressing to a very high degree, indeed the overstressing, of the non-rational or supra-rational elements in religion; and it is only intelligible when so understood. The various phases and factors of the non-rational may receive varying emphasis, and the type of Mysticism will differ according as some or others fall into the background.... As a provisional definition of Mysticism I would suggest that, while sharing the nature of religion, it shows a preponderance of its non-rational elements and an overstressing of them in respect to the 'overabounding' aspect of the 'numen' (*Idea of the Holy*, pp. 22 and 88, n. 1).

Otto defines the rational in a rather special way:

> Now all these attributes constitute clear and definite *concepts*: they can be grasped by the intellect; they can be analysed by thought; they even admit to definition. An object that can thus be thought conceptually may be termed *rational*. The nature of deity described in the attributes above mentioned is, then, a rational nature; and a religion which recognizes and maintains such a view of God is in so far a 'rational' religion (*Idea of the Holy*, p. 1).

I prefer not to postulate either compatibility or incompatibility between rational thought and mystical ideas. I assign the relation between the two terms to the probandum and so cannot specify it as a presupposition without incurring the error of circularity. It is not necessary to define the boundaries of the rational and the mystical a priori, but it is essential to designate some commonly acknowledged characteristics of the two terms.

Rational discourse is logical, that is, it is a field to which the science of logic refers. The logician can abstract from it groups of structures that participate in an axiomized or axiomizable deductive system. A logical structure is essentially mathematical, though it may have linguistic exponents. The exact relation between logical structures and linguistic exponents is still in dispute. As Robert E. Luce says:

> The question whether in addition to sentences there exist *propositions* in the sense of non-linguistic abstract objects such that each of them may be expressed by a sentence of which it then constitutes the meaning, and the analogous question concerning predicates and functions are among the most difficult and currently most controverted questions in the theory of logic. . . . Fortunately, for the immediate purposes of the text these questions need not be decided (Hilbert and Ackermann, *Mathematical Logic*, editor's note, p. 165, n. 1).

Modern formal logic, unlike Hegelian dialectic and traditional logic, is not concerned with the laws of thought or the laws of nature. Whether or not some mental events exhibit logical patterns, no consistent correlation between logical forms and mental events has been demonstrated, and thus logical considerations do not entail psychological ones. As Jan Lukasiewicz says:

> It is not true, however, that logic is the science of the laws of thought. It is not the object of logic to investigate how we are thinking actually or how we ought to think. . . . But the laws of logic do not concern your thoughts in a greater degree than do those of mathematics. What is called 'psychologism' in logic is a mark of the decay of logic in modern philosophy (*Aristotle's Syllogistic*, pp. 12–13).

In adopting Lukasiewicz's view, I suspend judgment on the thesis that the structure of right thought and the structure of reality are identical. In the modern logician's use of 'logic,' it is senseless to talk about a 'logic of nature,' except in the sense that the language of a nature poet might be called the 'language of nature,' that is, language which describes certain aspects of nature. Since the Mādhyamika position is that symbol systems do not actually and completely 'fit' any objective counterpart, any definition of logic that prejudged the rationality of the Mādhyamikas on the basis of whether or not they accept any particular thesis about the relation between fact and symbol would be worthless.

As Russell's statement (*Mysticism and Logic*, p. 26) takes for granted, "the logic of mysticism" means the logic of discourse about mysticism or discourse by mystics. The subject is contemplative experience, or other subjects as seen in the light of contemplative illumination. "The impulse to logic, not felt while the mystic mood is dominant, reasserts itself as the mood fades." This is the domain of pṛṣṭha-labdha-jñāna—after-obtained knowledge—(see La Vallée Poussin, *Siddhi*, and *Kośa*, references listed in indices), or pratyavekṣaṇā-jñāna (see Schayer, *Kapitel*, p. 70, n. 50). Of course, it cannot be assumed that everyone who writes about mystical ideas writes with pṛṣṭha-labdha-jñāna.

The frequent assertions in mystical literature notwithstanding, it cannot be granted a priori that the mystical domain is any less describable or analyzable than any other. Perhaps mystical experience can be described meaningfully in and from autobiographical accounts of great detail and precision. However, no such records are available for any of the Mādhyamikas to be discussed in the following pages. The documents refer now and then to trance-experience in general or to trance-experience as part of the empirical datum for discourse about the nature of being. Thus inquiry is limited to the field of mystical discourse. The problem is not whether rational thought characterizes trance-experience, but whether, as Otto asserts, there is a peculiar logic of mystical discourse that contradicts or abrogates the logic of rational discourse.

To return to the first question—how the Mādhyamika teaching was understood by the first Chinese who studied it—we will consider two significant components of the teaching, namely its modes of formal reasoning, and its mystical ideas. Taken together, these two are the terms of the second question—the relation between the rational and the mystical aspects. Taken separately, each of these components is a good index of assimilation, since both are complex and hence hard to assimilate and easy to identify.

There are many degrees of assimilation of a tradition, ranging from passive acquaintance and inert recognition to creative participation. On the concrete level, assimilating a system of thought means getting to know its literature, reading it occasionally, perhaps hearing or even giving lectures on it. This implies recognition but not acceptance. Quotations from the literature indicate influence of this degree, though absence of quotations does not mean absence of influence.

However, quotation does not prove that the quoter read the literary source, as he may have heard or seen the quotation through an intermediary. Furthermore, quotation only shows that the quoter is familiar with the quotation, and does not mean that he knew the rest of the work from which it is taken. Equally, non-quotation does not mean that the author did not know a text.

The piecemeal adoption of ideas is a somewhat deeper kind of assimilation than mere acquaintance, since it means partial acceptance. This sort of assimilation can often be inferred from terminology, but use of a term does not necessarily indicate acceptance of an idea, nor need a given term be used when a given idea is accepted. Patterns of relation are sometimes a good clue to ideas, but they too are not dependable indicators of provenance. By and large, the more complex an idea, the easier it is to identify, and the harder it is to assimilate.

Structural imitation is a yet deeper kind of assimilation, since it means partial acceptance of the system rather than merely of components. Stimulus diffusion of writing systems, political institutions, and religious ideas comes under this heading. It means either imperfect understanding of the model, or incomplete acceptance.

Exclusion of incompatible systems and correct manipulation of a system of ideas jointly constitute complete acceptance. This sort of assimilation is readily identified by a structural analysis. But 'incompatible' cannot be defined decisively in some borderline cases. Many people are able to think simultaneously in several idioms, and fail to see incompatibilities that the analyst claims to see. Incompatibility is in fact a term of the descriptive system and not of the object domain.

The final stage of assimilation is when the system has been critically assessed and transcended. In this, unlike the case of structural imitation, deviation from the model means not imperfect understanding or acceptance, but rather an understanding that sees its object too clearly to accept it as given. This is the operation of selection and rejection on the highest level.

One of the central topics in the Mādhyamika system is the relation between language and fact. This entails a theory of meaning and, as the exposition will show in due course, there is a considerable body of documents on Mādhyamika theories of language and meaning. Both on the philological and the philosophical level, both in methodology and in the content of the object-domain, this study is concerned with questions of language. Thus the following observations about language and meaning will be echoed in various ways throughout subsequent chapters.

The thoughts of men who lived fifteen centuries ago are imperceptible and only partially inferable. The only evidence for them is strings of written symbols representing a dead language for which only a limited corpus of texts now exists. This means that the writer's mood, his irony and humor, the triteness or novelty of his expressions, cannot be known with certainty, because the sample is defective. Not only are the lineaments of his literary mask discernible imperfectly, but the mental events that accompanied the composition of the text are even more inscrutable.

It cannot be assumed that the structure of language corresponds to the structure of thought,[16] or that all thoughts can be represented by symbols, or that language is the only kind of symbol-system. For example, the Chinese Buddhist of around A.D. 400 gave symbolic expression to his religion not only in his writings, but in the chant and gesture of his liturgy, in sculpture and painting, in architecture, and in the several disciplinary codes which monastics and laity observed. These considerations limit the scope of the inquiry to what can be inferred from literary materials. The domain of reference is not the mental life of Indian or Chinese Mādhyamikas, but a sample of their verbal behavior preserved in written artifacts. What these texts mean is a primary question, but it cannot be answered in terms of mentalist "meaning."

Meaning is inferred rather than perceived, and the object of inference for the meaning of a piece of language is the set of collocations in which it occurs.[17] This set is enumerable only for a limited text, and so the meaning of a piece of language can only be ascertained for a limited corpus, and predictions from this range of material to another collocation are to be worked out as a problem in probabilities. The postulate that words have an isolate true meaning is thus unnecessary to this inquiry.

Meaning is a function of different levels of constituents in a stretch of utterance or script, and meanings on one level are not strictly predictable from the inferred usual meanings of the components.[18] Thus meaning is not inherent in words as opposed to other units of language.[19] No smallest and no largest meaningful unit need be posited; neither a holistic nor an atomistic unit of linguistic meaning is necessary to inquiry into the meaning of texts. The complete single text is a given piece for analysis, but it is not postulated that a whole text is a whole and discrete unit in the descriptive system resulting from the analysis.[20]

Mādhyamika texts, both Indian and Chinese, exhibit a sizable technical vocabulary. A technical term is one that is specialized to an office in the system that the writer sets up to describe his object-domain. The office of the term is identified informally by the average reader and formally by the systematic reader through collocation of structures that belong to the system. The question whether a Chinese term conveys the technical meaning of its Indic equivalent depends on whether the translation represents the same formal system as the original, and on whether the reader of the Chinese understands the structures and system. If these two conditions are fulfilled, then the technical meaning of the term is understood, and whatever the term may or may not mean in Chinese texts from an earlier period is an extraneous question. However, the other meanings of a term may mislead the reader and prevent him from identifying its technical sense in the restricted context.[21]

There is not yet an adequate lexicon of the Buddho-Taoist vocabulary, which possesses a rich stock of formations that are unique to it. The work of such scholars as Demiéville, Liebenthal, Link, and Wright has furnished invaluable aids to the students of these texts, but it is still impossible to understand any piece of this style fully without doing a great deal of lexicography for oneself. This being the case, the theory of meaning sketched above finds numerous applications in the interpretation of the documents on which this study is based.

The primary operation for abstracting definitions is the collocation of passages. This, of course, is the technique that lexicographers have always used, but words are not the only meaningful units, and lexical meaning is not the only relevant kind of meaning. The technique of collocation applies equally to words, grammatical structures, rhetorical figures, figures of syntax, logical structures, citations from other texts, and abstract philosophical relations between terms. To understand this kind of text, a knowledge of lexical meaning alone does not suffice.

There are two kinds of definition, both necessary to the elucidation of Buddhist texts, whether Indian or Chinese. The first is the descriptive, which assembles its collocations from within a single text and seeks to extract a definition that is qualified in its consistency by nothing except the self-consistency of the author within that one text. This method works very well for fairly long and fairly repetitious texts, but is not too productive for texts that are short or that abound in singly-occurrent items. The definitions of certain key terms from the *Chao-lun* (T 1858), in chapter 6, illustrate this method of definition.

The second mode of definition is the comparative, either synchronic between contemporary texts by one or several authors, or diachronic between texts of different periods by one or any number of authors. As Régamey says:

There exist still other methods capable of guiding us on this difficult ground. A set of procedures that guarantee the maximum probability for correct understanding of ancient technical terms and formulas has been proposed by Maryla Falk in a study that is unfortunately too little known [*Il mito psicologico nell' India antica*, Rome: Dott. Giovanii Bardi, 1939]. She herself has demonstrated the efficacy of these methods in important monographs. While rejecting literal or etymological interpretations, she considers indispensable the monographic study of each technical term throughout its whole history where the maximum number of contexts permit one to delimit its precise value and to observe and note the fluctuations of its meanings. This is in fact the development of the method of the school of

> Leningrad, but furnished with an essential corrective: that of constantly taking into consideration the evolution of meaning in time. The function that a term acquired several centuries later can be very useful for determining its value in an ancient period, but only if we consider this ancient form as a previous evolutionary stage, not as identical with that which it has become. The interpretations obtained by this method are "constructs" based on extrapolations and comparisons; they rest, if you wish, on a constant speculation, but the incessant confrontation of each term with its previous and subsequent meanings as well as with those that it has at the same time "alongside," in other systems, provides guarantees of adequate interpretation that are infinitely greater than translation based exclusively on knowledge of grammar and etymological dictionaries ("Bouddhisme Primitive," p. 47).

This method has been utilized with manifest success by Johnston in his *Early Sāṁkhya*, Nagao in his "Saṁvṛtti," and Demiéville in, among other places, his study of 'li' in "Pénétration," pp. 28–31. To the corrective proviso that Régamey mentions, however, must be added another: that of plotting the meaning of each term within one text and then one system before comparing it with the meanings that it has in other systems before, after, and alongside. This is a counsel of perfection, no doubt, but as a goal it is no less valid for being difficult to reach.

The rhetorical structure of Mādhyamika works is varied and elaborate. Certain figures are common to most texts of the school—for instance, simile and oxymoron. Certain other features are not found in demonstrative texts but occur frequently in persuasive texts, for example, metaphor, climax, and double entendre. The latter in particular was highly developed by Chinese Buddhists in the late fourth and early fifth centuries. The principle is part of the doctrine of upāya (skilful means); the sūtras say that the Buddha spoke with one voice (sound), and each hearer understood whatever it was appropriate for him to understand.[22] The principle was also esteemed by Six Dynasties litterateurs, who relished systematic multivalence not only in poetry but in prose. The skilful Buddhist essayist could at once gain entrée to literary circles and cast unwelcome ideas in a welcome form by contriving his essay so that it would seem Taoist to the Taoist, Buddhist to those who understood, and aesthetically pleasing to everyone.

The value of rhetorical figures is identified in the same way as the offices of technical terms—by collocation of passages, and abstraction of systematic relations, within which the figures are plotted. The historic provenance of a figure may be a useful clue in analysis, but is not a part of formal analysis and has no place in a description based on such analysis. It is appropriate, however, to a comparison in which the text of provenance is the domain of one of the terms compared.

Figures and technical terms are constituents of the descriptive system and not of the text, which is merely a unilinear string of script symbols. But within the descriptive system bearing on the text, it is necessary not to confuse the rhetorical apparatus with the technical vocabulary. The first belongs to the devices of persuasion, and the second to the devices of exposition. When the figure is euphemism, the two structures may coincide. Terms more acceptable to the reader than the usual ones then occupy offices in a technical system. Thus, conclusions about the doctrinal affinities of a text that are based on an examination of vocabulary must take both the rhetorical and the technical systems of the text into account.[23]

For the Chinese texts to be considered in this study, it is not necessary or useful to distinguish figures of syntax from the normal grammatical apparatus, but it facilitates explanation to draw attention to certain frequent types of construction. The possibility of one 'word' occurring in several syntactic offices is systematically exploited. The noun role is played off against the verb role; the term as head-word is played off against the same term as adjunct; putative and factitive verb roles are contrasted with the noun roles of the same term. Since these structural features are not shared by most modern languages, the translator cannot employ the same syntactic devices, but must find equivalent ones.[24]

Another question involved in this study is that of comparative method, which enters the methodology of this study as of preceding works on both Indian and Chinese Mādhyamikas. Speaking about comparisons of modern European philosophers with the Indians, Schayer says:

> About the value of such juxtapositions people will probably be of different opinions. The danger lies in the arbitrary isolation of individual thoughts, which are only understandable in systematic connection, as elements of structural unities. If we wish to guard against this danger, we must show not only analogies and parallels, but also differences and contrasts (*Kapitel*, p. xxviii).

Since Schayer wrote, the comparative method and the significance of its results have been debated by linguists, and many of their conclusions are as relevant to non-philological as to philological comparisons. The following assumptions about comparative method reflect linguistic methodology as well as such views as Schayer's.

The primary object of description is the complete text attributed to one writer. The description abstracts structures from the text on the linguistic, rhetorical, logical, and philosophical levels, and then abstracts systems from these structures. These systems are then correlated and one overall system is derived from them.

My system is an abstraction from the Mādhyamika systems which in turn describe the views of their Hīnayāna, Tīrthika, and Chinese opponents, which systems in turn refer to the world. Some of the texts to be described refer to the views of other Buddhists or non-Buddhists, which in turn refer to the realm of facts. Thus a description of such a Mādhyamika text is a system about a system about systems about reality. There is a series of ranks in which the present exposition is quaternary and the Mādhyamika texts are tertiary. Each system is an abstraction from its domain of reference rather than a property of it. No matter how homologous system and meta-system may be, they are not the same system, and the distinct ranks must not be confused.

Before two texts are compared, each is analyzed and its systems described. Since the questions asked above refer to whole systems rather than to single components, they would not be answered by piecemeal comparisons. So one-system descriptions are prior to multi-system comparisons.

In comparison, a further rank of description is introduced, having as its domain of reference the previously established descriptions of the terms of the comparison. The number of terms compared is immaterial to the method however much it may affect the practicality of the procedure. This study excludes the comparison of Indian or Chinese Mādhyamika systems with Neo-Taoist systems, on grounds of convenience and arbitrary choice rather than from methodological principle. This does not preclude incidental observations on particular points of Neo-Taoism, but merely excludes systematic comparison.

The addition of another system to the set under comparison produces a different comparative system.[25] Features that were excluded from the systems established for the smaller set may be significant for the larger set. But since any system is potentially a term in an indefinitely large set of comparables, no comparison is comprehensive.

Furthermore, descriptive systems are non-unique and non-exhaustive.[26] Thus the present exposition is offered, not as *the* account of the subject, but as *one* account, aiming towards validity only for the structures abstracted and at completeness only for the categories selected from the set of possible ones. The three primary questions to be investigated concern Mādhyamika writers in India and China, and the similarities and differences between them. Other Indian systems, Buddhist or non-Buddhist, and the non-Buddhist Chinese systems are considered only in passing, on points where they are tangent to the primary questions, but the systematic comparison of Neo-Taoism with Mādhyamika of any sort, and the systematic comparison of Mādhyamika and the Tīrthika systems, are not within the scope of this study as I have defined it.

There is one last question to which Demiéville has drawn attention, but which I have chosen to treat only in passing, in spite of its importance:

> Finally, there is another disappointment of more general scope about which I cannot remain silent. After the almost exclusively philological annotation of the translation, I expected to find, in those of the "Studies" which are by philosophers, an analysis and an appreciation of the ***Chao-lun*** that would be more strictly

and at the same time more broadly philosophical. But the authors have been satisfied with a perspective that is narrowly Chinese and in great part historical, whereas Seng-chao would have merited, in my opinion, to be compared before the universal tribunal of the ***philosophia perennis*** (review of ***Jōron Kenkyū***, pp. 234–35).

Chapter II
Early Indian Mādhyamika

HISTORICAL PREAMBLE

The Chinese Perspective

Kumārajīva's pupils had a clearly formulated picture of the Mādhyamika founders and their role in the history of Indian Buddhism. Drawing an analogy between the state of affairs in China before Kumārajīva's arrival and in India before Nāgārjuna's advent, they regarded both teachers as saviors from bewilderment and contending views. As Hui-yüan said:

There was a Mahāyāna bodhisattva named Nāgārjuna. He was born in India, and came from the Brahman caste. Having accumulated virtue in bygone ages, his mind fitted existence in this [world]. He lived during the ninth century [A.N., i.e. after the (Pari)nirvāṇa], and at a moment when [the Dharma] was decadent and weak. He was grieved by the benightedness of the multitudes, and treading the steep (dangerous) track, he did not falter (Doc. 4.II.2).

Another disciple, Seng-chao, said of the second founder:

Eight hundred years and more after the Buddha's Nirvāṇa there was a bodhisattva monk named Deva.... He was able to unlock the double bars from the Tripiṭaka and level the abstruse road of the twelve [sections of the scriptures]. He strode alone through Kapilavastu, and became a moat to the City of the Dharma. At that time, the Tīrthikas ran riot, heterodoxies arose in conflict, and false debates imperilled the truth so that the Right Way was nearly lost in confusion. Then, looking up he lamented the decline of the Holy Teaching, and looking down he grieved that the strayed multitude were given over to delusion. With the intention of rescuing far and wide those who were drowning, he composed this treatise (Doc. 7.1–2).

Nāgārjuna's Life and Writings

Kumārajīva is given as the translator of a biography of Nāgārjuna (T 2047) which offers the following information: Nāgārjuna was born in a South Indian brahman family and received a brahmanical education in religious and secular subjects. By the time he reached manhood, he was renowned for his learning. He and three companions studied magic with a magician, learned the art of making themselves invisible, and used it to enter the royal palace and seduce the women. When the royal guards discovered them, the three companions were slain. This experience awakened Nāgārjuna to the knowledge that lust is the root of suffering and misfortune. He vowed to become a śramaṇa if he escaped alive, and when in fact he did escape, he went to a mountain, visited a stūpa, and took the rites of 'going forth.' In ninety days he recited and mastered the Tripiṭaka (some Hīnayāna canon), and then sought more scriptures. He obtained the Mahāyāna sūtras from an old bhikṣu at a stūpa in the Snowy Mountains (Himālayas), and recited, liked, and understood them. Then he continued his travels throughout India in search of scriptures, but without success. He won debates with Tīrthikas and Śramaṇas. The Tīrthikas persuaded him that the Dharma was deficient in formal reasoning, so he set up his own school, with its own rule and vestments. A 'Mahānāga bodhisattva' saw and pitied him, and took him to a place in the ocean where he presented him with the Vaipulya Sūtras. He recited and mastered them in ninety days. He came to understand the oneness of the sūtras, and gained the non-arising-patience. The nāga took him back to South India, where he propagated the Dharma extensively and defeated the Tīrthikas. He wrote a number of works and fostered the practice of Mahāyāna throughout India. One-hundred years after his death—apparently the time when the biography was written—he was worshipped as a Buddha at shrines dedicated to him in the states of South India.

That this biography was actually translated by Kumārajīva is attested by Seng-jui's reference (*GPWT Preface*, CST, p. 75a19) to an Indian biography, and by Hui-yüan's summary of this biography in his *Preface to the Great Perfection of Wisdom Treatise* (Doc. 4.II.2–4, CST, p. 75b–c). Ui says (*Vaiśeṣika Philosophy*, pp. 42–43) that Nāgārjuna lived about 750–850 A.N. "The date of the Nirvāṇa held by Kumārajīva and his disciples is 637 B.C. Hence we conclude the following dates: Aśvaghoṣa lived about 13 A.D., Nāgārjuna about 113–213 A.D., Deva about 163–263 A.D., and Hari-varman about 260 or 270 A.D." These dates are consonant with the supposition that the biography of Nāgārjuna translated by Kumārajīva was written during the first half of the fourth century, as it mentions the existence of shrines to Nāgārjuna one hundred years after his death.

Ui's Parinirvāṇa date is referred to Mochizuki (*Bukkyō Dainempyō*, first ed., p. 12, revised ed., p. 6, ll. 4, 5, 6), which in turn cites Tao-an of Later Chou, *On the Two Teachings* (KHMC, p. 142a19):

Further, according to the dharma-master Kumārajīva's chronicle and the *Stone Pillar Inscription*, both tallying with the *Ch'un-ch'iu*, the Tathāgata was born in the fifth year of King Huan of Chou, cyclical sign i-ch'ou [715 B.C.]. . . . and deceased in the fifteenth year of King Hsiang, cyclical sign chia-shen [637 B.C.]. From then until now is 1205 years.

This passage, then, was written in A.D. 568, a century and a half after Kumārajīva. Its authority is quite questionable.

There are various Chinese traditions about Nāgārjuna's date. The *Fa-hua-chuan-chi* (T 2068, p. 52c25) places Nāgārjuna at the end of the fifth century A.N. This text, however, is eclectic and incorporates doubtful items such as the putative Seng-chao preface to the *Fa-hua-ching*. Thus its testimony is not strong. Hui-yüan (Doc. 4.II.2) says that Nāgārjuna lived in the ninth century A.N. Seng-chao says in his preface to the *Hundred Treatise* (Doc. 7.1) that Āryadeva lived eight hundred and more years A.N.

Seng-jui says in his preface to the *Great Perfection of Wisdom Treatise* (T 1509): "Therefore Aśvaghoṣa arose in the remnant of the True Dharma, and Nāgārjuna was born at the end of the Counterfeit Dharma (p. 74c20—21).... Hence the *Indian Chronicle* says: At the end of the Counterfeit and of the True, Aśvaghoṣa and Nāgārjuna (p. 75a19).... Who but the two master-workmen could set it right? Therefore all the states of India set up temples to them and worship them like Buddhas (p. 75a23—24)."

Chi-tsang gathers together most of the evidence available to him and discusses it in commenting on Seng-chao's *Hundred Treatise Preface* (T XLII, 233a7—b1):

QUESTION: Did Deva and Nāgārjuna see each other, or not?
ANSWER: The sūtras and biographies disagree. Master Seng-jui's ***Preface to the Satyasiddhi***, written after Kumārajīva departed the world, quotes the Master Kumārajīva's words, saying: "Three hundred and fifty years after the Buddha's decease Aśvaghoṣa came into the world. At five hundred and thirty years, Nāgārjuna came into the world. Aśvaghoṣa flourished at the end of the True Dharma, and Nāgārjuna arose at the beginning of the Counterfeit Dharma." Emperor Wu of Liang, in the *Fa-p'u-t'i-yin-yüan*, says: "I bow reverently to Aśvaghoṣa Bodhisattva, who flourished in the True Dharma. I take refuge in Nāgārjuna Bodhisattva, who flourished in the Counterfeit Dharma." Seng-chao and Seng-jui both say that Deva appeared eight hundred and more years (A.N.), so it follows that they did not see each other. On the basis of three texts it is demonstrated that they did see each other. First, the ***Biography of Deva*** says: When Deva took out the god's eye and was going to subdue the Tīrthikas completely, he went to Nāgārjuna and received the dharma of leaving household life (T 2048, p. 187a18). Therefore they must have seen each other. Second, the ***Māyā Sūtra*** (T 383, p. 1013c) declares that at seven hundred years Nāgārjuna appeared. Now (Seng-chao) declares that at eight hundred years Deva appeared. They could thus have seen each other. Third, the *Fu-fa-tsang-ching*[1] (T 2058, p. 318c21—24) demonstrates that they did see each other. When Nāgārjuna was about to leave the world, he told his great disciple Kāṇadeva: "Listen, kulaputra. The Blessed One entrusted the supreme True Dharma to Kāśyapa, from whom it has been entrusted in succession down to me. Now, as I leave the world I entrust it to you. You shall raise up the cloud of compassion and pour down the Dharma which is elixir (amṛta)." Deva prostrated himself and answered: "I respectfully consent to [guard] the Venerable Teaching." Therefore we know that they saw each other.
QUESTION: Why do the bodhisattvas come into the world?
ANSWER: The main explanation is two points: first, demolition of Small (Vehicle)

beliefs, and second, demolition of the wrong and misdirected. As the *Great Perfection of Wisdom Treatise* says: at three hundred and some years there was Kātyāyana who composed the *Eight-Book* (*Jñānaprasthāna*, T 1543, 1544) (Lamotte, *Traité*, I, 110, note). Aśvaghoṣa then came into the world. So we know that Kātyāyana's believing in the Small [Vehicle] is a malady. Because Aśvaghoṣa demolished the Small's malady, he came into the world and propagated the Great [Vehicle]. Also possibly Kātyāyana lived at a time when predispositions (*nidāna*) were small and so declared the Small, so that worldlings would study the Small and so turn from the worldly and take the saintly. Thereafter Aśvaghoṣa came into the world and demolished the Small, so that they would turn from the Small and awaken to the Great Teaching. Therefore both men propagated the way to benefit beings. At the beginning of the six(th) hundred years the five hundred arhants in the Chipin country of North India commented on the *Eight-Book* (*Jñānaprasthāna*) and composed the *Vibhāṣā* (T 1546, 1547). Nāgārjuna at this time appeared.[2]

Chi-tsang goes on to say that about 800 A.N. Fa-sheng (Dharmaśrī or Dharmottara) and others were propagating Hīnayāna, when Deva arose, promoted the Mahāyāna and refuted heresies.

As Chi-tsang mentions, there are several predictions about Nāgārjuna in the Mahāyāna sutras. The *Laṅkāvatāra* says that there will be a venerable bhikṣu called Nāgārjuna in South India, that he will propagate the Mahāyāna, refute views of existent and inexistent, realize the pramudita-bhūmi (stage of rejoicing), and go to rebirth in Sukhāvatī. The Sanskrit text names Nāgāhvaya and says that he will appear four hundred years A.N. and will live for six hundred years.[3] The two Chinese translations that contain the prediction do not mention any dates (T 671, p. 569a; T 672, p. 627c). The *Mahāmegha-sūtra* contains a prediction about a bodhisattva who will live 1200 A.N. during the reign of a wicked Śātavāhana who will persecute the Dharma (T 387, pp. 1099c–100a). The *Mahāmāyā-sūtra* says that after 700 years A.N. there will be a bhikṣu named Nāgārjuna who will preach the Dharma well, extinguish false views, and hold aloft the torch of the True Dharma (T 383, p. 1013a). There is also a prediction in the *Mañjuśrī-mūla-tantra* (pp. 616–17, T. Ganapati śāstrī edition, Trivandrum Sanskrit Series, nos. 70, 76, 84, Trivandrum, 1920–22; Walleser, "Life of Nāgārjuna," p. 437).[4]

There are a few traces of Nāgārjuna in India. His name survives in the place name 'Nāgārjunikoṇḍa.' An inscription near the stūpa of Jaggayyapeṭa mentions the "Venerable Master Nāgārjuna." His Friendly Letter is dedicated to one of the Śātavāhana kings, possibly Yajñaśrī (See Lamotte, *Traité*, I, xi–xiv).

Walleser, after studying the Tibetan histories and the Chinese biography, expressed profound skepticism concerning their historical value. Nevertheless, he conceded, "In this case, Nāgārjuna must have lived in the third century A.D. which is not unlikely having regard to other reports of his co-existence with the kings Kaniṣka and Śātavāhana" ("Life of Nāgārjuna," p. 423).

Murti, remarking on the same subject, says:

Though the traditions of his life are greatly overlaid with legendary details, there is no reason to doubt that Nāgārjuna was a real person. The circumstances of his life are briefly told. He was, in all probability, a Brahman from the South who came to Nālandā and propagated the new ***Prajñā-pāramitā*** teaching. The legend which credits him with having brought the ***Śatasāhasrikā*** from the abode of the Nāgas means that he was the founder of a new and important phase in Buddhism. All our accounts agree in connecting his abode with Dhānyakaṭaka or Śrīparvata in the South, and of his personal friendship with the King Śātavāhana (Andhra) for whom he wrote the ***Suhṛllekha.*** Tradition places him four hundred years after the parinirvāṇa of the Lord, whereas the consensus of opinion among European scholars is that he lived about the middle of the 2nd century A.D. (***Buddhism***, pp. 87–88).

Winternitz says, "It is a good working hypothesis, though nothing more, that he lived in the latter half of the 2nd century A.D." (*History of Indian Literature*, II, 342).[5]

Lamotte has recently re-examined the dating of Nāgārjuna in his *Vimalakīrti* (pp. 70–77). He states that the attribution of the Chinese *Biography* (T 2047) to Kumārajīva is improper, but does not categorically reject its testimony. He reviews Chi-tsang's discussion of the case, and in the course of discussing the discrepant dates he makes the very plausible suggestion that the figure 530 means 530 years after Aśvaghoṣa rather than after the Nirvāṇa. On this supposition Nāgārjuna is 350 + 530 = 880 years A.N. This is congruent with the statements of Seng-chao, Seng-jui, and Hui-yüan which assign Nāgārjuna and Āryadeva to the ninth century A.N.

It would be hard to defend every item in the *Biography*, but it is easy to show that in substance it represents Kumārajīva's account. Seng-jui mentions the *Indian Chronicle(s)* (t'ien-chu-chuan), which probably means the biographies narrated by Kumārajīva. Hui-yüan's biographical sketch of Nāgārjuna in his *Preface to the Great Perfection of Wisdom Treatise* agrees with the *Biography* and many of his allusions are intelligible only with a knowledge of it. Seng-jui mentions the existence of temples to Nāgārjuna and Aśvaghoṣa, unfortunately without the date that occurs in the *Biography*. But the literary form and style of the *Biography* are typically Chinese. It has the standard opening which states the man's native region and class, and then indicates that the child was precocious and received a good education. The laudatory clichés are purely Chinese and transparently do not stand for Indic originals. Insofar as it is genuine, this *Biography* must consist of Kumārajīva's oral account as worded by his disciples. That Kumārajīva knew and told stories about the Indian patriarchs is shown by the tale of Aśvaghoṣa's conversion recorded in his *Vimalakīrti Commentary* (T 1775, pp. 399b5 ff. Cf. Lamotte, *Vimalakīrti*, p. 317, n. 43). In this case, the point one hundred years after Nāgārjuna's death would be some time during Kumārajīva's residence in Ch'ang-an (A.D. 401–13). Thus Nāgārjuna would have flourished in the third century A.D. This tallies with Lamotte's interpretation of Seng-jui's figure as 880 A.N., if it is equated with A.D. 243.

A side problem is that in the *Vimalakīrti Commentary* (p. 399b5) Kumārajīva says that Pārśva, Aśvaghoṣa's teacher, lived 600 A.N. This contradicts the date 350 A.N. for Aśvaghoṣa. But Chi-tsang gets the latter from a no-longer-extant *Satyasiddhi Preface* attributed to Seng-jui, which in view of the problems besetting the transmission of the *Ch'eng-shih-lun* (T 1646) is quite possibly spurious. Seng-jui's phrase in his *Preface to the Great Perfection of Wisdom Treatise* is 正法之餘, which could mean the period just after the Saddharma, i.e., the sixth century A.N.

There are divergent traditions about the number of works that Nāgārjuna composed. The Chinese *Biography* says:

> Explaining the Mahāyāna at great length, he wrote the *Upadeśa* in 100,000 ślokas. He also wrote the *Buddha-mārga-alaṁkāra-śāstra* (?) in 5,000 ślokas, the *Mahāmaitri-upāya-śāstra* (?) in 5,000 ślokas, and the *Madhyamaka-śāstra* in 500 ślokas, and caused the Mahāyāna doctrine to have a great vogue throughout India. He also wrote the *Akutobhayā-śāstra* (?) in 100,000 ślokas, out of which the *Madhyamaka-śāstra* comes (T 2047, pp. 184c17, 186b8, Walleser, "Life of Nāgārjuna," p. 447; cf. T 2058, p. 318b15).

Tāranātha mentions five works as Nāgārjuna's (Walleser, "Life of Nāgārjuna," p. 434):

1. *Mūla-mādhyamika-kārikās*,
2. *Yukti-ṣaṣṭika*,
3. *Śūnyatā-saptati*,
4. *Vigraha-vyāvartanī*, and
5. *Vaidalya*.

Buston lists six main treatises of Nāgārjuna (*History of Buddhism* I, 50–51; Murti, *Buddhism*, pp. 88–90):

1. *Prajñā-mūla (Mūla-madhyamaka-kārikās)*,
2. *Śūnyatā-saptati*,
3. *Yukti-ṣaṣṭika*,
4. *Vigraha-vyāvartanī*,
5. *Vaidalya-sūtra* and *prakaraṇa*, and
6. *Vyavahāra-siddhi*.[6]

Other texts attributed to Nāgārjuna are:

1. *Ratnāvalī*,
2. *Catuḥ-stava*,
3. *Pratītya-samutpāda-hṛdaya*
4. *Mahāyāna-viṁśaka*,
5. *Bhava-saṁkrānti-śāstra*,
6. *Prajñā-daṇḍa*, and
7. *Suhṛllekha*.[7]

Three treatises translated by Kumārajīva and extant only in Chinese are attributed to Nāgārjuna:

1. *Mahā-prajñā-pāramitā-śāstra* (GPWT, T 1509),
2. *Daśabhūmika-vibhāṣā* (T 1521), and
3. *Dvādaśa-mukha-śāstra* (*Twelve Topic Treatise*, T 1568).

In addition, there are a number of miscellaneous texts that survive only in Chinese translation:

1. *Eka-śloka-śāstra*, T 1573,
2. *Aṣṭādaśa-śūnyatā-śāstra*, T 1616,
3. *Bodhisambhāra-śāstra*, T 1660,
4. *Bodhicitta-nimitta-rahita* (?), T 1661,
5. *Bodhi[sattva-]caryāvatāra*, T 1662,
6. *Explanation of the Mahāyāna*, T 1668,
7. *Fu-kai-cheng-hsing-so-chi-ching*, T 1671,
8. *Dharmadhātu-stotra*, T 1675, and
9. *Kuang-ta-fa-yüan-sung*, T 1676.[8]

The question of which of these works are not authentic attributions has not yet been wholly resolved. However, if we define Nāgārjuna as the author of the *Middle Stanzas*, then there are no grounds for impeaching the authenticity of the other four works listed by Tāranātha, as their content agrees with that of the *Middle Stanzas*. In addition, the *Ratnāvalī*, *Catuḥ-stava*, *Pratītya-samutpāda-hṛdaya*, and *Bhava-saṁkrānti śāstra* (Murti, *Buddhism*, p. 90, n. 2; p. 91, n. 4) are attested by quotations in Candrakīrti, and the *Suhṛllekha* was translated into Chinese twice shortly after A.D. 430, once by Guṇavarman and once by Saṅghavarman. The *Mahāyāna-viṁśaka* may or may not be by the author of the *Middle Stanzas* (Murti, *Buddhism*, p. 91, n. 3; Tucci, *Minor Buddhist Texts*, pp. 199–200).

Āryadeva's Life and Writings

Kumārajīva is also given as the translator of a biography of Āryadeva (T 2048), which states the following: He was of brahman caste, and a native of South India. He was Nāgārjuna's disciple. He converted a hostile South Indian king, publicly debated with the Tīrthikas, defeating and converting them in large numbers, and subsequently withdrew with his disciples to the forest where he composed the *Hundred Treatise* in twenty chapters, and also the *Four Hundred Treatise*. He was murdered by the disciples of a master whom he had vanquished.

The sixth-century commentator, Candrakīrti, says:

> Āryadeva was born in the island of Siṁhala and was a son of the king of the land. After having become the crown prince he renounced the world, came to the South, and becoming a disciple of Nāgārjuna, followed his doctrine. Therefore the truth of his *Four Hundred Treatise* is not different from that of the *Middle Treatise*. Anyone who asserts that there is a difference simply shows his rashness, for it is a false imagination (Bhattacharya, p. XIX).

Four treatises extant in Tibetan are attributed to Āryadeva:

1. *Catuḥ-śataka* (Tib. mdo 'grel xviii, 1–20b),
2. *Hastavāla-prakaraṇa* (Tib. mdo 'grel xvii, 319a–21a; xvii, 24a–b),
3. *Akṣara-śataka* (Tib. mdo 'grel xvii, 157a), and
4. *Jñāna-sāra-samuccaya* (Tib. mdo 'grel xviii, 29a–31a).

Parts of the *Catuḥ-śataka* survive in Sanskrit. The Tibetans wrongly attribute the *Akṣara-śataka* to Nāgārjuna (Murti, *Buddhism*, pp. 92–94).

Five works in the present Chinese canon are attributed to Āryadeva:

1. *Catuḥśataka*—three versions:
   a. *Śata-śāstra (Hundred Treatise)*, T 1569, trans. by Kumārajīva,
   b. *Śata-śāstra-vaipulya*, T 1570, trans. by Hsüan-tsang, and
   c. Commentary by Dharmapāla on the *Śata-śāstra-vaipulya*, T 1571, also trans. by Hsüan-tsang,
2. *Akṣara-śataka*, T 1572,
3. *Mahāpuruṣa-śāstra*, T 1577,
4. *Refutation of the Four Theses of the Tīrthikas and Hīnayānists in the Laṅkāvatāra-sūtra*, T 1639, and
5. *Explanation of the Nirvāṇa of the Tīrthikas and Hīnayānists in the Laṅkāvatāra-Sūtra.*[9]

BIBLIOGRAPHICAL PREAMBLE

In China, Mādhyamika was known as the *Four Treatise School*, or the *Three Treatise School*, depending on whether the fourth of the treatises translated by Kumārajīva was accorded primary status. These four texts represent the state of the Mādhyamika tradition before Buddhapālita and Bhāvaviveka[10] reshaped it and founded the Prāsaṅgika and Svātantrika schools. Though the basic stanzas in the *Three Treatises* are the work of Nāgārjuna and Āryadeva and correspond fairly closely with counterparts in Sanskrit and Tibetan, the commentaries on them and the fourth *Treatise* are only extant in Chinese.

Kumārajīva's disciples considered the *Four Treatises* as a complementary set. As Seng-jui says:

> The *Hundred Treatise* disciplines outsiders (Tīrthikas) and shuts out falsehoods. This text [*The Middle Treatise*] frees insiders (Buddhists) and dissolves their obstructions. The *Great Perfection of Wisdom Treatise* is profound and vast. The *Twelve Topics* is concise and to the point. When you examine these four, it is indeed as if the sun and moon entered your bosom. There is nothing that is not mirrored forth clearly (Doc. 5.5).

The Middle Treatise (T 1564)

This is a commentary on Nāgārjuna's *Middle Stanzas (Madhyamaka-kārikās)*. Seng-jui says:

> It is said that in all the states of India there are none who venture to engage in studies who do not pore over this treatise [the *Middle Stanzas*] and take it for their canon. Very many of them have moistened their quills and written commentaries. The one that we are now issuing is the commentary by the Indian brahman named Pin-lo-chieh—in the Ch'in language, "Blue Eyes." Though he believed and understood the profound Dharma, his language is not elegant and apposite. The Dharma-master [Kumārajīva] edited and emended all the errors, deficiencies and redundancies in it, interpreting it according to the *Stanzas*, so that the principles are definitive, though in some places the language is not entirely excellent (Doc. 5.4).

The reconstruction of the author's name is problematic. Takakusu said (*Journal of the Royal Asiatic Society* (1903), p. 182):

> The first Indian author is not Piṅgala in reality. Mr. Suzuki seems to have been misled by the Chinese interpreter, who says in the preface to the vṛtti that its original was written by a Brahmacarī [*sic*] Tsiṅ-mu, lit. the 'blue-eyed,' the Indian original being Piṅgala, etc. Piṅgala, however, is not the 'blue-eyed,' but the 'tawny-eyed.' The 'blue-eyed' is a name of Candrakīrti, the actual author of the Sanskrit vṛtti, who is otherwise styled as Ārya Deva (Bodhisattva). . . .

Walleser (*Mittlere Lehre*, 1912, pp. X-XIII) discusses the matter at length. He says that fan-chi 梵志 is 'brahman,' not 'brahmacārin.' He says that the original reading of the name was *pin-lo-chieh* 賓羅伽 rather than *pin-chieh-lo*, which first appears in the 1881 Tōkyō edition of the Canon. He states that this oldest reading is preserved in the *Ch'u-san-tsang-chi-chi* and in the *Fan-i-ming-i-chi*. In the Taishō edition the editors seem to have remedied the matter by altering the reading in the *Fan-i-ming-i-chi* (T 2131, p. 1066c25) to *pin-chieh-lo*, giving no variant readings in footnote 21, but merely 'Piṁgara, Piṅgalanetra.' In the *Ch'u-san-tsang-chi-chi* (T 2145, p. 77a6), *pin-lo-chieh* stands unaltered. Walleser disposes of Takakusu's improbable suggestion that Pin-lo-chieh was Āryadeva or Candrakīrti. He thinks that the Chinese perhaps misunderstood the color-word *piṅgala*, and proposes to reconstruct *piṅgalākṣa* through a Prakrit *piṅgalakkha*. He adds that these characters can also be construed as a transcription of *vimalākṣa*. This is the name of Kumārajīva's vinaya-master. But 青 means "blue" rather than "pure," and furthermore Pin-lo-chieh is said to have been a Brahman. Hence Walleser rejects the reconstruction *vimalākṣa*.

A simple solution which I favor is to suppose that 青 (blue, green, azure) is an orthographic error for 清 (clear, pure). The two words are homophonous now, and in Ancient Chinese they were very close: 青 ts'ieng; 清 ts'iäng (Karlgren, pp. 812c', 812h'). Even if we allow that Karlgren's distinction is real rather than merely apparent, the two words might well have been identical in Ch'ang-an speech, or Kumārajīva's Kuchean accent may have obscured the difference. Or perhaps a scribe just omitted the water radical. 'Pure Eyes' would correspond exactly to 'Vimalākṣa.'

If this reconstruction is accepted, it is not necessary to identify the man with the vinaya-master; it is not a rare type of name, and probably designated some otherwise unknown Indian. The one remaining problem is why the transcription pin-lo-chieh was adopted rather than 卑摩羅叉 which is used for the vinaya-master. Inconsistencies in terminology and transcription are not rare in Kumārajīva's works, however, and this point is more a puzzle than a serious objection.

Kumārajīva, as reviser of the text, is author as well as translator.

The *Middle Treatise* contains twenty-seven chapters, like Candrakīrti's *Prasannapadā*, and 445 verses of the *Stanzas*, as against the 449 preserved in the *Prasannapadā*. Each chapter is a critical examination of one concept, in the following order:

1. the conditions (causation)
2. the gone and the ungone (motion)
3. the sense-faculties (perception)
4. the skandhas
5. the six dhātus (quality and substance)
6. the passion and the impassioned
7. the three marks of the conditioned
8. the act and the agent
9. the pre-existent
10. fire and fuel
11. beginning point and end point
12. suffering
13. the saṁskāras (composite things)
14. combination (the self-other relation)
15. own-being
16. bondage and release
17. deed and result
18. the ātman
19. time
20. conjunction (of causes and effects)
21. origin and dissolution
22. the Tathāgata
23. the misconceptions
24. the Holy Truths
25. Nirvāṇa
26. the twelve nidānas (dependent co-arising)
27. views (about whether the self is eternal or non-eternal).

The differences in number of verses between the *Middle Treatise* and the *Prasannapadā* are:

Chapter 7:	Chinese, 35	vs.	Sanskrit,	34
Chapter 8:	" 12	vs.	"	13
Chapter 13:	" 9	vs.	"	8
Chapter 21:	" 20	vs.	"	21
Chapter 23:	" 24	vs.	"	25
Chapter 26:	" 9	vs.	"	12

Gard, "On the Authenticity of the Chung-lun," summarizes these divergences and concludes:

Thus, contrary to most scholarly opinion, the *Mādhyamika-kārikā* is known to us only indirectly through commentaries and is therefore of questionable textual status.... In short, our present knowledge is too meager for the Chung-lun as a whole to be accepted as an authoritative statement of the *Mādhyamika-kārikā* without serious qualification.

Against this judgment there are several considerations: first, scholarly opinion has never held that the Sanskrit and Chinese *Stanzas* were known otherwise than as cited in the commentaries although the *Stanzas* do exist separately in Tibetan. The fact that the *Stanzas* are accompanied by commentaries diminishes the possibility of interpolations and hence strengthens the case for authenticity.

Second, there are rather few discrepancies in number of *Stanzas* between the *Middle Treatise* and the *Prasannapadā*. They occur in only eight of the total twenty-seven chapters. There are only eleven discrepancies, of which three are in Chapter 26, whose place in the structure of the whole work is unclear, and which is perhaps in its entirety an early interpolation. In the Sanskrit 7.7 corresponds to 7.7–8 in the *Middle Treatise*. Two Chinese verses—13.4 and 27.25—have no counterpart in the Sanskrit. Five Sanskrit verses—3.7, 8.11, 13.7, 23.20, and 26.11—have no counterpart in the Chinese. This is not a large measure of disagreement and though it shows the need for a text-critical treatment of the *Stanzas*, it does not impugn their testimony in the aggregate. The interpretation of Nāgārjunism is not affected materially by the presence or absence of any of the verses in question.

It cannot be assumed that a verse is an interpolation because it occurs in the Sanskrit and not the Chinese, or vice versa. It is a reasonable certainty that all verses common to the *Middle Treatise* and the *Prasannapadā* belong to a fairly primitive common text, but there is no way of telling whether any verses of the original text have been dropped by both commentaries. Thus we can never know the boundaries of the original text, if it had fixed boundaries.

A large part of the *Middle Treatise* commentary is prose paraphrase of the *Stanzas*, provision of opponents' questions and members of inferences not expressed in the *Stanzas*, and sundry other aids to the reader. There are also some original essays that take the *Stanzas* merely as their point of departure. The chief of these are the discourse on the series of becoming *(bhava-santāna)* in chapter 13 (pp. 17b4–18a25), and the refutations of ātman in chapter 18 (pp. 24a15–25b29) and chapter 27 (pp. 37a19–38a19). In the commentary there is some subject matter that does not occur in the *Stanzas*—some similes, the atom theory (ch. 1, p. 2a7), and the four pramāṇas (ch. 18, pp. 24a27ff.).

The Twelve Topic Treatise (T 1568)

This text, attributed to Nāgārjuna, is a systematic examination of twelve topics, namely:

1. causes and conditions
2. whether the effect exists or does not exist in the cause
3. conditions *(pratyaya)*
4. the marks—arising, enduring, and perishing
5. the marked and the markless
6. oneness and difference
7. existent and inexistent
8. nature *(svabhāva)*
9. cause and effect
10. the maker
11. the three times
12. arising *(utpāda)*

The text is in prose and takes its point of departure from twenty-six verses distributed throughout the chapters. The relation of these verses to those in other texts by Nāgārjuna tabulates as follows:

TT chapter and verse	MT chapter and verse	TT chapter and verse	MT chapter and verse
1.1	cf. 1.12, 15.4, 1.1–4	4.8	7.11
1.2	cf. 24.19, 7.17	4.9	7.12
2.1	1.9	4.10	7.13
3.1	1.13	4.11	7.14
3.2	1.5	5.1	5.3
3.3	1.14	6.1	
4.1		7.1	*Śūnyatā-saptati* 19
4.2		8.1	13.3
4.3	7.4	9.1	
4.4	7.5	10.1	12.1
4.5	7.6	10.2	1.15
4.6	7.7	11.1	cf. 11.2
4.7	7.10	12.1	cf. 7.15, 2.1

HT–MT identities	17
HT–MT similarities	4
Śūnyatā-saptati	1
unidentified	4
TOTAL	26

Twenty-one of the verses are identical or nearly identical with ones in the *Middle Stanzas*, and one verse is identical with a verse in the *Śūnyatā-saptati*. The prose section quotes the *Middle Treatise* by name and so was written afterwards, whether by Nāgārjuna or by someone else. "This matter has already been explained in the *Middle Treatise*" (p. 164c1), and "As it says in the *Middle Treatise*, . . ." (p. 165c22–23).

The content of the *Twelve Topics* is mostly a duplication of the *Middle Treatise*, but it contains some distinctive passages, in particular a little atheist tract in refutation of creation by Īśvara in Chapter 10 (p. 166a19–c9).

Chinese writers almost never quote the *Twelve Topics*.

The Hundred Treatise (T 1569)

This is a commentary on some stanzas by Āryadeva in refutation of Tīrthika theses. Seng-chao says:

> [The treatise's] final meaning being abstruse and tersely [expressed], few gained the gateway to it. The bodhisattva Vasu, wisdom and insight ripe within him, surpassing in sublime thought, from afar matched with the metaphysical footprints and wrote an expository commentary for it. He made manifest the hidden meaning with his fine pen (Doc. 7.3).

Nothing else is known for certain about Vasu. Péri, "Vasubandhu," pp. 362 ff., and Frauwallner, *Vasubandhu*, pp. 35 ff., want to identify Vasu with Vasubandhu. This is not impossible, but has not been demonstrated. Frauwallner, *Vasubandhu*, pp. 56–57, admits that we have not even determined which of the known Vasubandhu works were written by the Yogācārin Vasubandhu I and which by the Sarvāstivādin Vasubandhu II, and that this can be determined only when the works themselves are analyzed and compared. 'Vasu' may be an abbreviation for 'Vasubandhu,' but it might equally well be a complete name or an abbreviation for 'Vasudeva,' 'Vasumitra,' 'Vasubhadra,' etc. Péri pleads that, "It is hardly admissible that such praise should be addressed to a man who left no trace of his career except the pages of the Śataśāstra commentary" ("Vasubandhu," p. 364). But why should illustrious men not disappear and leave only one work? The *Hundred Treatise* alone would establish a man's fame. Nāgārjuna is not well attested from the standpoint of history, and Vasubandhu is so problematical that Frauwallner must conclude that there were two of him. In a country such as India where even great monarchs often fade from the record of history, bodhisattvas could quite easily flourish and then disappear from historical memory.

In this work, there are ten chapters with the topics:[11]

1. merit and demerit
2. the ātman
3. unity
4. multiplicity
5. sense-perception
6. objects
7. existence of the effect in the cause
8. inexistence of the effect in the cause
9. eternalness
10. emptiness

There are seventy-five or more similes in the *Hundred Treatise*, and a good proportion of them also occur in the *Nyāya Sūtras*:
Ch. I: salt and saltiness; the lamp lights self and others; mantras act at a distance; far-away stars affect men's luck; the elephant and its trunk; the dyer cleaning his cloth; the potter who makes and then breaks; washing and dyeing; the lamp lights but does not create.
Ch. II: the ox and the owner; fire and owner; sight and lamp; the horse' body and ātman; the black shawl; the man and the stick; sphaṭika changing colors; one potter, many pots; coals as fire without smoke; tortoise and hair; barren woman and child; the hand and taking; a corpse and feeling; sword and wound; the blind and the lame; the house-master's suffering; the reaper and the sickle; the house with six windows; potter and clay; burner and fire; wind igniting branches; corpse and seeing; fire and heat; right and left eyes; the body and its parts acting; cloth burning in one part.
Ch. III: existence, unity and pot; father and son; parts and whole of body; army and soldiers; forest and trees; long and short.
Ch. IV: existence reveals like a lamp; parts and whole of body; atoms and pot; threads and net; drops and water; barren woman and son; blind man and rūpa; sand and oil.
Ch. V: the eye does not see itself; finger and touch; manas, eye, and light.
Ch. VI: perceiving a pot; the man and his sabot; flower, fruit, seed, and bud.
Ch. VII: lump of clay; finger crooked and straight; man in childhood, youth, and age; pot emerges from lump of clay rather than willow; sprout, bud, and seed.
Ch. VIII: curds and butter in milk; mother giving birth to child; the youth becomes an old man; mirror and image; hare horns; barren woman and son; tortoise hair and cloth.
Ch. IX: the sun and the directions.
Ch. X: curds and ghee in milk; foetus in young girl; the house is distinct from beams and pillars; excrement in food; cloth distinct from threads; the house is empty of horses; mirage.

Kumārajīva, according to Seng-chao, was particularly fond of the *Hundred Treatise*. "He always pores over and recites this treatise, and considers it the mind's essential" (Doc. 7.5). Kumārajīva translated it once in 402, just after he arrived in Ch'ang-an, and then translated it again in 404. Seng-chao's *Preface* (Doc. 7.5) states that the language of the earlier translation was defective and thwarted attempts at comprehension.

Though Seng-chao wrote the official preface to the *Hundred Treatise*, it is not mentioned in any of his extant writings.

The Great Perfection of Wisdom Treatise (T 1509)

This treatise is a commentary on the *Pañcaviṁśati* (T 221, T 222, T 223), Kumārajīva's translation of which it incorporates. In the Taishō edition, the sūtra takes up two hundred pages, the remaining five hundred are occupied by the commentary. Kumārajīva and his disciples attributed the *Great Perfection of Wisdom Treatise* to Nāgārjuna. In recent decades, the validity of this attribution has been discussed rather widely.

Miyaji Kakue 宮地廓慧 (not Miyajima, as Demiéville has it), in "Ta-chih-tu-lun" cites twenty passages concerning India, its language, its customs, etc., in terms which would be inexplicable in a text destined for Indian readers. Demiéville (review of *Traité*, p. 386) says that Miyaji sometimes falls into an excessive mistrust.

Mano Shōjun, the *Kokuyaku Issaikyō* translator of the *Great Perfection of Wisdom Treatise*, says:

Though there are some who doubt that this *Treatise* which comments on the *Ta-p'in Prajñā Sūtra* is a genuine work of Nāgārjuna's, the magnificent content of the *Treatise* decisively drives away this doubt. Consequently, from of old it has been the universal opinion that this is an authentic work. However, because in this *Treatise* Nāgārjuna's other work, the *Middle Treatise*, is quoted by himself, its composition probably belongs to Nāgārjuna's later period, and it should be investigated as an expression of his mature thought (p. 2).

Tsukamoto Zenryū says:

Also, there is room to consider whether the *Ta-chih-tu-lun* (T 1509) whose Chinese translation is an abridgement in one hundred chüan from an original said to be several times as large should be recognized as being directly the composition of the author of the *Middle Treatise* ("Kumarajū no katsudō nendai ni tsuite," p. 607a).

Lamotte says:

We see that the triumph of "Kao tso" over the Tīrthikas, as it is related here in the Mppś, agrees perfectly with the biographies of Nāgārjuna written in the same spirit and with identical preoccupations. It would be rather tempting to identify "Kao tso" with Nāgārjuna. If the latter is really the author of the Mppś, he would thus have transmitted us an anecdote experienced by himself, designating himself not by his name, Lung-shu or Nāgārjuna, but by his title, Fa shih kao tso "the master of the law on the elevated seat," in Sanskrit *uccāsana dharmācārya.* But this hypothesis is so daring that it hardly deserves to attract attention (*Traité* I, 491, n.).

And again:

One may wonder whether the Nāgārjuna of the Mppś, who here shows himself so declared a partisan of the six gatis, is the same as the nihilist Nāgārjuna, author of the Madh. kārikā, who only admits five of them (cf. Madh. vṛtti, p. 269, l.9; p. 304, l.4). Counterwise, and contrary to the assertion of L. de La Vallée, in *Kośa* III, p. 11, the Nāgārjuna of the *Suhṛllekha* counts six gatis (cf. T 1673, p. 750cl) (*Traité* I, 614, n.).

And again:

It should be noticed that the Mppś, attributed wrongly or rightly to Nāgārjuna, does not manifest, in its refutation of the Ātman, any special resemblance to the Madh. kārikā of Nāgārjuna, and all said, seems to have neglected them, although in other places it has frequent recourse to them. (cf. ***Traité*** I, p. 36, 37, 69, 367, 378, 396). We have already stated above (***Traité*** I, p. 614 in n.) that the Mppś departs on certain points from the doctrines of the Madh. kārikā (***Traité*** II, 734, n. 1).

Demiéville says:

It is towards this region of the North-West that everything orients the ***Ta-chih-tu-lun***, it is with it that it "manifests a close acquaintance" (p. 706, n.), and not with Southern India where the legend of Nāgārjuna has its ties and where it has left, as M. Lamotte has shown in the preface of his translation (t. I, pp. xii–xiii) traces in the archeology and epigraphy of the Andhra country (review of ***Traité***, p. 381).

Further:

One certain fact has been brought to light by M. Lamotte, that the ***Ta-chih-tu-lun*** was written down in the North-West, and very probably by an author or authors who were brought up on the Sarvāstivādin or Mūlasarvāstivādin tradition. M. Lamotte indicates a mass of concordant evidences: the ***Ta-chih-tu-lun*** conceives prajñā and the other pāramitās from the viewpoint of the opposition of the Great Vehicle and the Little Vehicle (p. vii); it refers much oftener to the texts and personages of the Small Vehicle than to those of the Great Vehicle (pp. xiii–xv); in matters of Vinaya, it follows the recension of the Mūla-Sarvāstivādins (pp. xv–xvi); it assigns first place in the transmission of the scriptures to Maitreya, who in so many respects represents a "hinge," an index of transition between the Vehicles and whom another mahāyānist deviation of the Sarvāstivādin school, also made the inspirer of its scriptures (p. 939, n. 1); its doctrinal analyses develop within the framework of the rubrics and the terminology of Sarvāstivāda, for example in that which concerns morality (p. 782, n. 1), the hells (p. 811, n. 1), the recollections (p. 1035, n. 1), etc. These are only a few pieces of evidence taken at random from the second volume of M. Lamotte: doubtless he will give us in addition a general evaluation in the overall study which I hope will conclude his translation: but already the juxtapositions and comparisons which he has allowed himself in his valuable notes demonstrate with evidence that the ***Ta-chih-tu-lun*** must be the work of Sarvāstivādin adepts of the Small Vehicle converted to the Great Vehicle of the Mādhyamika school (review of ***Traité***, p. 382).

Waley says:

Throughout this note I mean by 'Nāgārjuna' the author of the Mādhyamika stanzas. It is not credible that other works (such as the *Prajñāpāramitā Śāstra*) are by the same author (***The Real Tripiṭaka***, p. 269, n. 1).

Hurvitz says:

One of Kumārajīva's most important translations (if indeed he was the translator, not the author, of this work) was that of the ***Ta-chih-tu-lun*** ("Render unto Caesar," p. 88, n. 20).

Hikata devotes twenty-three pages of the Introduction to his edition of the *Suvikrāntavikrāmi-paripṛcchā* to "The Author of 'Ta-chih-tu-lun.'" He says in summary:

My recent analysis of the 'Ta-lun,' a rather minute and thorough-going one, has led me to think it proper to divide the whole text into the following three classes:

(A) Clearly not Nāgārjuna's (*abbr.* Nāg's).
   1. Clearly not Nāg's but K-J's:
      a. Explanation of Sk. words, or of Indian customs, for Chinese readers.
      b. Not to be classed with (a), but not Nāg's own words either; acceptable only as K-J's words.
   2. Probably (if not clearly) not Nāg's but K-J's.

(B) (The reverse of A) Acceptable as Nāg's, but not as of other person, much less of a foreigner like K-J.

(C) Outside A and B; better be regarded as Nāg's, as has been traditionally held (Introd. Essay, pp. liii–liv).

In the *Great Perfection of Wisdom Treatise* there is one class of passage which is certainly Nāgārjuna's—the quite numerous quotations from the *Stanzas*. Hikata lists seven, and Lamotte identifies ten in the first eighteen chüan of the text. To date, without making a systematic search, I have found the following citations and quotations:

GPWT page	*Stanzas* chapter and verse	Listed by Hikata, *Suvikrāntavikrāmi-paripṛcchā*	Lamotte, *Traité*, page and note
57c13	15.10		3, 2
60b17	23.13	x	36, 2
60b26	8.2		37, 1
61b11	18.7	x	
61b14	18.8	x	46, 1
64b12	13.7		69, 1 & 2
64c7	17.29–30		72, 2
96c13	18.7	x	
97b12	1.1–2	x	
102c25	5.1–2		367, 1
104a7	7.34		
104b26	1.3		378, 2
104c26	13.6		380, 1
106c28	11.2		396, 1
107a11	24.18	x	
107a12	15.11	x	
198a6	25.19		
205b22	2.1		
205b23	2.2		

GPWT page	*Stanzas* chapter and verse	Listed by Hikata, *Suvikrāntavikrāmi-paripṛcchā*	Lamotte, *Traité*, page and note
205b25	2.4		
205b27	2.66–7a		
205c2	2.6		
205c4–7	2.8		
245c9	24.14		
338cl	18.8		
338c3	25.20		
427c27	2.1		
427c28–28al	2.2		
428a5	2.5		
428a7	2.66 & 96		
428a8	2.8		
439bl	7.4–8		
454c19	22.1		
455a15	22.2		
455a17	22.8		

At pages 64b12, 245c9, and 338cl, the *Middle Treatise* is cited by name. This establishes that at least there was a work called the *Middle Treatise* before the completion of the *Great Perfection of Wisdom Treatise*.

Tucci says:

The commentary by Vasu follows very often almost verbatim, the big work called *Ta-che-tu-lun, Mahāprajñāpāramitā-śāstra*, attributed to Nāgārjuna, which in its refutation of the Hīnayāna as expounded by Kātyāyanīputra seems to have been written with the purpose of opposing a Mahāyāna Abhidharma to that of the Sarvāstivādins (*Pre-Diṅnāga*, p. xiv).

Kumārajīva is reported to have said to Seng-jui:

If I applied my writing-brush and wrote a Mahāyāna Abhidharma, I would surpass Kātyāyanīputra. But now in the land of Ch'in the profoundly intelligent are rare. My wings are broken here, and what would I discourse about? (KSC, p. 332c4).

This statement is doubly puzzling, because the really intelligent were far from rare in Ch'ang-an at that time, and because the *Great Perfection of Wisdom Treatise* is in fact a Mahāyāna Abhidharma. One might perhaps conjecture that Kumārajīva had written some parts of the *Great Perfection of Wisdom Treatise* himself, either in Kuchā or during his two decades of leisure in Ku-tsang. As Demiéville says:

"It goes so far that some nasty minds wonder what, in the *Ta-chih-tu-lun*, is not by Kumārajīva" (review of *Traité*, p. 386)!

The *Great Perfection of Wisdom Treatise* is an all-embracing encyclopedia of doctrine, legends, and quotations. It quotes Hīnayāna and Mahāyāna sūtras and treatises, and even such non-Buddhist writings as the Upaniṣads. Among the Mahāyāna sūtras quoted or cited are:

1. *Pañcaviṁśati* (T 221, 222, 223)
2. *Vimalakīrti-nirdeśa* (T 474, T 475)
3. *Suvikrāntacintā-devaputra-paripṛcchā* (T 588)
4. *Kuśalamūla-samparigraha* (T 657)
5. *Saddharma-puṇḍarīka* (T 262–65)
6. *Ratnamegha* (T 658–60)
7. *Mahāmegha* (T 387)
8. *Dharmamegha* (10th bhūmi of *Daśabhūmi*)
9. *Maitreya-paripṛcchā* (T 349)
10. *Ṣaṭ-pāramitā* (T 261)
11. *Gaṇḍavyūha* (T 293, 300)
12. *Mahā-kāruṇa* (T 380)
13. *Upāya* (T 345)
14. *Anavatapta-nāgarāja-paripṛcchā* (T 635)
15. *Asura-rāja-paripṛcchā*
16. *Pratyutpannasamādhi* (T 416–19; Rahder's review of *Traité*, p. 124).

The *Great Perfection of Wisdom Treatise* was popular in the period immediately after its translation, partly because it was a commentary on the already well-known *Pañcaviṁśati*, and partly because it was a thesaurus of doctrine that could be used as a reference work. The elderly Hui-yüan prepared an abridgment in twenty chüan, wrote a preface, and corresponded with Kumārajīva about vexed points in the treatise. Seng-chao quotes the *Great Perfection of Wisdom Treatise*, though he ignores the *Twelve Topics* and the *Hundred Treatise*.

NĀGĀRJUNISM

The early Mādhyamika writings differ somewhat in subject matter but hardly at all in the system that they represent. An analysis and comparison of them would demonstrate this point, but it would be a digression from the main line of the present study. The following exposition of Nāgārjuna's teaching is based primarily on the *Middle Stanzas*, because they are one text, and the largest corpus of authentic Nāgārjunian authorship.

Doctrinal Structures

In this section, passages with similar structure and subjects are collated. In the next section, a system to be labelled 'Nāgārjunism' will be abstracted from them.

The structures are arranged in three broad groups, around the concepts of dependent co-arising *(pratītya-samutpāda)*, personality *(ātman)*, and nirvāṇa. Some other structures that pertain to the whole system are collected and placed before and after the three main groupings.

General Structures

1. I offer salutation to the best of preachers, the Buddha, who has taught that dependent co-arising has no ceasing, no arising, no nullification, no eternity, no unity, no plurality, no arriving, and no departing, that it is quiescent of all fictions, that it is blissful (1.1–2, cf. 18.11) (***Prasannapadā***, p. 11).[12]
2. It is dependent co-arising that we term emptiness; this is a designation overlaid [on emptiness]; it alone is the Middle Path (24.18) (***Prasannapadā***, p. 503).
3. The own-being of the Tathāgata is the own-being of this world; the Tathāgata is without own-being, and this world is without own-being (22.16) (***Prasannapadā***, pp. 448–49).
4. Saṁsāra has nothing that distinguishes it from nirvāṇa; nirvāṇa has nothing that distinguishes it from saṁsāra. The limit of nirvāṇa is the limit of saṁsāra; there is not even the subtlest something separating the two (25.19–20) (***Prasannapadā***, p. 535).
5. I bow reverently to Gautama, who, taking compassion, taught the True Dharma, in order to cut off all views (27.30) (***Prasannapadā***, p. 592).

These stanzas, the most widely-quoted of any in Nāgārjuna's works, state the central Mādhyamika positions on the problem of being, and the position of the Mādhyamika among the Buddhist sects. No duality is admitted and no monadic unity is affirmed. The Mādhyamikas revere Śākyamuni as the author of this teaching, and connect compassion with the elimination of wrong views. When the identity of the Tathāgata with the world and of nirvāṇa with saṁsāra is realized, then wrong views are not held.

Dependent Co-arising

6. No existents ever occur anywhere which have arisen from themselves, from others, from both, or without a cause (1.3, cf. 21.13) (***Prasannapadā***, p. 12, v. 1).
7. An "A" that comes into being dependent on "B" is not identical with "B" and not other than "B"; thus it is non-annulled and non-eternal (18.10) (***Prasannapadā***, p. 375).[13]
8. No dharma occurs that is not dependently co-arisen; hence no non-empty dharma occurs (24.19) (***Prasannapadā***, p. 505).

These stanzas relate dependent co-arising to the problem of

identity, to the problem of persistence, and to the concept of emptiness. No. 6 poses the question of cause-and-effect as one of source, and No. 7 treats it as a matter of identity. No. 8 connects the concepts of dependent co-arising and emptiness.

9. As realness does not occur for existents that lack own-being, "this being, that becomes" is not a fact, either (1.12) (*Prasannapadā*, p. 86, v. 10).
10. Whatever comes into being in dependence is quiescent by its own-being; therefore the now-arising is quiescent, and so is production (7.16) (*Prasannapadā*, pp. 159–60).
11. That existents are without own-being is because their alter-being is seen; an existent without own-being does not exist; hence the emptiness of existents. If own-being does not occur, to whom might alter-being belong? If own-being does occur, to whom might alter-being belong? (13.3–4) (*Prasannapadā*, pp. 240-41)
12. Emergence of own-being through cause-and-conditions is not valid; an own-being that had emerged through cause-and-conditions would be a made thing. How can own-being be a made thing, since own-being is unmade and not dependent on anything else? (15.1–2) (*Prasannapadā*, pp. 259–62)
13. When there is no own-being, whence might other-being be? For the own-being of other-being is called other-being (15.3, cf. 22.2 and 9) (*Prasannapadā*, pp. 265–66).
14. If existence [derives] from nature [*prakṛti*], its non-existence will not occur; for the otherwise-being of a nature [*prakṛti*] is never true to fact (15.8) (*Prasannapadā*, p. 271).
15. If the nature is inexistent, to what will otherwiseness belong? If the nature is existent, to what will otherwiseness belong? (15.9) (*Prasannapadā*, pp. 271–72)

These stanzas deal with the relation between change and nature (*prakṛti*). If an entity is real, it has own-being and cannot change; if an entity is unreal, it has no own-being which might change. Own-being is changeless, and dependent co-arising manifests a semblance of change. This fundamental incompatibility is the anvil on which Nāgārjuna hammers all his opponents' propositions. Here, incidentally, Nāgārjuna is attacking the Sāṁkhya concept of prakṛti by arbitrarily defining it in his own way. In the Sāṁkhya system, the modifications alter the form but not the own-being of prakṛti.

16. If an effect is born from the conjunction of cause and conditions, and if it exists in the conjunction, how can it be born from the conjunction?

If an effect is born from the conjunction of cause and conditions, and if it does not exist in the conjunction, how can it be born from the conjunction? (20.1–2) (*Prasannapadā*, p. 391)
17. If, having provided the cause for the effect, a cause is extinguished, then what is provided and what is extinguished would be two selves of the cause. If, without having provided the cause of the effect, a cause is extinguished, then, the cause having been extinguished, that effect would be born without cause. If the effect appears together with the conjunction, the absurdity ensues that producer and product are simultaneous (20.5–7) (*Prasannapadā*, pp. 394-95).
18. If the cause is empty of effect, how can it produce the effect? If the cause is not empty of effect, how can it produce the effect? (20.16) (*Prasannapadā*, p. 402)

19. For oneness of cause and effect is never a fact, and otherness of cause and effect is never a fact (20.19) (*Prasannapadā*, p. 403).

In the above stanzas, the procedure already applied to dependent co-arising and own-being is applied to the cause-and-effect relation. Two modes of dichotomy are effected: unity-versus-difference, and former-versus-latter. Each half of the dichotomy is shown to lead to contradiction of an accepted tenet of the opponent. Since the two propositions of each dichotomy are contradictories, a dilemma ensues whenever both are the antecedents of the same unwelcome consequent.

20. If present and future exist in relation to the past, then present and future should exist in past time; if present and future do not exist in it, how can present and future exist in relation to it? The establishment of the two does not occur without relation to the past; therefore present and future time do not exist (19.1–3) (*Prasannapadā*, pp. 382–83).
21. If time depends on an entity, then where is there time without the entity? Since there is no entity, where would time exist? (19.6) (*Prasannapadā*, p. 387)
22. Thus succession of becoming is not valid in any of the three times; how can that which does not exist in the three times be a succession of becoming? (21.21) (*Prasannapadā*, p. 427)

In these stanzas, the topic is the polarity of discrete and continuous (identity and difference) with reference to time. The method is the same as before—dichotomy, and reduction to the paradox that two entities in a relation are neither identical nor different. As temporal succession is one of the components of the concept of dependent co-arising, the problem of time belongs to the same class as those of identity, persistence, cause-and-effect, and own-being.

23. The gone is not arrived at, and the ungone is not arrived at; the just-being-gone is not arrived at separate from the gone and the ungone (2.1) (*Prasannapadā*, p. 92) (May, pp. 51–53, especially n. 7).
24. A goer does not go, and a non-goer does not go; what third one other than goer and non-goer goes? (2.8) (*Prasannapadā*, p. 97)
25. A goer does not stand still, and a non-goer does not stand still; what third one other than goer and non-goer stands still? (2.15) (*Prasannapadā*, p. 101)
26. A real goer does not go the threefold going; an unreal goer does not go the threefold going; nothing real-and-unreal goes the threefold going. Therefore going, goer, and what-is-gone-to do not occur (2.24–25) (*Prasannapadā*, p. 107).

These stanzas concern the problem of motion and rest. Going is treated as a relation between agent and locus, and so comes within the range of dichotomy and reduction to quandary as applied to all dyadic relations. Transit from one point in space to another, from one point in time to another, or from one state to another, are all construed as a mode of 'going.'

27. No space occurs previous to the mark of space; if it were previous to its mark, the absurdity would ensue that it is markless.

No markless existent occurs anywhere; when no markless existent exists, to what could the mark go? There is no emergence of the mark in the markless or in the markful; neither does it emerge anywhere other than in the markless and in the markful. When the mark does not emerge, the marked is not a fact; when the marked is not a fact, the mark too is impossible. Therefore the marked does not occur, the mark does not occur, and neither does any existent occur apart from marked and mark. When the existent does not occur, to what would the inexistent belong? Who apart from existent and inexistent knows the existent and inexistent? Therefore space is not an existent, not an inexistent, not something marked, and not a mark. The other five dhātus are [to be] the same as space (5.1–7) (***Prasannapadā***, pp. 129–34).

These stanzas deal with the fundamental elements of early Buddhist cosmology—the six dhātus (earth, water, fire, air, space/ether, and consciousness)—by examining the relation between entity and essential property (*bhāva* and *lakṣaṇa*). The mark is a universal concimitant of the entity. This relation is subjected to the same procedure as the binary relations of cause-and-effect, agent and locus, etc. The terms 'existent' *bhāva* and 'inexistent' *abhāva* refer to a presence and an absence with the same locus, or alternatively, to complementary extensions within a finite range.

28. If there were something non-empty, there might be something termed empty; there is no non-empty something, and so where might there be an empty something? The Victors have declared emptiness as the expeller of all views; but those who hold emptiness as a view they have pronounced incurable (13.7–8) (***Prasannapadā***, pp. 245–47).

29. A non-empty effect would not arise and would not perish; being non-empty, it would be unextinguished and unarisen. How would something empty arise or perish? The absurdity ensues that the empty, too, is unextinguished and unarisen (20.17–18) (***Prasannapadā***, pp. 402–3).

30. Emptiness wrongly seen destroys the slow-witted, like a serpent wrongly grasped or magic wrongly performed (24.11) (***Prasannapadā***, p. 495).[14]

These stanzas state that emptiness is not a term in the primary system referring to the world, but a term in the descriptive system (meta-system) referring to the primary system. Thus it has no status as an entity, nor as the property of an existent or an inexistent. If anyone considers it so, he turns the key term in the descriptive system into the root of all delusions.

31. If arising is conditioned, then it must have the three marks; if arising is unconditioned, how can it be a mark of the conditioned? (7.1) (***Prasannapadā***, pp. 145–46)

32. If there is another conditioned-mark of arising, abiding and perishing, then there is an infinite regression; if there is no [other], they are not conditioned (7.3) (***Prasannapadā***, p. 147).

33. It has already been demonstrated that neither of the real nor of the unreal nor of both-real-and-unreal is arising possible (7.20) (***Prasannapadā***, p. 162).

34. Abiding of a vanishing existent is not true to fact; but no non-vanishing existent is a fact (7.23) (*Prasannapadā*, p. 164).
35. When the arising of all the dharmas is not a fact, then the extinction of all the dharmas is not a fact (7.29) (*Prasannapadā*, p. 169).
36. The extinction of a real existent is not true to fact, since that existent and inexistent occur in a unity is not true to fact (7.30) (*Prasannapadā*, pp. 169–70).
37. Neither is the extinction of an unreal existent a fact, just as the cutting off of a second head is not a fact (7.31) (*Prasannapadā*, p. 170).
38. Because arising, abiding, and perishing are not established, there is no conditioned; since the conditioned is not established, how can the unconditioned be established? (7.33) (*Prasannapadā*, p. 176)
39. Like an illusion, like a dream, like a fairy castle, thus is arising, thus is abiding, thus is perishing declared to be (7.34) (*Prasannapadā*, p. 177).

Previous stanzas criticized the concepts of space, time, own-being, cause-and-effect, emptiness, and motion. These stanzas criticize the concept of the conditioned *(saṁskṛta)* and the unconditioned *(asaṁskṛta)*. Here the device of dichotomy-and-dilemma is combined with that of demonstrating endless regress *(anavasthā)*. The procedure is to show that a proposition implies an infinite regression, which is unacceptable to the opponent. If each moment has three sub-moments—arising, abiding, and ceasing—then each sub-moment has three sub-sub-moments of arising, abiding, and ceasing; arising has arising, abiding, and ceasing, abiding has arising, abiding, and ceasing, and ceasing has arising, abiding, and ceasing, and so on ad infinitum. Nāgārjuna imputes to his opponent the assumption that the three marks are of the same order as the conditioned dharma to which they pertain. Given this, they are segments of a linear continuum and are susceptible of infinite further segmentations. But an own-being is by definition indivisible, and so entity cannot be attributed to the dharmas, nor to their constituent moments.[15]

No. 37 belongs to the type of proposition in which one term is a member of the null class. It is taken for granted that the class of beings with two heads has no members. Other terms belonging to the null class are hare horns, tortoise hairs, and barren women's children.

The doctrine of momentariness *(kṣaṇikatva)* takes as axiomatic that no dharma occurs in two moments. Nāgārjuna shows that if each moment is segmentable into several sub-moments, then no dharma can occur at all. Here he strikes at a difficulty inherent in the concept of a continuous series of discrete points. Āryadeva employs this device to refute the theory of atoms (T 1570, p. 182b25–c1).

Personality

40. That I existed in past time is not a fact, because he who was in former lives is not identical with this one (27.3) (*Prasannapadā*, p. 573).
41. The ātman is not identical with the appropriation; the latter perishes and arises; how could the appropriator be the appropriation? (27.6) (*Prasannapadā*, p. 576)

42. Neither is it a fact that I did not exist in past time, for this one is not other than the one who existed in former lives (27.9) (*Prasannapadā*, p. 578).
43. It is not a fact that there is an ātman other than the appropriation, for it would then be apprehended without appropriation, and it is not [so] apprehended (27.7) (*Prasannapadā*, p. 577).
44. If former skandhas disintegrated and later skandhas did not arise dependent on the former, then the world would be finite (27.23) (*Prasannapadā*, p. 588).
45. If former skandhas did not disintegrate and later skandhas did not arise dependent on the former, then the world would be infinite (27.24) (*Prasannapadā*, p. 588).
46. Since this series of skandhas proceeds like the flames of a lamp, it is not valid to say that [the world] is finite or is infinite (27.22) (*Prasannapadā*, p. 587).

These stanzas treat the problem of personal continuity as a special case of the dharma-series *(dharma-santāna)*. The relation of ātman and skandhas is like the other binary relations between actor and deed, goer and locus, sense and object, etc. The relation between former person and latter person is like that between cause and effect. Thus this problem concerns the relation of simultaneous terms and that of successive terms.

Chapter twenty-seven of the *Stanzas*, from which the last group was taken, deals with the classic 'indeterminate questions' *(avyākṛta-vastūni)*. Nāgārjuna's treatment of these questions in some ways resembles Śākyamuni's as recorded in the *Nikāyas*. The same pattern of dichotomy-and-dilemma, and the same polarities of identity-versus-difference and continuous-versus-discrete are found in the *Stanzas* and in the *Suttas*.

47. The seer does not exist either apart from or non-apart from the seeing; when the seer does not exist, where are the seen and the seeing? (3.6) (*Prasannapadā*, pp. 117–18)
48. Because the seen and the seeing inexist, it is stated that the four—consciousness, etc.[16]—do not exist; so how can appropriation, etc. come into being? (3.7) (*Prasannapadā*, p. 119, v. 8)
49. You should know that hearing, smelling, tasting, touching, and thought, the hearer and the heard, etc. have been explained merely by the explanation of seeing (3.8) (*Prasannapadā*, p. 120, v. 9).
50. This existing dharma is declared to be without object-basis; then when the dharma is without object-basis, where else is there an object-basis? (1.11) (*Prasannapadā*, p. 84, v. 8)
51. Form, sound, taste, touch, smell, and dharmas are all nothing but appearances like fairy castles, resembling a mirage or a dream (23.8) (*Prasannapadā*, p. 457).
52. How can there be purity or impurity among them, since they are like a phantom man and like a reflection? (23.9) (*Prasannapadā*, p. 458)

This group of stanzas refutes the notion that some of the terms of epistemological relations might provide an Archimedean point of support for a system based on own-being.

53. Those that come into being in dependence on the pure, on the impure, and on misconception do not occur by own-being; therefore the passions (***kleśas***) do not [occur] in reality (***tattvatas***) (23.2) (***Prasannapadā***, p. 453).
54. Like the views of own-body, the passions do not exist in any of the five ways in the impassioned. Like the views of own-body, the impassioned does not exist in any of the five ways in the passions (23.5) (***Prasannapadā***, p. 454).
55. The pure, the impure, and misconceptions do not occur by own-being; dependent on what pure [things], impure [things], and misconceptions do the passions [exist]? (23.6) (***Prasannapadā***, p. 455)
56. Form, sound, taste, touch, smell, and dharmas, the sixfold object of lust, hatred, and folly, are [merely] conceived (23.7) (***Prasannapadā***, p. 456).
57. For if any passions belonging to anyone were real by their own-being, how could they be abandoned? Who will abandon own-being? (23.24) (***Prasannapadā***, p. 471)
58. If any passions belonging to anyone were unreal by own-being, how could they be abandoned? Who will abandon an unreal being? (23.25) (***Prasannapadā***, p. 471)

These stanzas refute the contention that since the Dharma talks about the passions *(kleśas)* and misconceptions *(viparyāsas)*, these must be existent. This contention is a typical example of the "doctrine of names" (See *Chao-lun*, Doc. 9. I.2, and Hui-yüan, Doc. 4. n. 71), the belief that words must mean something and thus that if there is a word, there must be a thing as its counterpart. Nāgārjuna denies this, and proceeds to apply his device of dichotomy-and-dilemma. Either the passions and misconceptions are real, in which case they cannot be destroyed, since the real is indestructible, or they are unreal, in which case they cannot be destroyed, since there is nothing to destroy in an illusion.

Nirvāṇa

59. He who sees this dependent co-arising sees suffering, arising, cessation, and path (24.40) (*Prasannapadā*, p. 515).
60. How would there be suffering that is not arisen in dependence? Since suffering is termed impermanent, it does not occur in own-beingness (24.21) (*Prasannapadā*, p. 506).
61. Why would something occurring by its own-being arise again? Therefore when you deny emptiness, there is no arising [of suffering] (24.22) (*Prasannapadā*, p. 506).
62. Cessation of suffering that exists by own-being is non-occurrent; because you persistently maintain own-being, you deny cessation (24.23) (*Prasannapadā*, p. 506).
63. If own-being existed, cultivation of the path would not be a fact; if the path is cultivated, then your "own-being" does not occur (24.24) (*Prasannapadā*, p. 507).
64. When suffering, arising and cessation do not occur, what path is supposed to be attained through the cessation of suffering? (24.25) (*Prasannapadā*, p. 508)

These stanzas work out the contradiction between the real and the changing as it affects the Four Holy Truths. The opponent has charged that Nāgārjuna denies the Four Holy Truths and all Buddhist doctrines because he asserts that they are empty. Nāgārjuna replies that a denial of emptiness entails denial of the Path, since change is impossible without emptiness.

65. In no way is nirvāṇa of the saṁskāras a fact; in no way is nirvāṇa of a living being a fact (16.4) (*Prasannapadā*, p. 288).
66. If appropriation is bondage, then one who has appropriation is not bound; one without appropriation is not bound; then how is any state bound? (16.6) (*Prasannapadā*, p. 290)
67. If bondage existed before the bound, then it might bind; but that is not so. The rest is stated according to the case of the being-gone, the gone, and the ungone (16.7) (*Prasannapadā*, pp. 291–92).
68. The bound one is not released and the unbound one is not released, either; if the bound one were being released, bondage and release would be simultaneous (16.8) (*Prasannapadā*, p. 293).
69. Those who grasp the notion, "I will enter nirvāṇa when free from appropriation, nirvāṇa will be mine," have a great grasp on appropriation (16.9) (*Prasannapadā*, p. 295).
70. Where there is no imposition of nirvāṇa and no repudiation of saṁsāra, what saṁsāra and what nirvāṇa are conceived? (16.10) (*Prasannapadā*, p. 299)
71. Nirvāṇa is defined as unabandoned, unattained, unannihilated, non-eternal, unextinguished, and unarisen (25.3) (*Prasannapadā*, p. 521).

In this group of stanzas, the binary relation between bondage and release is reduced to absurdity. These categories are no more properties of reality than are cause-and-effect, own-being, and the others. Saṁsāra and the appropriation (i.e., the skandhas) of the transmigrant are empty. Thus there is not even the slightest difference between nirvāṇa and saṁsāra.

72. He is not identical with the skandhas; he is not other than the skandhas; the skandhas are not in him, and he is not in them; the Tathāgata does not have skandhas; in this case, what Tathāgata is there? (22.1) (*Prasannapadā*, p. 432)
73. Thus in every way appropriation and appropriator are empty; how can an empty Tathāgata be designated by an empty [designator]? (22.10) (*Prasannapadā*, pp. 440-41)
74. Those who fantasize about the Buddha, who is beyond fancies and imperishable, are all slain by fancy and do not see the Tathāgata (22.15) (*Prasannapadā*, p. 448).
75. It is not asserted that after his final cessation the Blessed One exists, does not exist, or both, or neither (25.17) (*Prasannapadā*, p. 534).
76. It is not asserted that during his lifetime the Blessed One exists, does not exist, or both, or neither (25.18) (*Prasannapadā*, p. 534).

These stanzas state Nāgārjuna's Buddhological position. As he says, "The own-being of the Tathāgata is the own-being of this world; the Tathāgata is without own-being, and this world is without own-being."

Nāgārjuna's System

Mere inspection of the preceding examples suffices to show that the three groups of structures—dependent co-arising, personality, and nirvāṇa—differ somewhat in reference, but not at all in pattern. By substituting more general values for the terms, we may abstract one fundamental structure:

If a function has two terms, then they are either identical or different. You cannot admit that they are identical, because of your axiom that the two terms of a function are not identical.

You cannot admit that they are different, because of your axiom that real entities are not dependent on another. But if two entities are not in a relation of dependence, then they cannot be the terms of a function. If you assert that the two terms are both identical and different, then you contradict your axiom that identity is indivisible. Likewise if you assert that the two terms are neither identical nor different.

The axioms and definitions purport to be those commonly accepted by the disputants. The necessary properties of own-being are own-mark (intrinsic, individuating characteristic), independence (i.e., non-contingency), indivisibility (i.e., atomicity, necessary identity), and immutability. Properties are either necessary or contingent. If they are contingent, they do not really belong to the entity, and so Nāgārjuna refuses to admit them to his opponent's case.

The necessary properties of the existent are extension and succession. As the inexistent is the absence of an existent, it shares these necessary properties; it is an absence that is finite in extension and duration. This definition of 'existent' and 'inexistent' excludes universals and cannot accommodate a class of complex particulars. Being is restricted to the spatial, the temporal, the concrete, and the particular.[17]

By definition, own-being is incompatible with existence. Whatever is spatial and temporal has components, whether discrete or continuous. Thus it must stand as a term in the whole-part relation. But own-being is indivisible.

Given this contradiction, Nāgārjuna could either deny existence, or deny own-being. He chooses to deny own-being. This leaves him with a world-view in which there are no essences, and with a vocabulary every item in which implies an essence to some hearer or other. This is where his descriptive system and his description of it come into the picture.

77. The Buddhas' Dharma-explanation relies on two truths: the worldly, conventional truth, and the absolute truth. Those who do not know the distinction between these two truths do not know the deep reality in the Buddha's teaching. Without reliance on the expressional [truth], the absolute is not taught; without

arriving at the absolute, nirvāṇa is not reached (24.8–10) (*Prasannapadā*, pp. 492–94).
78. Everything is valid for that of which emptiness is valid; nothing is valid for that of which emptiness is not valid (24.14) (*Prasannapadā*, p. 500).

Worldly, conventional, or expressional truth means language and verbal thought. The absolute truth is said to be inexpressible and inconceivable. Yet realization of this fact depends on comprehension of expressional truth. All the doctrines taught by the Buddhas are compatible with emptiness; emptiness characterizes every term in the system of expressional truths.

That an entity is empty means that own-being is absent from it. When the entities are pieces of language, it means that they are symbols empty of object-content. Verbal thought and expression are 'constructed' or 'imagined' *(vikalpyate)*. They express only metaphorically, and there is no such thing as a literal statement, because there is no intrinsic relation of expressions to mystical experience and to worldly experience, since all alike are only figured but not represented by discursive symbols.

Once this is granted, the functional value of language is admitted by the Mādhyamika. As the *Hundred Treatise* says (Ch. 10, pp. 181c24–182a1):

OUTSIDER: If [things] are empty, you should not have a teaching. If everything is empty, then you must affirm a dharma devoid of teaching. How then do you now instruct people by teaching good and evil dharmas?
INSIDER: Because we accord with popular speech, there is no error. The Buddhas' Dharma-teaching always relies on the popular truth and on the absolute truth. Both these are true and not false speech. For example, though the Buddha knew that all the dharmas are markless, he told Ānanda, "Go into the city of Śrāvastī and beg food." A town cannot be perceived apart from earth, wood, etc. But because he accorded with popular speech, he did not fall into false speech. We, too, are without error, because we study according to the Buddha.

Emptiness is not a term outside the expressional system, but is simply the key term within it. Those who would hypostatize emptiness are confusing the symbol system with the fact system. No metaphysical fact whatever can be established from the facts of language. The question arises as to the relation between worldly truth and absolute truth. The term 'absolute truth' is part of the descriptive order, not part of the factual order. Like all other expressions, it is empty, but it has a peculiar relation within the system of designations. It symbolizes non-system, a surd within the system of constructs.

The quandaries into which the opponents are driven spring from the incommensurability of the descriptive order and the factual order. At least some of the opponents assumed commensurability, postulated a counterpart relation between verbal and factual units, and imputed the properties of own-being to facts. The matter is debated in the

Great Perfection of Wisdom Treatise (p. 147b8, Lamotte, *Traité* II, 726):

QUESTION: Just as the cloth which is donated really exists. For what reason? Since there exists the name of cloth, there exists an entity of cloth. If there were no entity of cloth, there would also be no name of cloth. But because the name exists, cloth must really exist. . . (p. 147b19).
REPLY: You say that because the name exists, [the entity] exists. But this is not true. How do we know it? There are two kinds of name: those that have actuals, and those that do not have actuals. Thus, there is a herb that is called 'caurī.' 'Caurī' translates as 'thief' in Chinese. The herb does not steal and does not rob. It is really not a thief, yet it is called 'thief.' Thus further, rabbit horns and tortoise hairs also have names only but do not have actuals. Though cloth is not inexistent like rabbit horns and tortoise hairs, yet it exists because causes and conditions combine and it inexists because causes and conditions disperse. It is like a forest and like an army, which all have names but do not have actuals.

Nāgārjuna's Logic

Analysis of the logical constructions in the *Stanzas* confirms the statement in the Chinese biography of Nāgārjuna that he adopted methods of formal reasoning from the Tīrthikas and utilized them to expound the Dharma. He also knew and used the early Buddhist repertory of dialectic devices, for which he found new uses.[18]

Nāgārjuna states explicitly that the form of his arguments may be abstracted from their content, that other proofs may be performed by substituting different terms within the same pattern. This comes rather close to recognition of the principle of variables. For example:

49. You should know that hearing, smelling, tasting, touching, and thought, the hearer and the heard, etc., have been explained merely by the explanation of seeing (3.8) (*Prasannapadā*, p. 120, v. 9).
67. The rest is stated according to the case of the being-gone, the gone and the ungone (16.7) (*Prasannapadā*, pp. 291–92).
79. By this method the remaining two [times] are to be treated mutatis mutandis. One should examine the top, bottom, and middle, etc., and the unity, etc. (19.4) (*Prasannapadā*, p. 384).
80. By the [example of the] fire and fuel is explained the whole method, omitting nothing, for [the examination of] self and appropriation, as well as for the pot, the cloth, and so on (10.15) (*Prasannapadā*, pp. 212–13).

In the *Stanzas*, the three "Laws of Thought" of traditional Western logic are not denied, and two of them are explicitly affirmed. The principle of contradiction is necessary to most of Nāgārjuna's arguments, because he relies heavily on dichotomies. This principle is stated rather generally in two places:

36. Existent and inexistent in a unity is not true to fact (7.30) (*Prasannapadā*, pp. 169–70).
81. . . . Since they are mutually contradictory; where are there both real and unreal in the same place? (8.7) (*Prasannapadā*, p. 185)

The law of the excluded middle is invoked explicitly in some places:

24. A goer does not go, and a non-goer does not go; what third one other than goer and non-goer goes? (2.8) (*Prasannapadā*, p. 97)
25. A goer does not stand still, and a non-goer does not stand still; what third one other than goer and non-goer stands still? (2.15) (*Prasannapadā*, p. 101)

Elsewhere, this law is assumed but not stated:

82. That existent would be either permanent or impermanent (21.14) (*Prasannapadā*, p. 421).

Candrakīrti renders the principle of chapter 2, verse 8 more explicit: "If you hold that one excluded *(vyatirikta)* from both [goer and non-goer] goes, it is not so, for what third one is there dissociated from goer and non-goer of whom it is conceived that he goes" (*Prasannapadā*, p. 98, ll. 4–5; May, *Prasannapadā*, p. 61)? The argument can be reformulated: There is no entity that is not either a goer or a non-goer. If *X* is an entity, then you must affirm either that *X* is a goer, or that *X* is a non-goer.

The possibility of finding multivalued logic has stimulated some recent interest in the role of the law of the excluded middle in Indian philosophy. Kevalādvaita Vedānta evidently sets up inexpressibility as a third truth-value (Ingalls, "Avidyā," pp. 69 ff.). Nāgārjuna does not do so. Nowhere does he acknowledge a third mode of judgment other than affirmation and negation, and nowhere does he refrain from negating a proposition. Candrakīrti states the conclusion to chapter 2, verse 8, not as "Therefore going is inexpressible," but as "Therefore there is no going."

The law of identity is neither affirmed nor denied anywhere in the *Stanzas*. However, unity and multiplicity are mentioned in a non-logical sense in many places:

83. Otherness does not occur in an other and does not occur in a non-other; and when otherness does not occur, there is neither an other nor an identity (14.7) (*Prasannapadā*, pp. 254–55).
14. The otherwise-being of a [specific] nature is never true to fact (15.8) (*Prasannapadā*, p. 271).
7. An "A" that comes into being dependent on "B" is not identical with "B" and not other than "B" (18.10) (*Prasannapadā*, p. 375).
84. If there were oneness of effect and cause, there would be oneness of producer and product. If there were difference of effect and cause, the cause would be the same as a non-cause (20.20) (*Prasannapadā*, p. 404).

In these passages, it should be noted, Nāgārjuna is discussing identity as an absolute, which he rejects because the concept of identity is definable only in relation to difference, and that which is not self-sufficient is not absolute. An absolute identity would be immutable. However, neither total identity nor total non-identity can be predicated of two things which stand in a relation to each other. This is not a denial of the concept of identity, but simply a denial that identity to the exclusion of difference, or vice versa, can be attributed to anything existential.

In the *Stanzas* there is a very large number of hypothetical syllogisms. In fact, demonstration by means of this form of inference is one of the features that distinguish the *Stanzas* most sharply from the Śūnyavādin sūtras. The two valid types of hypothetical syllogism—modus ponens and modus tollens—both occur, as well as the fallacious mode in which the antecedent is negated.

The form of modus ponens is: "*p* implies *q*; *p*, therefore *q*." Instances of this type are rare, and the antecedent which is affirmed is usually a negative proposition. For example:

85. Seeing does not see itself. When it does not see itself, how can it see others? (3.2) (*Prasannapadā*, p. 113)

Converted to standard form, this inference would be: "If something cannot see itself, then it cannot see anything else. Seeing cannot see itself. Therefore seeing cannot see anything else."

21. If time depends on an entity, then where is there time without the entity? Since there is no entity, where would time exist? (19.6) (*Prasannapadā*, p. 387)

Converting the question to a negation, an operation that is sanctioned by commentaries as well as Chinese translators' practice,[19] we obtain the implication, "Wherever there is no entity, there is no time." "There is no entity whatsoever" is then affirmed, and the conclusion, "time does not exist anywhere" is then drawn.

The rule of negating the consequent by which modus tollens is obtained is exemplified in the first half of 19.6, just quoted. "As the existence of time implies the existence of an entity, when there is no entity, there is no time." The general propositional form is: "*p* implies *q*; not *q*, therefore not *p*." Instances are quite common, for example:

86. If cause-of-form existed disjoined from form, then there would be an effectless cause [Therefore cause-of-form does not exist disjoined from form.] (4.3) (*Prasannapadā*, p. 124).

For other examples, see 5.1, 19.1, 25.5, and 27.7. It is quite common for the conclusion, and sometimes even the assertion of the negated consequent, to be left unexpressed.

Term negation in Nāgārjuna's system is the cancellation of a specific entity, rather than the class of everything except that entity. That is, the negation of a term is its "counter-twin" *(pratidvandvin)*.

87. If the existent is not established, then the inexistent is not established, either, since by the inexistent people mean the alter-existent of an existent (15.5) (*Prasannapadā*, p. 267).

Other examples occur in 7.33, 13.7, 23.10, 23.22, 25.7, and 27.18. An existent entity *(bhāva)* is conditioned and so it is neither universal nor null. Logically, it has a finite extension. Its negative counterpart *(abhāva)* is an absence in the place where the existent would have been if it had been present, or in the place where the existent was before it became inexistent.

Nāgārjuna distinguishes propositional negation from term negation, and uses special terms to negate propositions. A list of occurrences of these terms which serve as propositional functors is:

Na upapadyate— ('is not true to fact, is not proved').	1.12, 2.3, 2.6, 2.9, 2.16, 2.23, 4.4, 4.5, 5.4, 7.21, 7.23, 7.29, 7.30, 7.31, 8.6, 16.4, 17.12, 20.18, 20.22, 21.9, 21.10, 23.10, 24.13, 27.3, 27.7, 27.9, 27.27.
Na yujyate— ('is not valid, is not uncontradicted by a fact or a verified statement').	1.9, 2.18, 3.4, 6.3, 7.20, 7.25, 9.8, 10.11, 11.5, 12.1, 13.4, 14.8, 15.1, 15.8, 17.24, 21.17, 21.18, 21.20, 24.14, 25.10, 25.11, 27.22, 27.25, 27.26.
Prasajyate— ('leads to absurdity, contradicts what is taken as true').	2.4, 2.5, 2.6, 2.10, 2.11, 2.19, 4.2, 5.1, 8.6, 8.8, 10.3, 15.11, 17.23, 20.9, 21.14, 21.16, 24.13, 24.31, 25.4.

In the *Stanzas* there are many dilemmas. The commonest type has the form: "If *p*, then *q*; if not-*p*, then *q*." This is a special form of the "simple constructive" dilemma of traditional Western logic.

88. If there were co-being in oneness, then *X* would exist even without companion. If there were co-being in separateness, then *X* would exist even without companion (6.5) (*Prasannapadā*, p. 140).

89. When contact does not take place, how can a cause produce an effect? When contact does take place, how can a cause produce an effect (20.15) (*Prasannapadā*, pp. 401–2)?

Other examples are to be found in 4.6, 13.4, 15.9, 20.1–2, 20.16, 20.21, 21.9, 21.10, 21.18, 25.1–2, and 27.21.

A much rarer form of dilemma is: "If *p*, then *q*; if not-*p*, then *r*," where both *q* and *r* are unwelcome conclusions. This is a special form of the "complex constructive" dilemma of traditional Western logic.

90. If the fire is identical with the fuel, then there is oneness of agent and affectee. If the fire were different from the fuel, then the fire would exist even without the fuel (10.1) (*Prasannapadā*, p. 202).

It is a striking feature of the *Stanzas* that all predicates seem to be asserted totally of the whole subject. Existential quantifications are denied because the discussion is concerned, not with the denial or affirmation of commonsense assertions such as, "Some fuel is burning, and some is not," but with the concepts of own-being and essence. What pertains to part of an essence must of course pertain to the whole essence. A defining property is either essential or non-essential. If it is non-essential, it is not really a defining property of an essence. If it is essential, then the essence is never devoid of the property.

Many of Nāgārjuna's terms are explicitly bound and universally quantified. The usual quantifying expressions are "all," and "not... anything/anyone/anywhere/anywhen."

91. For impermanence never does not occur in entities (21.4) (*Prasannapadā*, p. 412).

This method of quantification emphasizes that the class quantified does not necessarily have any members, which perhaps accounts for Nāgārjuna's fondness for it.

From the Buddhist tradition which preceded him, Nāgārjuna inherited the tetralemma *(catuṣkoṭi)*. This venerable piece of dialectic apparatus is reported to have been in use in the time of Śākyamuni himself. In *Majjhima-nikāya* 63, Māluṅkyāputta says to himself:

... that the Tathāgata exists after death, that the Tathāgata does not exist after death, that the Tathāgata both exists and does not exist after death, that the Tathāgata neither exists nor does not exist after death—these the Blessed One does not explain to me (Trenckner I, 426).

In *Majjhima-nikāya* 72, Gotama answers a set of questions which Vacchagotta poses in tetralemma form:

Gotama, where is the monk reborn whose mind is thus freed?—Vaccha, it is not true to say that he is reborn.—Then, Gotama, he is not reborn.—Vaccha, it is not true to say that he is not reborn.—Then, Gotama, he is both reborn and not reborn. —Vaccha, it is not true to say that he is both reborn and not reborn.—Then, Gotama, he is neither reborn nor not reborn.—Vaccha, it is not true to say that he is neither reborn nor not reborn (Trenckner I, 486).

In the subsequent passage of this sutta, Gotama explains that just as a fire which is extinguished does not go anywhere, so when the five skandhas have been abandoned there is no subject of which rebirth can be predicated. Compare Nāgārjuna: "A real goer does not go the threefold going; an unreal goer does not go the threefold going" (2.24) (*Prasannapadā*, p. 107).

In both these suttas, the tetralemma occurs in the context of conversation about the undecided questions *(avyākṛta-vastūni)*. In the *Stanzas*, it occurs in the same context, in virtually the same words:

75. It is not asserted that after his final cessation the Blessed One exists, does not exist, or both, or neither (25.17) (*Prasannapadā*, p. 534).
76. It is not asserted that during his lifetime the Blessed One exists, does not exist, or both, or neither (25.18) (*Prasannapadā*, p. 534).
92. It should not be said that [the Tathāgata] is empty, or that he is non-empty, or that he is both empty and non-empty, or that he is neither empty nor non-empty. But it is said for the sake of designation (22.11) (*Prasannapadā*, p. 444).
93. If the man is identical with the god, he is thus eternal; the god would be unarisen, since the eternal is not born. If the man is different from the god, then he is non-eternal; if the man is different from the god, then succession is not a fact. If one part is divine and one part is human, then he is both eternal and non-eternal, and that is not valid.

If "both eternal and non-eternal" were established, then "neither eternal nor non-eternal" might be established too (27.15–18) (*Prasannapadā*, pp. 583–85).[20]

Chapter 27 of the *Stanzas* is devoted to the undecided questions. The *Middle Treatise*, commenting on the first two verses, says:

In past time, I was existent, or I was inexistent, or I was both existent and inexistent, or I was neither existent nor inexistent—these are called views of eternality, etc. which depend on past time. In future time, I will function, or I will not function, or I will both function and not function, or I will neither function nor not function—these are called views of finitude and infinitude which depend on future time (T XXX, p. 36a2).

The fourteen undecided questions are discussed at various places in the *Great Perfection of Wisdom Treatise*, and tetralemma formulas are given. See, for instance, T XXV, pp. 74c–75a (Lamotte, *Traité* I, 153 ff.); p. 110a (Lamotte, *Traité* I, 423); p. 170a (Lamotte, *Traité* II, 913) which quotes the equivalent of *Majjhima-nikāya* 63, 266a ff., and 545b ff.[21]

In all the examples so far, all four lemmas are to be rejected. If this were always so, then the tetralemma would be simply a more comprehensive and emphatic way of denying all forms of own-being. However, it has another use—as a pedagogical device.

94. Everything is either true, or not true, or both true and not true, or neither true nor not true; this is the adapted instruction of the Buddhas (18.8) (*Prasannapadā*, p. 369).

The *Middle Treatise* commentary on this verse (T XXX, 25a18–b2), is as follows:

As for "everything is real," when you analyze the real-nature of the dharmas, [you find that] they all enter the absolute truth, are all equal, are all of one mark, that is, they are markless. It is just like the different colors and different tastes of all the streams which become one color and one taste when they enter the great ocean.

As for "everything is unreal," when the dharmas have not entered the real-mark, they are contemplated analytically one by one, and they are all [seen to] have nothing real in them. They only exist because of the combination of many conditions.

As for "everything is both real and unreal," there are three classes of living beings—superior, medium, and inferior. The superior contemplate the marks of the dharmas as "not real and not unreal." The medium contemplate the marks of the dharmas as "all both real and unreal." The inferior, because their powers of knowledge are shallow, look on the marks of the dharmas as "partly real and partly unreal." Because nirvāṇa, and the [other] unconditioned dharmas are imperishable, they look on them as real. Because saṁsāra and the conditioned dharmas are counterfeit, they look on them as unreal.

As for "[everything] is not real and not unreal," [the Buddhas] declared "not real and not unreal" in order to refute "both real and unreal."

QUESTION: In other places, the Buddha declared "detachment from not-real-and-not-unreal." Why does it say here that "not existent and not inexistent" is what the Buddha declared?

ANSWER: In other places, it was declared in order to demolish the four kinds of attachment. But here there is no fiction (*prapañca*) regarding the tetralemma. When one hears the Buddha's declaration, then one attains bodhi. Therefore he says "not real and not unreal."

Candrakīrti, in the *Prasannapadā* (p. 370), gives a slightly different interpretation of *Stanza* 18.8. He considers the tetralemma as an expedient device *(upāya)* that the Buddha uses in giving progressively higher instruction to the different grades of living beings. First the Buddha speaks of phenomena as if they were real, in order to lead beings to venerate his omniscience. Next, he teaches that phenomena are unreal, because they undergo modifications, and what is real does not undergo modifications. Thirdly, he teaches some hearers that phenomena are both real and unreal—real from the point of view of worldlings, but unreal from the viewpoint of the saints. To those who are practically free from passions and wrong views, he declares that phenomena are neither real nor unreal, in the same way that one denies that the son of a barren woman is white or that he is black.

The *Middle Treatise* and Candrakīrti agree that the tetralemma is a therapeutic device, and that the lemmas form an ascending series in which each lemma except the first is a counteragent to the one before it. This is a dialectical progression, each lemma negating and cancelling its predecessor, and the whole argument moving forward to the negation of the fourth lemma, which is supposed to dispose of all "views."

It still remains to establish the logical form of the tetralemma. If we assume that the four lemmas are modes of one proposition, then the tetralemma is to be interpreted: "Either *p*, or not-*p*, or *p*-and-not-*p*, or not-*p*-and-not-not-*p*."[22] In this case, "*p*-and-not-*p*" would be absurd, by the rule of contradiction, and "not-*p*-and-not-not-*p*" is identical with "*p*-and-not-*p*" if we assume that "not-not-*p*" equals "*p*." Thus the third and fourth lemmas would be senseless. It would be very curious if early dialecticians from Māluṅkyāputta and Vacchagotta onwards had framed questions in two modes which they interpreted in a manner that they knew to be absurd.

The other likely possibility is that the four lemmas differ in the quantity of their constituent terms, that they are four propositions with different internal structures. In the first and second lemmas, the terms are obviously to be universally quantified—"All *x* is *A*," and "All *x* is non-*A*." *Stanza* 27.17, quoted in No. 93, interprets "both eternal and non-eternal" as "one part is divine and one part is human." The *Middle Treatise*, p. 3a7, says, "Existent-and-inexistent mean half existent and half inexistent." Thus there are grounds for interpreting the third lemma as: "Some *x* is *A* and some *x* is not-*A*." Accordingly, the fourth lemma may be construed: "No *x* is *A* and no *x* is not-*A*."

When the tetralemma is quantified in this way, it is analogous to the four Aristotelian forms in some respects. The similarities and differences tabulate as follows:

ARISTOTELIAN FORMS		TETRALEMMA	
A	All *x* is *A*	1	All *x* is *A*
E	No *x* is *A*	2	No *x* is *A*
I	Some *x* is *A*	3	Some *x* is *A*, and some *x* is not *A*
O	Some *x* is not *A*	4	No *x* is *A*, and no *x* is not *A*

Since "No *x* is not *A*" equals "All *x* is *A*," the fourth lemma is a conjunction of E and A forms. The third lemma is a conjunction of I and O forms. The fourth lemma is a conjunction of the contradictories of the conjuncts of the third lemma; "No *x* is *A*" is the contradictory of "Some *x* is *A*," and "No *x* is not *A*" is the contradictory of "Some *x* is not *A*." Thus there is a reciprocity between the third and fourth lemmas. Negation of the conjuncts of one always produces the other.

In these formulas, "*x*" stands for the attributes of the entity in question. According to the commentaries, which lemma is affirmed or denied depends on what set of attributes constitutes one's universe of discourse. In one frame of reference, a given lemma will be affirmed, and in another it will be denied. This is tantamount to saying that no proposition is valid except within a set of validating conditions. Consequently, no proposition is valid in an absolute sense.

There do not seem to be any real paradoxes in the *Stanzas*. The seeming paradoxes are easily resolved once the definitions and the fundamental absurdity of the concept of own-being are taken into account.

Mysticism in Early Mādhyamika[23]

In Kumārajīva's time, there was a belief in China that Nāgārjuna had been a mystic of high attainments. Hui-yüan says that during his Hīnayāna period Nāgārjuna dwelt in seclusion in the forest and practiced dhyāna (Doc. 4.II.3). He also says that after making the acquaintance of the dragon, Nāgārjuna arrived at the tenth bodhisattva stage and was endowed with non-arising-dharma-patience (Doc. 4.II.4). The Chinese biography of Nāgārjuna also says that after reading the dragon's library of sūtras and conversing with the dragon, Nāgārjuna attained the one-mark of all the sūtras, entered profoundly into no-arising, and was endowed with the two (three) patiences (T 2047, pp. 184c15, 186a15). These traditions, early though they are, are still separated from the lifetime of the master by one or two centuries. However, it is to be asked how even Nāgārjuna's contemporaries and close associates would have ascertained the degree of his attainment. Consequently, the Chinese tradition is valuable not as spiritual biography, but as evidence that the Mādhyamika school came at some early date to consider its founder as a great mystic.

The *Stanzas* contain no discussion of contemplative techniques or of the trances and absorptions. The empirical aspect of realization is treated in a drastically laconic fashion:

95. When ignorance is extinguished, the dispositions do not arise. The extinction of ignorance by knowledge [takes place] through meditation on [dependent co-arising] (26.11) (*Prasannapadā*, pp. 558-59).

This verse is lacking in Kumārajīva's translation of the *Stanzas* but it occurs in the Tibetan version and the Chinese *Prajñā-pradīpa*. Bhāvaviveka says:

"When ignorance has been cut off,
the dispositions do not arise again;
because one cultivates prajñā,
ignorance can be cut off."

COMMENTARY: This means that the dispositions do not arise because they lack conditions (*pratyaya*). Just as the sprout does not spring up because the seed has no entity (is absent). Now what knowledge (*jñāna*) does one cultivate to cut off ignorance? As it is stated in this treatise, the knowledge that cognizes dependent co-arising, the knowledge of emptiness that denies that all the entities have own-entity, that understands persons and dharmas to be sense-spheres without self (*nairātmya-gocarāḥ*). "Cultivate" means to practice repeatedly. As the *Treatise Verse* says:

"When each link is extinguished,
The next one does not arise;
The mere suffering-aggregate
Is (thus) termed forever and truly extinguished."

COMMENTARY: This means that each of the existence-links (***bhavāṅga***), the dispositions (***saṃskāras***) etc., because the counteragent way arises, then ceases. That these existence-links do not arise again is because the dispositions are extinct. When the dispositions cease, consciousness ceases, and so on until birth, old age and death, sorrow and grief cease. "The mere suffering-aggregate is (thus) termed forever and truly extinguished"—because this is comprised in the worldly truth. In the absolute truth, ignorance etc. have no arising and no cessation. [OBJECTION:] How then can you call it dependent co-arising? [REPLY:] The Buddha expresses the absolute truth by relying on the worldly truth. My meaning is like this. As a previous verse says: "If one did not rely on the worldly truth, one could not express the absolute" (24.10). Because of this the point that I have made is not refuted. . . (T 1566, XXX, 133a5–20).

The bodhisattva course and bodhi are only mentioned in passing as goals desirable to the opponent:

96. According to you, the Buddha would not be dependent on bodhi, which is absurd, and bodhi would not be dependent on the Buddha, which is absurd. For you, he who is non-Buddha by his own-being, even though he strives for bodhi, will not realize bodhi in the bodhisattva course (24.31–32) (***Prasannapadā***, pp. 510–11).

The content of enlightenment is stated with equal concision:

59. He who sees this dependent co-arising sees suffering, arising, cessation, and path (24.40) (***Prasannapadā***, p. 515).

The *Middle Treatise* comments on this verse (p. 34c8):

If a man sees that all the dharmas arise from conditions, then he is able to see the Buddha's dharmakāya and to augment his prajñā. He is able to see the Four Holy Truths—suffering, arising, cessation, and path. Seeing the Four Holy Truths, he obtains the four fruits and extinguishes all afflictions.

If one asks how philosophical reasoning conduces to this end, Nāgārjuna's answer is:

97. When the sphere of thought has ceased, the nameable ceases; Dharma-nature is like nirvāṇa, unarising and unceasing (18.7) (***Prasannapadā***, p. 364).

The *Middle Treatise* has nothing to say about samādhi in its commentary on this Stanza, but the *Great Perfection of Wisdom Treatise* (pp. 96b29 ff., Lamotte, *Traité* I, 321) quotes this verse in the context of a discussion on samādhi:

All the samādhis: the three samādhis are emptiness, wishlessness, and marklessness. Some say: emptiness means beholding that in the five skandhas there is no "I" and no "mine." Wishlessness means abiding in this samādhi of emptiness and not producing the three poisons towards subsequent lives. Marklessness means having an object without the ten marks, [that is] (a) the five sense-spheres, (b) male and female, (c) arising, (d) abiding, and (e) ceasing. Others say: the samādhi of emptiness means abiding in this samādhi and knowing the real-mark of all the dharmas, namely utter emptiness. When one has known this samādhi, one is wishless. What is wishlessness? Not to look on the dharmas either as empty or as non-empty, either as existent or as inexistent, etc. As the Buddhas declared in a stanza of the ***Dharmapada***: "When one sees existence, one is afraid; when one sees inexistence, one is also afraid. Therefore one should not be attached to existence and should not be attached to inexistence." This is called the samādhi of wishlessness. What is the samādhi of marklessness? All the dharmas are without marks. Not to accept and not to cling to all the dharmas is called the samādhi of marklessness. As the ***Stanza*** says: "When language has ceased, the spheres of thought also cease. It is non-arising, non-ceasing, and like nirvāṇa" [***Stanzas*** 18.7]. Further, the eighteen emptinesses are called the samādhi of emptiness. The mind not seeking anything in the various kinds of existence is called the samādhi of wishlessness. Obliterating all the marks and not cogitating about them is called the samādhi of marklessness.
QUESTION: There are many kinds of dhyāna and samāpatti. Why are these three alone called samādhis?
REPLY: Because in these three samādhis, thinking approaches nirvāṇa, so that men's thoughts are not too high and not too low, but even and immovable. In the other states [of trance] it is not so. For this reason, these three alone are called samādhis. In the other samāpattis, sometimes lust predominates, sometimes pride predominates, and sometimes views predominate. But in these three samādhis there is the real-truth, the real-benefit, and one can attain the gateways of nirvāṇa. Therefore, among all the dhyānas and samāpattis, these three samāpattis are the three gates of liberation. They are also called the three samādhis.

Notice that the samādhi of emptiness concerns ontology, that of wishlessness pertains to the affective and hence the strictly religious sphere, and that the samādhi of marklessness belongs to the domain of epistemology. The *Stanzas* have little to say about the affective problem which is supposed to find its solution in the second samādhi, but the noetic problems which the first and third samādhis would liquidate are the dominant subject of the *Stanzas*. The three samādhis, the gates to nirvāṇa, are manifestly psychological states in which the esoteric meaning of a gnosis reveals itself. The goal of the intricately patterned and rigorously rational argumentation of the *Stanzas* is thus avowedly an ecstasy in which determinate objects of thought are absent, where objects of designation are not apprehended, and where unarising and unceasing dharma-nature is realized. It is difficult to imagine the psychological content of such an experience, but the texts are remarkably explicit about its intellectual content. However mystical the cessation of misconceptions, of views of own-being, Nāgārjuna and his disciples talk about it in intellectual terms, in discourse whose structure is compatible with the logic of ordinary discourse.

It may be asked whether the cultivation of trances is essential to the solution of so eminently intellectual a riddle. The author of the *Stanzas* is silent on this point, but the *Great Perfection of Wisdom Treatise*, which discusses the contemplative stages at great length, insists that samādhi is indispensable to prajñā (p. 206c17):

QUESTION: In these three ways with prajñā one contemplates emptiness, contemplates marklessness, and contemplates wishlessness. Why is this prajñā called samādhi?
REPLY: If these three kinds of prajñā did not abide in samāpatti, they would be mad prajñā. One would fall into many falsehoods and doubts, and there would be nothing that one could do. If one abides in samāpatti, then one can demolish all the passions and attain the real-mark of all the dharmas. Further, this Way is different from everything mundane and is opposite to the mundane. All the holy men, residing in samāpatti, attain the real-mark. Their statements are not the utterances of a mad mind. Further, if these three dharmas were not in all the dhyānas and samāpattis, [the latter] would not be called samādhis.

So far, all the emphasis has been on the phase of withdrawal in the contemplative path. This is the prevailing note of the *Stanzas*, except for the salutations to Gautama in the first two verses of the first chapter and the last verse of the last chapter. However, the *Great Perfection of Wisdom Treatise* occasionally stresses the altruistic aspect of the contemplative life (p. 180b17, Lamotte, *Traité* II, 984):

QUESTION: The dharma of the bodhisattva is to take the salvation of all living beings as his duty. Why does he sit in seclusion among the woods and swamps and remain still and silent amid the mountains, only valuing his own person and abandoning living beings?
REPLY: Though the body of the bodhisattva is far away from living beings, his mind never abandons them. In a quiet abode he seeks samādhi and acquires real-prajñā in order to save everyone. It is like taking a medicine for the body. One temporarily quits one's household duties, but when one's health is restored one resumes one's tasks just as before. The tranquilization of the bodhisattva is similar to this. By the power of dhyāna and samādhi he takes the medicine of prajñā. When he has obtained the power of the super-knowledge, he returns to dwell among living beings and becomes a father, a mother, a wife, or a child; a master, a follower, or a leader; a god, a man, or even an animal. With many kinds of speech and expedient means he guides them.

NĀGĀRJUNISM AND THE PRAJÑĀ-PĀRAMITĀ-SŪTRAS

Tradition maintains that Nagarjuna systematized the teaching of the *Prajñā-pāramitā-sūtras*. La Vallée Poussin says:

We know that [Nāgārjuna] was the putative father of the Great Vehicle, or Mahāyāna, and, in particular, the revealer of the sūtras of the *Prajñā-pāramitā*, the teaching of which is akin to that of the Madhyamaka. It is even possible that several sūtras of the Great Vehicle were written with the sole purpose of stating the theories of the Madhyamaka philosophy under the guise of 'words of the

Buddha.' It is difficult to determine what part Nāgārjuna took in the redaction of the sūtras, but respect for tradition would lead us to believe that his share was a large one (*ERE* VIII, 235b–36a).

Murti says:

The Mādhyamika system is the systematized form of the Śūnyatā doctrine of the *Prajñāpāramitā* treatises; its metaphysics, spiritual path (*ṣaṭ-pāramitā-naya*) and religious ideal are all present there, though in a loose, prolific garb (*Buddhism*, p. 83).

Walleser says:

The systematic development of the thought of voidness laid down in the *Prajñāpāramitā Sūtras* is brought into junction with the name of a man of whom we cannot even positively say that he has really existed, still less that he is the author of the works ascribed to him: this name is Nāgārjuna ("Life of Nāgārjuna," p. 421).

Candrakīrti says:

The holy master Nāgārjuna, having the method of Prajñāpāramitā as known without misconception, out of compassion in order to enlighten others composed the *Treatise* (*Prasannapadā*, p. 3, ll. 1–2; cf. Stcherbatsky, *Nirvāṇa*, p. 83).

The preface to the Chinese translation of Asaṅga's *Madhyamaka-śāstra-anusāra* says, "The master Nāgārjuna who comprehended the Dharma wrote the *Middle Treatise* on the basis of the *Mahā-prajñā-pāramitā*" (T 1565, XXX, 39c9). The Asaṅga commentary itself says:

QUESTION: If the Master explained the meaning of the *Prajñā-pāramitā* in this way, through this skilful means, why did he first write the *Middle Treatise* (p. 40c10)? And again,
QUESTION: For what purpose did the Ācārya compose this treatise?
ANSWER: In conformity to valid reasoning he entered the meaning of the *Mahā-prajñāpāramitā* in order to lead living beings to . . . (p. 44c23).

Hui-yüan, writing in the early fifth century, says, "He (Nāgārjuna) considered the *Prajñā Sūtra* to be the sublime gate to the numinal treasury, the way to the Ideal Unity" (Doc. 4.5).

The Chinese biography of Nāgārjuna does not mention the *Prajñā-pāramitā-sūtras*, but it does state:

He said to himself, "Among the doctrines in the world there are very many roads and fords. Though the Buddhist sūtras are sublime, they are incomplete in respect to formal reasoning. What fault is there if in the respects where they are incomplete I expound them by inference and thus enlighten later students about not violating principles and not missing the facts!" (T 2047, p. 184c2)

The lower terminus for the earliest extant version of the *Aṣṭasāhasrikā-prajñā-pāramitā-sūtra* is A.D. 172, the date of Lokakṣema's first Chinese translation (Matsumoto, *Literatur*, pp. 22–23). The lower limit for the *Pañcaviṁśati* is A.D. 286, the date of Dharmarakṣa's translation. Thus some form of the *Aṣṭasāhasrikā* was established by Nāgārjuna's time, but it is possible that the *Pañcaviṁśati* was still in process of formation and may owe something to Nāgārjuna's influence. The *Aṣṭasāhasrikā* is the more suitable for the present comparison, since if it is connected with Nāgārjuna, he depends on it, not it on him.

Many of the most important religious and ontological terms in the *Aṣṭasāhasrikā* do not occur in the *Middle Stanzas*. Conversely, Nāgārjuna shares many terms with the Tīrthikas that are not found in the *Aṣṭasāhasrikā*, or that occur only in another sense, for instance the logical operators "yujyate" (is valid), "upapadyate" (is true to fact), and "sidhyate" (is established, proved, or made real). The following terms occur in the *Aṣṭasāhasrikā* and do not occur in the *Middle Stanzas*:

Term	Chapter and Page of Sanskrit Text
prajñā (wisdom, insight)	throughout.
tathatā (suchness)	12.271; 16; 18.342, 350.
bhūtakoṭi (reality-limit)	1.15; 4.94.
advaya (non-dual)	1.27; 2.38–40; 8.186–87; 12.265; 16.307–8; 17.323.
dharmadhātu (dharma-plane)	6.159; 9.206; 12.256; 17.327; 30.491.
dharmakāya (dharma-body)	4.94, 99; 17.338; 31.513.
rūpakāya (form-body)	31.513.
pāramitā (perfection)	throughout.
bodhicitta (thought of enlightenment)	1.5, 19; 8.190.
bhūmi (stage)	1.8; 17.336; 20.379.
karuṇā (compassion)	throughout.
upāya (skilful means)	11.247–48; 18.342.

'Bodhisattva' occurs once in the *Middle Stanzas* (24.32) and throughout the *Aṣṭasāhasrikā*.

Your choice of words depends on what you are talking about and who you are talking to. In the *Stanzas* Nāgārjuna was arguing with Tīrthikas and Hīnayānists who did not accept the Bodhisattva-yāna. He was trying to persuade them by reasoning on grounds that they accepted rather than to teach them the dharma-paryāyas of the Bodhisattva-yāna. Insofar as his purpose can be inferred from his performance, he was avoiding duplication of the techniques and content of the Śūnyavādin sūtras, which rely on rhetorical persuasion rather than inferential persuasion. So the conclusion drawn from the fact that the *Stanzas* do not use a dozen of the most important Śūnyavādin terms is that Nāgārjuna was not talking about those subjects to people who used those terms for them.

There are many similes in the *Aṣṭasāhasrikā* and only sixteen in the *Stanzas*:

1. Just as a lamp lights up its and another's self (7.8).
2. As the cutting off of a second head does not occur (7.31).
3. Like an illusion, like a dream, like a fairy castle (7.34).
4. As the woman takes the man and the man takes the woman (10.6).
5. The young man does not grow old, and the old man does not grow old (13.5).
6. The milk would be identical with the curds (13.6).
7. The series of the sprout, etc. that is set in motion from the seed (17.7).
8. (opponent's simile) Karma is like a debt that lasts as long as the account-sheet is not destroyed (17.14).
9. As a master created a phantom man by his magic powers, and the created phantom then created yet another (17.31).
10. Having the form of a fairy city, resembling a mirage and a dream (17.33).
11. (same as No. 10) (23.8).
12. Among those that are like a phantom man, and like a reflection (23.9).
13. (destroys) like a serpent wrongly grasped or a spell wrongly recited (24.11).
14. You have forgotten the very horse on which you are mounted (24.15).
15. Like light and darkness, the two do not exist together in one place (25.14).
16. This series of skandhas moves onward like the flames of a lamp (27.22).

Of these, five—Nos. 3, 9, 10, 11, and 12—are distinctly Śūnyavādin, though not peculiar to the *Prajñā-pāramitā-sūtras*.

Where these occur in the *Stanzas* is significant. No. 1 comes at the end of a section that attacks the Abhidharma categories of the conditioned and the unconditioned and the Hīnayānist concept of dependent co-arising. Nos. 9 and 10 conclude a refutation of the Hīnayānist charges that Śūnyavāda repudiates the traditional Buddhist ethic. No. 11 occurs in a refutation of the notion that the objects of the passions are real. No. 12 occurs immediately after No. 11. Thus all these similes are introduced against Hīnayānists who were familiar with this sort of simile in their own scriptures and so were likely to be persuaded by it.

The small number of these Śūnyavādin similes notwithstanding, Nāgārjuna is signalling his position as a Śūnyavādin when he quotes them, as they illustrate central doctrines of this faction.

The *Stanzas* and the *Aṣṭasāhasrikā* differ in their handling of the Two Truths. The *Aṣṭasāhasrikā* does not discuss the doctrine at any length, but systematically employs it as a rhetorical device. One of the interlocutors expounds a doctrine from the standpoint of expressional truth, and then another contradicts it from the standpoint of absolute truth. In the *Stanzas*, Nāgārjuna maintains one viewpoint throughout.

A selection of passages in the *Aṣṭasāhasrikā* that parallel ones in the *Stanzas* shows that Nāgārjuna and the Sūtra were in fundamental agreement on all topics that they have in common (see Doc. 1). To this extent the tradition is right that Nāgārjuna expounded the teachings of these sūtras. But aside from central tenets and a few commonplace similes, there is not much overlap between the *Stanzas* and the *Aṣṭasāhasrikā*. They differ radically in style, though each is systematic in its own way. Their meaning and purpose are the same, but their methods are different.

Sūtra Śūnyavāda reached China more than two centuries before the Mādhyamika treatises. So, to the degree that the sūtras resemble the treatises, they prepared the way for them. In investigating how well a Chinese writer had mastered the Mādhyamika system, it is immaterial how far the Śūnyavādin sūtras had contributed to his understanding, but it is essential to be able to identify components that are peculiar to the sūtras, and it is significant where items peculiar to the treatises are found.

EARLY MĀDHYAMIKA AND ITS ADVERSARIES

The Chinese biographies of Nāgārjuna and Āryadeva and the prefaces to Kumārajīva's translations of the *Four Treatises* unanimously and repeatedly state that these two aimed at the refutation of the errors of Hīnayānists on the one hand and of Tīrthikas on the other. The biography of Nāgārjuna also states that he received a brahmanical education before he became a monk, and a Hīnayāna education afterwards. The biography of Āryadeva credits him with great triumphs in debates against the Tīrthikas.

Since the other systems on which Mādhyamika preyed are so important a feature of the milieu in which this system arose and developed, some consideration of the adversaries is fitting at this point. It is not necessary to go beyond the *Middle Stanzas* to determine the theses which Nāgārjuna was attacking. However, the *Stanzas* do not mention the names of individuals or schools which maintained the refuted doctrines; Nāgārjuna simply refutes, and leaves his audience to decide who is guilty of what. A Chinese, Tibetan, or European who maintains the thesis that the effect is identical with the cause would not need to know that this was originally a Sāṁkhya doctrine in order to benefit from the antidote that Nāgārjuna provides. Nevertheless, the problem of whether the effect inheres in the cause is naturally more immediate and engaging for people in whose intellectual milieu the problem is already a live issue. One of the difficulties that the Chinese experienced in trying to understand Mādhyamika was that the Indian heretics were so different from any Chinese heretics. Another difficulty was that in China there were no entrenched Hīnayāna sects when Śūnyavāda was introduced. Abhidharma and Sūnyavādin sūtras alike were light from the West, both novel and both welcome.

In the first chapter of the *Middle Treatise*, there is an account of the historical and polemical setting of Mādhyamika:

QUESTION: Why was this *Treatise* composed?
REPLY: There are some who say that the myriad things arise from the god Maheśvara [*Śiva*]. Some say that they arise from the god Viṣṇu. Some say that they arise from combination (*saṁsarga*). Some say that they arise from time (*kāla*). Some say that they arise from world-nature (*prakṛti*). Some say that they arise from modification (*vikāra*). Some say that they arise from the self-so (*svabhāva, svayambhū*). Some say that they arise from the atoms (*aṇu*). Because they have such errors they fall into false views such as [that things are] causeless, have false causes, are annihilated, or are eternal. In many forms they assert "I" and "mine," and do not know the True Dharma. Because the Buddha wished to cut off all such false views and make them know the Buddha-dharma, he first in the śrāvaka-dharma declared the twelve nidānas. Further, for those who had already cultivated the great thought and who were worthy to receive the profound Dharma, with the Mahāyāna doctrine he declared the marks of the causes and conditions, namely that all the dharmas are unarising, unceasing, not single, and not plural, etc., utterly empty and devoid of any existent. As it is stated in the *Prajñāpāramitā*; the Buddha told Subhūti, "When the bodhisattva sits on the bodhimaṇḍa, he contemplates the twelve nidānas as inexhaustible like space."

After the Buddha's decease, during the latter five hundred years in the [period of the] Counterfeit Dharma, men's faculties were even duller, and they were deeply attached to all the dharmas. They sought for the real-being of the twelve nidānas, the five skandhas, the twelve āyatanas and the eighteen dhātus. They did not know the Buddha's intention and merely clung to the letter. When in the Mahāyāna dharma they heard utter emptiness declared, they did not know the reason why [things] are empty, and thus conceived views and doubts. "If everything is utterly empty, why do you particularize that there are sin and merit and recompense? In this case, there would be no worldly truth and no supreme truth." Grasping this mark of emptiness, they conceive addictions and produce many kinds of error about utter emptiness. For such reasons as these the Bodhisattva Nāgārjuna composed this *Treatise* (p. 1b18; *Kokuyaku Issaikyō*, Chūkanbu I, p. 57).

This account lists three classes of wrong doctrine—that of the Tīrthikas, that of the Hīnayānists who adhere to the reality of the dharmas, and that of the Hīnayānists who adhere to the emptiness of the dharmas. One representative of the last group is the Bahuśrutīyas, a splinter sect of the Mahāsanghikas, one of whose works, the *Satyasiddhi Śāstra* (T 1646) was translated into Chinese by Kumārajīva. Their presence in Andhra is attested by inscriptions from the third century A.D. at Nāgārjunikoṇḍa, and another inscription attests their presence near Peshawar in the fifth century A.D. (Bareau, pp. 81–83). The doctrines of this school are so close to Mādhyamika at some points that throughout most of the fifth century Chinese scholars thought that the *Satyasiddhi Śāstra* was a Māhāyāna work.

The chief representative of the group that adheres to the reality of the dharmas is the Sarvāstivāda in its various sects. The Abhidharma system criticized in the *Middle Stanzas* differs in some respects from the Vaibhāṣika system. It posits three marks of the conditioned rather than four (*Stanzas* 7.1 ff. Cf. La Vallée Poussin, *Kośa*, ch. ii, p. 222). This is the Sautrāntika position rather than the Vaibhāṣika. The *Middle Stanzas* particularly attack the doctrine of momentariness *(kṣaṇikatva)* and reject both the Sautrāntika and the Vaibhāṣika positions, which Stcherbatsky summarizes as follows:

When the Sarvāstivādin maintains that 'everything exists,' it means that all elements exist, and the emphasis which is put on the reality of elements refers to the conception that their past as well as their future transition represents something real. From this fundamental tenet the school derives its name. Since the conception of an element answers rather to our conception of a subtle force than of a substance, the reality, i.e., effectiveness of the past is not so absurd as it otherwise would appear. The Sautrāntikas denied the reality of the past and the future in the direct sense, they admitted the reality only of the present. The future, they contended, was not real before becoming present, and the past was not real after having been present. They did not deny the influence of past facts upon present and remote future ones, but they explained it by a gradual change in an uninterrupted sequence of moments, this sequence having a starting-point in a conspicuous or strong impinging fact; it was for them one of the laws of interconnexion between separate elements (*Central Conception*, pp. 35–36).

The first group of wrong doctrines, that of the Tīrthikas, is represented pre-eminently by the Sāṁkhyas and the Vaiśeṣikas. As the *Akutobhayā* says, commenting on the Salutation at the head of chapter 1:

Because the Sāṁkhyas accept that the cause and the effect are one, "not singular" [is declared] in order to refute them. Because the Vaiśeṣikas accept that the cause and the effect are different, "not plural" [is declared] in order to refute them (Walleser, *Mittlere Lehre*, p. 5).

Sāṁkhya is mentioned and a number of Sāṁkhya doctrines are stated in the *Hundred Treatise*. For example:

The disciples of Kapila, reciting the *Sāṁkhya Sūtras*, assert the general marks and the specific marks of all the good dharmas. In the twenty-five truths (*tattva*) the part of pure intelligence (*buddhi*) is called the good dharma (ch. 1, p. 168b6; *Kokuyaku Issaikyō*, Chūkanbu I, p. 254).

As it says in the *Sāṁkhya Sūtras*, the dharma of sacrifice is impure; it is non-eternal and marked by victory and capitulations (ch. 1, p. 170b23; *Kokuyaku Issaikyō*, Chūkanbu I, p. 266) [cf. *Sāṁkhya-kārikās*, 2].

Kapila says: From the occult beginning (*prakṛti? pradhāna?*) arises intelligence (*buddhi*); from intelligence arises the ego-mind (*ahaṅkāra*); from the ego-mind arise the five subtle particles (*sūkṣmabhūta, tanmātra*); from the five subtle particles arise the five great elements (*mahābhūta*); from the five great elements arise the eleven organs (*indriya*). The spirit (*ātman*) is the lord; it has the marks of eternality, and intelligence; it abides in the middle (is indifferent, *udāsīna* or *madhyastha*); it abides eternally, is not destroyed, and does not decay. It encompasses all the dharmas. He who knows these twenty-five truths (*tattva*) obtains liberation. He who does not know these will not escape from saṁsāra (ch. 2, p. 170c13; *Kokuyaku Issaikyō*, Chūkanbu I, p. 267).

As it says in the *Sāṁkhya Sūtras*: That which has intelligence as its mark is the spirit (ch. 2, p. 170c25; *Kokuyaku Issaikyō*, Chūkanbu I, p. 268).

The Sāṁkhyas say again: If knowledge and spirit were different, then we would have an error such as [you charge us with] above. But in our *Sūtras* there is no such error. For what reason? Because intelligence is the mark of spirit. We posit the spirit because of the mark of intelligence. Therefore it is eternally intelligent and in it there is no non-intelligence (ch. 2, p. 171c17; *Kokuyaku Issaikyō*, Chūkanbu I, p. 273).

In the *Sāṁkhya Sūtras*, a lump of clay is not a pot and not a non-pot (ch. 10, p. 181c21; *Kokuyaku Issaikyō*, Chūkanbu I, p. 336).

In the *Great Perfection of Wisdom Treatise* there is an explanation of the Sāṁkhya principles:

There is a dharma called world-nature (*prakṛti*). It is not known by the five senses, because it is extremely subtle. Within the world-nature there first arises intelligence (*buddhi*). Intelligence is identical with the intermediate-skandha-consciousness. From intelligence arises the ego (*ahaṅkāra*); from the ego arise the five kinds of subtle particles (*sūkṣmabhūta*) namely form, sound, scent, taste, and touch. From the subtle particles of sound arises the great element of space (*ākāśa*). From sound and touch arises the great element of wind (*vāyu*). From form, sound, and touch arises the great element of fire (*tejas*). From form, sound, touch, and taste arises the great element of water (*ap*). From form, sound, touch, taste, and scent arises the great element of earth (*pṛthivī*). From space arises the ear-organ. From wind arises the body-organ. From fire arises the eye-organ. From water arises the tongue-organ. From earth arises the nose-organ. In this way it proceeds by degrees from the subtle to the gross. As for world-nature: when coming from world-nature they have arrived at the gross, then from the gross they revert to the subtle and return to world-nature. It is like a lump of clay, within which the natures of pot and potsherd coexist. One makes a pot out of the clay. When the pot is broken, it becomes potsherds. In such transformations, nothing at all is lost. World-nature similarly transforms and becomes the gross. World-nature is an eternal dharma and does not come from anything. World-nature is explained at great length in the *Sāṁkhya Sūtras* (p. 545c17–29; Mano, p. 1610).

Vaiśeṣika is mentioned and a number of its doctrines are stated in the *Hundred Treatise*. For example:

The disciples of Ulūka recite the *Vaiśeṣika Sūtras* and say that among the six categories (*padārtha*), within the quality category (*guṇa-padārtha*) washing three times a day and worshipping fire twice [a day] etc. in combination produce the good dharmas that belong to the spirit (ch. 1, p. 168b8; *Kokuyaku Issaikyō*, Chūkanbu I, p. 254).

Ulūka says: Really the spirit exists and is eternal. Because of such marks as exhalation, inhalation, looking, blinking, and lifespan we know that the spirit exists. Further, because it is the place which supports desire, hatred, pain, pleasure, and intelligence, we know that the spirit exists (ch. 2, p. 170c18; ***Kokuyaku Issaikyō***, Chūkanbu I, p. 267–68).

The disciples of Ulūka recite the ***Vaiśeṣika Sūtras*** and say: Knowledge and spirit are different. Therefore the spirit does not fall into non-eternality and also is not without knowledge (ch. 2, p. 171b7; ***Kokuyaku Issaikyō***, Chūkanbu I, p. 271).

In the ***Vaiśeṣika Sūtras***, sound is not called large and not called small (ch. 10, p. 181c22; ***Kokuyaku Issaikyō***, Chūkanbu I, p. 336).

Vaiśeṣika Sūtra III, 2, 4, occurs without attribution of source in the *Middle Treatise*:

QUESTION: There are disputation-masters who say that exhalation, inhalation, looking, blinking, lifespan, thinking, pain, pleasure, hatred, desire, and inception-of-motion are the marks of the spirit. If there is no spirit, how can there be such marks as exhalation and inhalation? (ch. 9, p. 13b22; ***Kokuyaku Issaikyō***, Chūkanbu I, p. 122. Cf. Faddegon, p. 247)

Another version of this is given in the *Great Perfection of Wisdom Treatise*, p. 230c21. In the *Middle Treatise* there is a section on the pramāṇas which represents the Nyāya doctrine, since it posits four pramāṇas, while the Vaiśeṣikas only admit two, and the Sāṁkhyas three (see *Nyāya Sūtras* I, 1, 3–8, Vidyabhusana, pp. 3–5):

If you say that because there is a verification (***pramāṇa***) the spirit exists, this is not true. For what reason? There are four kinds of verification. The first is verification by manifestation of the thing (***pratyakṣa***). The second is verification by comparative knowledge (***anumāna***), as when one sees smoke and knows that there is fire. The third is verification by analogy (***upamāna***), as when, there being no natural copper in a country, one likens it to gold. The fourth is called verification by reason of the statements of the holy ones (***śabda***), as when they state that there is hell, that there is heaven, and that there is Uttarakuru (ch. 18, p. 24a27; ***Kokuyaku Issaikyō***, Chūkanbu I, p. 174).

In the *Nyāya Sūtras*, there is an objector who maintains a Mādhyamika position (II, 1, 8–12 and II, 1, 16–18; Vidyabhusana, pp. 32, 35). These Sūtras concern the pramāṇas, which topic is also debated between Nāgārjuna and a Nyāya opponent in the *Vigrahavyāvartanī*. Johnston and Kunst say:

The polemic against the validity of the Naiyāyika pramāṇas in verses 30–51 is important, because it raises by its parallelism with Nyāyasūtras, II, i, 8–19, the question whether Adhyāya ii of that composite work was in existence when Nāgārjuna wrote. The parallelism has already been dealt with by Yamaguchi in his notes, by Tucci on pp. 34 ff. of the notes of his translation, and by Rāhula Sāṅkṛtyāyana in his Introduction. Without going into details it may be remarked that Vatsyāyana's bhāṣya clearly has Nāgārjuna's position in mind, but it is not obvious that either Nāgārjuna knew the sūtras or vice versa; till the matter is more fully examined all that can safely be said is that the two works reflect the dispute between the two schools at much the same stage, but not necessarily with reference by one to the other ("Vigrahavyāvartanī," p. 8).

The stock of problems and methods that Mādhyamika, Nyāya, and Sāṁkhya share with each other indicates an intellectual environment where advocates of rival systems engaged in serious discussion and took each other's criticisms seriously. Many of the common problems, such as the atom theory, relation between cause and effect, whole and parts, agent and action, etc., whatever their bearing on moral philosophy, are certainly closer to science. Possibly the alchemical interests that appear in Nāgārjuna's biography are not entirely unrelated to his system and the scientific temper of his age.

Kumārajīva studied Tīrthika treatises, but his Chinese disciples did not. They drew their only knowledge of Nāgārjunism's opponents from piecemeal quotation in the very texts that refuted them. Thus what had been part of a live intellectual tradition as far abroad as the Central Asian cities was for the Chinese only a museum collection of curious foreign 'wrong views.'

Chapter III
KUMĀRAJĪVA

PERSPECTIVE

In the transmission of Mādhyamika from India to China, the intermediary agent was the great translator Kumārajīva (A.D. 344–413).[1] He was born in Serindia, where Indian and Chinese spheres of influence overlapped. As his father was an emigrant Indian aristocrat and his mother a Kuchean princess, his very parentage was international, and the environment was suitable for the birth of a great intercultural envoy.

Kumārajīva's native city of Kuchā was not a Mahāyāna area during the fourth century. The Sarvāstivādins were established along the Northern trade route. According to Hsüan-tsang, (Watters, pp. 53, 60, 64), Agni had 10 vihāras and 200 monks; Kuchā had 100 vihāras and 5000 monks, and Akṣu had several tens of vihāras and 1000 monks. All three cities were Sarvāstivādin. In Kuchā, there were numerous monasteries, splendidly decorated, each occupied by several dozen monks, and all observing strict discipline. There were also several thriving convents, and they too were famed for their strict discipline. Some of the monks and most of the nuns belonged to the Serindian aristocracy and royalty (Lévi, "Tokharien B," pp. 338–39). Thus the great Mahāyāna missionary grew up and spent his early manhood in a Hīnayāna stronghold.

At this time, Khotan was the great Mahāyāna center of Serindia. Indeed, Mahāyāna had been established there since at least as early as the third century A.D. (T'ang, *History*, pp. 283–84). Not only were Khotanese missionaries prominent in the work of translating the scriptures into Chinese, but many of the translations were made from texts of Khotanese provenance. For example, a *Pañcaviṁśati* translation (T 221) was made by Mokṣala from a text sent by Chu Shih-hsing from Khotan some time after A.D. 260. However, there is no record of Kumārajīva having been in Khotan, though in collaboration with Buddhayaśas he translated a Daśabhūmika text that came from there.[2]

Kumārajīva's studies abroad were first in North India and then in in Kashgar. Both places were Sarvāstivādin centers. When Hsüan-tsang visited Kashgar, it was still occupied by Sarvāstivādins, and had "hundreds" of vihāras and more than a thousand monks (Watters

II, 290). But Hsüan-tsang found the neighboring oasis of Yarkand a Mahāyāna center when he visited it in 644. This seems to have been the case in the middle of the fourth century, too, as it was a prince of Yarkand who first acquainted Kumārajīva with Mahāyāna. As the eastern borders of Yarkand adjoin Khotan, the Mahāyāna persuasion of the two countries probably had a common history.[3]

Mahāyāna influence emanated from Khotan in two directions: eastward to China, and northwards to the Tokharian area. Kumārajīva himself became a leader in this movement, though he was ultimately more successful in teaching Mahāyāna in China than in establishing it in his native Kuchā. As Lévi says:

> The biography of the monk Dharmagupta (Nanjio Catalog, Appendix II, 131) who passed through Kuchā in the first years of Sui, about 584, shows that at that moment the Great Vehicle was officially in favor there.... The controversy [of Hsüan-tsang] with Mokṣagupta illustrates with a vivid example the quarrel between the two Vehicles which was then agitating the Buddhist Church. The clergy of Kuchā, faithful to its old traditions, was obstinately defending the Small Vehicle; it practiced its rules, it studied its philosophical theories in the sanctified treatises: the *Saṁyuktahṛdaya* of Dharmatrāta . . . the *Kośa* of Vasubandhu and the *Vibhāṣā* of Kātyāyanīputra ("Tokharien B," pp. 348, 364).

KUMĀRAJĪVA'S EDUCATION AND CAREER[4]

Kumārajīva's father was an ex-monk, and his mother became a nun when her son was seven years old. Leaving lay life along with her, he spent the next two years studying the Āgamas and Abhidharma under a teacher. When he was nine, she took him to North India (Chipin) where under the dharma-master Bandhudatta (KSC, p. 330b6–16) he studied the *Dīrghāgama*, the *Madhyamāgama*, and the *Kṣudraka*. He is reported to have debated publicly against Tīrthikas, a surprising feat for so young a person. Perhaps his opponents were juveniles too. When he was twelve, he and his mother set out for Kuchā again. On the way, he stopped for more than a year in Kashgar, where he studied the Sarvāstivādin *Abhidharma-jñāna-prasthāna-śāstra* (T 1543) and also the Vedas, the Five Sciences, grammar, rhetoric and astrology.[5] In Kashgar, he became acquainted with Sūryasoma, a prince of Yarkand, who with his elder brother had relinquished his princely status and become a monk.[6] Sūryasoma was a Mahāyānist.[7] He explained the *Anavatapta-nāgarāja-paripṛcchā-sūtra* (T 635) to Kumārajīva. The latter was astonished to hear that the skandhas, dhātus, and āyatanas are all empty and without mark.[8] After thinking about it for some time, he became converted to Mahāyāna, and gave up adherence to Hīnayāna. At some point, perhaps while in Kashgar, he obtained and recited the *Middle Treatise*, the *Hundred Treatise*, and the *Twelve Topics*. In Kashgar, he also met and became friends with the North Indian (Chipin) brahman monk Buddhayaśas (KSC, pp. 334a9 ff.), a Dharmaguptaka master who read Mahāyāna sūtras (KSC, pp. 333c–34b; Bareau, pp. 190–200).

Upon leaving Kashgar, Kumārajīva and his mother passed through Akṣu, where he vanquished a famous teacher in debate. At the age of twenty, he received full ordination in the royal palace of Kuchā. He studied the *Sarvāstivādi-vinaya* (T 1435) with the North Indian master Vimalākṣa.[9] In due course, he went to live in the King's New Monastery, an honor reserved for those who had passed five years since their full ordination (Lévi, "Tokharien B," p. 339). Sometime after his ordination, he found a copy of the *Pañcaviṁśati* in an old palace beside the monastery. He then spent two years studying the Mahāyāna sūtras and śāstras. He is reported to have discoursed on the vaipulya sūtras to a saintly nun of royal blood. Eventually his old master Bandhudatta arrived from India, and Kumārajīva converted him to Mahāyāna.

A Chinese notice on Kuchā written in A.D. 379 mentions Kumārajīva as a brilliant young monk who studied the Mahāyāna, lived in the King's New Monastery, and was a disciple of the Āgama-master Fo-t'u-she-mi (Lévi, "Tokharien B," p. 339). In 379 Kumārajīva would have been about thirty-five.

Kumārajīva's studies in Mahāyāna were quite apparently in Śūnyavāda. His biography reports that he studied the *Three Treatises*, but says nothing about where he obtained them. When later Sino-Japanese tradition makes Sūryasoma a Mādhyamika master in the lineage "Nāgārjuna—Āryadeva—Rāhulabhadra—Pin-lo-chieh-Sūryasoma—Kumārajīva," it goes beyond the evidence.

In 383, when Kumārajīva was about forty years old, a Chinese expeditionary force seized Kuchā, and carried him away captive. He was held at the court of Later Liang, where he learned Chinese, for almost two decades. When Later Ch'in conquered Liang, he was escorted to Ch'ang-an and welcomed there in 401. He enjoyed the favor and support of Yao Hsing, the King of Ch'in, and spent the rest of his life in Ch'ang-an instructing an illustrious group of disciples and translating a large quantity of scriptures.

KUMĀRAJĪVA'S TRANSLATIONS

By the seventh century, more than a hundred titles were attributed to Kumārajīva as a translator (Bagchi, pp. 185–200). The catalogues of the early sixth century list only about thirty-five. Fifty-two extant works are attributed to him. These discrepancies hardly affect an assessment of Kumārajīva's work and thought, since most of the doubtful texts are small minor sūtras. The central corpus is very well attested by contemporary prefaces and colophons and by references in the Biographies. Dates of translation are known for twenty-three titles (Hatani, "Sanron Kaidai," pp. 19–20). There is some information on who solicited certain translations, and who the Chinese scribes and re-writers were.

Among Kumārajīva's translations, there are very few from the Āgamas. The largest group and the largest bulk of sūtras belongs to Śūnyavāda, chief among them being the *Pañcaviṁśati* (T 223), the *Aṣṭasāhasrikā* (T 227), the *Vimalakīrti-nirdeśa* (T 475), the *Vajracchedikā* (T 235), and *Prajñā-pāramitā-hṛdaya* (T 250). There are quite a few pietist texts, such as the *Saddharma-puṇḍarīka* (T 262), the *Smaller Sukhāvatī-vyūha* (T 366), and two Maitreya texts (T 454 and T 456). He translated the *Daśabhūmika* (T 286) in collaboration with Buddhayaśas.

There are five treatises on meditation in the extant Kumārajīva corpus. The chief one is the *Tso-ch'an-san-mei-ching* (T 614) also called the *Bodhisattva-dhyāna*. The first part of this work is a composite of pieces that Kumārajīva selected from treatises by Vasumitra, Saṅgharakṣa, Upagupta, Saṅghasena, Aśvaghoṣa, and Kumāralāṭa. These all propound Hīnayāna dhyāna. The last part, which explains the bodhisattva-dhyāna, Kumārajīva took from the *Vasudhara-sūtra* (T 482. See Nobel, "Kumārajīva," p. 230, n. 1).

Kumārajīva's additions to the Vinaya section of the Chinese canon are the *Sarvāstivādi-vinaya* (T 1435), the *[sarvāstivāda]-prātimokṣa-sūtra* (T 1436), and, according to tradition, the *P'u-sa-chieh-pen (bodhisattva-prātimokṣa)*, which is probably the second half of the present *Brahmajāla-sūtra* (T 1484).[10] The *Sarvāstivādi-vinaya* is the text that he learned from Vimalākṣa about the time of his full ordination.

Besides the *Four Treatises*, Kumārajīva translated three other śāstras: the *Daśabhūmika-vibhāṣā-śāstra* (T 1521) which is attributed to Nāgārjuna but is probably not by him;[11] the *Fa-p'u-t'i-hsin-ching-lun* (T 1659), attributed to Vasubandhu (see Frauwallner, *Vasubandhu*, p. 37); and the *Satyasiddhi-śāstra* (T 1646), a Bahuśrutīya treatise by Harivarman (Bareau, pp. 81–83).

The composition of this corpus shows that Kumārajīva's main interest was in the Śūnyavādin sūtras, particularly the Prajñā-pāramitā class, and the Mādhyamika treatises, but that his interests were broad enough to encompass pietist and miscellaneous sūtras, vinaya, dhyāna, and a masterpiece of the Mahāsāṅghika splinter sect, the Bahuśrutīyas. There is no evidence that Kumārajīva practised dhyāna other than in a ritual fashion, and the dhyāna texts were compiled and translated at the request of his disciples.[12]

Sixteen of Kumārajīva's translations are of sūtras already translated by Dharmarakṣa. They are (Hatani, "Sanron Kaidai," pp. 19–21):

1. *Pañcaviṁśati* (T 222–23)
2. *Saddharmapuṇḍarīka* (T 263–62)
3. *Bhadrakalpa* (T 425– ——)
4. *Viśeṣacintā-brahma-paripṛcchā* (T 585–86)
5. *Vasudhara-sūtra* (T 481–82)

6. *Vimalakīrti-nirdeśa* (—— –T 475)
7. *Pūrṇa-paripṛcchā* (—— –T 310, 17)
8. *Śūraṅgama-samādhi* (—— –T 642)
9. *Smaller Sukhāvatī-vyūha* (—— –T 366)
10. *Mi-lo-ch'eng-fo-ching* (T 453–54)
11. *Jen-wang-ching* (—— –T 245; authenticity dubious)
12. *Acintyaprabhāsa-nirdeśa-sūtra* (—— –T 484)
13. *Ta-fang-teng-ting-wang-ching* (T 477– ——)
14. *Vidhi-hṛdaya-vyūha* (—— –T 307)
15. *Ratnajāli-paripṛcchā* (T 433– ——)
16. *Sarva-puṇya-samuccaya-samādhi-sūtra* (T 381–82)

Eight of these were translated before or during 406, and the dates of the other eight are not known. It seems that Kumārajīva was expected to produce a complete set of the most important sūtras, whether they had previously been translated or not. Quite a few other sūtras that he did were repetitions of his predecessors' work.

The Indic and Serindian texts from which the translations were made were not the contents of one library. The Mādhyamika texts most likely came with Kumārajīva from Kuchā. Tsukamoto, "Kumarajū no katsudō nendai ni tsuite," p. 607, says: "He probably could not have brought a vast Buddhist canon with him when he was carried captive." But it is possible that Lü Kuang's armies looted the Buddhist libraries of Kuchā and carried their contents to Ku-tsang. Further, there must have been some Indic and Serindian texts in Ku-tsang, as only ten years before, in 373, Chih Shih-lun had translated the *Śūraṅgama-samādhi* and some other texts there. As two Mādhyamika texts are mentioned in Kumārajīva's biography in the episode of his conversion to Mahāyāna, they are established as sufficiently precious to him that he would naturally have taken his copies with him, or have carried them in his memory.

His *Saddharma-puṇḍarīka* is from a text of Kuchean provenance, and is more primitive than Dharmarakṣa's version translated in A.D. 286. The preface to the Jñānagupta version of the *Saddharma-puṇḍarīka*, T 264, p. 134c, says:

> I have examined the two translations, and they are certainly not the same text. Dharmarakṣa's resembles the tāla-leaf one; Kumārajīva's resembles the Kuchean text. I have searched through the sūtra-stores, and have studied the two texts. The tāla one agrees with the *Cheng-fa* [T 263] and the Kuchean is exactly the same as the *Miao-fa* [T 262].

There follows an account of the sections that each version lacks. That the Kumārajīva version is the more primitive has been established by K. Fuse, in his article "Genshi Hokke Shisō ga Teishutsu suru Mondai chū Hokke Genkeiron," *Osaki Gakuhō* (Bulletin of Risshō University), No. 76, summarized in *Bibliographie Bouddhique*, Vol. II, No. 136 (See Demiéville, "Yogācārabhūmi," p. 351, n. 5).

Perhaps Kumārajīva's *Saddharma-puṇḍarīka* had lain mouldering in an old library, like the *Pañcaviṁśati* mentioned in the *Biography*, from a time when Mahāyāna had enjoyed some vogue in Kuchā. There are records of Mahāyāna texts coming from Kuchā during the third century. For example, the *Avaivartikacakra-sūtra* (T 266) was translated by Dharmarakṣa from a sūtra presented to him in Tun-huang by an emissary from Kuchā (See CST, p. 50b).

The *Daśabhūmika* text was one of the more than two hundred sūtras that Chih Fa-ling brought back from Khotan (Liebenthal, *Chao*, p. 98, n. 382). The *Vimalakīrti* was done from a later and better text than Chih-ch'ien's primitive and corrupt one. A few confusions of voiced and voiceless stops in Chih-ch'ien's construing of personal names suggest that his text came from the Tokharian area and was perhaps in Tokharian. Among the mistakes are: 'Ratnakṛta' or 'Ratnakaṭa' for 'Ratnakūṭa,' 'Ratnātipradhara' for 'Ratnadīpadhara, 'Jalaprabha' for 'Jālaprabha,' and 'Dīpendra' or 'Dīparāja' for 'Devendra' or 'Devarāja.' He also misconstrues 'Nityodyukta' as 'Nityaṁ yujyate.'

With the centuries of lively importing of texts from Central Asia before Kumārajīva's time, there must have been plenty of texts in the monastery libraries of China awaiting translation or re-translation, so a priori surmises about the provenance of texts are not likely to be profitable.

Many of the translations are stated to have been undertaken at the request of a disciple or donor. Seng-jui requested a dhyāna text, and so prompted the production of the *Bodhisattva-dhyāna* in 402 (KSC, p. 364a22; Wright, "Seng-jui," p. 274). The *Pañcaviṁśati* was undertaken in 403 at the royal request of Yao Hsing (KSC, p. 332b4). Tao-jung is said to have requested the *P'u-sa-chieh-pen* translation (KSC, p. 363b29). As Seng-chao had a special personal fondness for the *Vimalakīrti-nirdeśa*, and as he was one of the secretaries and wrote the official preface for it, he probably had some share in inducing Kumārajīva to undertake the task (Bagchi, p. 188). In 407, Yao Hsien requested the translation of the *Tzŭ-tsai-wang-ching* (T 586), and in 411 he is said to have requested the translation of the *Satyasiddhi-śāstra* (CST, p. 78a8; Bagchi, p. 190).[13]

The order in which works were translated corresponds roughly to how highly Kumārajīva valued the texts, perhaps with the exception of the dhyāna text requested by Seng-jui. Kumārajīva discontinued translating the *Sarvāstivādi-vinaya* when his collaborator Puṇyatrāta died, and left it to be finished later by Vimalākṣa (Liebenthal, *Chao*, p. 99). He procrastinated about starting work on the *Daśabhūmika* until Buddhayaśas joined him in the undertaking (Kasugai, "Abhidharma," p. 695). However, after translating six texts in 402 and getting into his stride, he produced the twenty-seven-chüan *Pañcaviṁśati* and the hundred-chüan *Great Perfection of Wisdom Treatise* between the fourth month of 403 and the twelfth month of 405. It speaks for his devotion to the ***Hundred Treatise*** that he found time to revise his 402 translation in 404, in the midst of his great labor on the *Pañca-viṁśati* and its commentary.

That the *Middle Treatise* was not translated until 409 may be explained by Seng-jui's statement that Kumārajīva did not like Pin-lo-chieh's commentary, and that in translating he found it necessary to rewrite it somewhat (Doc. 5.4). There is no apparent reason why the *Twelve Topics* was not translated until 409.[14]

KUMĀRAJĪVA'S METHODS OF TRANSLATION

During the fourth century the growth of a native Chinese tradition of exegesis, particularly among the disciples of Fo-t'u-teng[15] had thrown into relief the linguistic and cultural problems of rendering the scriptures from Indic and Central Asian languages into Chinese. In 382, the seventy-one-year-old Tao-an gave the problem its classic expression in his *Preface to an Abstract of the Prajñā Sūtras*:[16]

In translating Hu into Ch'in, there are five deviations from the original. First: Turning the Hu utterances completely upside-down to make them follow the Ch'in [arrangement] is the first deviation from the original. Second: The Hu scriptures prize substance and Ch'in men love rhetoric. When the transmission conforms to the mind of the many and nothing is accepted if it is not rhetorical, this is the second deviation from the original.[17] Third: The Hu scriptures are repetitious. In recitative passages, they reiterate sometimes three times and sometimes four times. Disliking their prolixity and excising it is the third deviation from the original. Fourth: In the Hu there occur explanations of ideas which are correct but seem like disordered phrases. When one examines statements and looks at the words, the text has nothing that makes it different, yet sometimes a thousand or five hundred [words] are deleted and not retained. This is the fourth deviation from the original. Fifth: After a subject has already been completed [the text] may come to an ancillary [topic]. Having again used the previous phrases it then restates. To delete all [of this] is the fifth deviation from the original.

The ***Prajñā Sūtra*** is something that was uttered by the face-covering [tongue][18] of the one whose mind possesses the three knowledges. The Holy One certainly accommodated to his times, but there are changes in the customs of the times. Excising the elegant ancient [language] in order to adapt to modern [tastes] is the first difficulty. Stupidity and wisdom are heaven[-made] distinctions. The Holy Man cannot be a stairway. Then, wishing to transmit the subtle sayings of a thousand years ago and reconcile them with latter-day customs that are subsequent to the hundred [generations of] kings is the second difficulty.

When Ānanda was issuing the sūtras, the Buddha had not been gone for very long. [The time when] the Venerable Kāśyapa caused the five hundred [arhants] with the six super-knowledges to critically examine and write down [the Tripiṭaka] is separated from the present day by a thousand years, yet we conjecture [their meaning] with present-day ideas. When those arhants were so conflict-ridden, is it not the courage of those who do not know the Dharma for these men of saṁsāra to be so complacent? This is the third difficulty (CST, p. 52b23; Ui, ***Dōan***, p. 130).

Whether Tao-an meant that the five deviations are permissible, or illegitimate, or deplorable but unavoidable is not readily apparent. Ui says that *shih* 失 here means to miss, not to err. He takes the first point to mean changing the Sanskrit word order into Chinese word order, which is essential (*Dōan*, p. 133, n. 2). Zürcher says, ". . . he formulates some rules stating on what points the translator should be allowed to deviate from the original (five points, the 五失本), and where he should faithfully render the Sanskrit text (three points, the 三不易)" (*Conquest*, p. 203). Ōchō poses the question whether the five points are transgressions not to be committed or merely unavoidable deviations. The first is unavoidable, so it would be unreasonable to forbid it. The other four certainly cannot be called unavoidable, though. It is impossible to interpret all five consistently as neither forbidden nor allowed. These are the limits within which deviation, though not desirable, is permissible when necessary (*Chūgoku Bukkyō no Kenkyū*, pp. 248–49).

The anonymous colophon to the *Yogācārabhūmi* (CST, p. 71c5) supports Ōchō's interpretation: "Since regional fashions are different, we permit these five deviations from the Hu original. Outside of these, one must not deviate so much as a hair's breadth." Tao-an himself relates in the *Pi-ch'iu-ta-chieh-hsü* (CST, p. 80b14) that when Hui-ch'ang, the secretary on the translation team, was asked to delete the repetitions, he fled the mat and remonstrated against this sacrilege, saying: "If one word deviates from the original, there will be some offence without forgiveness. . . . How can one come to the Buddha's precepts, which have been honored by the saints and sages, and revise them to accord with regional language? . . . I wish not to excise [passages] for the sake of elegance." The assembly all voiced their approval, and it was written down according to the Sanskrit text. Only when there was an inversion of word order did they follow the principle of deviation.

Ōchō proposes that the *san pu i* 三不易, though they have been understood as "the three non-easy things" since early times, really mean "three reasons why the text should not be changed at will (*Chūgoku Bukkyō no Kenkyū*, p. 250). One must read *san fueki*, not *san fui* (*ibid.*, p. 251).

Quite clearly, the three points are reasons why any avoidable deviation should be avoided, why needless abridgment or adulteration should be eschewed. As for the five points, they should be understood in context of the earlier part of the preface, which compares various Chinese translations of the *Prajñā-pāramitā*. It is simply a catalogue of ways in which these differed from the Sanskrit text as Dharmapriya recited it and Buddharakṣa translated it. Points three to five describe the variations that occur between different Sanskrit versions of the *Prajñā-pāramitā*, and quite possibly the earlier translators were not abridging or rearranging at all. They may just have had markedly varying texts. Point two probably means that the translations of Mokṣala and Ḍharmarakṣa were more elegant than the bald translations that Buddharakṣa produced and which Tao-an took to represent the style of the original.

Whatever they may have been at first, the five points and the three points soon became guide rules for translators, confining deviations within strict limits, and prohibiting license with the Holy Word.

Kumārajīva's chief amanuensis during his most important translations—the *Pañcaviṁśati*, the *Great Perfection of Wisdom Treatise*, and the *Saddharma-puṇḍarīka*—was one of Tao-an's disciples, Seng-jui. In his preface to the *Pañcaviṁśati*, Seng-jui says: "While I held my writing-brush, I thought thrice about my deceased master's [Tao-an's] instructions concerning the five deviations and the three difficulties" (CST, p. 53a29; Ui, *Dōan*, p. 134).

Kumārajīva's group also wrestled with the vexed question of terminology, which Tao-an does not mention in his principles. Seng-jui says in his preface to the *Pañcaviṁśati*:

The technical terms are not the same as the old ones. All were corrected according to meaning by the dharma-master [Kumārajīva]. For example, the terms *yin* 陰 *ju* 入, and *ch'ih* 持 deviate from the meaning and so he changed them to accord with the meaning.

1. *Yin* 陰 [dark principle—*skandha*] became *chung* 衆 [group].
2. *Ju* 入 [entry—*āyatana*] became *ch'u* 處 [place].
3. *Ch'ih* 持 [hold—*dhātu*] became *hsing* 性 [nature].
4. *Chieh-t'o* 解脫 [release and take off—*vimokṣa*] became *pei-she* 背捨 [turr away and relinquish].
5. *Ch'u-ju* 除入 [removal-entry—*abhibhvāyatana*] became *sheng-ch'u* 勝處 [place of victory].
6. *I-chih* 意止 [idea-stop—*smṛtyupasthāna*] became *nien-ch'u* 念處 [place of recollection].
7. *I-tuan* 意斷 [idea-severance—*samyak-prahāṇa*] became *cheng-ch'in* 正勤 [right effort].
8. *Chüeh-i* 覺意 [awakening-idea—*bodhi*] became *p'u-t'i* 菩提.
9. *Chih-hsing* 直行 [straight-walk—*ārya-mārga*] became *sheng-tao* 聖道 [holy way].

There are very many like this which have been changed. Those whose Hu sound was wrong Kumārajīva corrected according to the Indian. Those whose Ch'i name was wrong, he decided according to the meaning of the graphs. Those that could not be changed, we simply wrote down (CST, p. 53b18).

The last paragraph means that Kumārajīva and his team revised the transcription of names and terms where the old Chinese transcription did not represent the pronunciation as Kumārajīva knew it. When the meaning of the archaic Chinese term was difficult to infer from the usual meanings of the component morphemes, they tried to coin another term whose technical sense would be easier to infer from its usual meaning or the usual meaning of its constituents. When the archaic terminology and translation needed no revision, it was simply adopted and incorporated into the new translation.

Examination of the nine examples of terminological revision shows several different principles. In No. 1 it is the substitution of a term with no established technical meanings for *yin*, which is ordinarily the antonym of *yang*. In No. 3 it is the substitution of an approximate semantic equivalent for the older etymological translation—*ch'ih* (hold) stands for the root of "dhātu," mistakenly identified as "dhṛ" (hold) rather than "dhā" (put, lay). In No. 2 it is the substitution of a semantic equivalent for "āyatana" (resting-place, support, seat, place, home, abode) for an etymological translation which interpreted "āyatana" as a derivative of "ā-i" (approach, enter). In No. 4 it is the substitution of a derivational translation for a semantic equivalence. *Pei* (turn away) corresponds to "vi" and *she* (relinquish) corresponds to "muc" and "mokṣa." In No. 5 it is the substitution of a more exact semantic equivalent for the first term, plus the replacement of *ju* by *ch'u* in accordance with No. 2. *Sheng* (overcoming, victory) corresponds to "abhi-bhū" (to overcome, conquer, surpass). Nos. 6 and 9 are simply substitutions of constituents whose normal meanings are closer to those of the Sanskrit immediate constituents. In No. 7, *tuan* (severance) in the archaic term corresponds fairly well to "prahāṇa" but it is also used for "uccheda" (annihilation), with consequent ambiguity. *Ch'in* (effort) corresponds to "vyāyāma" (exertion) rather than to "prahāṇa." *I* is perhaps based on a confusion of "samyak" (right) with "saṁjñā" (idea). No. 8 is the substitution of a transliteration for a reasonably good semantic equivalent.

The above statement by Seng-jui sets forth the policy of Kumārajīva's chief editor. It would lead us to expect translations in accordance with the philological and stylistic principles laid down by Tao-an, and with a standardized, rationalized terminology. The actual translations produced by this workshop fall somewhat short of this ideal. Seng-jui's biography recounts a case in point:

> Seng-jui participated in editing the sūtras translated by Kumārajīva. Formerly, Dharmarakṣa issued the *Saddharma-puṇḍarīka Sūtra*. The *Prediction Chapter* [*Saddharma-puṇḍarīka*, ch. 8, T 263, p. 95c28] says, "The gods see men, and men see the gods." When Kumārajīva was translating this sūtra, he came to this and said, "This sentence has the same meaning as the Serindian, but it keeps to the words and overpasses the substance." Seng-jui said, "Should it not be 'Men and gods are in contact and the two see each other?'" Kumārajīva was pleased and said, "It is really so." His commanding insights and exemplary utterances were all of this kind (KSC, p. 364b2; Wright, "Seng-jui," p. 276).

The Sanskrit text is "Devā api manuṣyān drakṣyanti, manuṣyā api devān drakṣyanti" (Kern-Nanjio edition, p. 202, ll. 3–4). As Kern translates, "The gods will behold men, and men will behold the gods" (*Sacred Books of the East* XXI, 194). The one defect in Dharmarakṣa's translation is that it does not indicate the future tense of "drakṣyanti." The normal device for translating Sanskrit futures is the modal *tang* 當.

The Kumārajīva translation does not remedy this omission. It simply illustrates Tao-an's second point and prefers the florid and rhetorical to the plain substance (see Ui, *Dōan*, p. 133, ll. 13 ff.).

The present text of the Dharmarakṣa version reads: "Gods above behold the world and the world can see the gods above. God-men and world-men go back and forth and contact each other." This is probably an emendation grafted into the text by some later editor who was familiar with the Kumārajīva text.

Tao-an's third, fourth, and fifth principles all concern deletions and abbreviations of one sort or another. Hui-yüan says:

> Because this Treatise [the *Great Perfection of Wisdom Treatise*] is deep and vast and difficult to study minutely in a short time, and because it is easy to abbreviate in the Chinese language, Kumārajīva abridged the original to a hundred chüan. An estimate of what was left out is that it was perhaps more than three times [what was translated].[19] Even so, literary gentlemen still considered it too verbose (Doc. 4.VI.14).

Ōchō ("Kumarajū no honyaku," pp. 21–23) draws attention to the fact that Kumārajīva also omitted the last half of the *Hundred Treatise*, rewrote the *Middle Treatise Commentary*, and proposed to prune the *Sarvāstivādi-vinaya* (T 1435). He concludes that Kumārajīva treated the integrity of the scriptures somewhat lightly. But surely the *Great Perfection of Wisdom Treatise*, *Hundred Treatise*, and *Middle Treatise* are not buddha-vacana, and probably Kumārajīva did not consider all the tales and excursions in the *Vinaya* to be holy writ rather than commentary. Furthermore, the only evidence for this last statement is a passage in the *Kao-seng-chuan*, written more than a century later. The incident does not occur in the slightly earlier *Ch'u-san-tsang-chi-chi* biography. It is also possible that what Kumārajīva on his deathbed regretted not having done was shaping up the rough draft of the Vinaya translation and crossing out all the notes and variant translations on the working copy.

On the whole, Kumārajīva and his team seem not to have abridged the sūtras, whether repetitious or not. Occasionally they left out titles or honorific vocatives, but not passages, however unesthetic. Even the non-sinologist can now observe this by comparing Idzumi's English translation of Kumārajīva's *Vimalakīrti* with Lamotte's French translation of the Tibetan version.

The quality of the translation was doubtless strongly conditioned by the organization of the workshop and the social circumstances in which the work was done. As Demiéville says:

> The translation proper was accompanied by numerous oral discussions and explanations. Kumārajīva and the emperor, we are told, "both glossed the different vocables (that is to say, the Sanskrit and Chinese words) and discussed the sense of the text"; the emperor "personally examined the texts, verifying the authentic terms of the original Sanskrit and seeking to penetrate the essential significance";

and in addition, the Chinese monks "scrutinized the text, plumbing in detail its doctrinal sense.... And it was only afterwards that they reduced it to writing." Let it be remembered that these monks numbered several hundreds: one may imagine the confusions, the mistakes, the interpolations that could have slipped into a translation made in such circumstances, inasmuch as the discussions took place in Chinese and must have referred essentially to the texts translated into Chinese rather than to the Sanskrit texts themselves. It happens, for example, that the *Ta-chih-tu-lun* commits errors that can only be explained as a faulty interpretation, not of the Sanskrit original of the sūtra, but of its Chinese translation badly understood by the translators of the śāstra. Also numerous glosses of Kumārajīva's have slipped into the text of the *Ta-chih-tu-lun*, to the point where one never knows very well which is his and which belongs to the Sanskrit original. Often these glosses take the form of replies and questions, and these questions were evidently those that his Chinese audience asked him in the course of the translation (review of *Traité*, pp. 385–86).

This state of affairs is reflected in the usage of terminology. In Kumārajīva's letters to Hui-yüan, the skandhas and āyatanas are referred to by the old terms—*yin* and *ju*, while the dhātus are termed *hsing*, the new term (Doc. 2.IV.5; T 1856, p. 137c6). Yet in the *Great Perfection of Wisdom Treatise*, at p. 288c22, the skandhas are termed *chung*, the āyatanas *ju*, and the dhātus *chieh* 界 (domain); that is, one new term, one old term, and one term not listed by Seng-jui at all. Both terms for "vimokṣa" are to be found in Kumārajīva's texts, for example, *chieh-t'o* in the *Great Perfection of Wisdom Treatise*, pp. 288c16, 96c2 and *pei-she* in the *Great Perfection of Wisdom Treatise*, pp. 215a7 ff.

A likely explanation is that many scribes employed in editing the translations were not sufficiently educated and indoctrinated in the method to be followed. If a new term puzzled or displeased them, they replaced it by the familiar one. Another possibility is that even senior editors like Seng-jui were not really used to the new terms, and when they were working under pressure, as they must have been during the production of the *Pañcaviṁśati* and the *Great Perfection of Wisdom Treatise*, they reverted to the terms that they knew so well, those of the old texts that they had memorized. Another possibility is that some of the re-writers were self-consciously opposed to certain of the new terms, and eliminated them from whatever they re-wrote. At any rate, the result betrays slipshod editing.

The foregoing considerations raise the question: to what degree did peculiarities of the translations affect the transmission of the Mādhyamika doctrine to China? This is most easily answered by studying Kumārajīva's translation of the *Middle Stanzas*, for which a Sanskrit original survives. The first chapter provides a fair sample. Including the salutation, there are sixteen verses in both the Sanskrit and the Chinese. However, the order of verses is somewhat different. Chinese 1.4 equals Sanskrit 1.5 and vice versa. Chinese 1.10 equals Sanskrit 1.11, and vice versa. (This is counting the salutation as verses 1 and 2.) A general comparison of the Sanskrit and the Chinese verses may be drawn from the following translation of the former into English and of Kumārajīva's version into "Chinglish," an ad hoc language which has Chinese grammar and English vocabulary:

1–2. SANSKRIT: **I offer salutation to the best of preachers, the Buddha, who has taught that dependent co-arising has no ceasing, no arising, no nullification, no eternity, no unity, no plurality, no arriving, and no departing, that it is quiescent of all fictions, that it is blissful.**
CHINESE: **Not arise, also not cease, not permanent, also not cut-off, not one, also not different, not come, also not go-out, able speak this cause condition, well quench all-the play discourse, I bow head revere Buddha, all-the speak among number one.**

Remarks: The Chinese does not make clear that the eight "nots" are all attributes of dependent co-arising. The Sanskrit order has been kept, but the syntactic relationship has not been preserved. The Chinese translates the Sanskrit privative bahuvrīhis by straight negative plus verb. It renders *ekārtham* (having one object, unity) by *i* 一 (one), and *nānārtham* (having diverse objects) by *i* 異 (different). In verse 2, *yin-yüan* (cause and condition) is more properly a translation of *hetu-pratyaya* or of *nidāna* than of *pratītya-samutpāda*, for which there is another and unambiguous term *yüan-ch'i* 緣起 (condition arising). *Neng shuo* 能說 (able speak, the speaker) translates *yaḥ deśayām āsa* (who has taught). "All-the speak among number one" renders *vadatām varam* (best of speakers/preachers). *Chu shuo* 諸說 (all-the speak) does not indicate that *vadatām* is "of *those who* speak." The word order "Buddha, all-the speak among number one" is Sanskrit, as an attributive phrase regularly precedes its head-word in Chinese. *Chu hsi-lun* 諸戲論 (all-the play discourse) corresponds to *prapañca-*, but the *chu* is interpretive. *Prapañca-* is the first member of the compound *prapañca-upaśamam* and is not marked for number. *Shan* 善 (well) in the second line perhaps renders *śivam* (blessed), but certainly does not convey the meaning of this highly important word.

3. SANSKRIT: **No existents ever occur anywhere which have arisen from themselves, from others, from both, or without a cause.**
CHINESE: **All-the dharma not self arise, also not from other arise, not both, not inexist cause; this reason know inexist arise.**

Remarks: "This reason know inexist arise" (therefore we know that they have no arising) is entirely added by the translators.

4. SANSKRIT: **For own-being of existents does not occur in the conditions, etc.; when own-being does not occur, other-being does not occur.**
CHINESE: **If all-the dharma own nature not be-there in condition inside, through inexist own nature reason, other nature also again inexist.**

Remarks: The Chinese translates *hi* (for) by *ju* 如 (if, as). The Chinese does not translate *ādi* (etc.) and does not show the plural of *-ādiṣu.*

5. SANSKRIT: There are four conditions—the cause, the object-basis, the immediate, and the dominant. There is no fifth condition.
CHINESE: Cause condition, next number condition, condition condition, increase over condition, four condition produce all-the dharma. Further inexist number five condition.

Remarks: "Produce all-the dharma" is added by the translators, probably because there is no verb in the first clause of the Sanskrit, where one would normally supply *asti.* The Chinese addition is interpretive, but valid. *Yüan yüan* 緣緣 (conditioned condition) stands for *ālambana pratyaya.* Kumārajīva more often than not translates *ālambana* by *yüan* rather than by the unambiguous *p'an-yüan* 攀緣 which he sometimes uses. As a consequence Chinese Buddhists have often confused the concepts of *ālambana* and *pratyaya.* See also verse 11.

6. SANSKRIT: Action is not condition-having; action is not non-condition-having; conditions are not non-action-having and are not action-having, either.
CHINESE: Effect is-it from condition arise? Is-it from non condition arise? This condition is-it have effect? This condition is-it have-no effect?

Remarks: The Sanskrit negates the alternatives, while the Chinese poses them as affirmative alternative questions. *Kuo* 果 (effect) points to a Sanskrit *kārya* rather than *kriyā* (Hatani, Chūkanbu I, p. 65, n. 27). If Kumārajīva read *kārya*, though, he could not have read the feminine *pratyayavatī.* Ts'ung . . . *sheng* 從 . . . 生 (from . . . arise) paraphrases *-vant* (having) inaccurately, and obscures the idea of the inherence of the effect, or the potency to produce it, in the cause. *Apratyayavatī* could be either "having a non-condition" or "non-having a condition." *Fei-yüan* means "non-condition." The other alternative would translate as *wu-yuan* (have-no condition). Compare *wu-kuo* 无果 (have-no effect, effectless) for *apratyayavatī* in the second half of this verse.

7. SANSKRIT: When [anything] arises having depended on these, these are indeed conditions. So long as this is not arisen, why are these not non-conditions?
CHINESE: Rest-on this dharma arise effect, this dharma name be condition. If/when this effect not-yet arise, why not name non condition?

Remarks: The translators supply *kuo* 果 (effect), which corresponds to a remote antecedent of *utpadyate* (arises), and *shih fa* 是法 (this dharma/dharmas), which corresponds to the pronouns *imān* and *ime.* This is a good explicative paraphrase.

8. SANSKRIT: It is not valid that an existing thing have a condition, nor that a non-existing one. What non-existing one has a condition? And what use is a condition to an existing one?
CHINESE: Effect before in condition inside, exist inexist together not OK. Before inexist sake-of who condition? Before exist what use condition?

Remarks: A good, clear paraphrase with the same explicative additions as in verse 7.

9. SANSKRIT: When neither an existing nor a non-existing nor an existing-and non-existing dharma generates, how can it be valid, this being so, that [there is] a generating cause?
CHINESE: If/when effect non exist arise, also again non inexist arise, also non exist inexist arise, how get say exist condition?

Remarks: The participles *sat* (existing) and *asat* (non-existing) are translated by *yu* 有 (exist, have) and *wu* 无 (inexist, have-no), which elsewhere do duty for a great variety of derivatives of *as* and *bhū*. *Ho te* 何得 (how get) translates *kathaṁ yujyate* (how can it be valid). *Nirvartako* (producer) is not translated by anything. The Sanskrit text of the second line is doubtful. La Vallée Poussin reconstructs from the Tibetan (*Prasannapadā*, p. 83): "kathaṁ nirvartako hetur ity evaṁ sati na yujate." The Chinese *yen* 言 (say) points to *iti* in the original. I suggest as a possible reading: "kathaṁ nirvartako hetur evaṁ satīti yujyate."

10. SANSKRIT: When dharmas have not arisen, cessation is not a fact. And what condition is there in the ceased? Hence the immediate [preceding condition] is not valid.
CHINESE: Effect when not-yet arise time, then not ought exist cease. Cease dharma how able condition? Reason inexist next number condition.

Remarks: Jo . . . shih 若...時 (when . . . time) renders the locative absolute. *Pu ying yu* 不應有 (not ought exist) stands for *nopapadyate* (is not a fact, is not true to fact). *Wu* 无 (inexist) stands for *na yuktam* (it is not valid). In the Sanskrit text the third and fourth pādas are reversed. As Candrakīrti says: "tenaivaṃ pāṭhaḥ—niruddhe ca pratyayaḥ kaḥ, nānantaram ato yuktam iti." My translation and the Chinese both follow this principle, the Chinese thus confirming Candrakīrti.

11. SANSKRIT: This existing dharma is declared to be without object-basis; then when the dharma is without object-basis, where else is there an object-basis?
CHINESE: As all-the Buddha what speak true real subtle marvelous dharma, in this inexist condition dharma, say how exist condition condition?

Remarks: Chu fo 諸仏 (all the Buddhas) is added by the translators. *Chen-shih wei-miao fa* 真實微妙法 (real, exquisite Dharma) is redundant by three characters in order to fill out the line. Kumārajīva seems to have read *saddharma* (True Dharma), thus making the verse a scriptural allusion. The *Prasannapadā* text is faulty here, and La Vallée Poussin supplies *san dharma* with the note, "Mss. sa dharma, sarvadharma."[20] Kumārajīva's reading may be preferable.

12. SANSKRIT: As realness does not occur for existents that lack own-being, that 'this being, that becomes' is not a fact, either.
CHINESE: All-the dharmas have-no own nature, reason no exist exist mark. Speak 'exist this fact reason, this fact exist' not so.

Remarks: Yu hsiang 有相 (exist mark) translates *sattā* (realness, being, the fact of being). This use of *hsiang* 相 (mark) to represent the abstract noun suffixes *-tva* and *-tā* is fairly common in Kumārajīva's works. *Wu yu* 无有 (has no existence) renders *na vidyate* (is not found, does not occur). *Pu jan* 不然 (is not so, is not true) renders *nopapadyate* (is not a fact, is not true to fact).

13. SANSKRIT: In the dispersed and the conjoined conditions there is not that effect. And how can that which is not in the conditions come into being from the conditions?
CHINESE: Brief expansive cause condition inside, seek effect not can get. Cause condition inside if inexist, say how from condition go-out?

Remarks: Lüeh-kuang 略廣 (briefly and at length) mistranslates *vyasta-samasta* (separately and together). It looks as if Kumārajīva read the Sanskrit text aloud and an assistant picked the wrong equivalent out of a bilingual glossary. At any rate, Kumārajīva did not revise this verse carefully. The *Middle Treatise* commentary says: "*Lüeh*—in the combined conditions there is no effect. *Kuang*—in the conditions [taken] one by one there is also no effect." If Kumārajīva understood this commentary, then he understood the verse. Yet neither he nor his assistants noted that *vyasta-samasta* here is not equivalent to Chinese *lüeh-kuang*. This seems to be a striking instance of mechanical mistranslation. *Ch'u* 出 (go-out, come-out) renders *bhavet* (may be, would/could come into being).

14. SANSKRIT: Then [if] even though non-existing [in them] that [effect] proceeds from those conditions, why does the effect not proceed from non-conditions, too?
CHINESE: If think condition have-no effect, but from condition inside go-out, this effect why not from non condition inside this-way go-out?

Remarks: Wu 无 (inexist) stands for the participle *asat* (not being, non-existing). *Kuo* 果 (effect) is clearer than the pronoun *tat* (it, that) which it stands for.

15. SANSKRIT: The effect is made out of the conditions, and the conditions are not made out of themselves. How can that effect which [emerges] from [condi-

tions] that are not made out of themselves be made out of conditions?
CHINESE: If effect from condition arise, this effect have-no own nature. From have-no own nature arise, how get from condition arise?

Remarks: The translation *ts'ung yüan sheng* 從緣生 (arise from condition/s) for *pratyaya-mayam* (consisting of conditions) obscures the concept of *satkāryavāda* (inherence of the effect in the cause) which Nāgārjuna is attacking. *Ho te* 何得 (how get, how can) renders *katham* (how can). *Wu tzŭ hsing* 无自性 (no own nature) paraphrases *asvamaya* and *asvayaṃmaya* (not made out of itself/themselves) obscurely but not incorrectly.

16. SANSKRIT: Therefore no effect occurs either made out of conditions or made out of non-conditions. Because of non-existence of the effect, how can conditions or non-conditions [exist]?
CHINESE: Effect not from condition arise, not from non condition arise. Through effect no exist reason, condition non condition also inexist.

Remarks: *Wu yu ku* 无有故 (because . . . has no existence) translates the nominal *-abhāvāt* (because of the non-existence/absence of . . .). *Wu* 无 (inexists) in the last clause renders *saṃvidyate kutaḥ* (where/how can it occur); a negative statement replaces an affirmative rhetorical question.

To summarize the virtues and faults of this translation: The Chinese is often more explicit than the Sanskrit. It relies less heavily on anaphora, and so is clearer. It sometimes supplies explanatory phrases such as one finds in the prose paraphrases of Sanskrit commentaries. In verses 6 and 11 the Chinese reflects Sanskrit variants which are as good as, or perhaps better than, those in the extant Sanskrit text. The Chinese copes successfully with syntactic features such as the locative absolute and statements of reason by means of ablative noun compounds. It possesses a device for handling the highly-important abstract-noun suffixes.

As for the defects: There are several lexical mistakes, and a number of renderings that misrepresent the meaning of the original. The terms *yu* and *wu* do duty for all the derivatives of *as* and *bhū* as well as for *upapadyate*, *yujyate*, *vidyate*, and their negatives. Sometimes a number-neutral Sanskrit term is pluralized in translation, and sometimes plurals are neutralized in translation. The worst defect in this chapter and also in the others is the handling of the logical operators—*upapadyate*, *yujyate*, and *prasajyate*. When the latter occurs, it is usually rendered by *shih shih pu jan* (this thing is not so/true), which fails to indicate the exact sense—the ensuing of a logical consequence that is unwelcome to the opponent. The translations of these three terms are not consistent, however, and *pu te* (is not got) may render *na vidyate* (is not found, does not exist) as well as *nopapadyate* and *na yujyate*. In the *Prajñā Sūtras*, *te* also does duty for *upalabdhi* (perception). This confusion of the existential, the modal, the logical, and the epistemological prevents anyone who does not know the Sanskrit from grasping the subtler points of the text.[21]

The substitution of rhetorical questions for negative statements and vice versa is neither a virtue nor a defect. Placing attributive phrases after the headword is un-Chinese, but it adds a certain flexibility to this translation style, and does not lessen the accuracy of the translation itself.

The defects of such a translation are bothersome to the scholar who wishes to reconstruct a Sanskrit original but, with the exception of the mishandling of logical terms, I do not think that the mistranslations prevent the reader from understanding the Mādhyamika system in the aggregate. Individual verses are wrong or misleading, but there is sufficient repetition in the text that if the student takes over-all consistency as his standard he will not be misled very much by blemishes in the translations. He will be more likely to miss right ideas than to conceive wrong ones.

KUMĀRAJĪVA'S WRITINGS

The most important evidence for Kumārajīva's thought is contained in the commentary on the *Vimalakīrti-nirdeśa-sūtra* (T 1775) taken down by disciples from his oral exposition, and in a collection of letters that he exchanged with Hui-yüan after A.D. 405. The latter, the *Correspondence* (T 1856; Doc. 2), is sufficient for this purpose and more convenient to use than the *Vimalakīrti Commentary*, which consequently will not be mentioned in the following exposition.

The topics in the *Correspondence* were chosen by Hui-yüan and reflect his interests in Abhidharma and Amitābhist pietism. Of the eighteen sections, the first eight are concerned with themes such as the dharmakāya, the thirty-two marks of Buddhahood, and arhants' receiving predictions of full enlightenment. The last ten sections deal with particular passages and problems from the *Great Perfection of Wisdom Treatise*, which Hui-yüan was in process of abridging from one hundred chüan to twenty (KSC, p. 360b5). Thus they discuss Mādhyamika ideas that Hui-yüan was puzzled about, or pretended for discussion's sake to be puzzled about. The over-all problematic of this correspondence may be seen in Zürcher's excellent summary (*Conquest*, pp. 227–29).

Kumārajīva refers to or quotes the *Pañcaviṁśati* seventeen times, the *Saddharma-puṇḍarīka* eight times, the *Vimalakīrti* twice, and the *Viśeṣacintā-paripṛcchā* three times. The *Tathāgata-guhya*, *Daśabhūmika*, and *Gaṇḍavyūhya* are only mentioned in the first sections where the subject is the dharmakāya. The general picture of the canonical texts that mattered to Kumārajīva is much the same as the one afforded

QUOTATIONS AND REFERENCES TO BUDDHIST SCRIPTURES IN THE *CORRESPONDENCE*

1. *Pañcaviṁśati-sāhasrikā-prajñāpāramitā* (T 221, 222, 223). 126a4 (191), 126a17 (105), h–129a17 (152), 129a29 (156), 129b24 (161), h–130c27 (182), 131b15 (194), 133c27 (cf. 230), h–135c16 (251), 138c10 (cf. 293), 138c13 (294), 139a11 (297), 139a24 (300), 139c9 (308), h–139c21 (311), 140a18 (317), h–140b7 (320), 140b12 (321), 140c1 (——), 141a18 (cf. 331), 142a12 (346).
   Hui-yüan, 5. Kumārajīva, 17. Total, 22.
2. *Ta-chih-tu-lun* (GPWT, T 1509). h–129c22 (163), 130b10 (171), h–130c8 (174), 131a25 (188), h–135a14 (243), 135c24 (253), h–136b23 (261), h–136b28 (263), h–136c10 (265), h–137b4 (271), h–138b20 (292), h–141a29 (334), h–141c16 (——).
   Hui-yüan, 10. Kumārajīva, 3. Total, 13.
3. *Saddharma-puṇḍarīka* (T 262, 263). 126a6 (102), 126c5 (116), 129c28 (165), h–130c12 (176), h–133a17 (211), h–133a20 (212), 133c21 (228), 134a3 (231), 134a21 (232), 137b23 (278), 141a16 (330).
   Hui-yüan, 3. Kumārajīva, 8. Total, 11.
4. *Tathāgata-guhya* (T 310, 3). 125c7 (98), 130b23 (173).
5. *Daśabhūmika* (T 286). 125c25 (99), h–126b11 (110).
6. *Gaṇḍavyuha* (T 278). 126a21 (106), 130a23 (170).
7. *Vimalakīrti-nirdeśa* (T 474, 475). 127c29 (140), 128c21 (146).
8. *Viśeṣacintā-brahma-paripṛcchā* (T 586). 126a24 (107), 128a6 (142), 140b29 (326).
9. *Pratyutpanna-buddha-sammukhāvasthita-samādhi* (T 417, 418). h–134b5 (233), h–134b15 (236), 134c5 (238), 134c22 (241).
10. *Fang-po-ching* (T 629). 126a7 (103).
11. *Mañjuśrī-buddha-kṣetra-guṇa-vyūha* (T 310, 15).[22] 126c24 (121).
12. *Tathāgata-jñāna-mudrā-[samādhi]* (T 632, 633, 645).[23] 127c10 (136).
13. *Shih-chia-wen-fo-pen-ch'u-fa-hsin-ching.* 128b1 (cf. 144).
14. *Anavatapta-nāgarāja-paripṛcchā* (?) (T 635). 129b14 (cf. 160).
15. *Śūraṅgama-samādhi* (T 624). 133c9 (225).
16. *Shih-chu-ch'u-kuo-ching* (T 309). h–141c14 (340).
17. *Various Abhidharma Texts.* 126c9 (119), 127c26 (138), h–131b20 (195), 131b27 (197), 132c21 (208), 132c28 (209), h–135a13 (242), h–136b25 (cf. 262), 143a20 (357).
   Hui-yüan, 3. Kumārajīva, 6. Total, 9.
18. *Āgamas* (T 1, 99, 100, 125). 131a22 (187), 136a17 (cf. 256), h–141c14 (340), h–124b5 (348), h–142c12 (cf. 350), h–142c17 (351).
   Hui-yüan, 3. Kumārajīva, 3. Total 6.
19. *Unspecified and Unidentified Sūtras.* 126c17 (120), 131a3 (185), 131a22 (187), 131a26 (189), 132b2 (204), 133b23 (cf. 221), 133c19 (227), 136a17 (256), 142c19 (352), 143a19 (356).
   Kumārajīva, 10.

---

h–141c14 (340) = mentioned by Hui-yüan, Taishō page 141, register c, line 14. See note 340 in *Eon Kenkyū.*

by the translation corpus—centered in the *Prajñā-pāramitā*, but accepting all known Māhayāna texts. The quotation from the *Saṁyukta-āgama* (T 99, p. 136a17) illustrates a Śūnyavādin point.[24]

The similes in the *Correspondence* are drawn chiefly from Śūnyavādin sūtras and Mādhyamika śāstras. "Lamp and darkness," "sprout and seed," "curds and milk," "jar and clay," "fire and burning," "reflected image (of the moon)," and "like a phantom, like a dream," occur in the *Middle Stanzas*. Only the last two of these occur in the *Aṣṭasāhasrikā*; the others belong to the realm of discourse with the Tīrthikas, and are the hallmark of Mādhyamika. The simile of iron and lodestone is taken from the *Nyāya Sūtras*.

Sections Twelve through Fifteen of the *Correspondence* (Doc. 2) are most directly concerned with Mādhyamika problems. In the next chapter these passages will be studied for the light they throw on Hui-yüan's thought. The subject here is Kumārajīva's own opinions, which his letters state clearly and in detail. No other Buddhist translator in China has left such substantial and revealing evidence of his own opinions. It is perhaps disappointing that he expresses no idiosyncratic or heretical views. He shows himself to be an orthodox Śūnyavādin and Mādhyamika, rejects the authority of the Abhidharma, and interprets the Āgamas in a Mahāyāna way, holds that the Buddha's statements are purely pragmatic and do not imply any real entities, and denies that real entities arise, because (a) neither inherence nor non-inherence of the effect in the cause is admissible, and (b) simultaneous and successive occurrence of cause and effect are alike untenable. He maintains that reality transcends the four modes of the tetralemma, and he holds Nāgārjuna's concept of negation.

Now to examine the evidence of the letters themselves.

Mahāyāna and Hīnayāna

Kumārajīva asserts his unqualified adherence to Mahāyāna: "Because the Mahāyāna Dharma is what I believe and assent to, I base my argument on it" (Doc. 2.I.5).

He rejects the authority of Abhidharma, though he employs it to illustrate doctrinal points: "It is Kātyāyana's disciples who say that conditioned dharmas have four marks, and not the Buddha who says so" (Doc. 2.I.3). "There are two kinds of śāstra. The first is the Mahāyāna śāstra, which declares the two kinds of emptiness . . . . The Hīnayāna śāstras declare the emptiness of living beings" (Doc. 2.III.3).

He accepts the authority of the Āgamas, but explains their statements about dependent co-arising as skilful means *(upāya)*: "Except for the Buddhas there is no man who can perceive and retain completely according to the real-principle. Therefore the Buddhas, accommodating to what living beings understand, explain three classes of doctrine within the one meaning *(ekārtha)*. For beings with dull faculties they

SIMILES THAT OCCUR IN THE *CORRESPONDENCE*

1. pp. 128a11, 131a18, lamp and darkness (*Middle Stanzas* 7.8).
2. pp. 130c14, 139b11, three animals crossing the stream (Hui-yüan) (*Lalitavistara*, T 186, p. 488b20; *Upāsaka-śīla*, T 1488, p. 1038b8).
3. p. 133c27, the two wings of prajñā and upāya (*Aṣṭasāhasrikā*, ch. 16, p. 312, also *Pañcaviṁśati* T XXV, 565b9 ff.).
4. p. 135b2, the new garment (Hui-yüan) (GPWT, p. 200b1).
5. p. 135b15, mother and child (*Hundred Treatise*, ch. 8).
6. p. 135b15, sprout and seed (*Middle Stanzas* 17.7; *Hundred Treatise*, ch. 8).
7. p. 135b29, like a dream, like a phantom (general śūnyavāda).
8. pp. 135c4, 136b23, 136c18, curds and milk (*Middle Stanzas* 13.6; *Hundred Treatise*, chs. 8, 10; GPWT, p. 59c9) (Hui-yüan).
9. pp. 136c5, 136c22, jar and clay (*Hundred Treatise*, ch. 7, p. 177c7; GPWT, p. 546c26; *Middle Stanzas* 10.15).
10. p. 135c3, bag and contents.
11. p. 136a24, the sun shining on all (*Saddharma-puṇḍarīka*, T 263, p. 85a18).[25]
12. p. 136b3, drinkers of the ocean.
13. pp. 137a6, 137a20, small remedy and great remedy (GPWT, pp. 60a16, 81a13).
14. p. 137b10, tortoise hairs (Hui-yüan) (GPWT, p. 147c26; *Hundred Treatise*, ch. 8, p. 179a27, etc., etc.).
15. p. 137c3, fingers and fist (GPWT, pp. 295c9, 747b20; *Middle Treatise*, p. 19b19–20).
16. p. 137c17, fire and burning (*Middle Stanzas*, ch. 10).
17. p. 138a27, moon's reflection (*Middle Stanzas* 23.9).
18. p. 138b10, remedy to cure the remedy's defects (*Middle Treatise* 13.8; *Kāśyapa-parivarta*, T 310, 43). p. 634a16, Stael-Holstein, section 65, p. 97; *Prasannapadā*, p. 248, ll. 4 ff.).
19. p. 138c4–5, calves and lambs going for milk like iron going to lodestone (not Kumārajīva's own view). (*Nyāya Sūtras*, 3.1.22. cf. GPWT, p. 298c3).
20. p. 140b16, dull and sharp axes (GPWT, p. 649c1; *Eon Kenkyū*, n. 323).
21. p. 141a7, rider controlling horse and vice versa.

declare impermanence, suffering and emptiness .... For beings with medium faculties, they declare that everything is without self.... For those with keen faculties, they declare that all the dharmas from the very beginning are unarising, unceasing, utterly empty and like nirvāṇa" (Doc. 2.3.7). "Therefore, the Buddha sometimes declares that beings are empty, and sometimes declares that dharmas are empty. When he says that form, etc. are real dharmas while milk, etc. are cause-and-condition existents, he commits no error" (Doc. 2.III.8).

Language and Truth

The Buddha's statements do not imply a set of entities corresponding to terms: "The Buddha has said in many places that they have nothing but names and letters. He has never said definitely that there is arising, much less arising of arising. This is other men's idea, and not to be believed and received" (Doc. 2.I.3). "Therefore the arising, ceasing, abiding, and altering declared in the Buddha's Hīnayāna sūtras are nothing but words and letters, and possess no real-being" (Doc. 2.I.4). "In the Mahāyāna sūtras, accommodating to worldlings [the Buddha] talks about the designation 'atom,' but does not say that its fixed-mark exists" (Doc. 2.IV.2). "To refute the false views of the Tīrthikas and the false arguments of the Buddha's disciples, we declare that the atoms have no fixed-mark and only have designation" (Doc. 2.IV.5). "Therefore, whether we talk about designations or about real-dharmas, there is no error" (Doc. 2.IV.6). "The Buddha sometimes saves living beings with the contemplation of no-self and sometimes saves living beings with the contemplation of emptiness" (Doc. 2.IV.7).

Cause and Effect

He denies the arising of real entities on the grounds that neither inherence nor non-inherence of the effect in the cause is admissible: "All dharmas are non-arising because if you seek for the real-being of arising you cannot find it. If there were a dharma within the cause, then it should not be called arising, just as the thing inside a bag is not produced by the bag. If it is not present previously in the cause, then why does a dharma not arise from a non-cause? Just as there is no curd in milk, so likewise there is none in water. If arising exists, then you say either that it exists in the first moment of the pot, or that it exists after the clay but does not exist at the time that the pot is not arisen" (Doc. 2.I.5).

Compare Nāgārjuna's arguments: "The effect is not in the dispersed and not in the conjoined conditions. How can that which is not in the conditions arise from the conditions (*Middle Stanzas* 1.13)? "If what is not present in them emerges from the conditions, why does the effect not emerge from non-conditions (1.14)? "The effect should have the substance of the conditions, and the conditions have no substance of their own. How can the effect arising from those which have no substance of their own have the substance of the conditions" (1.15)?

Kumārajīva also rejects the arising of real entities on the grounds that the three times—past, present, and future—are discrete. "If [dharmas arise] at one time, then they have no causes and conditions. If they arise in succession, then there is an infinite regress" (Doc. 2.I.4). "[The one] has already arisen, and [the other] has not yet arisen. The fault in the now-arising is the same" (Doc. 2.I.5).

Compare Nāgārjuna's argument: "When this arising is unarisen, how can it produce itself? If having arisen it is produced, what need is there for the arisen to arise again" (7.13)? "Neither while arising nor having arisen nor unarisen in any way is it produced, as explained in the case of the going, the gone, and the ungone" (7.14). "Going is not begun in the passed, going is not begun in the unpassed, and going is not begun in the being-passed; where does going begin" (2.12)?

Being

Kumārajīva has a concept of reality that excludes all existents and inexistents: "The real-mark of the dharmas is conventionally termed suchness *(tathatā)*, dharma-nature *(dharmatā)* and reality-limit *(bhūtakoṭi)*. In this [suchness] even the not-existent-and-not-inexistent cannot be found, much less the existent and the inexistent. It is only because of fantasy-conceptions that each one has difficulties about existence and inexistence" (Doc. 2.II.3). "Permanence is not real, and neither is impermanence real. As combining is not real, separation is not real, either. As existence is not real, inexistence is not real, either" (Doc. 2.IV.9). "Therefore the Buddha, because he wants to lead them out of existence and inexistence, declares the not-existent-and-not-inexistent, and that there is no dharma outside of these. Those that do not understand the Buddha's aim then become attached to the not-existent-and-not-inexistent. Therefore, the Buddha further demolishes the not-existent-and-not-inexistent. If 'not-existent-and-not-inexistent' is able to demolish views of existence and inexistence, then those who do not still crave the not-existent-and-not-inexistent do not need the demolition of the not-existent-and-not-inexistent. As for the not-existent-and-not-inexistent, if though existents and inexistents have been demolished people still figment fictions about the not-existent-and-not-inexistent, then the Buddha says, 'Abandoning the not-existent-and-not-inexistent is just like abandoning the existent-and-inexistent'" (Doc. 2.IV.14–15).

Statements of the type "If existence is not real, then inexistence is not real, either" show that Kumārajīva held to Nāgārjuna's concept of negation, namely that the negative of a term is an absence with the same locus. The occurrence of this distinctive concept is a good indication of the assimilation of Mādhyamika. Compare ***Middle Stanzas:*** "If existent is not established, then inexistent is not established, either, since by 'inexistent' people mean 'the alter-existent of an existent'" (15.5). "Independent of the pure there is nothing impure in dependence on which we may posit the pure. Therefore the pure does not occur, either" (23.10). "If Nirvāṇa is not an existent, it cannot be an inexistent; where there is no existent, there is no inexistent" (25.7).

Document Two reveals Kumārajīva's doctrine as derived chiefly from the *Great Perfection of Wisdom Treatise.* This fact is supported by the statement of Seng-jui, Kumārajīva's most eminent disciple, who says: "[Kumārajīva] always relies on (takes as his staff) this Treatise" (GPWT Preface, CST, p. 75a4). Because Parts Twelve to Fifteen of the *Correspondence* concern problems that Hui-yüan met while studying the *Great Perfection of Wisdom Treatise*, Kumārajīva's replies quite naturally draw heavily on that text. Nevertheless, the replies show him to be thoroughly familiar with the whole *Great Perfection of Wisdom Treatise.* He quotes and paraphrases passages from throughout the whole text. He affirms the teachings of this treatise against the Abhidharma that Hui-yüan brings forward. Thus it can be said that Kumārajīva's doctrine is the doctrine of the *Great Perfection of Wisdom Treatise.*

KUMĀRAJĪVA AND VAIŚEṢIKA

Two passages in the *Correspondence* (Doc. 2.IV.4 and 2.IV.11) resume doctrines that Kumārajīva ascribes to the Vaiśeṣikas. The first passage lists the great elements and their attributes. This corresponds to *Vaiśeṣika Sūtras* II, 1, 1–4, but is not unique to them, as it also occurs in Sāṁkhya and in Buddhist Abhidharma. The second doctrine in this passage—that the human body possesses only the nature of earth but is not an organized aggregate of the five elements— is distinctively Vaiśeṣika.

The second passage (Doc. 2.IV.11) is a précis of Vaiśeṣika doctrine. It reveals affinities with *Vaiśeṣika Sūtras* I, 1, 7; I, 2, 1–2; II, 1, 28; IV, 1, 8; IV, 1, 11–12; IV, 2, 1; IV, 2, 4; IV, 2, 5; VII, 1, 8–21; VII, 2, 1–8; VII, 2, 9,; VII, 2, 10–13; VII, 2, 21–25. The subject matter concerns the atom theory and the category of quality *(guṇa).* Aside from the thesis that the existence of a term can be inferred from the existence of its negative, there is no logico-epistemological material.

These rather crabbed resumés do not seem to serve much purpose in Kumārajīva's letter. They would not inform Hui-yüan about the Vaiśeṣika system, since as they stand they are not fully intelligible without reference to the *Vaiśeṣika Sūtras*. Their most likely purpose is to make Hui-yüan aware of the existence of the Tīrthikas and of the fundamental conflicts between them and the Buddhists.

KUMĀRAJĪVA'S CONVICTIONS

The preceding sections permit some conclusions about Kumārajīva as a Mādhyamika. He was an exclusive advocate of Mahāyāna, but did not oppose any sub-variety of Mahāyāna. He attached most importance to Śūnyavāda, whose criticisms of Sarvāstivāda he maintained. His principal authority was the *Prajñā-pāramitā-sūtras*. He did not reject the Āgamas, but interpreted them according to the distinction between expressional and absolute truth. He rejected all notions of existent and inexistent, while maintaining that the negation of these notions was simply a therapeutic device.

He did not prefer the Śūnyavāda of the sūtras to that of the śāstras, but accepted both. His critique of causation is the same as Nāgārjuna's. He used some similes that are characteristic of the Mādhyamika treatises but not of the sūtras. He accepted Nāgārjuna's concept of negation, one of the cornerstones of Mādhyamika. As this is a complex concept and not self-evident, it indicates a high degree of assimilation. Thus Kumārajīva had incorporated much of Mādhyamika into his own thinking, and on certain crucial problems his positions were distinctly Mādhyamika.

Since Lokakṣema's first translation of the *Aṣṭasāhasrikā* in A.D. 172, the *Prajñā-pāramitā* literature had been known and appreciated by thoughtful Chinese Buddhists. Thus Kumārajīva did not have the problem of converting people to Śūnyavāda. He and his disciples had a great deal of background in common. Much of his influence was due to the fact that he explained doctrines that were already known and valued, and resolved problems that were already perplexing his students. The sūtras had prepared the way for the śāstras.

There is no evidence that Kumārajīva attempted to found a lineage of any sort. His interests were catholic, and his sympathies were broadly Mahāyāna. Within limits, his teaching was in accordance with the interests of his disciples. In his language there is very little self-assertion, and it does not appear that he set himself up as the founder of any sect. As apparently he recognized no conflict between any two aspects of Mahāyāna, there would not have been much point in founding a Mādhyamika faction. For him, Mādhyamika was simply Mahāyāna in śāstra form.

Chapter IV
HUI-YÜAN

THE CHINESE SAṄGHA

About A.D. 400, the Chinese Saṅgha was a motley body of several tens of thousands of monks, only a small percentage of whom were intellectuals. Discipline was imperfect in even the best congregations, and non-existent in the worst. There was an elite, however, consisting chiefly of the sons of literati who had received a secular education before taking the robe. For this small group of learned and pious men, one crucial question was how to reconcile the civilization they had inherited with and to the religion they had adopted. An even more pressing problem for some was how to attain the Buddhist goal of enlightenment, to which members of their nation and class had in the past not even aspired. At this time, the grand old man of the Saṅgha was the saintly scholar Hui-yüan, who embodied the best of Chinese Buddhism as it had developed up to Kumārajīva's arrival, and whose moral and intellectual discipline were not typical of the average monk of the period.

As reported earlier, Kumārajīva is said to have told Seng-jui, "If I applied my writing-brush and wrote a Mahāyāna Abhidharma, I would surpass Kātyāyanīputra. But now in the land of Ch'in the profoundly intelligent are rare. My wings are broken here, and what would I discourse about" (KSC, p. 332c4)?

This theme of the unworthiness of the Chinese Saṅgha was widely current around A.D. 400. *The Life of Fa-hsien* presents the contrasting picture of the exemplary character of the Khotanese Saṅgha:

> The Saṅghārāma is called Gomati, and is a Mahāyāna monastery. At the sound of a gong, three thousand monks assemble to eat. When they enter the refectory, their deportment is sedate; they sit down in due order. All keep silent and make no noise with their bowls. When they wish more food, they must not call out to the attendants, but merely signal with their fingers (T 2085, LI, 857b8).

Earlier, the pilgrims had observed the strictness of the monastic rule in Karashahr (Agni):

> There are more than four thousand monks, all students of the Hīnayāna. Their dharma-rules are regular and proper. Śramaṇas from the land of Ch'in arrive at

that city and find themselves unprepared for the Saṅgha discipline (T 2085, p. 857a25).

Corruption in the Saṅgha was also a political problem. In A.D. 398, Huan Hsüan (who later usurped the Chin throne) wrote to Hui-yüan outlining a proposal for eliminating abuses. He charged that luxurious monasteries were being set up right in the market places and that bands of roving mendicants in the countryside were endangering civil order. To improve conditions, he proposed that only those who could read and explain the scriptures and who lived according to the code of discipline should be allowed the status of monks. In replying, Hui-yüan rejected the proposal saying that there were some monks who read the scriptures constantly but were not eloquent enough to explain them and that there were many virtuous monks who did not live in established monasteries. Some monks, he observed, were too old to do good works or study, but were innocent of any offence. All these groups would suffer injustice under Huan Hsüan's proposed measures (HMC, p. 85a–b; Ch'en, "Persecution," p. 264).

If this picture of the Chinese Saṅgha were both true and complete, its intellectual achievements during the fourth and fifth centuries would be inexplicable. But the very biography that reports Kumārajīva's low opinion of China also states that he had three thousand disciples (KSC, p. 332c20) and that more than eight hundred śramaṇas were appointed by royal decree to attend the translation of the *Pañcaviṁśati* (KSC, p. 332b5). Forty of his disciples are known by name and many of them are explicitly praised in the biographies for their intelligence and studious dispositions (Sakaino, pp. 404–9). In the next chapters it will be seen that the extant writings of these disciples render testimony to their high caliber.

In Kuchā, Kumārajīva had lived in a Sarvāstivādin community that numbered only a few thousands. There were ninety monks in the King's New Monastery, and only 700 monks and nuns altogether in the eight vihāras named in the Chinese report of 379 (Lévi, "Tokharien B," pp. 338–39). When Hsüan-tsang visited Kuchā, there were about 100 vihāras and 5000 monks, all Sarvāstivādins (Watters, I, 60). The three thousand Mahāyāna monks of Ch'ang-an, counting among them distinguished scholars from all of China, were not a poorer public for Kumārajīva than the Kuchean monks.

Intellectual monks were certainly a minority in the Chinese Saṅgha not only in Kumārajīva's day, but in other times as well. The *Kao-seng-chuan*, compiled about A.D. 530, gives main biographies for 101 dharma-teachers who lived during the fourth, fifth, and early sixth centuries. It also recounts the lives of contemplatives, experts in discipline, wonder-workers, sūtra-reciters, and self-immolators. In the proportion of the *Kao-seng-chuan* devoted to translators and exegetes, Hui-chiao shows the distinct bias of a literatus for men of letters. Nevertheless, he makes it quite clear that the non-intellectual wonder-workers, etc., represented the broad popular base of the Buddhist community. As they are less likely to come to the annalists' attention than preachers and writers, the number included in the *Kao-seng-chuan* actually testifies to their great importance.[1]

It is difficult to tell how many monks there were in China around 400, partly because the few statistics preserved are at best only as accurate as the censuses that they are based on, and partly because the status of a monk is hard to define. There were monks with official ordination certificates, and those without them; some who lived in large public and semi-public monasteries, others who lived in small village temples alone or with two or three companions; some who lived in mountain hermitages, and others who roamed through the country without having any fixed abode. There were bona fide men of religion, tax and draft evaders, farmers and merchants who had bought ordination certificates but continued in their lay professions and abodes, and mountebanks who for dishonest purposes assumed the robe and tonsure without the formality of ordination (Gernet, *Aspects*, pp. 1–11).

According to the *Pien-cheng-lun* (T 2109, p. 503a) there were 24,000 monks and 1,768 monasteries in Eastern China (A.D. 317–420). Assuming a comparable figure for North China, the size of the Chinese Saṅgha would have been somewhere in the order of 50,000. Probably not more than one out of ten monasteries was a public or semi-public one (Gernet, *Aspects*, pp. 2, 6). In this case, there were fewer than four hundred establishments of the type that averaged about fifty monks each. Very few smaller establishments would afford the library, the social climate, and the leisure for serious study of doctrine. Thus about half of the Saṅgha was almost automatically excluded from the intellectual life of the times.

Most of the exegetes who figure in the *Kao-seng-chuan* came from literate families and were able to read when they entered the Saṅgha. But the Saṅgha was composed chiefly of peasants (Gernet, *Aspects*, p. 2) who were handicapped by a lack of previous education. Thus the active doctrinal disputes and inquiries of the fourth and fifth centuries could not have had a public of more than five or ten thousand people. The participants in the debates of the times numbered a few hundred at most—a small and highly unrepresentative elite.

HUI-YÜAN'S LIFE AND WRITINGS (KSC, pp. 357c23ff.)

Hui-yüan was born in A.D. 334, and showed precocious gifts as a student. At thirteen he went along on study travel with his uncle, and learned the Classics and Taoist authors.[2] At twenty-one he went to hear Tao-an lecture, and became his disciple. On hearing Tao-an expound the *Prajñā Sūtras*, Hui-yüan exclaimed, "Confucianism,

Taoism, and the rest of the Nine Schools are only chaff" (KSC, p. 358a)! Tao-an once said of this diligent student, "Does not the propagation of the Dharma in the eastern country lie with Hui-yüan? "

At twenty-four Hui-yüan began to lecture and he made a great impression by using quotations from Chuang-tzŭ to explain the idea of 'real-mark.'[3] In A.D. 365, when Hui-yüan was thirty-two, he went south with Tao-an to Hsiang-yang. In 378, before the Ch'in forces took the city, Tao-an sent his disciples out in various directions. Hui-yüan with a few dozen disciples went to Ching-chou and eventually settled on Lu-shan, from which he did not depart for more than thirty years. In 391 he invited the Sarvāstivādin monk Gautama Saṅghadeva to come to Lu-shan and there helped him to translate the *A-p'i-t'an-hsin-lun* (T 1550) and the *San-fa-tu-lun* (T 1506). In 393 Hui-yüan sent Chih Fa-ling to the Western Regions to obtain scriptures, a move that eventually brought to China over 200 texts that Kumarājīva and others then translated. In 398 he entered into correspondence with Huan Hsüan (as mentioned above), keeping up the relationship that continued until Huan's death in 404. Huan visited Lu-shan in 399, and was much impressed by Hui-yüan and the spirit of his community.

In 402, Hui-yüan, then sixty-nine years of age, together with his disciple Liu I-min and others—123 people altogether—vowed before the image of Amitābha to seek rebirth in Sukhāvatī. Some of the devotees wrote poems on Buddha-recollection *(buddha-anusmṛti)*, which Hui-yüan collected and for which he wrote a preface. His Buddha-recollection was a kind of dhyāna, and was based on the *Pan-chou-san-mei-ching* (T 417, 418).

In about 405, Yao Sung (Yao Hsing's brother) wrote and told Hui-yüan of Kumārajīva's arrival (Zürcher, *Conquest*, p. 408, n. 75). A correspondence ensued, and Hui-yüan undertook to prepare an abridgment of the *Great Perfection of Wisdom Treatise*. In 406, Hui-yüan sent two of his disciples—Tao-sheng and Hui-kuan—to Ch'ang-an. Tao-sheng came back in 408, bringing a copy of Seng-chao's essay, *Prajñā Has No Knowing* (Doc. 8), which pleased Hui-yüan so much that he circulated it in the community. In 410 or 411, he welcomed Buddhabhadra after his expulsion from Ch'ang-an and wrote a letter to Yao Hsing pleading Buddhabhadra's case. He prevailed on Buddhabhadra to translate the *Dharmatrāta-dhyāna* (T 618) and wrote the preface to it himself. He died on Lu-shan in 416 (variant, 417; Zürcher, *Conquest*, p. 412, n. 129) at the age of eighty-three, after outliving both Kumārajīva and Seng-chao.

HUI-YŪAN'S BUDDHISM BEFORE KUMĀRAJĪVA

When the *Great Perfection of Wisdom Treatise* was translated in A.D. 405, Hui-yüan was seventy-two years old. In his youth, he

HUI-YÜAN'S WRITINGS

1. Preface and Eulogy to the Sixteen-foot Golden Image at Hsiang-yang in Chin. EK, pp. 61–62, 271–78; KHMC 15, p. 198b–c.
2. Preface to the Abhidharma-sāra (T 1550). EK, pp. 62–63, 278–83; CST, 10, p. 72b–c.
3. Preface to the San-fa-tu-lun (T 1506). EK, pp. 63–64, 283–87; CST, 10, p. 73a.
4. On Dharma-nature. EK, pp. 64, 287; KSC 6, p. 360a; Liebenthal, p. 258b.
5. Reply to Tai An. EK, pp. 66, 295–96; KHMC 18, p. 222b.
6. Letter to Tai An. EK, pp. 69–70, 309–10; KHMC 18, p. 224a.
7. On the Three Recompenses. EK, pp. 70–72, 310–18; HMC 5, p. 34b–c; Liebenthal, p. 255b.
8. Roamiṅg on Lu-shan (Poem). EK, pp. 72, 319–21; Lu-shan-chi (T 2095), 4.
9. Brief Memento on Lu-shan, EK, pp. 72–74, 321–26; Lu-shan-chi (T 2095), 1.
10. Memento on Roaming in the Mountains. EK, pp. 74, 326; Shih-shuo-hsin-yü Commentary.
11. Reply to Huan Hsüan's Letter Urging Suspension of Monks. EK, pp. 75, 331–34; HCM 11, p. 75a–b.
12. Explaining Recompense (Reply to Huan Hsüan). EK, pp. 76–78, 335-46; HMC 5, pp. 33b–34b; Liebenthal, p. 253a.
13. Preface to "Buddha-Recollection Poems." EK, pp. 78–79, 347–51; KHMC 30, p. 351b–c.
14. Reply to Huan Hsüan's Letter about Purging the Saṅgha. EK, pp. 80–81, 353–57; HMC 12, p. 85a–c; Ch'en, "Persecution," p. 264.
15. Letter of Cordiality to Kumārajīva. EK, pp. 81, 357–61; KSC 6, p. 259b25–c13; Zürcher, pp. 246–47.
16. Reply to Huan Hsüan. EK, pp. 82–83, 363–70; HMC 12, pp. 83c–84b.
17. On the Śramaṇa not Offering Obeisance to the King. EK, pp. 84–90; 370–400; HMC 5, pp. 29c–32b; Hurvitz, "Render unto Caesar," pp. 96–114; Liebenthal, pp. 248a, 251a; Doc. 3.
18. Letter to Emperor An of Chin. EK, pp. 91, 400; KSC 6, p. 361a14–17; Zürcher, p. 252.
19. Reply to Lu Hsün. EK, pp. 91, 401–2.
20. Reply to Wang Mi. EK, pp. 91–92, 402–3; CST 15, pp. 359, 110a11–14; KSC 6, p. 359b3–7; Zürcher, p. 246.
21. A Further Letter to Kumārajīva. EK, pp. 92–93, 405–8; KSC 6, pp. 359c27–360a8; Zürcher, p. 248.
22. Letter of Cordiality to Dharmaruci. EK, pp. 93, 408–10; KSC 2, p. 333b1–13; Cf. Zürcher, p. 248.
23. Reply to Yao Hsing, the Lord of Ch'in. EK, pp. 94, 411–12; CST 15, p. 110b9–14; KSC, p. 360a29–b5; Zürcher, p. 249.

HUI-YÜAN'S WRITINGS (continued)

24. On the Śramaṇa Baring His Right Shoulder. EK, pp. 94–95, 412–18; HMC 5, p. 32b–c.
25. Reply to Ho Chen-nan. EK, pp. 96–97, 421–26; HMC 5, pp. 32c–33b.
26. Letter to the Hermit Gentleman Liu I-min and others. EK, pp. 97–98, 427–33; KHMC 27, pp. 304a–b.
27. Preface to the *Great Perfection of Wisdom Treatise* Abridgment. EK, pp. 98–101, 433–43; CST 10, pp. 75b–76b; Liebenthal, p. 246b; Doc. 4.
28. Preface to the Dharmatrāta-dhyāna-sūtra (T 618). EK, pp. 101–3, 443–52; CST 9, pp. 65b–66a; Liebenthal, p. 249a.
29. The Buddha-shadow Inscription. EK, pp. 103–4, 453–64; KHMC 15, pp. 197c–98b; Liebenthal, p. 257b; Cf. Zürcher, pp. 224–25.
30. Correspondence with Kumārajīva. EK, pp. 5–57, 109–268; Doc. 2. Cf. Zürcher, pp. 225–29.

EK: *Eon Kenkyū*, vol. I.
Liebenthal: "Hui-yüan."
Zürcher: *Conquest.*

had studied the *Prajñā Sūtras* under Tao-an. In the process of collaborating with Gautama Saṅghadeva, he had acquired some familiarity with Sarvāstivādin Abhidharma. He was, furthermore, the leader of a cult of pietist dhyāna. As he was one of Tao-an's chief disciples and was the intellectual leader of the Chinese Saṅgha immediately before Kumārajīva's arrival, his doctrine at this time is particularly indicative of the highest achievements of Chinese Buddhist thought before the introduction of Mādhyamika.

In 404, while Kumārajīva was translating the *Pañcaviṁśati* and *Great Perfection of Wisdom Treatise*, Hui-yüan composed the essay *Spirit Does Not Perish* (Doc. 3), which culminated and concluded five years of correspondence with Huan Hsüan. This essay has long attracted the attention of Western and Japanese scholars, both for its intrinsic interest and because it seems to deviate widely from fundamental Buddhist principles. For purposes of the present exposition, its chief value is as one term in a comparison between Hui-yüan's doctrine before and after his contact with Kumārajīva and his study of the *Great Perfection of Wisdom Treatise*.

Spirit Does Not Perish is a difficult text linguistically, rhetorically, and philosophically. Consequently, in addition to the translation in Document 3, and the annotations to the translation, I furnish a periphrastic restatement in order to elucidate certain modes of meaning. This is particularly necessary because of Hui-yüan's penchant for innuendo.

Restatement of "Spirit Does Not Perish"

QUESTION: In our previous correspondence, you have argued that the goal of life is to be realized in a realm that transcends human life, and that consequently one who wishes to realize the *summum bonum* must renounce the customs of the world. To justify the monastic way of life, which actually violates the social code that is binding upon all Chinese, you advance the theory that this social code is not absolute, but relative to the conditions and needs of particular periods and times. You interpret the changes in dress, and manners, etc., from dynasty to dynasty as the operation of the Buddha's power, working through the imperial lineage to prepare China for the coming of the Dharma. However, this is not so, because the Chinese tradition, in particular the Taoist school, contradicts the doctrine of rebirth, on which your whole justification of monasticism is founded.

The basic principle is the vital ether. At birth, a man receives an endowment of this ether. When this endowment is exhausted, the man dies, and the vital forces disperse again. This process is limited to one individual life. Psychic and physical are merely different gradations of the one ether, so there is no reason to assume that the fate of the spirit differs from that of the body.

You Buddhists talk about the existent and the inexistent. If these terms mean anything, they refer to phases of the transformations. When vital ether collects, a thing becomes existent. When vital ether disperses, the thing becomes inexistent, and its energies revert to the matrix of the Inexistent. This is Chuang-tzŭ's point of view, and he surely must have known what he was talking about.

I conclude that the individual has only one life, and that the supreme end of man is something that must be achieved within the limits set by one birth and one death.

REPLY: You are wrong when you say that the Chinese tradition contradicts my doctrine. The concept of spirit is fundamental to the ***I-ching***, where it is defined as that which subtly pervades the myriad things. It is on the plane of spirit that the omens subsist, and the diviner receives the portents by tuning in on the numinal plane. However, the figures of the ***I-ching*** represent the behavior patterns of things, and spirit is not a thing. Therefore, the hexagrams cannot chart it. Concrete things have a destiny which is allotted to them when they come into being, which is worked out in accordance with the patterns of destiny that the hexagrams symbolize. But spirit is expressly stated to be not a concrete thing and not even an ordinary psychic thing. It is not accessible to commonsense knowledge, and only the Holy Men in their trances are able to discover how it works, to remember their own and others' past lives, and to realize the condition of nirvāṇa, where spirit is free from karmic fetters. Yet you, a mere worldling, assert your commonsense doctrine of man, equating spirit with those psychic factors such as sense-consciousness that are dependent upon the body. How dare you deny the revelation of the Chinese sages and the Indian saints?

Spirit is essentially indescribable, but in the following description I will try to give some idea of it. It is all-pervasive, and it is not controlled by any other principle, since it is itself the highest principle. In its relations with phenomena, it acts automatically and unfailingly. It is an unmoved mover which activates determinate entities. Its power is manifested through the phenomenal modes which it activates. But it is not a determinate mode, it is not a phenomenal entity, and thus when the allotted lifespan of a determinate thing is exhausted, the spirit which activated this entity and which informed it is not affected by the dispersal of ethers which you mentioned. Since spirit operates through phenomena, it can be known by contemplating phenomena. It is endowed with affections, feelings, and predispositions which determine the character of subsequent rebirths. Consequently, when the contemplative practices the four abodes of recollection and realizes the true nature of body, feelings, thoughts, and dharmas, he attains knowledge of spirit.

There are differences between individuals as to physical endowment and also as to mental endowment. These cannot be explained if each destiny emerges from the undifferentiated matrix of the Inexistent. Difference does not come from sameness. But these individual differences can be explained quite easily if we assume, as the doctrine of karma teaches, that differences in this life are determined by differences in a previous life. Difference in the effect presupposes difference in the cause.

We can now proceed to describe the cycle of saṁsāra. Birth and death are brought about by the predispositions (*saṁskāras*), which are the volitional component of personality. Spirit is a continuity that accompanies the volitional forces, affections, etc., in their transmigration. The process of migration from skandhas that die to the skandhas that are born is, however, not discernible by commonsense observers. It is occult, unmanifested (*avijñapti*). The predispositions find a set of skandhas that is appropriate to them, and thus spirit precipitates a new destiny, a new determinate mode.

As long as you are not aware of this process, as long as you ignore the effect of the predispositions which bind people to recurrent rebirth, you will continue to be bound. You will only break the fetters of karma and return to the essentially free condition of spirit, the state of nirvāṇa, when you contemplate the process of saṁsāra and recognize the forces of karma for what they are.

You say that Chuang-tzŭ maintained that there is no transmigration, but you are wrong. Those passages in which he talks about life and death really mean that life and death alternate in a series of rebirths and re-deaths. You err because the exegetical tradition has degenerated, and people no longer remember the original, true meaning of these passages, which I have now re-discovered with the help of the Buddhist doctrine. The operation of transmigration is extremely subtle and so can only be known by those who are accomplished contemplatives, which, of course, you and the Taoist commentators of recent generations are not. Consequently, the recovery of the true meaning of Chuang-tzŭ had to wait until the arrival of the Buddhist revelation.

For example, the simile of the fire and the wood is from Chuang-tzŭ. You interpret this to mean that the spirit is dependent on the body, just as the fire is dependent on the fuel, and that when the wood is used up, the fire comes to an end. But fire can burn an endless number of pieces of wood. As long as the fire-tender continues to provide fresh wood, the fire does not go out. The fire is transmitted from the old fuel to the new fuel without loss of continuity. Fire is potential in every piece of fuel. It pervades fuel, just as spirit pervades the myriad things. Your notion is based on a shallow interpretation of Chuang-tzŭ, such as is current among those Neo-Taoists who belong to the cult of longevity. You simply do not understand the profound, metaphysical meaning of the text.

If we suppose, as you wish to, that spirit and body arise together and perish together, then several serious problems ensue. The celestial matrix is impartial and would not endow different individuals differently. Further, if the body is the vehicle of one's celestial endowment, then the body should become spirit when it reverts to the celestial origin at death. But this is not so. If, on the other hand, the celestial endowment of character that an individual receives belongs to his spirit, the pure spirit, coming directly from the celestial origin, would not have any gradations and everyone should be equally intelligent and equally holy. But this is not so. Therefore, I conclude that the endowment of character does not come from the celestial origin, since it would have to come either through the body or through the spirit, and both alternatives are absurd.

Since your explanation of the differences between people's characters is wrong, there is no alternative to my explanation, the Buddhist doctrine of karma. Karmic inheritance from previous lives decides one's intelligence, and the body is only adopted after the karmic forces have selected it. The principle of self-so-ness is really the principle of karma, and not the principle of a spontaneous, immediate origin from a celestial matrix.

Thus the theory that I support accords with the Taoist classics, and it explains the facts of human character as well as the course of destiny. You really have no alternative but to accept the doctrine of transmigration, and the principle of monasticism which follows from it.

Hui-yüan's Doctrine of Spirit

It is indeed curious that Hui-yüan, in A.D. 404, seventy-one years old and a student of Buddhism for more than fifty years, the most eminent Buddhist in China, and articulate spokesman for the Saṅgha in its dealings with the state, a paragon of strict observance of the Vinaya, an earnest contemplative and an outstanding intellectual, should have maintained such a gross and elementary heresy as ātmavāda. It is not possible that he was unaware of a doctrine which is repeated endlessly in the *Prajñā Sūtras* to which he must have been exposed during his many years with Tao-an and which is expressly taught in the *Abhidharma-sāra* that he helped Gautama Saṅghadeva to translate. In view of the anecdote about his refusing on his deathbed to drink even a mixture of honey and water without first verifying that the Vinaya permitted it (KSC, pp. 360b1 ff.), it is unlikely that in doctrinal matters he deliberately rejected the authority of scriptures just as holy as the Vinaya.[4]

It might be objected that belief in a spirit was a carry-over from the Taoist classics that Hui-yüan had studied in his youth and continued to study throughout his life. However, the Neo-Taoist belief was that spirit perished. The seekers for longevity, such as Ko Hung, author of the *Pao-p'u-tzŭ*, held only that this one life might be transformed into an immortal one. The opponent in *Spirit Does Not Perish* is in fact an orthodox Taoist, while Hui-yüan reads the Buddhist doctrine of transmigration into Chuang-tzŭ.[5]

The problem is more complex than it appears superficially. In the first place, Hui-yüan's talk about spirit seems confined to those portions of his extant writings that are addressed to laymen and monks in training. The word *shen* 神 (spirit) occurs dozens of times in the letters to Huan Hsüan and in the *Prefaces*, which were addressed obviously to thoroughly literate Chinese and evidently were designed to encourage them to read the actual text. However, in the correspondence with Kumārajīva, *shen* only occurs as a member of binomial compounds. Of these, *shen-t'ung* 神通 (*abhijñā*, superknowledge), *shen-tsu* 神足 (*ṛddhipāda*, magic powers), and *wei-shen* 威神 (*anubhāva* or *adhiṣṭhāna*, pervading power or grace), are all technical terms used in translating Indian texts, and they do not concern the question of transmigration. There are also two other compounds—*shen-pen* 神本 (spirit-origin) and *shen-ku* 神骨 (spirit-bone)—but they do not designate any factor in the process of transmigration (T 1856, pp. 123b29, 133a28). In these same letters to Kumārajīva, though, Hui-yüan often uses other Buddho-Taoist terms. It appears that he did not assert his theory of spirit when communicating with an Indian-trained Buddhist dharma-master.

Adaptation of one's doctrine to the malady of the listener is an orthodox Buddhist principle, and it even sanctions the assertion of an ātman under some conditions. As Nāgārjuna says:

> The Buddhas have taught that there is an ātman, that there is no ātman, and that there is neither ātman nor non-ātman (*Middle Stanzas* 18.6).

Candrakīrti's commentary on this verse says:

> There are people in this world . . . who are situated in the expressional truth and who strive to conform to the view that the only reality (*tattva*) is earth, water, fire, and wind. They say that the mind (*buddhi*) is nothing but the product of the maturation of the great elements. . . . They say, "This world does not exist, the other world does not exist, there is no maturation of the fruits of good and evil deeds. . . . It is to stop the false views of these people that the Buddhas . . . have sometimes spoken of an ātman" (La Vallée Poussin, *Prasannapadā*, p. 356; De Jong, *Chapitres*, p. 15. For the *Middle Treatise* commentary on this verse, see Doc. 2.III.n.20).

This view, as Candrakīrti's phrasing reveals (see La Vallée Poussin's note, *Prasannapadā*, p. 356, n. 6) is that which the heretical teacher Ajita is made to express in the *Sāmañña-phala Sutta*:

> There is no such thing, O King, as alms or sacrifice or offering. There is neither fruit nor result of good or evil deeds. There is no such thing as this world or the next. There is neither father nor mother, nor beings springing into life without them. There are in the world no recluses or Brahmans who have reached the highest point, who walk perfectly, and who having understood and realised, by themselves alone, both this world and the next, make their wisdom known to others.
>
> A human being is built up of the four elements. When he dies the earth in him returns and relapses to the earth, the fluid to the water, the heat to the fire, the windy to the air, and his faculties pass into space. The four bearers, on the bier as a fifth, take his dead body away; till they reach the burning-ground men utter forth eulogies, but there his bones are bleached, and his offerings end in ashes. It is a doctrine of fools, this talk of gifts. It is an empty lie, mere idle talk, when men say there is profit therein. Fools and wise alike, on the dissolution of the body, are cut off, annihilated, and after death they are not (*Dīghanikāya*, No. 2, *Sacred Books of the Buddhists* II, 73–74).

Ajita's doctrine was abhorred because it denied the value of the religious life and the efficacy of donations made to men of religion.

This is precisely the contention of Huan Hsüan in the correspondence. Hui-yüan wrote *Spirit Does Not Perish* to convince this politician that the life of religion is directed towards a real and valid goal; that it is more important to mankind than the affairs of the state and the secular world. Hui-yüan maintained that the monk is engaged in a task so important that the government should accept him as a burden on the national economy and should even allow monks of doubtful character to go unmolested rather than hinder some bona fide monk in his progress. He argues that karma follows the individual relentlessly from life to life, and that only the hard-striving monk can obtain release and help others towards release. His doctrine of spirit must be viewed as an antidote to the mundanism of his opponent.

The next question is whether Hui-yüan's concept of *shen* really corresponds to *ātman* and *ātman* only. Two different conditions of spirit are to be considered. When involved in saṁsāra, it is bound to life. When not bound to life, it "merges" (冥) and the resultant condition is described as nirvāṇa. This is reminiscent of *Middle Stanzas* 25.9: "The entity which when appropriating or dependent wanders to and fro, is declared to be nirvāṇa when non-dependent and unappropriating."

In the process of transmigration as Hui-yüan describes it, birth (life) depends on transformations; transformations depend on predispositions (feelings); and predispositions depend on spirit. *Ch'ing* 情, which I translate 'predispositions,' corresponds among other things to *saṁskāras*, the second of the twelve *nidānas* and the fourth skandha. The saṁskāras involve *cetanā* (volition), so that Liebenthal's translation of *ch'ing* as "volition" is apt. In the *I-ching*, which Hui-yüan often quotes, *ch'ing* means the inner tendencies of a thing before any overt action is manifested. (Compare Stcherbatsky's statement: "Volition *(cetanā)* is defined as the mental effort that precedes action." *Central Conception*, p. 16.) Hui-yüan draws an analogy between the changes of fortune in this one life that the *I-ching* diagrams, and the destinies in transmigration that the doctrine of karma explains. His account of the cycle of births and deaths, with predispositions forming during lifetimes and conditioning the transition from one life to another, is a restatement of the same basic doctrine that the Indian teaching of the twelve nidānas represents. Seen from another viewpoint, it is restructuring of Neo-Taoist terms into a system that is equivalent to, but not homomorphous with, the Indian Buddhist formula for transmigration.

Throughout his life, Hui-yüan strove to pour foreign wine into native bottles, to find "hidden" meanings in *Chuang-tzŭ* and the *I-ching*, to interpret the Chinese tradition as an upāya by which the Buddhas had prepared the way for the Dharma.[6] When he heard Tao-an preach, he declared that the whole native philosophical tradition was mere chaff (KSC, p. 358a3), but when he began to lecture he found that visitors who questioned him about the principle of reality (real-mark) got more and more confused the more he explained, and so he quoted *Chuang-tzŭ* and by a series of analogies succeeded in leading them to comprehension. These visitors (*k'o* 客) were probably laymen, in which case Hui-yüan began his teaching career, as he finished it, as the apostle to the gentry.

Hui-yüan was preoccupied with the problem of gradual attainment versus sudden attainment (see Doc. 4. n. 11). He recognized that some advanced adepts leap suddenly to perfection, but he was concerned with the plight of those who could only advance step by step. He worked out an ideology[7] in which the secular traditions of China and the Buddhist tradition were comprehended in a unitary schema. This unitary edifice had two storeys, the lower one being the secular world, the world of the layman who obeyed the laws and customs of the land as well as the precepts, who studied the Confucian and Taoist classics preparatory to embarking on the study of the Buddhist scriptures, and who supported the second storey, the monastic order. This transformulation of the doctrine of transmigration is evidently one of Hui-yüan's attempts at a synthesis that would ease the transition between Neo-Taoism and Buddhism for the literate gentlemen so many of whom seem to have been converted.

For all that, the doctrine of spirit is still peculiar. Spirit is different from the body, but transforms along with it. It rotates through transmigrations automatically and involuntarily. It is the ultimate of the psychic, subtly pervading all things. It is indescribable and marvelously consummate. However, when incited by predispositions, it transmigrates.

Hui-yüan does not say that spirit exists after death. He merely says that it does not perish. Furthermore, he does not say that spirit is born when an individual is born. He merely says that birth (life) binds spirit. As it is not a thing, it is quite natural that it should not be born. The word *shu* (number, destiny, determinate mode) sometimes renders *saṁskṛta* in archaic translations, and its negation equals *asaṁskṛta*. As an Abhidharma scholar, Hui-yüan was undoubtedly familiar with the distinction between conditioned and unconditioned. Spirit is unconditioned, because it does not perish, and all conditioned things perish. This leads to the conclusion that spirit, though in essence unconditioned, is bound to the course of transmigration, that it is nirvāṇa which wanders in saṁsāra. Compare *Middle Stanzas* 25.19, "There is not the slightest difference between saṁsāra and nirvāṇa."

In Hui-yüan's terms the release of spirit is "returning to the Origin." This is achieved by cutting off predispositions or volitions, which bind spirit to life. Spirit is then concentrated, focused unwaveringly, and becomes clear and bright. Then all abstruse matters and mysteries are illuminated, the path of spirit and the occult operations of karma are clearly apprehended, and spirit "merges," that is, transcends the sense spheres and object-spheres of the relative world. Thus it is consummated.

Spirit is defined as unfathomable, indescribable, and metaphysical. Thus it may be added to the long roster of designations for the absolute—*śūnyatā*, *prajñā*, *bhūtakoṭi*, *dharmatā*, *nirvāṇa*, *buddhatā*, *tattva*, etc. It seems superficially to be a biological soul, and on deeper analysis it turns out to be not a thing, not a substance and not a soul. It is a venerable Chinese term with familiar and favorable connotations which Hui-yüan uses as an expedient device in order to lead his readers by a congenial way to an otherwise uncongenial conclusion.

The great weakness in Hui-yüan's interpretation of Buddhism at this stage is not his concept of spirit, but his failure to define the relation between saṁsāra and nirvāṇa, between the relative world and the absolute. Spirit is at once absolute and entangled in transmigration. Yet the state of the transmigrating spirit and that of the free spirit are both described in terms of a commonsense epistemology. At this time Hui-yüan evidently did not realize the importance of epistemology and of the doctrine of the Two Truths.

Hui-yüan's Letters to Kumārajīva

In the course of abridging the *Great Perfection of Wisdom Treatise*, Hui-yüan became puzzled about a number of problems, and communicated them to Kumārajīva. It is possible that some of his queries were submitted on behalf of his disciples, and it is certain that if he had possessed the whole text of the *Great Perfection of Wisdom Treatise* and had studied it carefully his questions to Kumārajīva would have been superfluous. In fact, Kumārajīva's replies consist largely of digests of the *Great Perfection of Wisdom Treatise*. To a certain degree Hui-yüan may have been raising objections simply for the sake of having Kumārajīva's own authoritative pronouncements, but when all allowances have been made the letters indicate that he was genuinely perplexed on a series of fundamental points.

In Section 12 (Doc. 2.I), Hui-yüan recounts the Vaibhāṣika theory of the four marks of the conditioned and the four secondary marks which are in a reciprocal relation with the primary marks. He evidently understood this theory, which occurs in the *Abhidharma-sāra*, and he was puzzled by the Mādhyamika refutation of it. In the second part of this letter, he retells the Mādhyamika critique of the marks of the conditioned and lands himself in a dilemma.

In Section 13 (Doc. 2.II), Hui-yüan asks how three terms for the absolute—dharma-nature, suchness, and reality-limit—differ in meaning. He goes on to ask whether dharma-nature is existent or inexistent. He lists the unacceptable conclusions that follow from either alternative, expresses puzzlement about the relation between existent and inexistent, and suggests, if I understand the last sentence in the letter correctly, that the doctrine of dependent co-arising may provide a solution to the problem.

In Section 14 (Doc. 2.III), Hui-yüan takes up the question of the theory of atoms and the distinction between primary and secondary matter which the Vaibhāṣikas maintained. He was evidently having trouble reconciling Abhidharma with Śūnyavāda, but persisted in the attempt. He ascribes the thesis that form, scent, taste, and touch are real to the *Great Perfection of Wisdom Treatise*, which he could only do by mistaking an opponent's objection for the author's words.

In this letter, Hui-yüan asserts the thesis that real-dharmas and causes and conditions are the same. He asserts that the four great elements and secondary matter are created by cause-and-condition. It appears that he still held staunchly to a form of realism and expected answers in terms of physics rather than metaphysics. He still showed no awareness of the principle that what is to be asserted depends on the point of view of the speaker and the listener. In reply, Kumārajīva spelled out the distinction between Hīnayāna and Mahāyāna, which apparently was not clear to Hui-yüan, and took pains to emphasize that commonsense realism is in fact based on false imagination.

In Section 15 (Doc. 2.IV), Hui-yüan again presses his queries about the atoms. Are they existent or inexistent? If they exist, then eternalism ensues. If they inexist, then annihilism ensues. He asks again for an explanation of the existent, the inexistent, the both existent and inexistent, and the neither existent nor inexistent. In his reply, Kumārajīva makes it plain that Śūnyavāda rejects all postulations of an ultimately small entity. He then explains that the tetralemma is a piece of therapeutic dialectic, not a piece of physics.

Throughout these four sections, Hui-yüan's questions betray a preoccupation with objective problems and an obliviousness to the crucial place of epistemology in the Buddhist world-view. He had learned some parts of his Abhidharma well, but he had certainly not acquired any idea of what the *Prajñā-pāramitā Sūtras* mean. It would be unwarranted to assume that other members of Tao-an's school were equally uncomprehending of Śūnyavāda, but it is significant that so eminent a scholar as Hui-yüan should have been so much in the dark.[8]

HUI-YÜAN'S DOCTRINE AFTER THE GREAT PERFECTION OF WISDOM TREATISE ABRIDGMENT

It is fortunate for the purposes of this study that one of the extant later writings of Hui-yüan is his *Preface* to the abridgment of the *Great Perfection of Wisdom Treatise*, which he and his colleagues prepared on Lu-shan from Kumārajīva's translations. This *Preface* is a piece worthy of the *Great Perfection of Wisdom Treatise* in every way. It is three times as long as the average preface, is rich in historical data, abounds in rhetorical embellishments, presents Hui-yüan's summary of the philosophical essence of the *Great Perfection of Wisdom Treatise*, and contains a rather full discussion of the literary problem of translating Indic texts into Chinese. It is a giant among prefaces just as the *Great Perfection of Wisdom Treatise* is a giant amont treatises. That the elucidation of this *Preface* requires a periphrastic restatement in addition to heavy annotation is simply another tribute to its richness and profundity.

Restatement of Preface to the Abridged Great Perfection of Wisdom Treatise

There is order and structure in the cosmos. This order proceeds from the realm of the unconditioned, which is the abode of the Holy Men, the sages who discovered the fundamentals of civilization in high antiquity, as well as the Buddhas and Bodhisattvas. A feature of this order in the cosmos is the recurrence of cyclical alternations. There are cycles in nature, such as the seasons, and there are also cycles in human destiny, both in the lives of individuals and in the lives of societies. These cycles are not chance occurrences, but proceed from the power of the Buddhas' providence, which has nurtured Chinese culture from the beginning, educating the people by degrees to the point where they could receive the Dharma. In antiquity, there were the Chinese culture-heroes and wise kings. For some time, the pendulum has swung the other way, and recent generations have been overwhelmed with disorder. Now we have reached a turning-point in the cyclical movement. Providence, the operation of the divine order in history, has brought the Dharma to China. It has been contended that the quest for a transcendental goal is inimical to the interests of Chinese society. On the contrary, it is precisely because the Enlightened Ones have taken up their position in the non-localized, actionless, and transmundane realm of nirvāṇa that their power pervades the mundane order. The Truth is revealed through the perfect response of providence to the readiness of men. As this readiness develops little by little, the Truth is learned gradually.

Nāgārjuna was the Indian equivalent of a Chinese literatus. He was born a Brahman, and spent his youth in acquiring secular learning. Then, like many Chinese gentlemen of this last century, he was moved by compassion for the multitudes and desire for higher wisdom, and became a bhikṣu. Through the practice of dhyāna, he came to realize the limitations of Hīnayāna, and set out in search of a higher doctrine. When he had found the Mahāyāna, he became a famous teacher, and excelled in polemics. Nāgārjuna esteemed the ***Prajñā Sūtras*** most highly of all the scriptures, and wrote a commentary on the ***Pañcaviṁśati*** in order to make its meaning more accessible.

According to the ***Great Perfection of Wisdom Treatise***, the ultimate principle is that there are no real objects corresponding to ideas or words, that cognition is not a relation between real objects and real perceivers. This truth clears away all false notions, and enables the spirit in samādhi to realize its goal, which is beyond affirmations and negations. In this samādhi, the identity of conventional truth and absolute truth is realized, and the bodhisattva path culminates in the realization of final unity.

Nāgārjuna's achievement in restoring the vogue of the Mahāyāna and revealing the true meaning of the ***Pañcaviṁśati*** is so great that it is comparable to the Buddha's achievement in preaching the Sūtra. Nāgārjuna is virtually another Buddha

I, Hui-yüan, have studied this treatise respectfully and carefully. Allow me to summarize its essence insofar as I understand it.

Transmigrations have their source in emptiness, which is beginningless. The existent arises from the inexistent. Before you are born, you are inexistent. Afterwards, you are existent, until you die, when you become inexistent again. Thus existence and inexistence are successive phases of the same entity. They alternate, but neither is the source of the other, and they share a common source, which is emptiness. Entities are mere appearances and are not endowed with intrinsic reality. In order to attain the samādhi in which the absolute is realized, one contemplates phenomenal entities, and realizes that one's own true nature is the same as the nature of empty things. One introspects and sees one's body, feelings, thoughts, and dharmas as they really are. Introspection frees the mind from passions and prejudices, and allows the profound and metaphysical truths to shine forth. One thus enters the extremely abstract realm, where neither one's concepts nor what one knows corresponds to anything in the commonsense world. This vision of the absolute is prerequisite to the understanding of the fourth lemma of the tetralemma, "not-existent-and-not-inexistent."

The ordinary worldling takes existence to be existence, and inexistence to be inexistence. He affirms each naïvely and totally. But mundane existence is not real existence, and mundane inexistence is not real inexistence. The existent is not self-existent, and the inexistent is not self-inexistent. This is so because the nature of every thing is dharma-nature, and the nature of all the dharmas is their lack of intrinsic nature. In spite of the absence of own-being in dharma-nature, however, it is because of dharma-nature that things arise through causes and conditions. As the conditions through which a thing arises have no intrinsic characteristics, they are existent in the mundane sense but inexistent in the absolute sense. Yet, though they are inexistent in the absolute sense, they are not dissociated from existence, because of the identity of the conventional truth and the absolute truth. Emptiness is identical with dependent co-arising.

Consequently, emptiness is that from which things arise and into which they cease. The existent does not return to the inexistent, and the inexistent does not return to the existent, but both revert to emptiness. Therefore, the enlightened contemplative does not apprehend determinate characteristics. He does not obliterate any determinate marks, nor does he cultivate trances, and yet he abides effortlessly in the knowledge of the highest truth, the emptiness of emptiness.

The *Great Perfection of Wisdom Treatise* is a treatise of such vast proportions and manifold literary artifices that only a supremely learned man is qualified to translate and interpret it. Kumārajīva is such a man of eminent qualities and has specialized in the study of this treatise for a long time. It is fortunate that the Prince of Ch'in has provided him with the opportunity and inducement to perform the feat of translation.

The sheer volume and inherent difficulty of the *Great Perfection of Wisdom Treatise* constitute a serious obstacle for the Chinese reader. Kumārajīva abridged the original while he was translating it, but one hundred chüan still daunts most readers. Under these circumstances a further abridgment is desirable.

The *Great Perfection of Wisdom Treatise* utilizes a series of typically Indian rhetorical devices to accommodate its message to its audience. These devices are by no means congenial to the Chinese reader, who values brevity and dislikes the refrains, climaxes, concatenations, and expansions of Indian "vaipulya" rhetoric. Consequently, in abridging the text, I and my collaborators have eliminated repetitions and have arranged the contents topically, correlating the

Treatise with the Sūtra. The resulting abridgment is still twenty chüan long. We offer it somewhat diffidently to the reader, hoping that it will be of some small value in a modest way.

Mādhyamika in the Great Perfection of Wisdom Treatise Abridgment Preface

The philosophical section of the *Preface* begins with an apparent contradiction of Mādhyamika: "Everything exists when it arises from the not-yet-existent and inexists when it has ceased from the already-existent" (Doc. 4.IV.8). This is annihilism, and is explicitly condemned by Nāgārjuna *(Middle Stanzas):* "Annulment—'it existed formerly but does not exist now'—is absurd" (15.11). Although the *Preface* continues: "Existent and inexistent alternate in the one entity" (Doc. 4.IV.8), Nāgārjuna says: "There is no dissolution without origin or with origin; there is no origin without dissolution or together with dissolution" (21.1). "Thus the succession of becoming is not admissible in any of the three times; how can that which does not exist in the three times be a succession of becoming" (21.21)?

The *Preface*, however, continues:

Though they shine in the void, they have no lord (Doc. 4.IV.8). . . . The nature of no-nature is termed dharma-nature. Dharma-nature has no nature, yet causes and conditions arise through it. As the conditions of arising have no own-mark, though existent, they are forever inexistent. Though forever inexistent, they are not cut off from existence. It is like a fire which, being transmitted, does not cease (Doc. 4.IV.9).

This string of stock Śūnyavādin propositions combines Nāgārjuna's critique of own-being with the alternation of popular and absolute viewpoints that characterizes the *Prajñā Sūtras* and Seng-chao. Things are inexistent from the own-being viewpoint, though existent from the non-own-being viewpoint. Hui-yüan applies his simile of the fire again, in the same way that Nāgārjuna applied the simile of the flames of the lamp (Ch. 2, No. 46; *Stanzas* 27.22).

The *Preface* also says:

Therefore, one identifies with [the transformations] in order to achieve vision, and reverses the mirror in order to find the Ideal.[9] When the mirror is bright, sense-dust does not alight on it, and the images of the primal dichotomy are visible. When the vision is profound, then understanding penetrates the subtle, and names and actuals alike are metaphysical (Doc. 4.8). . . . Therefore, the minds of those who roam in the recondite do not depend on cogitation. They do not make an object of anything. Without extinguishing marks, they are still; without cultivating samādhi, they are at rest. . . . They know the metaphysical [truth] of the emptiness of emptiness. This is the utmost point; this is the ultimate. No one can know anything beyond this (Doc. 4.IV.10).

Here Hui-yüan is engaged again in explaining the *Prajñā Sūtras* in Neo-Taoist language, an operation that is facilitated by a great degree of actual agreement between the two transcendentalist systems. This passage is so close to Seng-chao's *Prajñā Has No Knowing* (Doc. 8) that it may have been written after Hui-yüan saw Seng-chao's paper in A.D. 408.[10] The basic distinction here is between mundane knowing, which cognizes marks, and transcendental knowing, which identifies with the markless.

After the statement that "Names and actuals alike are metaphysical," the *Preface* continues:

If you are going to find its essentials, you must put this first, before you can speak about the not-existent-and-not-inexistent. . . . To reside in the existent while existing is to make (consider) the existent existent. To reside in the inexistent while inexisting is to make (consider) the inexistent inexistent. Existence of the existent is not existence; inexistence of the inexistent is not inexistence" (Doc. 4.IV.8–9).

Here Hui-yüan states an affirmation of the fourth lemma of the tetralemma, 'not so and not not so,' and posits markless vision as a prerequisite for understanding this final negation of the existent and the inexistent. He then explains it in terms of absence of own-being in the dharmas, and asserts that the dharmas are both existent and inexistent, which is the third lemma of the tetralemma, namely 'both so and not so.' This is admissible in expressional truth, where terms may be quantified existentially, but it is inadmissible from the absolute viewpoint, since own-being is defined as indivisible. Hui-yüan seems to contradict himself by asserting both 'existent and inexistent' and 'not existent and not inexistent,' because he fails to signal a change of viewpoint. His position can be explained clearly and consistently, but he did not do so.

The theme of the cycle of destiny runs through the whole *Preface*:

The path of the living begins in the beginningless region; the transformations interlink through arenas of good luck and bad luck (Doc. 4.8). Existent and inexistent alternate in the one entity (Doc. 4.8). The entities do not have different destinies. First and last sink into the void (Doc. 4.IV.10).

The earlier part of the *Preface* explains the advent of Nāgārjuna and the transmission of his system to China as the mysterious working of destiny. In this conception, the Neo-Taoist notion of fate is fused with the Buddhist doctrine of karma, which appears as a dominant idea in most of Hui-yüan's writings. Both doctrines are admissible as expressional truth, for the edification of living beings, but neither is admissible as anything more. The idea that existent and inexistent alternate is not Buddhist at all, and arises from a confusion between inexistence and death.[11] Emptiness is conceived as the matrix of dependent co-arising, from which things emerge and to which they revert. The Mādhyamika conception is that emptiness is identical with dependent co-arising. Hui-yüan's interpretation makes emptiness a term in the object-system rather than in the descriptive system. Thus he did not really understand the emptiness of emptiness.

CONCLUSIONS

Before Hui-yüan studied Mādhyamika his doctrine posited an ultramundane goal for the religious life, but this goal and the world process were both conceived in realistic terms. Hui-yüan's doctrine was a physics of the absolute rather than a metaphysics, for he showed little interest in the cognitive process and next to no awareness of the bearing of epistemology upon ontological questions.

During his correspondence with Kumārajīva, Hui-yüan was instructed in the essentials of Śūnyavāda and was told expressly that the objective in Mahāyāna metaphysics is not to establish a set of ultimate constituents of the universe, but to understand the emptiness of all the dharmas. He was told that the tetralemma is a device for counteracting wrong views and that when wrong views have been eliminated, one does not maintain views of existence, inexistence, both, or neither.

After studying the *Great Perfection of Wisdom Treatise* and abridging it, Hui-yüan summarized his conception of its message in the *Preface*. Here he affirms the principle of the Two Truths and states that the absolute truth is known in mystic vision, and that it is devoid of object-counterpart, marks, and determinate nameables (Doc. 4.III.6). But when he proceeds to discuss existence and inexistence in the tetralemmic form he fails to signal shifts from the expressional to the absolute standpoint, and he persists in maintaining that existence and inexistence alternate in successive phases of an entity.

Hui-yüan, his advanced age notwithstanding, had learned a great deal from Kumārajīva and the *Great Perfection of Wisdom Treatise*. However, certain features of the synthesis which he had labored more than fifty years to build were not exactly congruent with Mādhyamika. His doctrine as of A.D. 404 was Mahāyāna in spirit, but Hīnayāna in philosophy. Consequently, he did not assimilate the śāstra variety of Śūnyavāda perfectly.

Chapter V
SENG-JUI

LIFE AND WRITINGS

Six days after Kumārajīva arrived in Ch'ang-an, a fifty-year-old dharma-master named Seng-jui[1] came and asked him to translate some material on the practice of dhyāna. Kumārajīva accordingly compiled the ***Bodhisattva-dhyāna*** (Nobel, "Kumārajīva," p. 230, n. 1) from various sources, and translated it. Seng-jui became Kumārajīva's chief disciple and remained with him throughout the dozen years of the master's career in Ch'ang-an. He wrote the prefaces to most of the important translations and figured prominently in both the teaching and the translating activities of Kumārajīva's 'academy.' As the biography of Kumārajīva says, "The śramaṇa Seng-jui possessed great talent and a clear intellect. He always accompanied Kumārajīva and served as his scribe" (KSC, p. 332b23).

Seng-jui was born in the area of Northern Honan where Fo-t'u-teng had promoted the Dharma during the Later Chao period. He was born in A.D. 352, four years after Fo-t'u-teng's death, in the general region where Tao-an was teaching until 365.[2] Seng-jui while still a boy conceived the desire to become a monk, and at the age of eighteen he left the household life and became a disciple of Seng-hsien, who is otherwise unknown. Seng-jui listened to Seng-lang,[3] one of Fo-t'u-teng's great disciples, lecture on the *Pañcaviṁśati*, and distinguished himself by his intelligent questions. When he was twenty-four (about 375) he set out on a study-travel tour, during which he probably met Tao-an for the first time. Although Seng-jui's biography does not mention any connection with Tao-an, he claims in his prefaces that Tao-an was his master (*Ta-p'in Preface*, CST, p. 53a29; *Vimalakīrti Commentary Preface*, CST, pp. 58c24, 59a7; *Yü-i-lun*, CST, p. 41b15). At this time, Seng-jui achieved fame as a lecturer. In 382 he was in Yeh, the old capital of Later Chao, where he served as scribe in the team that assisted Kumārabodhi to translate the *Ssŭ-a-han-mu-ch'ao-chieh*[4] (T 1505). This enterprise was apparently directed by Tao-an, who went to Yeh from Ch'ang-an in 382 and visited Fo-t'u-teng's tomb. Perhaps Seng-jui had been with Tao-an in Ch'ang-an.

Tao-an died in 385. There were political disturbances in North China at that time, and perhaps because of them Seng-jui went to Szechwan. In Western Szechwan, he was captured by some herdsmen who made a slave of him and set him to tending sheep. A travelling merchant discovered that he was a monk and ransomed him, whereupon he resumed his travels. He spent some time in Hui-yüan's community on Lu-shan, with which he shared an interest in dhyāna and pietistic leanings. Under Tao-an he had been exposed to the Maitreya cult. On Lu-shan he was in contact with the Amitābha cult.

Seng-jui, like Tao-an and Hui-yüan, was seriously concerned with dhyāna practice, and lamented the inadequacy of the dhyāna manuals then current in China.[5] After Kumārajīva provided him with the *Bodhisattva-dhyāna*, he applied himself ardently to the practice of contemplation and soon achieved a reputation for holiness. He appeared before Yao Hsing and made a great impression on the court. During 402, he assisted in translating the *Viśeṣa[-cintā]-brahma-paripṛcchā*. In 402, he was the senior editor in the *Pañcaviṁśati* translation. He also acted in this capacity during the *Great Perfection of Wisdom Treatise* translation, completed in 405. In a letter to Hui-yüan, Yao Hsing stated that the monks of Ch'ang-an deferred to one another about writing the preface to this important work. Ultimately, though, it was Seng-jui who wrote it (KSC, p. 360a24). Seng-jui was present during the *Saddharma-puṇḍarīka* translation in 406. He assisted in translating the *Tzŭ-tsai-wang-ching* in 407, and in the same year wrote a preface to the revised *Bodhisattva-dhyāna*. In 408, he was on the team that translated the *Aṣṭasāhasrikā*. In 409, he participated in translating the *Middle Treatise* and the *Hundred Treatise*. He lectured on the *Vimalakīrti*, translated in 406 and, although he did not play any prominent part in translating the *Satyasiddhi-śāstra* in 411 and 412, he lectured on this text at Kumārajīva's request.

In 418, at the age of sixty-seven, he moved south to Chien-k'ang and took up residence in the Wu-i-ssŭ,[6] where he lectured on the sūtras. The Prince of P'eng-ch'eng, a powerful Sung official, became his disciple. In his dealings with this prince, Seng-jui, now known by his "Southern" name of Hui-jui, showed strict devotion to the Vinaya in the face of rich temptations. At the request of the famous layman, Hsieh Ling-yün,[7] he wrote a treatise on Sanskrit phonology. He died in 436, devoutly expecting rebirth in Amitābha's paradise.

DOCTRINAL POSITION

Evidence of the Biography

Seng-jui's early education was in *Prajñā* studies. He lived at a time when Neo-Taoist studies flourished in this area, and his prefaces

SENG-JUI'S WRITING

Prefaces to:

1. *Ta-p'in* (CST, pp. 52c–53b)—*Pañcaviṁśati*, T 223.
2. *Hsiao-p'in* (CST, pp. 54c–55a)—*Aṣṭasāhasrikā*, T 227.
3. *Fa-hua-ching* (CST, p. 57b–c)—*Saddharma-puṇḍarīka*, T 262.
4. *Ssŭ-i-ching* (CST, pp. 57c–58a)—*Viśeṣacintā-brahma-paripṛcchā*, T 586.
5. *Vimalakīrti Commentary* (CST, pp. 58c–59a).
6. *Tzŭ-tsai-wang-ching* (CST, p. 59a–b)—*Īśvara-rāja-bodhisattva*, T 420.
7. *Tso-ch'an-san-mei-ching* (CST, p. 65a–b)—*Bodhisattva-dhyāna*, T 614.
8. *Ta-chih-tu-lun* (CST, pp. 74c–75b)—*Great Perfection of Wisdom Treatise*, T 1509.
9. *Chung-lun* (CST, pp. 76c–77a)—*Middle Treatise*, T 1564 (see Doc. 5).
10. *Shih-erh-men-lun* (CST, pp. 77c–78a)—*Twelve Topic Treatise*, T 1568 (see Doc. 6).

Independent Works:

11. *Vimalakīrti Commentary*—fragments preserved in T 1775, 2777 (vol. LXXXV).
12. *Erh-ch'in-lu* (Catalogue of translations produced under the Former and Later Ch'in regimes)—not extant, but incorporated into the *Ch'u-san-tsang-chi-chi.*
13. *Yü-i-lun* (CST 5, pp. 41b–42c).

support the supposition that he studied the Taoist classics carefully. His interest in dhyāna indicates that he shared the concern of Tao-an and Hui-yüan for vigorous practice as well as study. The account of his death shows him as an Amitābha devotee of considerable fervor.

The anecdotes in his biography and in Kumārajīva's show plainly that Seng-jui was the chief spokesman among Kumārajīva's disciples. Renowned for his intelligence and eloquence, he was Kumārajīva's constant companion, assisted with his most important works, and received the master's approval for his teaching. Since Seng-jui had been an established teacher in his own right for many years before Kumārajīva arrived, it is to be expected that he would grasp Kumārajīva's teaching and the Mādhyamika system better than most of the other disciples.

Evidence of the Prefaces

Seng-jui's prefaces to the *Middle Treatise* and the *Twelve Topic Treatise* are the most direct evidence for his understanding of Mādhyamika (Docs. 5 and 6). These two brief essays combine elegant rhetoric and doctrinal precision. Their great merit is attested by the fact that Chi-tsang honored them with full commentaries as if they had been Nāgārjuna's own words (T 1824, pp. 1a–5b; T 1825, pp. 171a–174b).

These prefaces can be read as Six Dynasties essays, or as Buddhist tracts, as Neo-Taoist discourse, or as an incisive attack on Buddho-Taoist ideas. The vocabulary is chosen from both the sūtras and the *hsüan-hsüeh* writings. Likewise, the metaphors and allusions are a deliberate blend of Buddhist and non-Buddhist. But if one picks out only the Buddhist figures and terms, then Seng-jui seems to be purely Buddhist. If one lists only the Taoist figures and terms, then Seng-jui seems to be a Taoist. Quite evidently he was trying to say different things to different people at the same time. Consequently, his meaning is not to be confused with his language.

Restatement of the Middle Treatise Preface

In the title, *Middle Treatise*, "middle" refers to the Middle Path, and "treatise" refers to the text which expounds the Middle Path. This Middle Path is only to be understood through designations and must be expounded in some literary form or other. Absolute Truth is inexpressible, yet we can only arrive at it through expressional truth. This treatise does this so successfully that it enables one to follow the bodhisattva course right up to complete, perfect enlightenment.

Passions and wrong views arise from mistaking impermanence for permanence, no-self for self, impurity for purity, and suffering for pleasure. These misconceptions enslave worldlings in the domains of desire, form, and the formless. The Hīnayānist conceives aversion to the world, and thus escapes from bondage to lust, but falls into one-sided views and stops short of the goal of supreme, perfect enlightenment. Final bodhi requires the realization that all the dharmas are non-arising and utterly empty, but the Hīnayānist clings to the view that though persons are empty, dharmas are not. Thus he fails to transcend the dichotomy of existent and inexistent, and rests in the dualism of religious versus worldly. Because his knowledge is imperfect, he cannot attain the Middle Path which resolves all antitheses between extremes such as existent and inexistent, nirvāṇa and saṁsāra, religious and profane. For this reason, Nāgārjuna wrote the *Middle Stanzas*, to obliterate all dualisms, and so that Hīnayānists who had given up the quest would enter the bodhisattva course. With the doctrine of the identity of saṁsāra and nirvāṇa, he confounded the ratiocinations of the Tīrthikas, who are comparable to our Chinese Taoists, and flooded them with the light of the true teaching.

This treatise is truly a world-shaking work. It clears the obstacles from the bodhisattva way and opens the gateway to supreme enlightenment. It awakens prajñā and confers great gifts on those who have been languishing for the true teaching.

By comparison with this treatise, Hīnayāna texts, such as the Abhidharma that has been studied in Ch'ang-an recently,[8] all seem very inferior. We Chinese are extremely fortunate to have this landmark of Indian Buddhist thought introduced into our provincial culture and to share in the benefits of the work that Nāgārjuna originally composed for the sake of the Central Lands of India. Hitherto, scholar-monks such as Chih Tao-lin, Tao-an, and myself, have tried to interpret the ***Prajñā Sūtras***, but our systematic background has been Neo-Taoist, and we have not really got to the heart of the matter. Now, though, we have an authentic Indian exposition of Śūnyavāda, and we can tell what the Sūtras really mean.

Nāgārjuna's ***Middle Stanzas*** are said to be very popular in India, and dozens of scholars have written commentaries on them. The commentary that we have translated is by Pin-lo-chia who, though a learned and devout Buddhist, was not a very good writer. Kumārajīva has revised this commentary, adding, deleting and amending, and bringing it into line with the ***Stanzas***. From the point of view of doctrine, it is now quite correct, though its style is still not perfect.

Each of the Four Treatises has its special purpose. The ***Hundred Treatise*** is concerned with refutation of the Tīrthikas, and with the demolition of false views. The ***Middle Treatise*** is concerned with remedying the misconceptions of Buddhists, with the refutation of Hīnayānist false views. The ***Great Perfection of Wisdom Treatise*** is distinguished by its gigantic size and profound and thorough-going expositions of doctrine. The ***Twelve Topics*** is characterized by brevity and succinctness. These four texts, taken together, provide for any and every requirement. They illuminate every point of doctrine.

I have studied this ***Middle Treatise*** avidly and continually and though I am probably not qualified to write a preface worthy of such a work, my enthusiasm for the text has led me to write these few lines.

Restatement of the Preface to the Twelve Topic Treatise

This little text is a guide to supreme enlightenment, because with the principle of the Middle Path it demolishes all dualistic extremes. "Twelve" is a number that symbolizes completeness. "Gate" is a metaphor for anything that provides access where otherwise one could not pass through. The purpose of this treatise is to reduce all heterodoxies to the one truth. Otherwise, the various Buddhist sects would continue to wrangle back and forth.

Nāgārjuna was deeply grieved that heterodoxies—Hīnayānist and Tīrthika—prevented people from progressing to supreme enlightenment and led them to seek false nirvāṇas. That is why he wrote this treatise. The key terms, the all-embracing categories, are "existent" and "inexistent." The treatise works out the Śūnyavādin ontology in terms of these two concepts. Then it proceeds to refute the concept of a Creator God. The supreme principle in Śūnyavāda is emptiness, suchness, dharma-nature, or reality-limit. This principle subsumes all dualistic antitheses and dispels all notions of self. But, when emptiness has served to dispel notions of self, the verbal teaching of emptiness must be abandoned, and one must not cling to the reasoning by which emptiness of self and dharmas was realized. Only when object and vision are both purified of falsity can the reality be seen. In this reality, there is no difference between the empty and the real, because emptiness is the real-nature of the dharmas. In this way, one succeeds in passing out of transmigration and attaining enlightenment.

This little treatise is actually of vast significance. It is composed with a skill like that of Wen-hui's butcher, and it expresses the inexpressible. It provides a ford to the Other Shore of enlightenment and it leads out of the mundane realm.

We are fortunate indeed to have this guide to the Mahāyāna. It is destined to clear up our misunderstandings and to facilitate great progress among us. I personally hope to gain a lot from studying this text. Better people will of course gain much more than I. Nevertheless, someone has to write a preface, and so I have ventured to do so, and have added a table of contents.

Main Doctrinal Positions

The main outlines of Seng-jui's doctrinal position can be extracted from the prefaces, chiefly those to the *Middle Treatise* and the *Twelve Topics Treatise*.

1. He esteemed Nāgārjuna as the great teacher of the age of the Counterfeit Dharma and understood Nāgārjuna's task to have been both the destruction of wrong doctrines and the revelation of the right doctrine.

Therefore Nāgārjuna Bodhisattva opened up a road for those who wish an exit, and wrote the ***Twelve Topics*** to set them right (Doc. 6.2).

It is said that in all the states of India there are none who venture to engage in studies who do not pore over this treatise and take it for their canon (Doc. 5.4).

If knowledge is not consummate, then with it one cannot traverse the Middle Path and obliterate the two limits. That the religious and the profane are not unified and that the two limits are not obliterated is what grieves the bodhisattva. Therefore the great man (***mahāsattva***) Nāgārjuna equalized them with the Middle Path (Doc. 5.2).

2. He accepted the Mādhyamika criticism of Hīnayāna.

When the hundred-beamed (cedar-beamed) mansion arises, it makes the tumble-down thatched cottage seem mean. When you behold how grand this treatise is, then you know how inferior one-sided understanding is (Doc. 5.3).

This text frees insiders (Buddhists) and dissolves their obstructions (Doc. 5.5).

Therefore, the great man (***mahāsattva***) Nāgārjuna equalized them with the Middle Path, enabling students who have erred from the goal (meaning) to look at the metaphysical pointer and totally change. He encompassed them with [the principle of] identity with transformations, and caused the clients of metaphysical understanding to lose their plans and deliberations in the morning's clear rays (Doc. 5.2).

That heterodox ideas are not razed to the ground and that deviations from the goal are not obliterated is what grieves the great man (***mahāsattva***) (Doc. 6.2).

One-sided understanding springs from knowledge [characterized] by aversion, and through it their resolve errs from the goal. Thus we know that great bodhi resides in vast intuition, and small knowledge is bound by the constricted mind (Doc. 5.2).

3. He esteemed the teaching that he had inherited from Tao-an's school, but avowed that it was merely preparatory to Kumārajīva's explanations of Śūnyavāda.

When I first put forth the thought [of bodhi] I received my elementary instruction in this [i.e., the ***Vimalakīrti***]. I recited and studied it and took it as my canon.

I received the metaphysical pointer from my former master [Tao-an].... When I received Kumārajīva's correction of the metaphysical text and his pointing with the abstruse pointer, I understood for the first time how defective was the text of the earlier translation, and how the wrong language erred from the goal (meaning) (*Vimalakīrti Commentary Preface*, CST, p. 58c23).

4. He condemned the practice of "matching concepts" (*ko-i* 格義) and the theories of the fourth-century dharma-masters.[9]

Since the wind of insight has been fanning the dharma-words eastward and making the chants flow, "matching concepts" has caused deviations from the origin, and the Six Houses, being one-sided, have not realized the thesis (Ideal) of the emptiness of natures (*Vimalakīrti Commentary Preface*, CST, p. 59a1).

5. He considered the *Prajñā-pāramitā Sūtras* and the *Saddharma-puṇḍarīka* as the two complementary mainstays of the *Sūtra-piṭaka*.

Thus the *Saddharma-puṇḍarīka* and the *Prajñā* in mutual support tend towards the End (*Aṣṭasāhasrikā Preface*, CST, p. 54c26).

Therefore, as for praising depth, the power of the *Prajñā* is mighty; as for glorifying the real, the service of the *Saddharma-puṇḍarīka* is exquisite (*Aṣṭasāhasrikā Preface*, CST, p. 54c29).

6. He was personally interested in the Mādhyamika texts, and accorded a high place to them.

I have handled [this book] and have pored over it and have not been able to let it out of my hand. So, forgetting my lowness and ineptness, I have expressed my insights and feelings in a preface, and have put a table of contents at the beginning. But how can I hope to explain it! It is merely to express delight at my own sentiment of agreement (Doc. 5.6).

7. He maintained the identity of nirvāṇa and saṁsāra, of holy and profane, and assigned a key function to understanding "existent" and "inexistent."

If the intuition is not vast, then it does not suffice to raze the existent and the inexistent, to unify the religious and the profane (Doc. 5.2).

When they are set right with the Twelve, then the existent and the inexistent are both made clear, and no problem is not consummated. When problems are consummated in the existent and the inexistent, then the work of a Creator-of-transformations is denied (Doc. 6.2).

Truly it may be termed . . . going forth from the existent and inexistent, going beyond the [worldly] domain (Doc. 6.3).

8. He considered emptiness as the expeller of views which in its turn must not be held as a view.

The *Phantom Chapter* forgets the support (object) and then forgets its forgetting. (*Aṣṭasāhasrikā Preface*, CST, p. 54c18).

CONCLUSION

Insofar as his biography and literary remains permit a conclusion, Seng-jui may be said to have adhered to Kumārajīva's main positions. He esteemed the same scriptures, held the same attitude towards Hīnayāna and "divergent views," affirmed the Mādhyamika tradition as founded by Nāgārjuna and transmitted by Kumārajīva, advocated a Middle Path that transcended existent and inexistent, and envisaged the path of liberation as the refutation of wrong views which reveals the right vision. He rejected the exegetical theories of the "Six Houses" and the practice of "matching concepts," but affirmed that Tao-an's school prepared the way for Kumārajīva's resolution of the central problem of the existent and inexistent.

The prefaces do not permit any conclusions about Seng-jui's knowledge of Mādhyamika formal reasoning, or about his view of language and fact. However, the frequent pairing and contrasting of terms such as "word" and "meaning" in the prefaces does show that he was interested in the question of meaning and expression.

Altogether, Seng-jui's profile is that of a Mādhyamika. It indicates that he probably understood much more than is evidenced by his literary remains.

Chapter VI
SENG-CHAO

LIFE AND WRITINGS

While Kumārajīva was in Ku-tsang, a brilliant young monk named Seng-chao came from Ch'ang-an to become his disciple. Thus when Kumārajīva entered Ch'ang-an in A.D. 401, he was accompanied by the first and youngest of the distinguished men who in due course constituted his school.

Various reasons lead to the conclusion that Seng-chao is the crucial figure in the transmission of Kumārajīva's teaching in China. He was naturally brilliant, and met Kumārajīva while he was still quite young. The fact that he ventured to go to Ku-tsang in spite of the difficult diplomatic relations between Later Ch'in and Later Liang shows both his adventurous spirit and his early devotion to Kumārajīva. Not only did Seng-chao write prefaces to some of the most important translations, but he composed essays that were acclaimed by Kumārajīva, by Hui-yüan, and by other contemporaries, and that were transmitted to later generations. These essays were formative in the thinking of the New Three Treatise Sect, during the sixth century. They constitute the largest surviving set of documents on the earliest Chinese Mādhyamika thought.[1]

Seng-chao was born in 374[2] in the vicinity of Ch'ang-an (KSC, p. 365a, Liebenthal, *Chao*, pp. 4–6). As his family was poor, he went to work as a copyist, an occupation that enabled him to read widely in secular literature. In his youth he was fond of Neo-Taoism, but not entirely satisfied with it. Reading the *Vimalakīrti* converted him to Buddhism and prompted him to become a monk. By the time he reached manhood[3] he had achieved fame and the jealousy of others because of his wide learning and brilliant debating. Later, he went to follow Kumārajīva in Ku-tsang and when Kumārajīva came to Ch'ang-an, Seng-chao came back with him. He was appointed by Yao Hsing to assist Kumārajīva in his translations, which gave him the opportunity to learn Kumārajīva's interpretations of the doctrine. After the translation of the *Pañcaviṁśati*, he wrote an essay of more than two thousand characters, entitled *Prajñā Has No Knowing* (*Chao-lun*, part III) and showed it to Kumārajīva, who praised it, saying, "My understanding does not differ from yours, and in phrasing we might borrow from each other" (KSC, p. 365a26).[4]

In 408 Tao-sheng took this essay to Lu-shan where he showed it to the recluse Liu I-min. He commented "I did not suspect that there might be a Ho Yen[5] among the Buddhist clergy, too" and passed it on to Hui-yüan, who also praised it, and circulated it in the Lu-shan community where it was very favorably received. Liu I-min then wrote a letter to Seng-chao, who replied at some length.

Afterwards, Seng-chao wrote *Emptiness of the Non-Absolute* (*Chao-lun*, part II) and *Things Do Not Shift* (*Chao-lun*, part I). He also wrote a commentary on the *Vimalakīrti*, and some prefaces. While mourning the death of Kumārajīva, Seng-Chao composed *Nirvāṇa Is Nameless* (*Chao-lun*, part IV) and presented it to Yao Hsing who praised it and had it copied for circulation among the royal relatives. Seng-chao also wrote an obituary of Kumārajīva.

PRAJÑĀ HAS NO KNOWING

This essay, according to the *Biography* and the preamble of the essay itself, was inspired by the *Pañcaviṁśati* translation in which Seng-Chao participated during 403 and 404. When the paper was written, the *Hundred Treatise* had already been translated, and the translation of the *Great Perfection of Wisdom Treatise* had at least begun. Thus Seng-chao was acquainted to some degree with Mādhyamika.

Restatement of Prajñā Has No Knowing

Introduction

Prajñā is the essence of the Three Vehicles, but has not been understood correctly in China. Kumārajīva is well qualified to expound its true significance. Yao Hsing was the right man to bring Kumārajīva to Ch'in and to serve as *dānapati* to the translation project. Since I, Seng-chao, was present when the *Pañcaviṁśati* was translated, I am in a position to attempt a statement of its message as rendered by Kumārajīva.

Exposition

According to the *Prajñā-pāramitā Sūtras*, Prajñā is devoid of the marks of arising and ceasing, devoid of all marks of existing things. It has no thing that it knows and no thing that it sees. Since in fact there is a markless knowing, the intuition of not-knowing is demonstrated.

This thesis is proved by three arguments, one based on a distinction between universal cognition and particular cognitions, one based on the concept of non-purposive activity, and one based on the definitions of the terms "real," "unreal," "existent," and "inexistent." These arguments are supported by further quotations from the Sūtras.

OBJECTION 1: The Sage knows and acts, so you are wrong in denying him these functions.

REPLY: What I actually said was that he knows without apprehending objects,

EXTANT WRITINGS ATTRIBUTED TO SENG-CHAO

1. *Prajñā Has No Knowing, Chao-lun*, part III, written between 404 and 408 (T 1858, XLV, 153a–54c). Liebenthal, *Chao*; *Jōron Kenkyū.*
2. *Emptiness of the Non-Absolute, Chao-lun*, part II, written probably after 408 (T 1858, XLV, 152–53a). Liebenthal, *Chao*; *Jōron Kenkyū.*
3. *Things Do Not Shift, Chao-lun*, part I, perhaps written after part II (T 1858, XLV, 151a–c). Liebenthal, *Chao*; *Jōron Kenkyū.*
4. *Nirvāna Has No Name, Chao-lun*, part IV. Written between the fourth month of 413, and Seng-chao's death in 414 (T 1858, XLV, 157a–61b). At least parts of the present text of this essay are spurious. Liebenthal, *Chao*; *Jōron Kenkyū.*
5. *Correspondence with Liu I-min*,[6] included in the present *Chao-lun* (T 1858, XLV, pp. 154c–57a). Liebenthal, *Chao*; *Jōron Kenkyū.* Seng-chao's answer was written in 410.
6. *Introductory chapter of the Chao-lun* (T 1858, XLV, pp. 150c–51a). Probably written by the compiler of the collection rather than by Seng-chao. Liebenthal, *Chao*; *Jōron Kenkyū.*
7. *Vimalakīrti-Nirdeśa Commentary*, written between 406 and 410 (T 1775). Zürcher has a manuscript translation of most of this, which he did a dozen years ago.
8. *Obituary of Kumārajīva*, written in 413 or 414 (KHMC, pp. 264b–65b).
9. *Preface to the Vimalakīrti-nirdeśa-sūtra*, translated in 406 (CST, p. 58a–b). Link, "Shih Seng-yu," p. 36.
10. *Preface to the Hundred Treatise*, translated in 404 (CST, p. 77b–c).
11. *Preface to the Brahmajāla-sūtra* (T 1484, XXIV, 997a).[7]
12. *Preface to the Dīrghāgama*, translated in 413 (CST, pp. 63b–c).
13. *Postface to the Saddharmapuṇḍarīka Translation*, extant in *Fa-hua-chuan-chi* (T 2068, pp. 54b ff.).[8]
14. *The Jewel-Repository Treatise (Pao-Tsang-lun)* (T 1857, pp. 143b–50a).[9]

---

and acts without directing purposive emotion towards the beneficiary.
OBJECTION 2: When you say that "The Holy Mind is devoid of knowing" and also that "There is nothing that it does not know," you contradict yourself.
REPLY: The Sūtras define Prajñā as nameless, inexpressible, not existent, not inexistent, not real, and not void. Language cannot convey it, but to suggest it we cannot avoid using language.
OBJECTION 3: Since Prajñā has the Absolute Truth for its object, it is wrong to say that Prajñā has no object, and thus wrong to say that Prajñā has no knowing.
REPLY: Prajñā has no knowing precisely because it knows the Absolute Truth, which is not an object.

OBJECTION 4: If Prajñā does not apprehend, then either it does not apprehend because it has no knowing, or it knows first and then does not apprehend. Thus the Holy One either is totally blind, or his knowing is distinct from his not apprehending.
REPLY: Both alternatives are wrong. His knowing is identical with his not apprehending, and so he can know while not apprehending.
OBJECTION 5: Do you mean by "not apprehending" that the Holy Mind does not consider things to be things, and so does not apprehend falsely? In that case, it neither affirms nor matches (particular things), and who is it that, matching the Holy Mind, says that there is nothing which it does not know?
REPLY: I agree. As there is nothing that it matches, there is no thing that is not matched. Thus while it matches, there is no thing that it matches.
OBJECTION 6: It is not that the Holy Mind cannot affirm, but rather that it affirms nothing-to-affirm. It is consonant with the Absolute Truth that Prajñā should consider the markless to be markless.
REPLY: The Holy One is devoid of any "markless," because if he considered the markless as markless, then the markless would become a mark. The Perfect One dwells in the existent without being existent, and in the inexistent without being inexistent. He neither apprehends nor abandons the existent and the inexistent.
OBJECTION 7: Do you agree, then, that the Holy Mind responds when response is fitting, and does not respond when it is not fitting, and so that the Holy Mind sometimes arises and sometimes ceases?
REPLY: The course of the Holy One's responses is as dependable as the regular course of the four seasons. But, as he has emptiness as his own-being, he cannot arise and cannot cease.
OBJECTION 8: The inexistence of Holy Knowledge and the inexistence of deluded knowledge are both inexistence of arising and ceasing. What is the difference between them?
REPLY: The "inexistence" of Holy Knowledge is "nothing known." The "inexistence" of deluded knowledge is "knowing nothing." As the Holy Mind is void and still, it has no knowing that can inexist. Deluded knowing has a knowing, and so it has a knowing that can inexist. "Nothing known" is the "inexistence" of Prajñā. "Knowing nothing" is the "inexistence" of Absolute Truth. Therefore, the relation between Prajñā and Absolute Truth is that considered as function, they are different while the same and considered as calmness, they are the same while different. Since they are the same, they have no mentation about self and other. Since they are different, intuition does not fail.
OBJECTION 9: Do you mean to say that within Prajñā there is a distinction between function and calmness?
REPLY: The function is identical with the calmness. Function and calmness are one in their own-being. While springing from sameness, they are named differently.

Quotations

The titles of the scriptures and the frequency with which they are cited indicate a pattern similar to that found in Kumārajīva's *Correspondence.* The *Pañcaviṁśati* is the most important. The *Lalitavistara* allusion is the one that Hui-yüan mentions in the *Correspondence.* The *Middle Treatise* quotation is interesting as evidence that Seng-chao knew this text before the supposed date of translation in 409.

Terms and Concepts

There are two procedures for arriving at a definition of Seng-chao's terms: the historical, in which each term is sought out in the writings of his predecessors, contemporaries, and successors; and the descriptive, in which each term's place is plotted in the pattern of his writings, and its significance elicited by collation of the environments in which it occurs. As the *Chao-lun* offers a much larger context than do the surviving earlier writings, and since Seng-chao uses his key terms extremely often and in widely varied environments, it is more productive in this case to rely chiefly on the descriptive procedure.

The theme of *Prajñā Has No Knowing* is the contrast of the Holy Man's cognitive processes with those of ordinary men. The central group of terms is that which concerns the Holy Man. It is pointless to ask whether he is a Buddha, a bodhisattva, or a Taoistic sage. He is simply one who is endowed with Prajñā and concomitant attributes, and so might equally well be any of the three. The Holy Man: is endowed with numen by virtue of Holy Knowledge ⌜19⌝;[10] keeps his mind empty and intuits with non-apprehending Prajñā the markless Absolute Truth ⌜36⌝; does not have marklessness as an attribute, since it would thus be a mark ⌜64, 65⌝; dwells in existence yet is not existent, resides in inexistence yet is not inexistent, apprehends neither the existent nor the inexistent yet does not leave them ⌜66⌝; is devoid of action yet is devoid of non-action ⌜67⌝; has a mind without thoughts ⌜69⌝; responds with a non-responding response ⌜70⌝; has void-nothing as his essence, so neither arises nor ceases ⌜71⌝; and exercises the distinct functions of knowing the Absolute Truth and being the Absolute Truth while remaining essentially undifferentiated ⌜79, 81, 83⌝.

The Holy Man has the properties of Holy Mind, Holy Spirit, Holy Response, and Holy Knowledge.

Definitions

Holy Spirit exercises the function of response, and so is the agent of Holy Response ⌜9, 15, 86⌝. It contrasts with Holy Knowledge ⌜10–11, 12–13⌝, and is active (affective) rather than cognitive. Holy Response is ubiquitous and unceasing, non-arising and non-stopping ⌜13, 14, 71⌝.

Holy Mind exercises the function of Prajñā, Holy Knowledge, or Absolute Knowledge, which intuits, or mirrors, Absolute Truth ⌜51, 59⌝. Since Absolute Truth is devoid of determinate characteristics (marks), the cognitive relation between Prajñā and Absolute Truth is not the same as mundane cognition ⌜23, 24, 56, 59, 61, 62, etc.⌝. Like Holy Spirit, Holy Mind is ubiquitous and neither arises nor stops ⌜12, 69, 71, etc.⌝. It is omniscient ⌜4, 5, 37⌝, devoid of erroneous notions ⌜23, 30, 33⌝, empty of mundane existents and inexistents ⌜42, 46, 47,

48, etc.⌝. In some respects it is the same as Absolute Truth and in some respects it is different. The differences pertain to function, and the identity pertains to essence ⌜78⌝. The opposite of Holy Knowledge is deluded knowledge, which perceives marks and objects, and cognizes things that are not really so ⌜76, 34, 33, 53, 54, 55, 57, 58⌝.

Absolute Truth is the transcendental object of Prajñā, and the real nature of the myriad dharmas ⌜23, 24, 36, 52, 56, 59, 77, 79, 80, 82⌝ It is devoid of marks, and can be known only by Prajñā ⌜24, 51, 56⌝. Since there is nothing real except Absolute Truth, Prajñā knows everything in knowing Absolute Truth. Thus, to know everything, it does not have to apprehend the marks of mundane objects, since they are delusions, and not anything to be known absolutely ⌜4, 5, 6, 73, 74, 75, 76⌝. The subject-object relation between Prajñā and Absolute Truth is termed "inside" and "outside" ⌜79, 81, 82, 83⌝ though this cannot be taken spatially.

Intuition and *Mirroring* are the regular terms for Prajñā's cognitive function ⌜1, 2, 6, 7, 8, 11, 15, 20, 21, 23, 31, 36, 37, 43, 47, 79, 80, 81, 86⌝. A distant or abstract knowable is dark, obscure, abstruse, and Prajñā's power is shown by its ability to illuminate (intuit) the most obscure knowables[11] ⌜11, 15, 37, 86⌝.

The key metaphysical terms are the five polar pairs "void—real," "existent—inexistent," "sameness—difference," "calmness—function," and "stillness—motion."

Void is the opposite of "real" ⌜6, 42⌝ and the opposite of "obscure" ⌜7⌝, but it is not the opposite of "existent" and is not the same as "inexistent" ⌜16⌝. It is predicable of both Prajñā and deluded knowledge ⌜32, 75⌝. It is compatible with the function of intuition ⌜23, 43⌝. It is formless and nameless ⌜21⌝.

Real is the opposite of "void" ⌜6, 42⌝ and compatible with "obscure" ⌜6, 7⌝, but it is not the opposite of "inexistent" and is not the same as "existent" ⌜16⌝. It is predicable of the myriad dharmas qua Absolute Truth ⌜79, 80, 82⌝. It does not imply having marks ⌜82⌝.

Existent is the opposite of "inexistent" ⌜42⌝. It means having form and name ⌜18⌝, and being non-subtle ⌜45⌝. The existent is the domain of the name-doctrine ⌜46⌝. It is predicable of Prajñā ⌜42⌝. From the Absolute standpoint, it is not the mark of any thing ⌜53b⌝. It is pervaded by the Holy Man but is not his locus ⌜66⌝.

Inexistent is the opposite of "existent" ⌜42⌝. It is not compatible with being numinal ⌜19⌝. It is not compatible with functioning ⌜45⌝. It is denied of Prajñā and the Holy Mind ⌜42, 46⌝. It is predicated of the objects of deluded knowledge ⌜76⌝. From the relative standpoint, it is not the mark of things perceived ⌜53a⌝. It is pervaded by the Holy Man but is not his locus ⌜66⌝. The use of this term as a synonym of "empty" in ⌜26⌝ and ⌜83⌝ is not consonant with its meaning according to other contexts, and is probably a lapse into the usage of the earlier period when existent and real, inexistent and empty, were equated.

Sameness is the relation between terms that differ in function but not in essence ⌜85⌝. It applies to subject and object (inside and outside) in their calmness, namely emptiness, but not in their functions as the terms of cognition ⌜81, 82⌝. When Prajñā and Absolute Truth are considered from the standpoint of calmness, it is their dominant trait, though it does not exclude difference ⌜78b⌝. It implies absence of self and other ⌜78b⌝.

Difference is the relation between terms that are identical in essence but not in function ⌜81⌝. It applies to subject and object in their function as the terms of cognition, but not in their state of essential emptiness. It is a mode of designation rather than a mode of being ⌜85⌝. It is not a universal predicate ⌜78a, 84⌝, and it is not a predicate of the Holy Mind in its essence ⌜50⌝. When Prajñā and Absolute Truth are considered from the standpoint of function, it is their dominant trait, though it does not exclude sameness ⌜78a⌝.

Calmness is the passive mode of being. It is the aspect in which sameness is dominant and difference is subordinate ⌜78b⌝. In calmness, Prajñā and Absolute Truth are identical, though their difference is not excluded thereby ⌜78b⌝. In essence, calmness is identical with function, though they differ in designation ⌜85⌝. Calmness does not occur apart from function ⌜85⌝.

Function is the active mode of being. It is the aspect in which difference is dominant and sameness is subordinate ⌜78a⌝. In function, Prajñā and Absolute Truth are different, though their identity is not cancelled thereby. Function is identical in essence with calmness ⌜85⌝. Spirit has the function of responding ⌜9⌝. Prajñā has the function of intuition ⌜43, etc.⌝.

Stillness is the mode of things in essential voidness. Since everything is void, nothing is incompatible with stillness, not even motion ⌜25, 86⌝. In stillness, subject and object coalesce in unity [83].

Motion is related to stillness as function is related to calmness. It is compatible with stillness ⌜25⌝, and the more profound the stillness of the essence, the more powerful the action of the function ⌜86⌝.

These metaphysical polar pairs are of course extremely common in translations from Indic languages. "Void" corresponds to "śūnya" and "asadbhūta"; "real" corresponds to "sadbhūta" and "tattva" (also to "artha"); "existent" equals "bhāva," and "inexistent" equals "abhāva"; "sameness" is "ekatva" or "ekārtha"; "difference" is "pṛthaktva" or "nānārtha"; "stillness" and "motion" compare to "acala" and "cala"; "state" and "function" correspond more or less to "śānta" and "kriyā" or "nivṛtti" and "pravṛtti," but the correspondence is not complete.

It will be necessary to return to these definitions in the next section when considering the principles of negation and quantification. Seng-chao's statements about identity and difference may seem to assert a suprarational identity of opposites, but in fact they only state that none of the categories can be predicated universally of their subjects.

Logical Structure

A very high proportion of *Prajñā Has No Knowing* consists of rhetorical exposition rather than demonstration. Each section contains at least one quotation from a Sūtra, which lends the support of canonical authority to the exposition. Aside from the quotations, a large part of the essay consists of definitional statements and substitution of terms in such statements. The primary aim of the essay is the clarification of terms, and so logical inference appropriately plays a minor part in it. The rhetorical structure is very complex indeed, but the logical structure is rudimentary. In the whole essay, there are six arguments that are worth examining as logical specimens.

Argument One (p. 153a27; Doc. 8. II.2)

If there is something that is known, then there is something that is not known. Because in the Holy Mind there is nothing that is known, there is nothing that is not known.

This is a hypothetical syllogism of a form familiar in traditional Western logic, and of the kind that occurs so frequently in the *Middle Stanzas*. The first interesting fact about this syllogism is that it is invalid, since it is the antecedent that is negated.[12] Its form is:

A implies *B*; not-*A*, therefore not-*B*.

Nāgārjuna occasionally negates the antecedent. It is likely that Seng-chao was imitating the *Stanzas* and either imitated a fallacious syllogism or erred in attempting to imitate a valid one. Since this is the only complete hypothetical syllogism in this essay, it is especially significant that it is fallacious.

The second point of interest is the initial implication. It has the same form as Nāgārjuna's *Stanzas* 13.7 and 27.18, and is the converse of *Stanzas* 15.5, 23.22, and 25.7.

13.7: If something non-empty existed, then there might be something termed empty.

27.18: If "both eternal and non-eternal" were affirmed, then "neither eternal nor non-eternal" might be affirmed.

15.5: If entity is not established, then non-entity is not established, either.

23.22: If self, purity, permanence, and felicity do not occur, then non-self, impurity, impermanence, and suffering do not occur, either.

25.7: Where there is no entity, there is no non-entity.

This is Nāgārjuna's concept of negation as the complement of a finite extension, universal and null terms being excluded from consideration.

Seng-chao's argument seems most likely to have been formed on the model of *Stanzas* 13.7, since it exhibits the same concept of negation, and the same fallacy. This supports the evidence of the one quotation from the *Middle Treatise* indicating that the text of *Prajñā Has No Knowing* was finished after Seng-chao had learned something about the *Middle Treatise*.

Argument Two (p. 153b9; Doc. 8.II.4)

If you wish to say it exists, it is formless and nameless.
If you wish to say it inexists, the Holy One is numinal because of it.
The Holy One is numinal because of it, so though empty it does not fail to intuit.
It is formless and nameless, so though it intuits it does not fail to be empty;
though it intuits it does not fail to be empty, so it is manifold [together with the myriad things] but it does not change;
though empty it does not fail to intuit, so it moves to contact concrete things.
Therefore, the function of Holy Knowledge never ceases even for a moment; yet if you seek it in shapes and marks, you can never perceive it even for a moment.

The propositional structure of this argument is:

not *A*, because *B*.	not *C*, because *D*.
D so *E*;	*B* so *F*;
F so *G*;	*E* so *H*;
therefore *I* and *J*.	

It is to be noted that there is not a single implication in the whole argument. All statements of reason are simply made categorically. This is elaborate rhetoric, not logical inference. Since there are no conversions, it is impossible to tell whether Seng-chao at this time distinguished equivalence from implication, or knew how to manipulate conversions.

Argument Three (p. 153b19; Doc. 8.III, First Objection)

OBJECTION: [*A*] The Absolute Mind of the Holy Man, shining in solitude, intuits each and every thing; [*B*] his intercourse [with things] being limitless, his movements meet events. Because [*A*] he intuits each and every thing, [*C*] there is nothing that his knowing omits. Because [*B*] his movements meet events, [*D*] his meeting does not miss the crucial instant. Because [*D*] his meeting does not miss the crucial instant, [*E*] meeting of the meetable certainly exists. Because [*C*] there is nothing that his knowing omits, [*F*] knowing of the knowable certainly exists. Because [*F*] knowing of the knowable certainly exists, [*G*] it is not in vain for the Holy One to know. Because [*E*] meeting of the meetable certainly exists, [*H*] it is not in vain for the Holy One to meet. Since [*G*] he knows and since [*H*] he meets, why do you say that he has no knowing and no meeting?

This chain of reasons and consequences is of the same structure as Argument Two. Note that it is the opponent's point of view, a fact that shows the care with which Seng-chao framed the objections that he proposed to answer. The propositional structure is:

A and *B*; *A* so *C*; *B* so *D*; *D* so *E*; *C* so *F*; *F* so *G*; *E* so *H*;
G and *H*, so not not-*G* and not not-*H*.

The cross-order of the propositions is one of Seng-chao's favorite patterns. Restated in straight order, the argument consists of two chains; starting from the conjuncts of the initial conjunction, and concluding with the conjunction of the last terms of the two chains.

$$A \text{ and } B \begin{cases} \text{(a) } A \text{ so } C;\ C \text{ so } F;\ F \text{ so } G; \\ \\ \text{(b) } B \text{ so } D;\ D \text{ so } E;\ E \text{ so } H; \end{cases} \Bigg\} \begin{array}{l} G \text{ and } H, \\ \text{so not not-}G \\ \text{and not not-}H. \end{array}$$

Argument Four (p. 153c27; Doc. 8.III, Second Reply)

The Holy Mind, being ethereal and markless, cannot be considered existent; being extremely vigorous in functioning, it cannot be considered inexistent. Because it cannot be considered inexistent, Holy Knowledge has being in it. Because it cannot be considered existent, the "doctrine of names" does not concern it at all. Therefore: When we call it "knowing," it is not that we consider it to be "knowing," but that we wish by this to explain its mirroring. "Not knowing" is not "not knowing," but we wish by this to specify marks. As we specify its marks, we do not consider it inexistent; as we explain its mirroring, we do not consider it existent. Because it is not existent, while knowing it has no knowing; because it is not inexistent, while having no knowing it knows. Therefore: Knowing is identical with no-knowing; and no-knowing is identical with knowing. You should not impute differences to the Holy Mind because the words ["knowing" and "no-knowing"] are different.

The interesting features of this piece of dialectic are that the chains of reasons are interrupted by four definitional sentences, and that the final conclusion is a formal statement of identity. This is in the common Śūnyavādin form, with conversion to show that the first statement is convertible (*A* is *B*, and *B* is *A*). This form clearly distinguishes equations from predications, equivalences from implications. It is instanced in the *Prajñā-pāramitā-hṛdayasūtra*:[13] "Form indeed is emptiness; emptiness indeed is form; form is not other than emptiness; emptiness is not other than form; that which is form is emptiness; that which is emptiness is form" (T 250, VIII, 847c13). It also occurs in the *Middle Treatise*, for example: "Nothing of saṁsāra is different from nirvāṇa; Nothing of nirvāṇa is different from saṁsāra" (25.20).

Argument Five (p. 154a7, 10; Doc. 8.III, Third Reply)

When you seek for knowledge because of [the existence of] its object, [you see that] knowledge is not knowing. For what reason? The knowing and the known exist conjointly, and inexist conjointly. Because they inexist conjointly, no thing is existent.
Because they exist conjointly, no thing is inexistent.
Because no thing is inexistent, [knowing] is aroused by its object.
Because no thing is existent, [knowledge] is not something that objects can arouse.

Because [knowledge] is not something that objects can arouse, though it intuits its object, it is not a knowing.
Because [knowing] is aroused by its object, knowing and its object arise in mutual dependence.
Therefore: Knowing and no-knowing arise from the known.

The first statement is not part of the argument proper. The structure of this piece is similar to the preceding ones, with two strings of statements of reason and consequence, stated in cross order.

A and B; B so C; A so D; D so E; C so F; F so G; E so H; therefore H and G.

The conclusion is a conjunction of two propositions that are more or less equivalent in meaning to H and G, though they differ considerably in form. This argument, like the third one, begins with a conjunction and concludes with a conjunction.

In straight order, the argument runs:

$$A \text{ and } B \begin{cases} B \text{ so } C;\ C \text{ so } F;\ F \text{ so } G; \\ \\ A \text{ so } D;\ D \text{ so } E;\ E \text{ so } H; \end{cases} \text{therefore } H \text{ and } G.$$

Argument Six (p. 154c2; Doc. 8.III, Eighth Reply)

Therefore: As for Prajñā and Absolute Truth:
If you speak about their function, then while being the same they are different.
If you speak about their state, then while being different they are the same.
Because they are the same, there are no thoughts of self and other.
Because they are different, they do not fail in the process (results) of intuition.
Therefore: If you specify sameness, it is sameness in difference.
If you specify difference, it is difference in sameness.
Thus they cannot be considered as different, and they cannot be considered as the same.

This argument shares some of the features of the second, third, fourth, and fifth ones, but lacks others. The terms of the propositions are permuted rather than the propositions themselves. Only two of the propositions consist of reason and consequence. Certainly this argument is not dependent on any principles of formal logic.

A number of apparent paradoxes seem superficially to support the view that Seng-chao and those who use similar negational patterns are hinting at "an ultimate reality . . . which cannot be subsumed under the categories of logic."[14]

The knowing of unknowing is termed all-knowing (p. 153a28; Doc. 8. II. 1).

Knowing is identical with no-knowing; no-knowing is identical with knowing (p. 154a3; Doc. 8. III, Third Reply).

Though he always knows, he never knows (p. 153b1; Doc. 8. II.2).

The Holy Man always speaks and never speaks (p. 153c27; Doc. 8. III, First Reply).

The solution is that Seng-chao is using both "knowing" and "speaking" in two different senses—mundane knowing and transcendental knowing; mundane speaking and transcendental speaking. This is made explicit in a passage of Argument Five:

> In saying "knowing" it is not that we consider it to be "knowing," but that we wish by this to explain its mirroring.
> "Not knowing," is not "not knowing," but we wish by this to specify its marks.

Yet the point remains that Seng-chao thought that language was inadequate to his message. The advocate of "the doctrine of names" holds that names are established to communicate about things, and that there are really things that correspond to the names, so that the Holy Mind cannot be said both to have no knowing and to have nothing that it does not know (p. 153c15; Doc. 8.III, First Objection). In reply, Seng-chao says: "[Prajñā] is a nameless dharma, so it is not something that language can express. Yet, though language cannot express it, nothing other than language can communicate it. Therefore the Holy Man always speaks and never speaks" (p. 153c24, Doc. 8.III, First Reply). This means that names apply to marks, and that marks are the property of the existent. The label theory of names that is given by the opponent confirms the supposition that the "doctrine of names" involved positing the existence of things as counterparts for names. You cannot impute difference to the Holy Mind because of differences of words (p. 154a3, Doc. 8.III, First Reply). As Seng-chao's standpoint is that names are mere designations, he means "Though the Holy Man always speaks in designations, he never posits any entities corresponding to the designations that he uses." This must be taken together with the statement, by the opponent in Objection 3: A Sūtra says that if you do not obtain Prajñā, you will not see the Absolute Truth." For those who have Prajñā, the designations used by the Holy Man are meaningful, while for others they are mere expressions that do not correspond to anything in the realm of "deluded knowledge." When it is said that Prajñā is nameless, the paradox is only superficial. The word "Prajñā" is a designation, and not the label of an entity possessed of svabhāva.[15]

The philosophical problem here is that of the ontological status of abstractions. The "name-doctrine" that Seng-chao cites tries, like the Indian realists, to solve the question by either concretizing or denying them. Seng-chao understood the relationship between language, abstractions, and actualities that is fundamental to both Sūtra and Śāstra Śūnyavāda. Thus, when he wrote this essay he was well on the way to understanding Mādhyamika.

Mādhyamika in "Prajñā Has No Knowing"

When he wrote this essay, Seng-chao was thoroughly familiar with Sūtra Śūnyavāda, of which he gives a competent exposition in a novel literary form. He understood the epistemology, ontology, and theory of language of the *Prajñā-pāramitā-sūtras* and of the *Vimalakīrti-nirdeśa*. His concepts are metaphysical rather than cosmological, thus he successfully made the transition from cosmic cycle theory to abstract philosophy. This is a transition that Hui-yüan never quite made.

The Seng-chao of *Prajñā Has No Knowing* knew the *Middle Treatise* and presumably knew the *Hundred Treatise*, though he does not quote it. The influence of these texts is not too strong in this essay, however. Only one invalid hypothetical syllogism reveals the influence of Mādhyamika logic. Seng-chao had assimilated a feature of real importance, but had done so inaccurately, and neglected to exploit its potentialities in his debating. He shows no knowledge of the tetralemma, and the rules of contradiction, excluded middle, and conversion. He knows how to state an identity, but probably learned this from the Sūtras, where it is more frequent than in the Mādhyamika treatises.

Seng-chao seems to violate the Mādhyamika ban on existential quantifications, but, since he is speaking in mere designations rather than in svabhāva terms, his procedure is quite compatible with Nāgārjuna's.

LETTER TO LIU I-MIN

When Tao-sheng left Ch'ang-an and returned to Lu-shan in the late summer of 408, he took with him a copy of Seng-chao's *Prajñā Has No Knowing* which circulated among Hui-yüan's disciples and excited great admiration as well as some perplexity. The lay recluse Liu I-min wrote to Seng-chao and posed a series of questions, to which Seng-chao replied in the eighth month of 410.

One passage in Seng-chao's reply (p. 156b26) furnishes information about his grasp of logic and dialectic that is not to be found in his other writings.

> To say that [prajñā] is not existent is to say that it is not affirmed as existent, but does not mean that it is affirmed as not existent. To say that it is not inexistent is to say that it is not affirmed as inexistent, but does not mean that it is affirmed as not inexistent. It is not existent and it is not not existent. It is not inexistent, and is not not inexistent.

This passage obviously concerns the tetralemma, though its doctrine of affirmation and negation appears rather enigmatic. Yüan-k'ang explains it in a way which makes the quantity of the terms the key factor (T XLV, 188a9).

> It is like the three positions—east, west, and middle—with regard to each other. When we say that the middle is not the east, we do not say that it is identical

with the west. On the basis of the preceding statements, we should say, "To say that it is 'not east' is to say that it is not affirmed as 'east,' but does not mean that it is affirmed as 'not east' and that 'not east' is determined as 'west.' To say that it is 'not west' is to say that it is not affirmed as 'west,' but does not mean that it is affirmed as 'not west' and that 'not west' is determined as 'east.'" (Question omitted).
ANSWER: If "the not existent and not inexistent" is affirmed as the middle, why labor to use the term "middle" separately? East, west, and middle are like this, too. Further, "not east" is not necessarily identical with "not east." [i.e., one "not east" is not identical with any other "not east."] "South" and "north" are also "not east." "Not west" is not necessarily identical with "not west." "South" and "north" are also "not west." If you pattern "not existent and not inexistent" on "not east and not west," then you can understand it.

The analogy of the directions poses the problem as one involving the different kinds of opposition. 'Not east' is the contradictory of 'east,' but 'west' is not the contradictory of 'east,' but only its contrary. Yüan-k'ang seems to be aware of the problem of extension and of a kind of indeterminacy of complements. However, his analogy leads him astray, since 'existent and inexistent' is a two-term pattern, while the directions constitute a five-term system. The spatial illustration presents the concept of contrariety vividly, but obscures the principle of the quantity of terms on which the distinction between different kinds of opposition depends.

The question is how to interpret the term *shih* 是 (affirm) in Seng-chao's passage. One possibility is to consider that it means total affirmation of the predicate. In this case, Seng-chao's statement that "it is not existent" means "it is not affirmed as existent" furnishes a rule that all unquantified terms are to be taken as if quantified universally. This rule produces the following table:

A	All *X* is *A*	ch'i shih . . .其是 . . .
E	No *X* is *A*	ch'i shih fei . . .其是非 . . .
I	Some *X* is *A*	ch'i fei shih fei . . .其非是非 . . .
O	Some *X* is not *A*	ch'i fei shih . . .其非是 . . .

The last two statements in the passage, (1) "It is not existent and it is not not existent," and (2) "It is not inexistent and is not not inexistent," have the form of the fourth lemma of the tetralemma—"No *X* is *A*, and no *X* is not *A*." However, interpreted according to the value that has been supposed for ***shih***, they exhibit the form of the third lemma, "Some *X* is *A*, and some *X* is not *A*." The calculation, substituting from the table, is as follows:

(1) ch'i fei yu, fei fei yu (It is not existent, and it is not not existent).
= ch'i fei shih yu, ch'i fei shih fei yu.
= Some *X* is not *A*, and some *X* is *A*.

This is the third lemma, a conjunction of I and O forms.

(2) ch'i fei wu, fei fei wu (It is not inexistent and is not not inexistent) (same procedure as for (1)).

This result is curious, but it tallies with Seng-chao's general treatment of the tetralemma and the terms "existent" and "inexistent." In accordance with varying points of view, he asserts sometimes the third lemma and sometimes the fourth lemma. The decisive factor here, as with "self" and "other," is the point of reference. Compare the *Middle Treatise* explanation of the tetralemma, which has been translated above in Chapter Two.

Yüan-k'ang supports the hypothesis that this passage should be interpreted as involving quantification. Thus it appears that Seng-chao, in addition to having some idea of the tetralemma, was aware of the fact that the quantity of the terms is significant in this logical form.

THE VIMALAKĪRTI COMMENTARY

In his reply to Liu I-min, Seng-chao mentioned that he had written a commentary on the *Vimalakīrti-nirdeśa Sūtra*:

In the year *wu* (406) the dharma-master Kumārajīva issued the *Vimalakīrti Sūtra*. At that time I attended and heard the proceedings. In the time when I was free from attending the sessions, I wrote down the true words [of Kumārajīva] and made them into a commentary. Though the phrasing is not literary, the ideas that I have received have a foundation. Now I use the occasion of this letter to send a copy south (p. 155c27; *Jōron Kenkyū*, pp. 44–45; Liebenthal, *Chao*, p. 101).

This commentary was evidently completed within three or four years of the translation of the Sūtra. Tsukamoto says that it was probably written in 407 or 408 (*Jōron Kenkyū*, pp. 147–48). The main general interest of this text is that it is a specimen of early Chinese exegetical literature. It also possesses a special value as evidence on how Seng-chao understood the scripture that had converted him to Buddhism.

Some passages in the Commentary show that Seng-chao utilized the Mādhyamika treatises in explaining the sūtras:

SŪTRA: Mañjuśrī said, "So it is, householder. The already come does not come again. The already gone does not go again. For what reason? The comer has nowhere to come from, and the goer has nowhere to go to. What is seen cannot be seen again" (T XIV, 544b15, ch. 5).

SENG-CHAO: Departing and coming and seeing each other are all nothing but cause-and-condition designations. The not-yet-come (future) is non-coming. The already-come does not come again. Apart from the already-come and the not-yet-come where further is there coming or departing? Seeing also is so. You should consult the critique of this matter in the Treatises (*Vimalakīrti Commentary*, T XXXVIII, 371c10).

This is the general theme of *Middle Stanzas*, chapter two. The distinctive feature is the principle that there is no third apart from the gone and the ungone. Seng-chao could have read this in the *Great Perfection of Wisdom Treatise*, pp. 205b–c and 427c–28a, where chapter two of the *Stanzas* is paraphrased. Even if the *Middle Treatise* was translated in 409, the Commentary need not have been completed before then.

SŪTRA [Vimalakīrti to Maitreya]: In what birth did you obtain a prediction? In the past? In the present? In the future? If it is a past birth, the past birth has already ceased. If it is a future birth, the future birth has not yet arrived. If it is the present birth, present birth does not abide (T XIV, 542b3).
SENG-CHAO: Separately analyzing the three times, [Vimalakīrti] explains no-arising. Past arising (birth) has already ceased, and the already-ceased cannot be called arising (*Vimalakīrti Commentary*, p. 361b5).
SENG-CHAO: Present dharmas flow quickly and do not abide. What do you consider as arising? If arising and ceasing are at one time, then the two marks are both destroyed. If arising and ceasing are at different times, then at the time of arising there is no ceasing, then dharmas do not have the three marks. If dharmas do not have the three marks, then they are not conditioned. If they have all three marks, then there is the error of infinite regression. This statement of no-arising is also furnished in the *Treatises*. Since the three times are inexistent, in which does [Maitreya] obtain a prediction (*Vimalakīrti Commentary*, p. 361b10)?

Here Seng-chao glosses the *Vimalakīrti* with a paraphrase of *Middle Stanzas*, chapter seven. He produces a perfectly acceptable Mādhyamika refutation of the three times, except for his statement that present dharmas flow quickly. This is interesting since one of his later essays (*Chao-lun*, part I) is on the thesis that things do not shift. This passage is important evidence on the problem of time in *Chao-lun*, part I, since it shows that Seng-chao knew the Mādhyamika doctrine on this point.

In the *Commentary* there are two passages in particular that expound Seng-chao's doctrine of samādhi, a subject on which the *Chao-lun* has very little to say:

SŪTRA: While not arising from the trance of cessation (*nirodha-samāpatti*) to display all the postures [i.e., walking, standing, sitting, and lying down]—this is samādhi (still-sitting) (ch. 3, T XIV, 539c21).
SENG-CHAO: When the Hīnayānists enter the trance of cessation, then their bodies are like dry wood and lack the power of moving and functioning. When the mahāsattva enters the real-mark-samādhi his mind-knowledge ceases forever, and his body fills the eight directions. He acts in compliance with crucial occasions, and his responding and meeting are endless. In rising, moving, advancing, and halting, he does not forsake correct deportment. His practice of samādhi is also according to the ultimate. When it says above that he does not manifest body or mind in the three planes, it means that he displays all the postures. Now, because he has no displaying, he is able to have nothing that he does not display. Nothing not displayed is identical with the essence of no displaying. I hope that gentlemen who investigate the metaphysical will have the means to understand

the respects in which the two are the same, and to make the same the respects in which the two are different (*Vimalakīrti Commentary*, p. 344c14–21; Liebenthal, *Chao*, p. 39).

The Hīnayāna samādhi is described in Taoist terms. Possibly Seng-chao classed the Taoist adepts and the Hīnayāna arhants together. The use of the term 'real-mark-samādhi' is more significant for his own doctrine. The source of the term is the *Great Perfection of Wisdom Treatise*:

Before, it stated the names of the samādhis, but did not tell their marks. Now it wishes to tell their marks. Therefore it says that [they are] coursing in emptiness, wishlessness, and marklessness. If there is anyone who courses in emptiness, wishlessness, and marklessness, he is said to have attained real-mark-samādhi (GPWT, T XXV, 97a18; Lamotte, *Vimalakīrti*, pp. 324–25).

The samādhi that Seng-chao proceeds to describe could only belong to a dharmadhātu-kāya bodhisattva or Buddha. His body is omnipotent and omniscient, yet uncharacterized by visible body or determinate mentation. Quite evidently this is not to be construed as a report on Seng-chao's own experience. If he ever experienced any such exaltations, his writings do not say so.

SŪTRA: "As for samādhi, not to manifest body or mind in the three planes is samādhi" (ch. 3, T XIV, 539c20).
SENG-CHAO: Now, in the samādhi of the dharmakāya, body and spirit have both ceased. The Way (*bodhi*) is dissociated from ordinary sense-spheres and it is something that seeing and hearing cannot reach. How then is it samādhi when one manifests a body in the three planes and cultivates thoughts? Śāriputra still had a worldly-retribution-born body and a worldly-retribution mind-organ, so he considered human company an annoyance, and "sat still" under a tree. He was not able to make his body and spirit devoid of traces, and so he incurred this criticism. The general intention behind [Vimalakīrti's] criticism [of Śāriputra] is to benefit [him] greatly. It is not that [Vimalakīrti] held onto other and self and had thoughts in terms of affirmation and denial (*Vimalakīrti Commentary*, p. 344b23–29).

In Seng-chao's view, the samādhi of the dharmakāya is a supersensuous mode of illumination. It is devoid of "traces," i.e., of discursive symbolisms and conceptions. It is not a mere trance state experienced by a human being sitting still under a tree. It is not purely subjective, but affects one's whole mode of being. This is not uniquely Seng-chao's notion, but is the explicit doctrine of the *Vimalakīrti Sūtra* of which the passage is an exposition. Vimalakīrti criticized Śāriputra's samādhi because contemplation that depends on the senses or the imagination or bodily postures is not the dharmakāya contemplation.

It is a reasonable surmise that Seng-chao's doctrine of samādhi was essentially the same as that of the *Great Perfection of Wisdom*

Treatise. About his own experience, we can either speculate without hope of proving our hypotheses, or maintain a silence as complete as, but not as knowledgeable as, Vimalakīrti's.

EMPTINESS OF THE NON-ABSOLUTE
(Chao-lun, part II, pp. 152a–53a)

This essay was written at some time in or after 409. Unlike *Prajñā Has No Knowing*, it is not in the form of a disputation, but of an exposition entirely in the author's person. It consists of three introductory sections and six sections forming the essay proper. There are no quotations in either the introductory sections or conclusion, but each of the other sections contains quotations either as a point of departure for, or as a confirmation of, the reasoned exposition. The theme of this essay is emptiness, and consequently it deals with the Two Truths, entity, identity and difference, existence and inexistence, and other concepts relating to emptiness. Throughout this paper, the relation between utterances and events, or language and facts, is dominant, just as the relation between knowledge and facts was dominant in *Prajñā Has No Knowing*. The text is briefer and even more laconic than *Chao-lun*, part III.

Restatement

I.1 Introduction: The Holy Man's intelligence is all-pervading and unobstructed because he identifies with the self-voidness of the myriad things.

Since forms are not self-made, they do not individuate themselves, and thus are not absolute. Though they are forms in the relative sense, they are not forms in the absolute sense.

I.2 Refuting Divergent Views: There are three current misconceptions about what emptiness is.[16] The *first view* holds that emptiness is blotting out the images of external objects and thus emptying the mind. This view rightly understands that stillness of spirit is the condition in which emptiness is realized, but mistakenly holds that things are actually existent whether the mind is empty of them or not. The *second view* is that form is emptiness, because form does not make itself, but is made by emptiness. This view rightly sees that forms are not self-made, but errs in attributing a self-nature to emptiness. The *third view* is that emptiness is the primordial inexistence from which all existent things have arisen. This view rests on fascination with the idea of inexistence, and involves a misinterpretation of the Sūtras' words that dharmas are "not existent and not inexistent," which are misconstrued as meaning "the existent is inexistent and the inexistent is inexistent too, so the inexistent is the matrix of everything."

I.3 The Point of the Essay: You can call things "things," but you cannot call names "things." Things are not names, and do not coincide with actuals; names are not things and do not coincide with true concepts. Absolute Truth is a name, so it cannot be called a thing. The theory that names correspond to things does not apply to it. Nevertheless, though language cannot refer to it as an object of reference, I propose to talk about it.[17]

II.1 Quotations on Emptiness

The *Great Perfection of Wisdom Treatise* and the *Middle Treatise* both state that the dharmas are not existent and not inexistent, which refers to the Absolute

Truth. This Absolute Truth is not realized, however, by stopping up the senses and erasing all images of things from the mind, but rather it is achieved by realizing one's identity with things.

The counterfeit and the absolute are identical in nature, so when one realizes this identity, there is no change of nature. The dharmas exist though inexistent, because no nature changes, and inexist though existent, because they do not obstruct the Holy One's intelligence. This is what "not existent and not inexistent" means.

Thus a Sūtra says, "Form is empty by nature, not by destruction." Further, the *Vimalakīrti-sūtra* says that the bodhisattva's sickness is not absolute and not existent. The *Chao-jih-ching* (T 638) says that the four elements are identical with voidness.

"Having attainment" is the counterfeit name for "having no attainment"; "having no attainment" is the absolute name for "having attainment."

What is called "absolute" never exists; what is called "counterfeit" never inexists.

The two terms are never the same, and the two principles are never different.

II.2 Reasoning about Emptiness

Things are existent in some respects and inexistent in others. Thus they both exist and inexist. As the existent does not coincide with the Absolute and the inexistent is not a blanking out, existent and inexistent differ in name, but are one in their reference.

Thus Ratnakūṭa in the *Vimalakīrti-sūtra* says that according to the Buddha the dharmas are neither existent nor inexistent, because they arise dependently. The *Keyūra-sūtra* (T 656) denies that there is either a turning or no turning when the Dharma-wheel is turned. These texts mean that annullist views are erroneous because things are not inexistent, while eternalist views are incorrect because things are not existent. "Not existent and not inexistent" applies to Absolute Truth.[18]

II.3 Further Quotations

"Not existent and not inexistent" is asserted by the *Prajñā-pāramitā-sūtra* and the *Middle Treatise*. We can give a rational account of this, too.

If existence were absolute, it would be self-existent, and not dependent on causes and conditions. But it is dependent on causes and conditions, so we know that it is not self-existent, and so is not absolute.

If inexistence were absolute, it would be motionless and its subjects should not arise. But since the myriad things arise from conditions, we know that they do not inexist, and so inexistence is not absolute.

If existence were a necessary property of the existent, then inexistence could not be a property of it. If inexistence were a necessary property of the inexistent, then existence could not be a property of it.

We state this by saying that "not inexistent" explains "existent" and "not existent" explains "inexistent." The fact is one and the terms are two.

II.4 Further Reasoning

Things do not really exist, since in some ways they are inexistent, and do not really inexist, since in some ways they are existent.

Because they arise non-absolutely, they do not really exist.

Because they have form, they do not really inexist.

As the *Fang-kuang* (T 221) says, it is like a phantom man who is not inexistent, but merely not a real man.

II.5 Names and Reals

The thing has no actual that matches the name, so the thing is not a real thing. The name has no efficacy to obtain the thing, so the name is not a real name. Thus there is no matching between names and actuals.

As the *Middle Treatise* says, "self" and "other" have no fixed reference. The self is other for another, and the other is self for itself.

Thus the myriad things are not absolute, but figurative appellations.

II.6 Conclusion

The Holy Man is ubiquitous and immutable because he coalesces with the intrinsic voidness of things, and not because he imposes any adventitious voidness on them. Thus he is both the support of all the dharmas, and identical with them. He is immanent in the myriad things.

Quotations

The quotations and allusions to Buddhist texts in the first three parts of the Chao-lun tabulate as follows:

Taishō	Title	Part III	Part II	Part I	Total
T 221, 223	Pañcaviṁśati-p.p.	7	4	1	12
T 474, 475	Vimalakīrti-nirdeśa	2	3		5
T 1564	Middle Treatise	1	3	1	5
T 630	Sampanna-prabhāsa-samādhi	1	1	1	3
T 1509	Mahāyāna-śāstra (GPWT)		2	1	3
T 224	Aṣṭasāhasrikā-p.p.		1	1	2
T 656	Bodhisattva-keyūra		1		1
T 638	Chao-jih-ching		1		1
T 262	Saddharma-puṇḍarīka			1	1
T 586	Viśeṣacintā-brahma-paripṛcchā	1	1		2
T 186	Lalita-vistara or Upāsaka-Śīla (T 1488)	1			1

The chief difference in the pattern of ***Emptiness of the Non-Absolute*** compared with ***Prajñā Has No Knowing*** is that the ***Middle Treatise*** is mentioned three times and the ***Great Perfection of Wisdom Treatise*** twice. The quotations from these two texts do not correspond exactly with passages in the present texts. They may have been quoted from memory, rephrased for quotation, or rephrased so that one statement alludes to several passages in the text cited.

Terms and Concepts

The key terms of ***Chao-lun***, part III—the Holy Man, Holy Spirit, Holy Mind, Absolute Truth, Void, Real, Existent, Inexistent, Sameness, Difference, Calmness, Function, Stillness, and Motion—are also fundamental to ***Emptiness of the Non-Absolute***, ***Chao-lun***, part II. However, there is almost no mention of 'knowing' and considerably less mention of 'intuition' and 'response.' There is less emphasis on epistemology and soteriology, and more on ontology. Furthermore, many terms are defined from aspects other than those considered in ***Prajñā Has No Knowing*** (***Chao-lun***, part III).

Meaning-shifts signalled by shift of syntactical role are essential to the essay. 'Form' (*se*, 色) and 'thing' (*wu*, 物) in particular switch back and forth between their noun roles and their factitive and putative verb roles—'to cause (something) to be a form/thing' and 'to consider/call (something) a form/thing.'[19] Reflexive constructions occur frequently in both noun and verb roles: *tzŭ-hsü* 自虚—making itself empty; *tzŭ-i* 自異—differentiating itself; *tzŭ-se* 自色—making itself into form; *tzŭ-yu* 自有—making itself existent. *yu* 有 (exist) and *wu* 无 (inexist) run the gamut of their functions, serving as existential copulas, as prefixes meaning 'having' and '-less,' as substantives ('existence' and 'inexistence'), and as predicates.

The term *chi* (卽) requires special notice since it exhibits both grammatical and lexical behavior of a peculiar kind. It is the copula of complete identity between a given and a new term, a usage in which it occurs from Late Chou onwards. There are two variants of the structure, namely:

(a) 'shih X chi Y' or 'chi X shih Y,' e.g. 'chi shen shih fo' 卽身是仏.

(b) 'X chi shih Y,' e.g. 'se chi shih k'ung' 色卽是空.

The structure 'chi X chi Y' is merely a variant of (a), e.g. 'chi wei chi chen' 卽僞卽真.

In the *Chao-lun*, *chi* frequently functions as a full verb, with either a resultative sense ('become identical with') or a stative sense ('remain identical with'). In either usage it may often be translated by 'coincides.' It does not occur as an intransitive predicate.[20]

Identity, *chi*, is a function of the Holy One. He identifies with things ⌜11⌝,[21] and identifies with the self-voidness of things ⌜18, 57⌝. In samādhi, the devotee identifies with the Spirit ⌜61⌝. *Identity* is the relation between the counterfeit and the absolute ⌜12⌝, but not the relation between the existent and the absolute ⌜33⌝. The Buddha's establishing the dharmas is identical with his being absolute ⌜59⌝. This relation was ascribed to function and calmness, and to knowing and not apprehending, in *Chao-lun*, part III.

The theme of this paper is emptiness and so the attendant concepts of the Two Truths—absolute and relative, of the relation between language and fact, and of essence versus quantification, are all prominent in the exposition. In *Chao-lun*, part III, Absolute Truth was mentioned, but not relative (popular) truth. The discussion of language and fact is much more precise in this paper than in the preceding one.

Absolute Truth is outside the sphere of the "doctrine of names" ⌜8⌝, is referred to by the statement that the dharmas are not existent and not inexistent ⌜9, 36⌝, is asserted to explain "not inexistent" ⌜28⌝, is realized without blanking out images of the myriad things from the mind ⌜10⌝, and in it there is no achieving and no attaining ⌜20⌝. It coincides with popular truth in the essential nature (emptiness) of its referent ⌜27, 29⌝.

Popular Truth affirms achievement and attaining of Absolute Truth ⌜20⌝, is asserted to explain "not inexistent" ⌜28⌝, and coincides with Absolute Truth in the essential nature of its referent ⌜27, 29⌝.

The theory of language and fact assumes three terms—the name, which is a linguistic entity, the thing, which is a phenomenal entity, and the actual, which is a noumenal entity. "Name" (*ming* 名) and "actual" (*shih* 實) are the Chou Logicians' terms.[22] The "doctrine of names" is that names match things and things match actuals. Seng-chao, like Kumārajīva and Nāgārjuna, denies this, and asserts that names are "borrowed" to designate things and actuals ⌜43, 49, 57⌝. Thus they are counterfeit ⌜12, 21, 24, 26⌝, and do not succeed in designating what is true ⌜7⌝. Things (phenomena) are the appearances of actuals, but like a phantom are not what they seem ⌜47, 48, 52⌝, and are thus not real or absolute things ⌜56, 45, 46⌝.

The term "name" has some connotations that might escape the modern theorist on language. A true name, according to the notion attributed to the "doctrine of names," should have an efficacy or power ⌜51, 53⌝. This power evokes the thing when the name is uttered. Since Brahmanical ritual and Buddhist mantric practice alike affirm this power of names to conjure up things, the Śūnyavādin denial of the connexion between words and things would seem inimical to such religious practices, and yet the *Prajñā-pāramitā Sūtras* proclaim their own efficacy as spells.

Logical Structure

In this essay, apparent paradoxes are even commoner than in the preceding one. The interpretation of these is decisive for the important question whether Seng-chao was a clear philosophical thinker or an ecstatic. The question need not be stated as an exclusive disjunction, since it is possible that Seng-chao was both a philosophical thinker and an ecstatic. But since feeling is more private than thought Seng-chao's emotions are unlikely to appear through the literary mask that he composed fifteen centuries ago. He wrote philosophical essays, not autobiography, and he wrote in a language that is now known only from a few literary artifacts. On the other hand, the question of paradoxes is within the customary field of formal logic and can be resolved.[23]

(a) "Not existent and not inexistent" is indeed speech about Absolute Truth ⌜36⌝ (Doc. 9.II.2).
(b) Existent and inexistent differ in name but are one in their reference ⌜33⌝ (Doc. 9.II.2).
(c) That though existent they inexist is what "not existent" means ⌜15⌝ (Doc. 9.II.1).
(d) That though inexistent they exist is what "not inexistent" means ⌜16⌝ (Doc. 9.II.1).
(e) Though forms, they are not forms ⌜2⌝ (Doc. 9.I.1).
(f) A thing without an actual to match its name is not a thing ⌜52⌝ (Doc. 9.II.5).

(g) A name without efficacy to obtain a thing is not a name (Doc. 9.II.5).

These seem to say that an entity can be both existent and inexistent, that forms are not forms, that things are not things, and that names are not names. However, (e), (f), and (g) are resolved when construed, as "counterfeit forms are not real forms," "counterfeit things are not real things," and "borrowed names are not true names." The other paradoxes are resolved when the subjects are quantified existentially.

(h) There are some respects in which the myriad things are not existent ⌜30⌝ (Doc. 9.II.2).

(i) There are some respects in which [the myriad things] are not inexistent ⌜31⌝ (Doc. 9.II.2).

(j) Since there are some respects in which the myriad dharmas do not exist, they cannot really exist ⌜45⌝ (Doc. 9.II.4).

(k) Since there are some respects in which they do not inexist, they cannot really inexist ⌜46⌝ (Doc. 9.II.4).

(l) Inexistence is not utter voidness, and existence is not absolute existence ⌜32⌝ ⌜cf. 3⌝ (Doc. 9.II.2).

This says that all the marks of existence must be predicable of a subject for it to exist absolutely. As this condition is not fulfilled by any things, their existence is only partial, and the inexistence that precedes their arising and follows their ceasing and accompanies their phenomenal existence from the noumenal standpoint is a "borrowed" attribute, not an intrinsic one.

The idea of dependent co-arising plays an important part in this paper ⌜37, 38, 40⌝. It is evident that Seng-chao has thoroughly mastered the meaning of *Stanzas* 24.18: "We declare that dependent co-arising is emptiness; it serves as a designation; it is identical with the Middle Path." The chief point of this idea is that universals and nulls are incompatible with the observed panorama of change.

This paper shows that since writing *Chao-lun*, part III, Seng-chao had made some progress in assimilating the structure of the hypothetical syllogism. There are two examples of the fallacy of the antecedent at the end of Section II.2 (Doc. 9.II.2):

(converting cross order of propositions to straight order),
(a) Would you say that things are inexistent? Then annullist views would not be erroneous. Because things are not inexistent, annullist views are erroneous.
(b) Would you say that things are existent? Then eternalist views would be correct. Because things are not existent, eternalist views are not correct.

In the following syllogism, Seng-chao performs a valid conversion, and then infers a conclusion which is valid from either the first implication or the second, its conversion:

(c) If the myriad things were inexistent, then they should not arise; as they arise, they are not inexistent; (negation of the consequent). Thus it is clear that because they arise from conditions, they do not inexist (Doc. 9. II.3).

There are two valid examples of *modus ponens*, though they are stated in an oblique way and their structure is only apparent after restatement (Doc. 9.II.4).

(d) If the existence of things arises non-absolutely, then the things do not really exist; the existence of things arises non-absolutely; therefore things do not really exist.
(e) For things to have shapes implies that things do not really inexist; things have shapes; therefore they do not really inexist.

The fact that in this essay there are no long chains of "becauses" like those in *Chao-lun*, part III may indicate an increased understanding of the patterns of formal reasoning.

The paradoxes in this paper are all perfectly logical, and the formal reasoning, though bad, is a good deal better than in the preceding paper. In Seng-chao's work, we can observe a trend towards more mature systematic thought rather than towards an ecstatic inebriation, forgetful of reason.

Summary

In comparison with *Prajñā Has No Knowing*, *Emptiness of the Non-Absolute* shows much greater familiarity with Mādhyamika literature, a somewhat deeper grasp of certain concepts such as the Two Truths and the relation between language and fact, and a slightly better control of the hypothetical syllogism.

THINGS DO NOT SHIFT

This paper was written later than *Chao-lun*, part III and perhaps later than *Chao-lun*, part II. Because it deals with the problems of time, change, and motion rather than with Prajñā and Absolute Truth, it seems unlike Seng-chao's other essays, and more like the *Middle Stanzas*. It is noteworthy that the term "emptiness" does not occur in *Chao-lun*, part I. There are very few references to the Holy One, and little attention is paid to the soteriological themes that are so prominent in *Chao-lun*, part III and *Chao-lun*, part II. This is the most purely philosophical of all the essays.

Restatement of "Things Do Not Shift"

I. Introduction: The common opinion is that when change takes place, things move through time. But this is not so. The *Fang-kuang* [T 221] says that the dharmas

do not move to or from anywhere. Though moving they are always still, and though still they are always moving.

But contemporary disputants never agree on the never-changing identity of motion and stillness. When they talk about the Absolute, they contradict popular opinion, and when they conform to popular usage, they do violence to the Absolute. In the first case, their arguments fall flat, and in the second they lose sight of the true nature of things. Consequently people either stay bewildered, or cease to care about the problem.

If we examine the relationship between stillness and motion, however, it is possible to resolve the problem.

II.1 and 2 Quotations and Commonsense Examples

The ***Tao-Hsing*** (T 221) and the ***Middle Treatise*** both state that the dharmas do not depart from any place and do not arrive at any place, and so we know that things do not shift from one time-point to another.

The common idea of motion is that past things move and are not still because they do not move from the past to the present. My idea of motion is that past things are still and do not move because they do not move from the past to the present. Because they do not come, they are moving and not still, and because they do not depart, they are still and not moving.

What differs is not the fact, but people's interpretation of it.

II.3 Dismissing Errors

People know that past things do not come to the present, but they still imagine that present things go to the past. But if past things do not move, neither do present things.

Past things are never inexistent in the past and are never existent in the present. So we know that they do not leave the past and do not come to the present. This applies mutatis mutandis to the present.

Thus past things abide in their own proper place in the past, and present things occupy their own proper place in the present. Neither arrives at its position from another position.

Thus even the great movements in the phenomenal world are not really movements, but are at rest while they move.

II.4 Reconciling the Teachings

The Śrāvakas reach attainment when they awaken to the fact of impermanence. The Pratyeka-buddhas attain liberation when they realize detachment from dependent co-arising. But if there is no change in dependent co-arising, then the Śrāvaka's attainment is vain because he imagines change, and the Pratyeka-buddha's liberation is vain because there is no stillness detached from motion.

Stillness while moving is like staying while leaving. It must be realized with the intellect.

When the scriptures say "depart," they do not affirm a dharma of departure, but simply counteract the wrong notion of permanence. When they say "stay," they do not affirm a dharma of "staying," but simply counteract the wrong notion of impermanence. The terms are used as popular truth, not as absolute truth.

Thus, though things are called permanent, they do not stay, and though said to depart, they do not move from one time to another. They are still in the sense that they do not move from one time to another. They pass in the sense that they do not abide from one time to another. This is the point of view of the Holy Mind, which conforms to absolute truth and differs from popular opinions.

The popular notion is that the identity of a person persists throughout the successive phases of a lifetime. They know that the years pass, but they think that the substance of the person remains. Witness the astonishment of the old recluse's neighbors when he said, "I resemble the former 'me,' but I am not the former 'me.'"

The Tathāgata adjusts the language that he uses to the particular prejudices that have to be overcome in living beings. His mind is non-dual, while his teachings are multifarious. Thus in the absolute sense he says "do not shift from one time to another," while in popular parlance he says "move" and "flow." The differences of verbal expression all refer to the same fact.

Literalists misunderstand and think that "moving and flowing" means that present things leave the present and move to a past time.

Thus each nature abides in its own proper time-point, and things do not move back and forth between time-points.

This is the common reference of the varying statements in the scriptures. If one understands it, then the errors of the hundred schools can be avoided.

II.5 Contradicting Permanence

What is commonly called abiding I call departing, and what is commonly called departing I call abiding. That is, by "abiding" others mean that the past is not to be found in the present; I know that the present does not depart from the present moment, and the past does not depart from the past moment. There is no present thing in the past moment and no past thing in the present moment. Each event abides in its own time, and nothing departs or comes.

So, the seasons are still while they fly past, and the Great Bear does not move as it revolves.

II.6 Conclusion

Since each event abides in its own proper moment, deeds abide, and the efficacy of the Tathāgata's influence endures.

Karmic influence does not move from past moments to later ones, and so it is immutable.

The explanation of this is that effect and cause do not occur simultaneously. The cause occurs in moment 1, and the dependent effect occurs in moment 2. Thus the efficacy of karmic causes consists in their abiding in the cause-moment and not shifting to the effect-moment.

This should settle perplexity about rest and motion. If your intelligence identifies with the nature of things, then it will understand.

Quotations

The quotations from Buddhist scriptures in *Chao-lun*, part I are remarkably few and commonplace, in comparison with *Chao-lun*, part II and *Chao-lun*, part III. The only deviation from the pattern of preceding papers is the *Saddharma-puṇḍarīka* paraphrase.[24]

Terms and Concepts

"Absolute" and "popular," "existent" and "inexistent," "stillness and "motion," are all terms met and defined in the previous two essays. Notably absent are "real" and "empty," "Prajñā," "knowledge," "response," "matching," "intuition," "mirroring," and "marks." As these absences from the vocabulary indicate, there is no epistemological discussion and nothing about the language-and-fact problem.

Unlike the preceding two papers, this one offers almost no instances of syntactical permutations employed to effect meaning-shifts There are only one or two putatives, no reflexives, and no affirmative copulas of identity. This, of course, highlights the fact that these devices were specialized to the discussion of the problems of knowledge, language, and fact, which are absent from this essay.

Some terms indicating binary relations merit special mention. They are "resemble" (*yu* 猶), "occur with" (*chü* 俱), and "depend on" (*yin* 因). "Resemble," the copula of partial identity, occurs parallel to *fei* 非, the negative copula, with which it is compatible ⌜28⌝.[25] Thus Seng-chao qualifies identity. "Occur with" and "depend on" are treated as incompatible ⌜46⌝.[26]

In this essay, the question of change is approached in the Mādhyamika fashion, in terms of the relations between past moment, the locus of the cause, and present moment, the locus of the effect. The cause does not inhere in the effect and the effect does not inhere in the cause, and yet there is no cause without effect and no effect without cause ⌜46, 47, 48⌝. Change is popularly considered as the non-transition of an entity from one time-point to another time point, and non-change is considered as the transition of the entity from one time-point to another ⌜8, 36⌝. This is the question of going and staying, the topic of *Middle Treatise*, chapter 2.

Each event pertains to one moment of occurrence, with which it is inalienably associated ⌜33⌝. Seng-chao takes it as an unexpressed axiom that no event occurs at two different moments. This principle is basic to Nāgārjuna's system. "There is no second cutting off of a head" (*Stanzas* 7.31), and "If the goer goes, then the two goings are absurd" (*Stanzas* 2.10). Thus no event can depart from its moment of occurrence and move to another moment of occurrence. The terms "move," "shift," "depart," "pass," "arrive," and "reach" all refer to such a transition from one moment to another, while "abide," "remain," "stay," and "be still" all refer to the ineluctable togetherness of the event and its moment of occurrence.

As stated above, this essay contains no discussion of the language-and-fact question. However, Seng-chao's view on this point is crucial to the essay, since the key terms have two senses, one the "absolute" sense ("what I mean by . . .") and the other the "popular" sense ("what other people mean by . . ."). Thus the fact that past things do not reach the present is termed "moving" in the popular sense, and "stillness" in the absolute sense ⌜8, 9⌝. The fact that past things are permanently tied to their moment of occurrence is termed "departing" in the popular sense, and "abiding" in the absolute sense ⌜34, 35, 36, 37⌝.

This doctrine of the Two Truths is applied as a principle of exegesis. When the scriptures talk about "departing," they may or may not mean "departing" in the popular sense. If they do, it is a therapeutic counteragent to delusions of permanence, that is, to the idea that things occur at more than one moment. If they do not mean "departing" in the popular sense, then they mean it in the absolute sense, which is of course negated ⌜19, 20, 21, 22, 23, 29, 30, 31⌝.

The pseudo-paradoxes in this essay are ones where the same term is used in both the absolute and the popular sense in the same proposition. The striking asseverations about the great forces of the phenomenal world not moving as they roll onwards are instances to the point.

Seng-chao uses his Mādhyamika conception of cause and effect to explain the Tathāgata's pervading power ⌜43, 44, 45⌝. One great trouble that Hui-yüan had was that of understanding how the Buddha could respond without acting. This stemmed from his conception of response as a sort of motion, in which the Buddha's power leaves one point and shifts to another. This problem does not trouble Seng-chao, since for him ordinary causation does not operate through a shift of entity from one point to another. In modern terms, he considers causation as a relation between events rather than as an event. The Tathāgata, the Holy One, identifies with the self-voidness—the nature—of all the dharmas. Thus he is all-pervasive, all-knowing, and able to exert influence without acting, that is, without shifting from one point to another.

There is the question whether Seng-chao's conception of time agrees with Nāgārjuna's. The latter devoted one short chapter of the *Middle Stanzas* (Chapter Nineteen) to a refutation of a certain notion of time. Since this chapter is actually quoted without citation in *Chao-lun*, part I, it is worth quoting it in full here:

> If present and future depend on the past, then present and future should exist in past time; if present and future do not exist in it, how can present and future exist in dependence on it? The establishment of the two does not occur without dependence on the past; therefore, present and future time do not exist. By this method the remaining two [times] are to be treated mutatis mutandis. One should examine the top, bottom, and middle, etc., and the oneness, etc. Non-abiding time is not perceived, and abiding time does not occur; how can imperceptible time be designated? If time depends on an entity, where is there time without the entity? No entity exists, so where would time exist?

Nāgārjuna is demonstrating the absurdity of conceiving the three times as isolate entities *(svabhāva)*. Nāgārjuna holds consistently to one sense for each term—that of a svabhāva, while Seng-chao switches back and forth between the two senses of his terms. It is not that Nāgārjuna was only interested in refuting things while Seng-chao was trying to prove "positive" propositions,[27] but rather that Nāgārjuna maintained a consistent and single point of view, while Seng-chao films the same scene with two different cameras.

Logical Structure

There are five highly structured arguments in this paper. Each is a refutation of an opponent's proposition, though this fact is disguised somewhat by the literary form of the text. These arguments are the most sophisticated of all in Seng-chao's surviving writings, so they merit detailed examination. The original structure of these arguments may be seen in Document 10. For purposes of logical analysis, it is more convenient to recast some of them in a more formal shape.

Argument One (p. 151a22–28; Doc. 10.II.2)

OPPONENT: Because past things do not reach the present, they move and are not still.
AUTHOR: Because past things do not reach the present, they are still and do not move.
You say that in moving they are not still, because they do not come.
I say that being still they do not move, because they do not depart.
So what we meet (experience) is never different, and what we see never agrees.

The first two propositions seem to constitute a dilemma. Seng-chao may have taken his model from some of Nāgārjuna's dilemmas, such as:

OPPONENT: If all this [world] is empty, there is neither arising nor falling apart; thus there is no one of whom to assert nirvāṇa through abandonment or cessation.
NĀGĀRJUNA: If all this is non-empty, there is neither arising nor falling apart; thus there is no one of whom to assert nirvāṇa through abandonment or cessation (*Stanzas* 25.1–2).

As in Nāgārjuna's example, the dilemma is solved when it is recognized that the key terms are being used in two different senses.

Seng-chao's dilemma is an inference of contradictory consequents from the same antecedent. Most of the dilemmas that I have identified in the *Stanzas* are inferences of the same consequent from opposite antecedents (cf. *Middle Stanzas* 13.4, 15.9, 20.1–2, 20.16, 20.21, 21.9, 21.18, 25.1–2, 27.21). It does not conform to any dilemmas that I have found in the *Stanzas*.

Argument Two (p. 151a28–65; Doc. 10.II.3)

OPPONENT: [*A*] Past things do not come, so [*B*] present things pass.
AUTHOR: [*A*] Past things do not come, so [*C*] present things do not pass to anywhere.
[*D*] Past things never inexist in the past.[28]
[*E*] Past things never exist in the present.
[*E*] Past things never exist in the present, so [*F*] things do not come.
[*D*] Past things never inexist in the past, so [*G*] things do not depart.
Thus [*H*] past things reside in the past and do not reach the past from the present.

In this argument, there is the unexpressed proposition that a thing that does not leave its locus and does not go to another locus stays in its locus.

As *C* and *B* are contradictories, Seng-chao here accepts the opponent's antecedent and infers a contradictory conclusion. This does not correspond in form to Nāgārjuna's dilemmas, mentioned above.

The demonstration (*D* to *H*) proceeds from the two assumptions *D* and *E*, through the two expressed inferences *E*—*F* and *D*—*G*, and the unexpressed inference by *F*, *G*, and the hidden assumption, to the conclusion, *H*.

In restating the argument, I omitted the proof that present things reside in the present and do not go from the past to the present, since this is formally identical with the proof of *H*.

Argument Three (p. 151b11–12; Doc. 10.II.4)

OPPONENT: [*A*] You contradict the scriptures because you deny change.
[*B*] If the myriad things do not change, one cannot attain bodhi through understanding change.
AUTHOR: Things seem to move but actually are still, seem to depart but actually remain.
[*C*] When the scriptures say that things depart, they mean that they seem to depart, not that they actually depart.
[*D*] When the scriptures say that things abide, they mean that they seem to abide, not that they actually abide.
[*E*] Thus by abiding and departing the scriptures mean apparent rather than real abiding and departing.

This argument differs from the preceding one in that the author does not begin by contradicting the opponent. It is an elliptically expressed demonstration, in which the connections between *B* and *C*, *B* and *D* are assumed rather than stated. The sequence of connections is:

B so *C*; *B* so *D*; thus *C* and *D*.

Argument Four (p. 151c3; Doc. 10.II.4)

OPPONENT: [*A*] Because things do not shift, [*B*] past things do not reach the present.
[*C*] Because things move, [*D*] present things can reach the past.
AUTHOR: [*E*] Because you have assigned each thing to the past or the present,
[*F*] it is not necessary for things to shift from one time to another.
[*G*] What the scriptures call passing is not necessarily passing.
[*H*] Things always subsist in the past and in the present,
[*I*] because they do not move.
[*J*] What the scriptures call departing is not necessarily departing.
[*K*] Things do not go to the past from the present,
[*L*] because they do not come.
[*L*] Because they do not come, [*M*] they do not travel between past and present.
[*I*] Because they do not move, [*N*] each nature abides in one time.

The author's argument is a refutation of *D*. He accepts the opponent's conclusion that past things do not reach the present, but denies the opponent's conclusion that present things go to the past. *G* and *J* are repeated from Argument Three and though they are explained here, they do not perform any function in the chain of reasoning. The sequence of inference is:

I so *H*; *L* so *K*; *L* so *M*; *I* so *N*.

In the Chinese, it is not wholly certain whether *I* is the reason of *H* and *L* the reason of *K*, or vice versa. Thus there is the alternative possibility of the sequence:

H so *I*; *K* so *L*; *L* so *M*; *I* so *N*.

At any rate, it is obvious that "because," *ku* 故, in these chains of propositions does not signal a clear-cut dependence, and that a reversal of the roles of the two constituent clauses would not make much difference. Quite possibly the particles in question indicate little more than sequence, and certainly their value is less clearly defined than that of a true logical functor.

Argument Five (p. 151c13–17; Doc. 10.II.5)

OPPONENT: [*A*] Because the past is not found in the present, [*B*] it does not abide.
AUTHOR: [*C*] Because the present is not found in the past, [*D*] it does not depart.
[*E*] If the present reaches the past, the present should exist in the past.
[*F*] If the past reaches the present, the past should exist in the present.
[*G*] Because there is no past in the present, things do not come.
[*H*] Because there is no present in the past, things do not depart. Thus things do not depart or come, and each abides in one time.

The proof here consists of two hypothetical syllogisms in cross order. *E* belongs with *H*, and *F* belongs with *G*. In both syllogisms, the consequent is negated. This adds two valid examples of *modus tollens* to Seng-chao's score. As observed above, these two syllogisms are modelled on *Stanzas* 19.1, which provided not only the idea but the logical form.

Summary

Things Do Not Shift differs markedly in subject matter from *Prajñā Has No Knowing* and *Emptiness of the Non-Absolute*. Its content is closer to that of the *Middle Treatise* than theirs is. But since there is no actual incompatibility between the first two essays and Nāgārjuna's system, it cannot be said that *Chao-lun*, part I is truer to Mādhyamika than *Chao-lun*, part II and *Chao-lun*, part III.

The quotations in this paper do not prove anything not proved already by the quotations in the other two papers. However, the paraphrase of *Stanzas* 19.1 in the Conclusion is highly significant, since it indicates the source both for the expression of a key concept and for a valid logical model.

This essay shows that Seng-chao mastered the Mādhyamika conception of dependent co-arising and momentariness, and of the connection between this and the doctrine of the Two Truths. When comparing Nāgārjuna with Seng-chao, one must keep in mind that Nāgārjuna's refutations are made from one point of view—the absolute one—while Seng-chao alternates between the popular and the absolute standpoints. Since this is also the practice of the Sūtras that Nāgārjuna accepted, and since Seng-chao is careful to say which point of view he adopts in each case, it must be admitted that this procedure, though not Nāgārjuna's, is perfectly admissible for a Mādhyamika.

From the standpoint of formal reasoning, *Things Do Not Shift* exhibits an interest in turning the opponent's proposition into a dilemma, but only presents two dilemmas and they do not conform to Nāgārjuna's models. The hypothetical syllogism is used rarely but correctly.

CONCLUSIONS

In *Chao-lun*, parts III and II, Seng-chao handles the epistemology of Prajñā and the device of the Two Truths with considerable skill. He writes like an accomplished metaphysician, and from the point of view of content he passes muster as a Śūnyavādin. However, *Chao-lun*, part III does not exhibit much influence of the form of the Mādhyamika dialectic, and for its proofs it relies chiefly on rhetorical rather than logical exposition. *Chao-lun*, part II shows somewhat greater reliance on logical demonstration and though the logic is bad, it is nevertheless Mādhyamika.

In *Chao-lun*, part I, Seng-chao treats a question that belongs strictly to the Indian Mādhyamika problematic. His treatment differs from Nāgārjuna's because he switches back and forth between the expressional and the Absolute standpoints, which makes the essay read like a mixture of Sarvāstivāda and Mādhyamika. However, this same shift of viewpoint also characterizes the *Great Perfection of Wisdom Treatise*, one of the treatises from which Seng-chao probably learned his Mādhyamika.

Those writings of Seng-chao's that have been examined in this chapter permit these conclusions about his logic:

a. His paradoxes are only apparent, and are easily resolved by the doctrine of the Two Truths and by determining the quantity of the terms.

b. He understood the tetralemma and thus had some knowledge of the logic of classes.

c. He employed the hypothetical syllogism, though not as frequently as Nāgārjuna did. Like Nāgārjuna, he sometimes violated and sometimes observed the rules of conversion. Thus his control of simple propositional logic was poor.

d. He constructed very few dilemmas, and none of the same type as Nāgārjuna's.

In view of the foregoing, I conclude that Seng-chao was not anti-logical, though his manipulation of logical forms was imperfect. The point is not that he reasoned badly, however, but that he reasoned at all.

Seng-chao's writings provide a philosophy of mysticism, but not a psychology, and not a case-book. His stated goal was the standard Mahāyāna one of supreme, perfect enlightenment. This goal transcends the commonsense world, but is at the same time the true nature of the worldly manifold. This thesis is not rational if the rational be defined as a reality which is homomorphous with the commonsense notion of things. However, there are theories in the impeccably rational fields of mathematics and astro-physics that are every bit as contrary to naïve realism as Seng-chao's system is.

On the rhetorical, logical, and philosophical levels, Seng-chao's writings are highly patterned. He was a master of verbal design, he experimented with logical patterns, and he worked out the definitions of his terms in their structural relations to one another. He stated explicitly that language is mere designation, mere fiction, and yet according to his biography and the evidence of his writings he spent the greater part of his life in working with language—listening, discussing, reading, copying, and composing. There is no record of his having been noted for attainments in the practice of dhyāna, and during the years that he worked with Kumārajīva the busy schedule of the translation workshop would not have left room for this time-demanding and attention-absorbing task. However, this does not preclude his having experienced dhyānas and samādhis. According to the *Great Perfection of Wisdom Treatise*, the three great samādhis, the gates of liberation, are noetic, consisting of intuition into emptiness, wishlessness, and marklessness.

In the course of so many years spent in intense work with Śūnyavādin texts, study may well have produced the same insights as contemplation. But this is only supposition, and as Seng-chao says:

> The flourishing of words and traces (footprints) produces heterodox paths. But words have something that cannot be expressed and traces have something that cannot be traced. Therefore the skillful speaker of words seeks to express what cannot be expressed, and the skillful tracer of traces seeks to trace what cannot be traced (*Letter to Liu I-min*, *Chao-lun*, p. 157a6; Liebenthal, *Chao*, p. 109).

Chapter VII
General Conclusions

In preceding chapters, Kumārajīva and three of his Chinese contemporaries have been studied individually, while comparisons between thinkers have been merely parenthetic. In this chapter, the introduction of Mādhyamika to China will be viewed synoptically. With the preceding individual studies as a basis, the several interpretations of the Mādhyamika system can now be summarized, compared, and contrasted.

Kumārajīva's mind and personality were more decisive for the outcome than were those of his best pupils. It was inevitable that there would be some intelligent and receptive minds among the three thousand monks who were assembled in Ch'ang-an to hear the great Serindian master. But though many disciples were prepared to receive, there was only one teacher who possessed the Mādhyamika teaching. If Kumārajīva had been poor at learning languages or had disliked Śūnyavāda, then the monks of Ch'ang-an would have had no opportunity to learn anything about Nāgārjuna's doctrine.

His writings and translations establish Kumārajīva as an expert on Mādhyamika. He does not appear as an original thinker, but he was thoroughly versed in the tradition that he represented. Furthermore, he was not merely a transmitter; he also advocated Mādhyamika. Intellectually, he was a remarkably good missionary for his chosen system.

Though Kumārajīva wrote and translated manuals on contemplation, he apparently did not distinguish himself in the practice of this discipline. He was noted for his ability in prognostication, but not for the attainment of mystic trances. His mysticism was theoretical rather than applied, and he advocated many things which he did not practice.

As the work of this one translator constituted the sole route of access to Mādhyamika for several generations of Chinese, it is particularly important to ask how much of the content of the *Four Treatises* was lost in the course of translation. There is no intrinsic reason why the translations should not have been fully satisfactory. It is apparent from the best of his translations that Kumārajīva must have known both languages very well. His technical terminology was adequate in most respects, and there is no reason why, given the resources of the Chinese lexicon at that time and the known devices for coining new terms, the terminology should not have been perfected in those respects where it was defective. Chinese is capable of conveying all the significant lexical and structural meanings of a Sanskrit original. Even with regard to the difficult problem of "cultural meanings," Kumārajīva and his associates realized the nature of the problem, and utilized the device of interpolated glosses to explain Indian matters that translation alone did not make clear to the Chinese reader. They might have exploited this device more than they did.

In actual fact, blemishes that need not have occurred are frequent in Kumārajīva's translations. They are due to haste in translation, too many collaborators, and too little attention to re-checking the edited copy against the original. The damage is not serious in most instances, but where mistranslation confuses the epistemological, ontological, and logical levels, it prevents the Chinese reader from grasping the formal precision which is one of the finest qualities of the original. In this respect, it must be admitted that defects in the translations materially hindered the assimilation of Mādhyamika in China.

Hui-yüan moved in a world that differed profoundly from Kumārajīva's. By education and inclination, he was wedded to the pre-Buddhist culture of China. Kumārajīva's problem was not one of reconciling two cultures but of communicating the religion of the one to the other. Hui-yüan, though, devoted himself to the task of reconciling secular China with the Buddhist religion, both socially and intellectually. He also set himself the objective of fidelity to the Dharma on the levels of ethics, contemplation, philosophy, and worship. It can be deduced from his biography that he was a gentleman, a saint, and a philosopher, but he never did understand Mādhyamika. Undoubtedly he was too old and had too many ingrained notions when Kumārajīva arrived. A further factor is that his interests and activities were so diverse that he probably never settled down to the prolonged and intense intellectual endeavor that is required to master Śūnyavāda. Consequently, in his last writings he was still thinking in terms of the origination of things rather than of causation, was still confused about the Two Truths, and still misconstrued emptiness as a sort of cosmic matrix. His mysticism, though, was quite in accord with Śūnyavādin doctrines of contemplation. He held that the fruit of advanced contemplation is insight into the arcanum of the emptiness of emptiness, that the highest mysticism leads to the solution of an intellectual riddle.

Hui-yüan's rhetoric varies with his audience. He alludes to sūtras when writing to Kumārajīva, but not in his letters to Huan Hsüan. He loads his prefaces with allusions to the *I-ching*, but does not quote it to Kumarajiva. The Indian figure that he uses most—the fire and the fuel—is also found in the Chinese classics. His other favorite Indian figure—the three animals crossing the stream—does not occur in

Śūnyavādin literature. Thus, although his rhetoric varies, it is uniformly free from Mādhyamika influence.

Seng-jui was twenty years younger than Hui-yüan, and had been a specialist in the *Prajñā Sūtras* for thirty years when Kumārajīva arrived. Thus he had a better background and was at a more receptive age than Hui-yüan. Seng-jui, like Hui-yüan, evidently had a good classical education, but he did not undertake, as Hui-yüan did, to reconcile the native tradition with the imported one. His allegiance to Kumārajīva's doctrine was not impaired by other loyalties such as Hui-yüan had. Furthermore, Kumārajīva satisfied Seng-jui's dominant interests. At least one of the meditation manuals was produced at Seng-jui's request. The Vinaya translations must have pleased Seng-jui, who was a strict disciplinarian. The *Saddharma-puṇḍarīka* and *Smaller A-mi-t'o-ching* translations must have appealed to Seng-jui's pietism. Thus the interests of master and disciple were easily reconciled.

In his prefaces, Seng-jui advocated all the positions which Kumārajīva himself maintained. He belittled Hīnayāna, though the only Hīnayānists he knew were broadminded missionaries to some extent tinged with Mahāyāna. He disparaged the Tīrthikas, although no Indian Tīrthika schools were established in China. In philosophical matters he shows himself as a thoroughgoing Śūnyavādin, but it is not possible to establish that his doctrine derives from the śāstras rather than the sūtras, because there is next to no logical inference in the prefaces. Seng-jui himself stated that the Mādhyamika treatises made Śūnyavāda clear to him for the first time, but in evaluating this statement it is necessary to allow for deference towards Kumārajīva on Seng-jui's part.

Seng-jui's rhetoric is distinguished by abundant double-entendre, and in using Taoist clichés to state the superiority of Mādhyamika over non-Buddhist systems he is ironical. His secular allusions are to *Chuang-tzŭ*, *Lao-tzŭ*, and *Analects*, but seldom to the *I-ching*. Seng-jui's prefaces, in contrast to Hui-yüan's, often allude to sūtras. The impression is that Seng-jui was more exclusively Buddhist than Hui-yüan, and less inclined to compromise with and accommodate to the values of the literati.

Seng-jui is reputed to have been an accomplished contemplative and a systematic practicer of dhyāna. However, his doctrine of contemplation does not seem to differ from that of Kumārajīva and Seng-chao, who were not noted for the practice of contemplation. Seng-jui maintains that the concept of emptiness is a fish-trap, to be abandoned when the fish of insight is obtained. It may be inferred that he saw no incompatibility between the exercise of reason and the attainment of insight, but viewed the one as an aid to the other.

Seng-chao, before becoming a Buddhist, acquired a secular education by reading the texts that he was transcribing in his job as a copyist. In this way, he was perhaps less heavily indoctrinated than if he had studied the classics in a secular school. His first introduction to Buddhism was by way of a Śūnyavādin text. Thus he had comparatively little to unlearn when he went to study with Kumārajīva, and yet he was sufficiently informed to appreciate the master's lectures.

The most striking features of Seng-chao's rhetoric are the parallelisms, climaxes, antitheses, and refrains. He excels in formal design more than in richness of vocabulary or subtlety of allusion. Nevertheless, his writings are strewn with allusions. He refers often to *Chuang-tzŭ* and *Lao-tzŭ*, sometimes to *Analects*, and rarely to the *I-ching*. He quotes the sūtras much more frequently than either Hui-yüan or Seng-jui do, though the comparison is incomplete since we have no essays by Seng-jui. The quotations confirm that Seng-chao was familiar with Śūnyavādin sūtras and the Mādhyamika treatises, a fact that is known from his biography.

Whereas Hui-yüan's pamphlets employ Buddhist technical terms very sparingly, Seng-chao's essays use them in fair numbers and quite freely. At the same time, both the *Chao-lun* essays and the *Vimalakīrti Commentary* also use a sizeable array of Taoist terms, many of them standing as glosses or euphemisms for Buddhist terms. Seng-chao's terms are defined contextually in relation to each other, and many of them have specialized meanings not found in other Buddho-Taoist writings. A case in point is *chao*, which means "cognition" in Hui-yüan, but in the *Chao-lun* has the more restricted sense of "intuition."

Seng-chao's rhetoric reinforces his use of technical terms, since the extensive parallelisms and refrains furnish contexts in which terms can be identified as each other's synonyms and antonyms. This is also true of Hui-yüan, but to a lesser degree.

In Seng-chao's essays there are almost no stock Śūnyavādin similitudes such as "tortoise hairs," "rabbit horns," "the phantom man," or "the fire and the fuel." Seng-chao probably avoided using them so as not to shock his lay readers by outlandish figures. He certainly must have known these similitudes; Hui-yüan knew them, and used some of them in his letters to Kumārajīva. The non-occurrence of these figures obviously proves nothing about the degree of Śūnyavādin influence that Seng-chao had undergone.

The epistemology, ontology, and theory of language in the *Chao-lun* are thoroughly Mādhyamika. This is not true of Hui-yüan, though he had probably read Seng-chao's first essay before he wrote his later prefaces. Thus we can conclude that the young disciple assimilated Mādhyamika well, while the old saint did not.

Though logical arguments do not constitute a high proportion of the material in Seng-chao's essays, the fact that they occupy any place at all is extremely significant. Hui-yüan's few attempts to reason syllogistically are poor imitations of Mādhyamika syllogisms. Seng-chao's hypothetical syllogisms are good imitations, though often of fallacious models. His manipulations of quantification are fairly sophisticated, and carry a heavy function load in his philosophy. The rarity of dilemmas in the *Chao-lun* need not indicate failure to understand Nāgārjuna's numerous examples, but may only mean that this form did not serve Seng-chao's purposes. It must be noted that Seng-chao, unlike Nāgārjuna, displays no awareness of logical rules. If he had really understood the theory behind the logical patterns with which he experimented, he would probably have exploited them more extensively.

Seng-chao's statements about contemplative experience are orthodox Śūnyavāda. He maintained that the enlightened Buddhas and Bodhisattvas have insight into the truth of emptiness, which is the real nature of all things, and he held that their saving power proceeded from this noetic illumination. The texts which he knew and to which he alludes in his passages on samādhi maintain that this intuition has a transcendental but nevertheless intellectual content.

By writing a formally reasoned exposition, Seng-chao affirmed that reason is a means towards illumination. He still stated that words were inadequate to convey his meaning. This plea, though, does not make him anti-rational; after all, the same plea is made even by non-mystical philosophers. As a Śūnyavādin, Seng-chao did not expect the structure of language to conform to the facts of experience, nor did he believe that hearing about a transcendental experience was the same as having the experience. In short, he attempted to be rational, he aimed at a mystical goal, and he did not assert that there is any incompatibility between these two objectives.

In Chapter One, it was asked which aspects were Indian and which were Chinese in the writings of the first Chinese who encountered Mādhyamika. This question can now be answered in part. The cosmological system is Indian, even in Hui-yüan, who is the least Indianized of the three authors considered. The doctrine of transmigration establishes a gulf between the world-view of Buddhist and non-Buddhist Chinese. However, Hui-yüan's ontology never became genuinely Buddhist, while Seng-chao's is always unmistakably Śūnyavādin. Seng-chao understood the Śūnyavādin epistemology, but Hui-yüan did not, though in his later prefaces he shows some awareness of the subject. In theory of language, both Hui-yüan and Seng-chao had some understanding of the Mādhyamika position, but since there are close analogues in Taoism this does not make their philosophies more distinctively Indian.

The most Indian element in Seng-chao's writings is the logical. But he apparently learned his logical reasoning by imitating concrete examples. There is no evidence that he possessed any theoretical treatise on the art of reasoning. Under the circumstances, it was natural that even he should not have realized the full value of this new instrument of demonstration.

A number of Indian features were not adopted by the early Chinese Mādhyamikas, the most obvious of which is Indian literary forms. The Chinese at this period declined to write śāstras and continued resolutely to prefer the native literary modes—the preface, the essay, and the commentary. The śāstra, though, is a valuable component of the Indian tradition, and the Chinese in the early fifth century would have profited by its adoption. The full architectonic intricacy of Indian Buddhist philosophy can only be conveyed through extensive and systematic expositions. The exercise in reasoning at length and correlating numerous components would have been instructive for Chinese students of the Dharma. The reason for their failure to adopt the Indian literary form at this time may be detected in Hui-yüan's discourse on Indian and Chinese literary modes. Evidently the gentlemen of the time found it easier to change their religion than their literary tastes.

Another literary feature that did not transfer well is the Indian dṛṣṭānta. These similitudes serve a useful pedagogical purpose in Indian philosophical literature, and one would expect that they might make the new ideas more intelligible to the Chinese reader. These figures are quite common in the Ch'an literature centuries later, but apparently the literary norms of the early fifth century militated against the introduction of such figures into Buddho-Taoist essays.

A more fundamental and serious element that was lost in transmission is the Indian philosophical problematic. Seng-chao, the most Indian of the Buddho-Taoist authors, only mentions the problem of cause and effect once in the first three essays of the *Chao-lun*. Hui-yüan never notices the Indian problem of time and the temporal series, while Seng-chao only treats it in *Chao-lun*, part I. Seng-chao only mentions the problem of the marks of the conditioned in the *Vimalakīrti Commentary*, where the problem is posed by the sūtra itself. It is natural for people in different ages and places to have different problems, but it is difficult to understand and assimilate a foreign philosophy if it answers questions that one has never asked.

The Chinese documents studied in this inquiry were all written within fifteen years after Kumārajīva's arrival. They represent the views of men who had had only a short time in which to assimilate a radically strange philosophy. It should not be concluded either that what Seng-chao understood became a permanent property of Chinese Buddhist thought, or that what the first Chinese students of the *Four Treatises* failed to master did not eventually penetrate the Chinese philosophical tradition. These questions could only be answered by investigating the works of later masters such as Chi-tsang.

Chapter VIII
Epilogue: The Lineage Of The Old Three Treatise Sect

Sino-Japanese scholarship has a tradition about the fortunes of the Mādhyamika teaching in China between Kumārajīva and the rise of the New Three Treatise Sect in the early sixth century. Hatani summarizes it as follows:

Among Kumārajīva's disciples, Seng-tao wrote the ***San-lun-i-shu*** and wrote the ***Essay on the Two Truths of the Empty and the Existent***, concerning the central problem of the ***Three Treatises***, and he was thus a pioneer in establishing the Three Treatise Sect. T'an-ying wrote a commentary on the ***Middle Treatise***, and Tao-jung lectured on the ***Middle Treatise***, so tradition says. Seng-tao, together with Seng-jui who wrote prefaces to the ***Middle Treatise*** and the ***Twelve Topics Treatise***, and Tao-sheng who wrote an ***Essay on the Two Truths***, founded the Three Treatise School which transmitted the ***Three Treatises*** in Chiang-nan. Seng-chao, who wrote the preface to the ***Hundred Treatise***, and Tao-jung, who lectured on the ***Middle Treatise***, together established the so-called Four Treatise School, centered in Kuan-nei, which propagated in Chiang-pei the ***Three Treatises***, along with the ***Great Perfection of Wisdom Treatise***, also translated by their master. Subsequently, however, the Abhidharma School held sole sway in Chiang-pei, and the Four Treatise School gradually declined. The Three Treatise School in Chiang-nan was crowded out forcefully by ***Satyasiddhi*** studies, but after Seng-lang and Seng-ch'üan came on the scene, the fortunes of the Three Treatise School gradually revived. Continuing during Fa-lang's career, the teaching of the Three Treatise Sect became firmly established during the time of Chi-tsang, the great master of Chia-hsiang, of the Sui dynasty. It is Chia-hsiang Ta-shih who actually completed the Three Treatise Sect. He wrote thorough, erudite, and voluminous commentaries on each of the ***Three Treatises***, thus bestowing on posterity the orthodox guide to the ***Three Treatises***[1] ("Sanron Kaidai," p. 3).

Fortunately, the lineage table of the Three Treatise Sect is recorded at the beginning of the *Sanronshōsho* (三論章疏) in the *Nihon Daizōkyō*, *Ronzōbu*. With the addition of some corrections, it serves to indicate the transmission of the Three Treatise lamp in the three countries ("Sanron Kaidai," p. 5).

The *Genealogy* lists fifteen immediate disciples of Kumārajīva. It only lists disciples for six of these. Hatani's "tradition" mentions six of Kumārajīva's disciples who promoted the *Three Treatises*. Of these, only one—Seng-tao—is shown in the *Genealogy* as having disciples. Furthermore, the line of descent to the New Three Treatise

THE THREE TREATISE GENEALOGY FROM NĀGĀRJUNA TO CHI-TSANG ACCORDING TO HATANI ("Sanron Kaidai," p. 6)

Nāgārjuna ↓	-Tao-jung			
	-Seng-jui			
Āryadeva ↓	-T'an-ying			
Rāhula ↓	-Seng-chao			
Pingala(?)→Sūryasoma	-Seng-tao →	T'an-chi		
↓ Bhāvaviveka ↓ Kumārajīva	-Hui-kuan →	Fa-yüan →	Seng-tsung	-Tao-chuang
	-Tao-sheng →	Seng-chin		-Fa-an
	-Tao-heng	Tao-yu		-Fa-ch'eng
	-Seng-sung →	Seng-yüan →	Fa-tu ↓	-Hsiao-ming Fa-shih
	-Hui-yen →	Fa-chih	Seng-lang ↓	-K'uang Fa-shih
	-Tao-piao		Seng-ch'üan→	-Chi-tsang, etc.
	-Seng-ch'i	T'an-ti		-Hui-chüeh
	-Seng-pao			-Lo-yün
	-T'an-wu-ch'eng			-Hui-che
	-Tao-wen			-Chih-chü
				-Ming Fa-shih
				-Chen-kan

(Tao-sheng ↘ Tao-yu)

Sect according to the *Genealogy* is by way of Seng-sung, who is not mentioned in the "tradition." These discrepancies indicate a confusion in the traditions and necessitate an examination of their sources.

Seng-sung is mentioned in the appendix to Tao-wen's biography (KSC, p. 373a11).

At the same time in the Chung-hsing-ssŭ there were Seng-ch'ing, Hui-ting, and Seng-sung, all renowned for their doctrinal studies. Seng-ch'ing was expert in the Three Treatises, and was honored by the scholars of the time. Hui-ting was expert in the *Nirvāṇa Sūtra* and Abhidharma. Seng-sung was equally versed in the Sarvāstivādin treatises. In his last years, he held the heresy that the Buddha does not abide constantly. The day that he died, the root of his tongue burned up first.

This notice shows that as far as Hui-chiao, the author of the *Biographies*, knew, Seng-sung was not a Three Treatise scholar. There is no evidence that he was a disciple of Kumārajīva. The fact that he is relegated to an appendix does not indicate that he did not deserve a separate biography, since Hui-chiao makes it quite apparent that he disapproves of Seng-sung's "heresy."

This quotation also reveals a Three Treatise master who is not listed in Hatani's "tradition"—Seng-ch'ing. It shows that the Mādhyamika tradition was cultivated in the Chung-hsing-ssŭ at this time. There is no evidence that Seng-ch'ing was a disciple of Kumārajīva (Sakaino, pp. 408–9).

Seng-yüan is honored by a separate biography (KSC, p. 375a) according to which during his wander-years he stayed in the Pai-t'a-ssŭ in Hsü-chou. Later he studied *Satyasiddhi* and Abhidharma under Seng-sung. He eventually achieved a great reputation. The retired gentleman, Liu Yin-chih, donated the mountain on which he lived to Seng-yüan for a monastery. Seng-yüan's disciples were T'an-tu, Hui-chi, and Tao-teng. Hui-chi was an Abhidharma expert. Tao-teng was expert in the *Nirvāṇa Sūtra* and *Saddharma-puṇḍarīka.* Both were esteemed by the Wei emperor Hsien Wen Ti and were famed throughout Wei. Seng-yüan died at the age of sixty-eight in 481.

From this account it appears that Seng-yüan, like his master Seng-sung, was an Abhidharma and *Satyasiddhi* specialist, not known for any connection with the *Three Treatises.* It should be noted that he spent his later life in Wei and that his disciples were famed throughout the North. This means that the line from Seng-sung to Chi-tsang could not be considered a completely Southern one.

Fa-tu is listed in the *Genealogy* as a disciple of Seng-yüan. According to his biography (KSC, p. 380b) he spent his early wander-years in the North, studying the scriptures and practicing austerities. Later he went to Chien-k'ang towards the end of the Liu Sung dynasty. He took up residence in the haunted monastery on Mount She near Lang-ya, and succeeded in taming the resident vampire. Fa-tu desired rebirth in Sukhāvatī and lectured specially on the *Sukhāvatī-vyūha Sūtra*. He died on his mountain in A.D. 500 when he was sixty-four.

Contrary to the *Genealogy*, there is no evidence that Fa-tu was a *Three Treatise* scholar and no evidence that he was a disciple of Seng-yüan.

Seng-lang is noted in an appendix to Fa-tu's biography (KSC, p. 380c15).

Fa-tu had a disciple, Seng-lang, who succeeded him as abbot of the mountain temple. Seng-lang was a native of Liao-tung. He was a scholar of broad erudition, able to lecture on all the Sūtras and Vinayas. He was especially noted for the *Avataṁsaka* and the *Three Treatises*. The present emperor [Liang Wu Ti] saw how talented he was, and decreed that all the students of doctrine should receive the teaching on his mountain.

Thus Seng-lang was a disciple of Fa-tu, and a Three Treatise scholar, although he probably did not receive the Mādhyamika teaching from Fa-tu. According to Chi-tsang, Seng-lang first went to Kuan-nei, where he studied the teachings of Kumārajīva and Seng-chao. Later he went to the South, took up residence in the Ts'ao-t'ang on Chung-shan, met Chou Yung,[2] and, according to Chi-tsang, gave him the doctrine. A mid-T'ang tradition recorded in the *Fa-hua-hsüan-i-shih-ch'ien*(T 1717, p. 951a18) states:

Since the Sung period, the several teachers who transmitted the *Three Treatises* all derived their teaching from Kumārajīva. But as the years went by, the literature was lost, until by the Ch'i period, the metaphysical line was almost extinct. In Chiang-nan the *Satyasiddhi* was vigorously promoted, and Ho-pei was partial to the Abhidharma. Then the Korean Seng-lang arrived in Chiang-nan during the Chien-wu period of Ch'i (494–97), and refuted the *Satyasiddhi* masters, tying their tongues so that they had no answers. Thereupon Seng-lang himself promulgated the *Three Treatises*.

Seng-ch'üan is mentioned in the continuation of the above passage from the *Fa-hua-ch'ien*.

When Liang Wu Ti decreed that Seng-ch'üan and nine others should study the *Three Treatises*, nine treated it as child's play, and only Chih-kuan Seng-ch'üan carried the study through to fulfillment. There were four students who entered Seng-ch'üan's chamber. They were Crouching Tiger Lang of Hsing-huang-ssŭ, Get-Ideas Pu of Hsi-hsia-ssŭ, Cause-to-awaken Pien of Ch'ang-kan-ssŭ and Literary Yung of Ch'an-chung-ssŭ.

According to the *Kao-seng-chuan* (p. 369c), Seng-ch'üan was a native of Liao-hsi. During childhood, he entered Yen and Ch'i, and studied secular books. Before attaining manhood, he left the lay life and studied the Tripiṭaka, in which he excelled. He crossed the Yang-tzŭ and lived in Chien-k'ang, where he set up as a teacher.

On the invitation of a patron, he went and lectured in Wu, where he was widely esteemed. At first he lived on the Hsien-chü-ssŭ and later he lived on Hu-ch'iu-shan. Before he left Huang-lung-wo (Northern Yen), he had set up a sixteen-foot image. Later he set up a golden image on Hu-ch'iu-shan. He was a charitable giver and lived very frugally. Later Meng K'ai of P'ing-ch'ang established the Fang-hsien-ssŭ in Yü-k'ang, and invited Seng-ch'üan to reside in it. Seng-ch'üan lost his eyesight while here, but continued to lecture. He traveled through Lin-an County, and while he was staying with a lay disciple, Tung Kung-ts'ao, he fell seriously ill. He had visions of the images which he had made coming to him, and of deva hosts attending his sickbed. His disciple Fa-lang dreamed that he saw a crowd and on asking where they were going was told that they were going to welcome Seng-ch'üan. Next morning, Seng-ch'üan died.

Thus Seng-ch'üan was the outstanding disciple of Seng-lang, was a teacher of the *Three Treatises*, and was a monk with considerable support from eminent laymen. He had received a gentleman's secular education, and was already learned in the scriptures when he came South and was sent by imperial decree to study the *Three Treatises* under Seng-lang.

Seng-ch'üan and his disciple Fa-lang were both pietists as well as *Three Treatise* scholars, since Seng-ch'üan undertook to set up images, and since both he and Fa-lang believed firmly in welcoming hosts coming to meet the dying.

Seng-ch'üan's death date must be later than Fa-lang's leaving lay life, which was in A.D. 528.

Fa-lang, who is known from a biography in the *Hsü-kao-seng-chuan* (HKSC, pp. 477b–78a) was the son of an official of the Liang dynasty. In 528, at the age of twenty-one, he left lay life, and studied in the Ta-ming-ssŭ in Yang-tu, learning dhyāna from the dhyāna-master Pao-chih and Vinaya from the Vinaya-master T'uan. He studied *Satyasiddhi* with master Hsien of Nan-chien-ssŭ, and Abhidharma with master Ching of Chu-chien-ssŭ. He received instruction in the *Four Treatises*, *Avataṁsaka*, and *Pañcaviṁśati* from Seng-ch'üan of the Chih-kuan-ssŭ. In 558 he received an imperial decree to reside in the Hsing-huang-ssŭ in Chien-k'ang. He lectured more than twenty times on each of the *Four Treatises*, the *Avataṁsaka*, and the *Pañcaviṁśati*, during a period of twenty-five years. He died in A.D. 581, at the age of seventy-five.

Chi-tsang, whom Hatani calls "The completer of the Three Treatise Sect" ("Sanron Kaidai," p. 4), is the first master in this lineage whose writings have survived. His biography is given at some length in the *Hsü-kao-seng-chuan* (pp. 513c–15a). When he was a boy, his father took him regularly to hear Fa-lang lecture and at the age of seven, he became a novice under Fa-lang. At nineteen, he lectured before the assembly. In 580, he moved to the Chia-hsiang-ssŭ. In 606, he moved at imperial request to the Hui-jih-ssŭ in Yang-chou, and later to the Jih-yen-ssŭ in Ch'ang-an, where he died in 623, at the age of seventy-five.

In summary, the lineage from Fa-tu to Chi-tsang is attested in the earliest sources. It is certain that the Three Treatise tradition was transmitted in this lineage from Seng-lang onwards. But there is no evidence that Fa-tu taught the *Three Treatises*, or that he was a disciple of Seng-yüan. Neither Seng-yüan nor his teacher Seng-sung can be established as a teacher of the *Three Treatises*, and Seng-sung cannot be established as a disciple of Kumārajīva. Thus the *Genealogy's* version of the Three Treatise lineage is not substantiated.

The next step is to examine the others given in the *Genealogy* as disciples of Kumārajīva, to see whether the evidence shows any other lineage through which the Three Treatise teaching might have passed to Seng-lang.

Seng-tao is one of Kumārajīva's disciples mentioned in Hatani's "tradition" who is shown as having disciples in the *Genealogy*. His biography (KSC, p. 371a–c) states that he left lay life at ten. His teacher gave him the *Kuan-shih-yin-ching* to read, and he inferred that it was part of a larger work, much to the amazement of his teacher who then gave him the entire *Saddharma-puṇḍarīka*.[3] By the time he was eighteen, his knowledge and zeal were outstanding. Seng-jui noticed him, and predicted that he would become a great teacher. Yao Hsing became fond of him, and eventually assigned him to help in Kumārajīva's translations. He later wrote commentaries on the *Satyasiddhi* and the *Three Treatises*, and an essay on *The Two Truths of the Empty and the Existent.* Later, when Sung Kao-tsu attacked Ch'ang-an and captured the ruler of Ch'in, Kao-tsu met Seng-tao and was pleased with him. When the Sung occupation forces were driven out of Kuan-nei, Seng-tao interceded to save the emperor's son from the "barbarians," for which he received imperial gratitude, in the form of the Tung-shan-ssŭ at Shou-ch'un.[4] He had more than a thousand pupils. During the persecution of Buddhism in T'o-pa Wei after A.D. 444, he provided food, clothing, and shelter for several hundred refugee monks. He also performed liturgical services in memory of those who were killed in the persecution. When Hsiao Wu Ti ascended the throne he issued a decree that Seng-tao should reside in the Chung-hsing-ssŭ. Later Seng-tao lectured on the *Vimalakīrti* at imperial request in the Wa-kuan-ssŭ. Later he returned to Shou-ch'un, and died in the Shih-chien-ssŭ at the age of ninety-six. He had two disciples, Seng-wei and Seng-yin, who were both expert in *Satyasiddhi.*

T'an-chi, listed as Seng-tao's disciple in the *Genealogy*, is mentioned in the biography of T'an-pin (KSC, p. 373b6): "At that time in the Chuang-yen-ssŭ there were also T'an-chi and T'an-tsung, both revered by their contemporaries for their learning and talent."

T'an-chi wrote the *Essay on the Seven Schools*. T'an-chi is also mentioned in the *Ming-seng-chuan* (16.5), which says that he left lay life at thirteen, was a disciple of Seng-tao, and lived in the Tung-ssŭ (eastern temple) on Pa-kung-shan in Shou-yang. In A.D. 458 he crossed the Yang-tzŭ and went to live in the Chung-hsing-ssŭ (Huang, *History*, p. 100; Liebenthal, *Chao*, p. 147, n. 641).

There is no evidence that T'an-chi taught the *Three Treatises*, or that he had any disciples of any importance. Thus we cannot trace any lineage by way of him.

Tao-jung (KSC, p. 363b–c) left lay life at twelve. His teacher was impressed by his intelligence, and so had him study some secular books first. By the time he was thirty, he was highly learned. Hearing that Kumārajīva was in Ch'ang-an, he went to study under him. Kumārajīva got a good impression of him, and mentioned him to Yao Hsing, who issued a decree that he should enter the Hsiao-yao-yüan and take part in the work of translation. He requested Kumārajīva to translate the *P'u-sa-chieh-pen*, which was extant during Hui-chiao's time. Later when the *Middle Treatise* was translated, Tao-jung lectured on it. Kumārajīva also assigned him to lecturing on the new *Saddharma-puṇḍarīka*, and on hearing him lecture, said "If the Buddha's doctrine is to flourish, Tao-jung is the man to effect this." A brahman from the Lion-country[5] came riding a camel to Ch'ang-an, bearing a letter to Yao Hsing, who had misgivings about the stranger. The brahman challenged the monks of Ch'in to a debate, and Kumārajīva instructed Tao-jung to accept the challenge. In preparation, he read through and memorized the Tīrthika books on which the brahman relied. Tao-jung vanquished his opponent who then left the country. Tao-jung later went back to P'eng-ch'eng, where he lectured continually to several thousand enquirers. He had about three hundred steady pupils. He died in P'eng-ch'eng at the age of seventy-four. He wrote commentaries on the *Saddharma-puṇḍarīka*, *Pañcaviṁśati*, *Suvarṇa-prabhāsa*, *Daśabhūmika*, and *Vimalakīrti*, all of which were current still in Hui-chiao's time.

T'an-ying (KSC, p. 364a) first distinguished himself as a teacher of the *Kuang-tsan-ching* (Dharmarakṣa's *Pañcaviṁśati*, T 222), and the *Cheng-fa-hua-ching* (Dharmarakṣa's *Saddharma-puṇḍarīka*). He drew crowds of a thousand monks and laymen. Later, he went to Kuan-chung and was well received by Yao Hsing. When Kumārajīva arrived, T'an-ying went and followed him. Kumārajīva told Yao Hsing, "Yesterday I saw T'an-ying. In manner he is a paragon among the monks of this country." Yao Hsing appointed him to live in the Hsiao-yao-yüan and assist Kumārajīva. When the *Satyasiddhi* was translated, T'an-ying summarized its main points and showed his summary to Kumārajīva, who approved of it. When the *Saddharma-puṇḍarīka* was translated, T'an-ying played an important role, since he was well versed in the old translation. He wrote a four-chüan commentary on the *Saddharma-puṇḍarīka*, and a commentary on the *Middle Treatise*. Afterwards, he lived as a hermit in the mountains, devoting himself more and more to strict discipline. He died in the I-hsi period (405–18) at the age of seventy. Since he took part in the translation of the *Satyasiddhi*[6] in 412, he died between 412 and 418. There is no evidence that he had any disciples. However, his commentary on the *Middle Treatise* seems to have survived, at least in parts, until the sixth century, since Chi-tsang quotes it occasionally, and approvingly, in the *Chung-lun-shu* (T 1824).

T'an-ying was at least fifty-three years old when Kumārajīva arrived. He was at least sixty-four when he served as rewriter in translating the *Satyasiddhi*.

Tao-sheng, according to one version of the lineage (Huang, *History*, p. 196) transmitted the Three Treatise teaching to T'an-chi, who transmitted it to Seng-lang. This probably stems from a confusion of Seng-tao and Tao-sheng. T'an-chi is last mentioned as residing in Chien-k'ang, in 458. Seng-lang did not arrive in Chiang-nan until 494–97, at least thirty-six years later, and by that time it is said that he had already learned the Three Treatise teaching in Kuan-nei. It is highly unlikely that he was ever a disciple of T'an-chi.

Tao-sheng was born in 360, in P'eng-ch'eng. He was a disciple of Fa-t'ai. Later he spent seven years in Hui-yüan's community on Lu-shan where he studied Sarvāstivādin Abhidharma. In 405 or 406, he went to Ch'ang-an and studied under Kumārajīva. Leaving Ch'ang-an in 408, he stopped a short time on Lu-shan, and arrived in Chien-yeh in 409. In 428 or 429, he was expelled from Chien-yeh for maintaining that icchantikas have Buddha-nature. In 430 he arrived on Lu-shan. When the "Northern Edition" of the *Nirvāṇa Sūtra* vindicated him, he returned to the capital. He died in 432 (KSC, p. 366b; T'ang, *History*, pp. 601–76; Liebenthal, "Biography of Tao-sheng").

Tao-sheng seems to have spent a mere two years under Kumārajīva in Ch'ang-an. He arrived after the *Great Perfection of Wisdom Treatise* translation and left before the *Middle Treatise* was translated. His earlier interests were in Gautama Saṅghadeva's Abhidharma and in the topics that Hui-yüan's community discussed. In his latest years, he was concerned with the *Nirvāṇa Sūtra*. The extant fragments of his writings show him as an independent thinker[7] and his biography confirms that he neither followed a school nor founded one.

The lineage table in Mochizuki's *Bukkyō Dainempyō* (appendix, p. 28) traces the Three Treatise Sect from Kumārajīva to Tao-sheng to T'an-chi to Tao-lang to Seng-ch'üan to Fa-lang to Chi-tsang. It has been assumed that 'Tao-lang' is a mistake for 'Seng-lang' (Huang, *History*, p. 196). However, there was such a monk during the early fifth century, and some maintain that he is the Ho-hsi master whom Chi-tsang cites (e.g., *Chung-lun-shu*, p. 528).[8] He is mentioned several times in the biography of Dharmakṣema: "At this time the śramaṇas Hui-sung and Tao-lang were pre-eminent (strode alone) in Ho-hsi" (KSC, p. 336a24). "Hui-sung and Tao-lang further requested [Dharmakṣema] to issue a large quantity of the sūtras. Then he translated the ***Mahāsannipāta Sūtra***, etc." (KSC, p. 336a28; ***Bagchi***, p. 215). "The translation [of the *Nirvāṇa Sūtra*] began in the third year of the illegitimate Hsüan-shih (A.D. 414) and was finished in the tenth year of Hsüan-shih, tenth month, twenty-third day, which equals Sung Wu [Ti], second year of Yung-ch'u (A.D. 421)" (KSC, p. 336b5). "At that time the śramaṇa Tao-lang excited praise throughout Kuan-hsi. On the night when Tao-chin had a visionary experience of the precepts, Tao-lang also shared the dream. Then he humbled himself to his superior in the precepts and sought to become [Tao-chin's] younger brother in the Dharma. Thereafter, more than a thousand people received [the bodhisattva precepts] from Tao-chin. This Dharma has been passed right down to the present. It is all the persisting example of Dharmakṣema" (KSC, p. 336c27).

There is a preface to Dharmakṣema's translation of the *Nirvāṇa Sūtra* written by Shih Tao-lang of Liang-chou (Ho-hsi) (CST, pp. 59b–60a). As the translation of this work began in 414, and as Tao-lang was already eminent, he was old enough to have been a student of Kumārajīva's. The congregation observing the bodhisattva precepts survived until the sixth century, so continuity of the community to which Tao-lang belonged is attested. It is thus possible that Seng-lang obtained the Mādhyamika doctrine somewhere in the North-West before he went South, but the lineage of this North-Western school is not known, and the survival of the Mādhyamika doctrine in the North-West is evidenced solely by Chi-tsang's statement.

As the *Kao-seng-chuan* was written in the South, it is only natural that it provides somewhat better information about Three Treatise studies in Sung and Ch'i than in Wei. Thus it is possible to trace a tradition through from Kumārajīva almost to the arrival of Seng-lang.

Seng-jui survived well into the Sung period, and was resident in Chiang-nan from 418 until his death in 436. "Afterwards in the Chih-huan-ssŭ[9] there was also Shih Seng-jui, who was expert in the *Three Treatises* and was honored by Sung Wen Ti" (KSC, p. 369a3).

Seng-ch'ing, mentioned above, was a contemporary of Tao-wen who died at the beginning of T'ai-shih (A.D. 465–71), aged sixty-nine. He is thus about a generation later than Kumārajīva's chief disciples. Tao-wen is said to have been Kumārajīva's disciple. He first left lay life at the age of sixteen when he entered the community of Lu-shan under Hui-yüan. Later he went to Ch'ang-an and studied under Kumārajīva. As he must have been sixteen no later than 412, he must have stayed a very short while on Lu-shan and could only have been in Ch'ang-an a very short while before Kumārajīva's death. Thus Tao-wen is not likely to have transmitted the Three Treatise teaching.

Seng-chung was born in the commandery of Lu, and left lay life at sixteen. He met Seng-tao at Shou-ch'un and impressed him with his ability. Later an official requested Seng-chung to lecture on the *Hundred Treatise*, and Seng-tao attended the lectures. Seng-chung was reported to be remarkably expert in *Satyasiddhi*, *Three Treatises*, *Nirvāṇa Sūtra*, and *Daśabhūmika*. Later he went South to the capital and resided in the Chung-hsing-ssŭ. At the beginning of Yung-ming (A.D. 483–93) he distinguished himself by his brilliant repartee in a debate with an envoy from Wei. He was honored by the crown prince Wen Hui and by Wen Hsüan, prince of Ching-ling. He died in Yung-ming 7 (A.D. 489), aged sixty (KSC, p. 375c13).

Two contemporaries of *Tao-yu*, the disciple of Tao-sheng who died during Yüan-hui (A.D. 473–76) at the age of seventy-one, are also noted for their Three Treatise studies:

> At that time Hui-cheng of the Pei-to-pao-ssŭ and Chüeh-shih of Ch'ang-lo were equally famous and equally virtuous. Hui-cheng was especially versed in the *Three Treatises* and was venerated by scholars. Chüeh-shih was expert in the *Ta-p'in* and the *Nirvāṇa Sūtra*. He established the idea that the non-empty is mere designation (KSC, p. 374c25).

Chih-lin came originally from Turfan. He spent some time in Ch'ang-an and then made his way to the southern capital. He was a disciple of Tao-liang whose exile in Nan-yüeh he shared (KSC, p. 372b). About 465, at the beginning of Ming Ti's reign, he was summoned back to the capital where he took up residence in the Ling-chi-ssŭ and lectured to large audiences. He explained the Two Truths, about which there were three different theses. At that time, Chou Yung of Ju-nan also wrote his *Essay on the Three Theses*, which tallied with Chih-lin's ideas. Chou Yung was reluctant to publish his essay, so Chih-lin wrote to him and urged him to. In a letter to Chou Yung, he mentioned that when he was twenty, that is, about 428, he heard an old man in Ch'ang-an say that this idea had once been well-known in Kuan-chung. He eventually persuaded Chou Yung to give him a copy of his essay. Afterwards Chih-lin departed and returned to Turfan, where he died in Yung-ming 5 (A.D. 487) aged seventy-nine. He wrote an *Essay on the Two Truths*, and a Notebook on the *A-p'i-t'an-tsa-hsin* (T 1552). He also commented on the *Twelve Topic Treatise* and the *Middle Treatise* (KSC, p. 376a20).

Hsüan-Ch'ang was a man from Ho-hsi. He was orphaned in childhood and became a disciple of Hsüan-kao in Liang-chou. In 445 he fled the persecution of Buddhism in Wei and escaped south to Yang-chou. He is said to have thoroughly understood the Sūtras and the Vinaya, and to have been an expert on dhyāna. He prophesied the future, apparently with remarkable accuracy. He studied the *Avataṁsaka* and the *Three Treatises* and was highly respected by scholars. When Sung Wen Ti (A.D. 429–53) requested him to be tutor to the crown prince, he refused, and left the capital. He moved to Ching-chou and lived in a temple near Ch'ang-sha, probably the Ch'an-fang-ssŭ which was the residence of the śramaṇa Kung-te-chih whom Hsüan-ch'ang assisted in the translation of the ***Nien-fo-san-mei-ching*** (T 414). This sūtra was translated in about 462. Later Hsüan-ch'ang moved to the Ta-shih-ssŭ in Ch'eng-tu, probably together with Kung-te-chih (*Hōbōgirin*, fasc. annexe, p. 143b, Kudokujiki). Hsüan-ch'ang traveled in the Min Shan range, where he built a hut, and in 479 build a temple. The prodigies preceding and attending the founding of this temple were construed as a good omen for the new Ch'i regime, and 100 households were assigned to support the temple. After Ch'i Wu Ti ascended the throne (A.D. 483) Hsüan-ch'ang was summoned to the capital and soon after arriving he died, in Yung-ming 2 (A.D. 484) aged sixty-nine. Prince Hsien of Lin-ch'üan set up a stele for which Chou Yung of Ju-nan wrote the text (KSC, p. 377a3).

Hui-tz'ŭ was born in Chi-chou, and left lay life under Chih-hsin. Later he transferred to the master Fa-ch'ien, in whose company he went to the Southern capital and lived in the Chu-lin-ssŭ. When he was fifteen he went to P'eng-ch'eng along with Fa-ch'ien, and at eighteen he was learned in the sūtras and śāstras and was outstanding among the religious of Hsü-chou. After full ordination, he distinguished himself even more. He often lectured on *Satyasiddhi* and the *Three Treatises*. During Ta-ming (A.D. 457–64) he moved out of the capital and lived in the Hsieh-ssŭ. Around the end of Sung and the beginning of Ch'i, he had a high reputation and numerous disciples. He was honored by the crown prince Wen Hui and by Wen Hsüan, prince of Ching-ling, with the rites due to a teacher. In Yung Ming 8 (A.D. 490) he was lecturing on the *Hundred Treatise*. When he came to the "Chapter Refuting Atoms" (ch. 6) he suddenly dropped dead; he was fifty-seven years old (KSC, p. 379b23).

The turning point in the history of the *Three Treatise* tradition is *Chou Yung's Essay on the Three Theses*. Chou Yung was a prominent layman—Chih-lin addresses him as "dānapati" in his letters. Chi-tsang says:

> Mr. Chou's 'designations are emptiness' originally came out of Seng-chao's ***Emptiness of the Non-Absolute*** (***Chung-lun-shu***, p. 29b29).
>
> The dharma-master Great Lang (Seng-lang) got this idea in Kuan-nei and gave it to Mr. Chou, who used it to write the ***Essay on the Three Theses*** (p. 29c5).

The "three theses" are three different concepts of what the Two Truths are. As Chi-tsang shows in the passage following those quoted, Chou Yung does owe his basic insights to Seng-chao. However, it is not true that he learned about Seng-chao's doctrine from Seng-lang. As the Chih-lin letters show, the Three Theses was written while Chih-lin was alive, hence before 487. Seng-lang arrived in Chiang-nan shortly after 494. Chou Yung was friendly with two of the *Three Treatise* scholars of the times, namely Chih-lin and Hsüan-ch'ang. Furthermore, the essays that later constituted the *Chao-lun* were known in Chiang-nan at this time. *Chao-lun*, essays two, three, and four are listed in Lu Ch'eng's *Fa-lun-mu-lu*, compiled at the decree of Sung Ming Ti between 465 and 472 (CST, pp. 83a8, 83b3, 83a22; *Jōron Kenkyū*, pp. 272–73).

Thus Seng-lang arrived too late to teach Chou Yung what he wrote in his essay, and the doctrine that Seng-lang was supposed to have brought to Chiang-nan had been there all the time.

What is remarkable about Chou Yung is that he seems to have understood *Emptiness of the Non-Absolute*. Chüeh-shih, who established the thesis that it is the non-empty which is mere designation, in spite of his fame and expertise, must not have understood Seng-chao's doctrine. Chih-lin, in his letters, tells how "The sublime sound has been interrupted for sixty or seventy years" (KSC, p. 376b5). Under these conditions, though the study of the *Three Treatises* had not actually lapsed, it is rather misleading to speak of an Old Three Treatise Sect.

DOCUMENTS

DOCUMENT 1

AṢṬASĀHASRIKĀ PASSAGES THAT PARALLEL THE MIDDLE STANZAS

Translations are based on those of Edward Conze, with some modifications. The two page numbers in parentheses after each excerpt refer respectively to Conze's translation and to Rajendralal Mitra's edition of the Sanskrit text.

I. General Structures

1. The marks are fixed on to the fact that they are empty, signless, wishless, not brought together, not produced, not stopped, not defiled, not purified, that they are non-existence, Nirvāṇa, the realm of Dharma, and Suchness (98; 273).
2. Tathāgatahood, Buddhahood, Self-existence, and the state of all-knowledge are unthinkable (100; 277). . . . Also the skandhas, and all dharmas are unthinkable (100; 278).
3. All dharmas are situated in space, they have not come, they have not gone, they are the same as space. Space has not come, nor gone, is not made, nor unmade, nor effected; it has not stood up, does not last, nor endure; it is neither produced nor stopped (110; 297).

II. Dependent Co-arising

4. The bodhisattva surveys dependent co-arising in such a way that he avoids the duality of the extremes. He surveys it without seeing any beginning, end, or middle. . . . When he thus surveys dependent co-arising, he acquires the cognition of the all-knowing (194; 469).
5. A bodhisattva who thus surveys dependent co-arising certainly does not regard any dharma that is being produced without a cause, nor does he regard any dharma as permanent, stable, eternal, not liable to reversal, nor does he regard any dharma as a doer or a feeler (195; 470).
6. For the absence of own-being in beings should be known as belonging to the very essence of the perfection of wisdom. One should

know that the perfection of wisdom is without own-being because beings are without own-being (56; 175).

7. And the isolatedness of the essential nature of all dharmas is identical with the perfection of wisdom. . . . And the nature of all dharmas is no-nature, and their no-nature is their nature (65; 192).

8. For the five skandhas have emptiness for own-being, and, as devoid of own-being, emptiness cannot crumble nor crumble away (94; 256).

9. As a matter of fact, however, the true nature of dharmas is not past, nor future, nor present; it lies quite outside the three periods of time; and for that reason it cannot possibly be converted, cannot be treated as a sign, nor as an objective support, and it cannot be seen, nor heard, nor felt, nor known (65; 191).

10. If a person who belongs to the vehicle of the bodhisattvas does not seize on past, future, and present dharmas, . . . if he considers them with the conviction that all dharmas are fabricated by thought-construction, unborn, not come forth, not come, not gone, and that no dharma is ever produced or stopped in the past, future, or present, . . . then his jubilation is in accordance with the true nature of those dharmas (52; 161–62).

III. Personality

11. For the Tathāgata is one who has forsaken all reflections and discriminations. Space on its own cannot raise a deed or a thought without the help of objective support *(ālambana)*. A deed can arise only with an objective support, not without one. Intellectual acts must refer to dharmas which are seen, heard, felt, or known. In respect of some objects, intellectual acts take defilement upon themselves, in respect of others, purification. Acts of will and deeds can therefore arise only with objective support, not without. . . . Even so, objective supports are isolated. The act of will is isolated from the sign, and it arises only in reference to the conventional expressions current in the world (137; 358).

IV. Nirvāṇa

12. The perfection of wisdom cannot be expounded or learned . . . by means of the skandhas, or by means of the dhātus, or by means of the āyatanas. . . . Nor can the perfection of wisdom be understood otherwise than by the skandhas, etc (57; 177).

13. Form is neither bound nor free, because form has no own-being (62; 185).

14. To demonstrate that is to demonstrate all dharmas. But no one has demonstrated it, no one has heard it, no one has received it, and no one realises it, in the past, present, or future. Nor by this demonstration of dharmas does anyone ever go to Nirvāṇa (71; 204).

15. If we take such statements as 'the Tathāgata continues to exist after death,' 'the Tathāgata does not continue to exist after death,' 'the Tathāgata does and does not continue to exist after death,' 'the Tathāgata neither does nor does not continue to exist after death,' then these statements refer to the skandhas only, and they have no basis in the true reality of the Tathāgata (97; 269).
16. That which is the suchness of the skandhas is the suchness of the world; that which is the suchness of the world is the suchness of the fruit of a streamwinner; and so on up to that is the suchness of pratyeka-buddhahood, that is the suchness of the Tathāgata (97; 271).
17. The isolated cannot be known by the isolated, and nevertheless a bodhisattva knows full enlightenment and he does not know it without resorting to the perfection of wisdom (180; 440).

V. Language and Truth

18. For names and signs are also sources of attachment (64; 190).
19. To call it 'perfection of wisdom' is merely giving it a name. And what that name corresponds to, that cannot be got at. One speaks of a name with reference to a merely nominal entity. . . . In so far as it is a word, it is perfect wisdom; in so far as it is perfect wisdom, it is a word (68; 200).
20. It is also a deed of Māra if after one has written down the perfection of wisdom one should either think that it is the perfection of wisdom which is written down, or that it is not the perfection of wisdom which is written down, or if one should adhere to the perfection of wisdom either in the letters or as something not in the letters (87; 240).
21. Therefore then, according to ultimate reality, no distinction or difference can be apprehended between these dharmas. The Tathāgata has described them as talk. One just talks when one speaks of 'immeasurable,' or 'incalculable,' or 'inexhaustible,' or 'empty,' or 'signless,' or 'wishless,' [etc.] (132; 347).
22. From the fact that all dharmas are beyond words (198;476).

VI. Similes

23. It is as with a phantom man. Praise does not penetrate into him or win him over (67; 196).
24. This is a perfection of a dream, an echo, a reflected image, a mirage, or an illusion, because it is informed about non-production (71; 205).
25. Is the wick of a burning oil lamp burned up by the first incidence of the flame, or by the last incidence of the flame (134; 352)?
26. Like a dream is all that which belongs to the triple world (149; 381).

27. A phantom creature performs its work but remains without discrimination.... A puppet which could be moved by pulling the strings. Whatever action it were made to perform, it would perform. And yet that wooden machine would have no discriminations (181; 443).

Document 2: Part I

THE CHIEF IDEAS OF THE MAHĀYĀNA
(Ta-ch'eng-ta-i-chang) (T 1856, pp. 122a–43b)

Section 12: The Four Marks

Texts: T, p. 135a12–c14.
Shan-tao-ssŭ edition, pp. 62–65.
Eon Kenkyū, pp. 36–39.
Japanese translation: *Eon Kenkyū*, pp. 169–73.

1. *Hui-yüan asks*: The scripture[1] says that the former [i.e., primary] four marks each act on eight dharmas,[2] and that the latter [i.e., secondary] four marks act on one mark [i.e., one dharma]. Because the two marks [primary and secondary] effect each other, one does not incur the difficulty of infinite regression. But the *Great Perfection of Wisdom Treatise* says that if arising can produce arising, then arising has a further arising. If it has a further arising and then has arising, then, arising and producer of arising being thus, there is an infinite regression.[3] If the result is infinitely regressing, then the cause has no limits. If [the result] is finite in regression, then cause and conditions arise without a source. If their arising happens in dependence on the present [moment], then one does not incur the difficulty of infinite regression. If one does not incur the difficulty of infinite regression,[4] then the four marks will in turn effect[5] each other and enable the former [i.e., primary] to produce dharmas. If arising is produced again, then in the repetition there is the power of producing. If former arising is able to repeat [the act of arising], then it should not set a limit of inability for the latter [arising]. In this case, we are led again into infinite regression.
2. *A further question*: The four marks are causes[6] for the mental *(caitasika)* dḥarmas. If they have causes, is there the distinction of former and latter, or do they function together at the same time? If they function together at the same time, then [one objects that] the natures of arising and of ceasing are contradictory. While ceasing, [a thing] should not be arising. While arising, it should not be

ceasing. If there is distinction of former and latter, then [one objects that] in arising there is no ceasing, and in ceasing there is no arising. If in arising there is no ceasing, then arising falls into views of existence *(bhavadṛṣṭi)*. If in ceasing there is no arising, then ceasing falls into views of inexistence *(vibhavadṛṣṭi)*.[7] If existence and inexistence are parted, then annulling and permanence both persist separately.[8] If in arising there is a little ceasing and in ceasing there is a little arising, then former arising and latter arising would overlap, and former ceasing and latter ceasing would tread on each other. In this case you should not say arising and ceasing ever anew are mutually separate and have no previous [entity] in them (p. 135b1). If indeed they have no previous [entity] in them, then it is clear that dependent co-arising is not overlapping or treading on one another. If arising is the cause of abiding, and abiding is the cause of ceasing, then in arising there is no abiding, and in abiding there is no ceasing. If you suppose it to be like the example of the new garment,[9] then in arising there is already abiding, and in abiding there is already ceasing. This means that the effect is in the cause, and the effect is not different from the cause. Cause and effect are ranged side by side, and there is no distinction whatsoever. In this case, whether you advance or retreat, you fall into a place of doubt. You fall repeatedly into errors of reasoning *(nigraha-sthāna)*.[10]

3. *Kumārajīva answers*: It is Kātyāyana's disciples who say that conditioned dharmas have four marks, and not the Buddha who says so.[11] In all the sūtras, there are two main categories, namely conditioned dharmas and unconditioned dharmas.[12] Conditioned dharmas have arising, ceasing, abiding, and altering. Unconditioned ones are unarising, unceasing, unabiding, and unaltering. The Buddha has said in many places that they have nothing but names and letters.[13] He has never said definitely that there is arising, much less arising of arising. This is other men's idea, and not to be believed and received. How can I answer? When other men are in error, then it is something that they did not know. The Buddha declared that all dharmas are either permanent or impermanent. Impermanent means formerly inexistent and now existent, formerly existent and then inexistent.[14] Permanent means being free from such marks. The impermanent are conditioned dharmas. The permanent are unconditioned dharmas. For living beings the Buddha declared that the causes and conditions produce mundane dharmas and called it 'arising,' like mother and child, like the sprout arising from the seed.[15] This, a matter that appears and is seen, is called arising. Ceasing means that the conditions disintegrate. In living beings it is called death. In the myriad things it is called decay. The alteration in the interval between arising and ceasing is called abiding and altering. In living beings it is called aging, death, sickness, and wasting. In non-living things it is called transmutation. In this way, inner and outer things are

said to arise and cease, to abide and alter. The man of straight faith, having heard this, conceives aversion and obtains release. This explains the Buddha's main intention. Such is its purport. However, bhikṣus who in their deep minds cling to dharmas figment fictions *(prapañcayanti)* about the marks of the conditioned dharmas and imagine *(vikalpayanti)* that there are eight of them.[16]

4. The idea that dharmas arise together also misses the target (the middle). It is a storehouse of many difficulties. If [they arise] at one time, then they have no causes and conditions. If they arise in succession, then there is an infinite regress. Furthermore, there should not be any arising apart from dharmas. For what reason? Arising is the mark of the conditioned. If there is a dharma apart from arising, then it is not a conditioned dharma. If arising can combine with dharmas and effect arising, why cannot dharmas combine with arising and effect non-arising? There are many errors of this sort in the objection that you have sent. Therefore, the arising, ceasing, abiding, and altering declared in the Buddha's Hīnayāna sūtras are nothing but words and letters, and possess no real-being *(sadbhūta)*.

5. In the Mahāyāna sūtras [the Buddha] declared that arising is utterly empty, like a dream, like a phantom, nothing but the thoughts of deluded[17] worldlings (p. 135c1). Because the Mahāyāna Dharma is what I believe and assent to, I base my argument on it. All dharmas are non-arising because, if you seek for the real-being *(sadbhūta)* of arising, you cannot find it. If there were a dharma within the cause, then it should not be called arising, just as the thing inside a bag is not produced by the bag.[18] If it is not present previously in the cause, then why does a dharma not arise from a non-cause?[19] Just as there is no curd in milk, so likewise there is none in water.[20] If arising exists, then you say either that it exists in the first moment of the pot, or that it exists after the clay but does not exist at the time that the pot is not arisen.[21] It is not so in either of these two times. For what reason? Because [the one] has already arisen and [the other] has not yet arisen.[22] The fault in the now-arising is the same.[23] If [you say that] the completion *(siddhi)* of the pot is arising, this also is not [so].[24] When there is no arising part there is no pot. You should not consider completion to be arising.[25] Why? When the three factors[26] are separated, then [arising] is inexistent. If [arising occurs] at one time, then it is without cause and condition. Each [thing] that is without cause and condition should produce itself.

6. There are countless errors of this kind. Therefore, the Buddhas, the Tathāgatas, know that the dharma of arising has no real-being. The scripture[27] deludes the eyes of worldlings. Like events in a dream, [dharmas] have no origin or end. For this reason, [the Buddhas] declare that all the dharmas are non-arising, non-ceasing, dissociated from verbalism, quenched of all workings of thought, and the same as Nirvāṇa.[28] As soon as you get this sublime principle, you attain non-arising-dharma patience.[29]

DOCUMENT 2: PART II

THE CHIEF IDEAS OF THE MAHĀYĀNA
(Ta-ch'eng-ta-i-chang) (T 856, pp. 122a–43b)

Section 13: Suchness, Dharma-nature, and Reality-limit[1]

Texts: T, pp. 135c15–36b10.
Shan-tao-ssŭ edition, pp. 65–68
Eon Kenkyū, pp. 38–39.
Japanese translation: *Eon Kenkyū*, pp. 173–76.

1. *Hui-yüan asks*: When the sūtras talk about dharma-nature *(dharmatā)*, then they say that whether there is a Buddha or is not a Buddha, the nature abides in suchness.[2] When they talk about suchness *(tathatā)*, they explain receiving a prediction to become a Tathāgata.[3] When they talk about reality-limit *(bhūtakoṭi)*, they say that the reality-limit is not the receiving of realization.[4] The three statements are each different. Might I hear what their meaning is?
2. *A further question*: Is dharma-nature in constantly abiding inexistent or existent? If it is inexistent like space *(ākāśa)*, then it is dissociated from existence, and one should not say that the nature abides. If it exists and abides constantly, then one falls into the eternalist view. If it is inexistent and abides constantly, then one falls into the annihilist view. If it is neither existent nor inexistent, then is there necessarily any difference? In distinguishing and connecting existent and inexistent, the deeper one's perception, the more obscure it becomes. In thinking about the limit of existent and inexistent, it may be found through cause and conditions.[5]
3. *Kumārajīva answers*: These three ideas have already been explained in [the section on] non-arising patience.[6] Further, the *Great Perfection of Wisdom Treatise* explains the matter at length.[7] It says that dissociation from all verbalism and quenching all workings of thought is termed the real-mark of all the dharmas.[8] The real-mark of the dharmas is conventionally termed suchness, dharma-nature, and reality-limit.[9] In this [suchness] even the not-existent-and-not-inexistent cannot be found, much less the existent and the inexistent.

It is only because of fantasy-conceptions that each one has difficulties about existence and inexistence. If you conform to the cessation-mark *(niruddhatva?)* of the Buddha's Dharma, then you will have no discursive fictions *(prapañca)*. If you figment fictions about existence and inexistence, then you depart from the Buddha's Dharma (p. 136a1). The *Great Perfection of Wisdom Treatise* with many reasons demolishes existence and demolishes inexistence. You should not grasp the dharmas that are refuted and raise objections.

4. As for the further answer [to Hui-yüan's further question], it does not differ in meaning from the previous one. If anyone answers with a different idea, then it is not the Buddha's intention, and resembles [that of] the Tīrthikas.

5. Now, to explain again briefly: the marks of the dharmas are named according to time.[10] If one obtains the mark of the nature of the dharmas, as it truly is *(yathābhūtam)*, which cannot be demolished by any arguments, then it is called suchness, as it is like the dharma-mark and not something made by the power of thought.[11] The bodhisattvas whose faculties are keen investigate the suchness of the dharmas. For what reason? Suchness has the mark of cessation. It cannot be taken and cannot be rejected.[12] So we know that it is because the suchness of the dharmas is self-so by nature.[13] It is like earth's firm nature, water's moist nature, fire's hot nature, and wind's moving nature.[14] Fire's function is to blaze upwards, water's function is to flow downwards, wind's function is to move horizontally.[15] In this way, the nature of the dharmas is self-so by nature. This is called dharma-nature. One does not seek further for a higher thing.[16] At such a time, when the mind is fixed [in samādhi], having exhausted the extremes, this is called reality-limit. Therefore their basis is one, but the meaning and names are three.[17] The Dharma of suchness is one. Because it is distinguished as upper, middle, and lower, it is termed the Three Vehicles.[18] The first is suchness. The middle one is dharma-nature. The last is reality-limit. Reality-limit is the upper, dharma-nature is the middle, and suchness is the lower.[19] There are distinctions according to the power of contemplation. Further, they have names that have similar sounds in the Indian language. Therefore, it is said that he who knows the suchness of the dharmas is the Tathāgata,[20] just as he is called Buddha because he correctly and comprehensively knows *(samyaksambudh-)* all dharmas.[21]

6. Furthermore, the Hīnayāna sūtras also speak about suchness and dharma-nature. As in the Saṁyuktāgama,[22] a bhikṣu asked the Buddha, "Blessed One, these twelve nidānas, are they created by the Buddha, or are they created by someone else?" The Buddha said, "O bhikṣu, these twelve nidānas are not created by me and are not created by another. Whether there is a Buddha or is not a Buddha, the suchness, the dharma-nature, and the dharma-position[23] of the dharmas constantly

abide in the world. That is to say—because this dharma exists, this dharma exists; because this dharma arises, this dharma arises. 'On ignorance depends consciousness' and so on to 'on birth depends aging-and-death, on which depend all sufferings.' 'If ignorance ceases, saṁskāras cease,' and so on to 'if aging-and-death ceases, all sufferings cease.'" The Buddha only explains and makes this clear to men, just as the sun manifests and illumines the myriad things, long and short, beautiful and ugly, though they are not made by the sun.[24]

7. Thus the śrāvaka-sūtras declare that in the world there are always dharmas of birth and death. At no time are they not existent. This is called, "Whether there is a Buddha or is not a Buddha, the marks constantly abide."

The idea of reality-limit is only declared in the Mahāyāna dharma.[25] Because the dharma-nature is immeasurable, like the waters of the great ocean,[26] all the saints and sages accord with what their wisdom-power obtains. Since the wisdom-power of men of the two vehicles is scanty, they are not able to enter deeply into dharma-nature, and then take their realization (p. 136b1). They realize the sublime ultimate principle of dharmas as they truly are *(yathābhūtam)*, deeply loathe the conditioned, and firmly decide that this is the absolute, without anything surpassing it. But the bodhisattvas, possessing the power of great wisdom, enter deeply into dharma-nature. They do not take arrival to be realization and though they forego profound entry [into bodhi], they have no different affairs, just as those who drink the great ocean, though their quantity may differ, do not differ in affairs.[27]

8. Further, the bodhisattvas, when they have mounted compliant-patience *(ānulomikī dharmakṣānti)* and have not yet obtained no-arising-dharma-patience, contemplate the real-mark of the dharmas.[28] At this time, [the real-mark of the dharmas] is called suchness. When they have obtained the no-arising-dharma-patience, because they have already profoundly contemplated suchness, at this time it is renamed dharma-nature. When they sit on the bodhimaṇḍa and realize dharma-nature, then dharma-nature is renamed reality-limit.[29] While they have not realized reality-limit but have entered dharma-nature, they are called bodhisattvas, as long as they do not have the holy fruit *(āryaphala)*. When they reach the bodhimaṇḍa, because the Buddhas with their all-knowledge [know] the measureless dharma-nature, they then emerge from the bodhisattva-way and realize[30] the Buddha-way.

Document 2: Part III

THE CHIEF IDEAS OF THE MAHĀYĀNA
(Ta-ch'eng-ta-i-chang) (T 1856, pp. 122a–43b)

Section 14: Existence of Real Dharmas (pp. 136b22–37b2)

Texts: T, pp. 136b22–37b2.
Shan-tao-ssŭ edition, pp. 69–72.
Eon Kenkyū, pp. 40–42.
Japanese translation: *Eon Kenkyū*, pp. 177–80.

1. *Hui-yüan asks*: The *Great Perfection of Wisdom Treatise* considers that form, scent, taste, and touch are real-dharma-existents, while milk and curds are cause-and-condition existents.[1] Please analyse to the basis, discover the law, and define the terms. Cause-and-condition arising arises from real-dharmas.
2. *A further question*: From what do real-dharmas arise? The scripture says that form, scent, taste, and touch are secondary matter.[2] Form *(rūpa)* then has the four great elements *(mahābhūtas)* for its basis. Why does it proceed originally from the four great elements and not from cause and conditions? If from cause and conditions, then in what sense are they real-dharmas? If you seek real-dharmas in analysing the four great elements, the query is the same. Why? The śāstra says that none of the dharmas has fixed-mark. Therefore, one who obtains magic powers can make water become earth, or earth become water (p. 136c1). The marks of the four great elements change according to his power. They are grounded in the contemplation of friendliness.[3] Therefore, we know clearly that the four great elements and secondary matter all are created by cause and conditions. If the four great elements and secondary matter are not cause-and-conditional, then they lack the three marks.[4] If they lack the three marks, the Blessed One should not declare that he regards them as impermanent. If they are impermanent, then they arise and cease ever anew. Therefore it is said, "One does not see an existent dharma that arises without cause and conditions."[5] One does not see an existent that is constantly arising and does not cease. In this case, all that

arise have causes and conditions. So is there any longer a distinction between cause-and-condition and real-dharmas? The śāstra's explanation means that existence from cause and conditions differs from that which exists as a real-dharma. Though the two are the same in cause and conditions, that by which they are existent is not the same. In that case, that which is transformed by cause and conditions should have no fixed-mark, and what is not transformed by cause and conditions should have fixed-mark. But in the *Magic Powers Chapter*[6] of this śāstra it says that the four great elements have no fixed-mark. Because their fixed-mark is inexistent, following their cessation they change. When they change, they leave their original [state]. Form, scent, taste, and touch come forth from the four great elements, so the principle is the same as for what is created by cause and conditions. When they are transformed, they change into different things. From this I infer that real-dharmas and cause and conditions are not at all different. The śāstra seems to explain the meaning, but it is not an exhaustive account. Therefore I will accept [instruction] from you.

3. *Kumārajīva answers*: There are two kinds of śāstra. The first is the Mahāyāna śāstra, which declares the two kinds of emptiness—emptiness of living beings, and emptiness of dharmas. Of the two, the Hīnayāna śāstras declare the emptiness of living beings.[7] For what reason? Because the skandhas, āyatanas, and dhātus, combining, provisionally form a living being, but in it there is no separate reality.[8] Thus the śāstra say that milk, etc. are cause-and-condition existents while form, etc. are real-dharmas.

4. Further, [beings] conceive two kinds of attachment towards the dharmas. The first is attachment to living beings *(pudgala)*. The second is attachment to dharmas. Because they are attached to living beings, [the Buddha] preaches that there is no dharma of self, that it has only name-and-form[9] as a basis. In name-and-form the deluded perceive marks and imagine "This is a living being, this is a man, this is a god, this is something living, this is a house, these are mountains and woods, this is a river, etc." All such views do not pass beyond name-and-form. Just as the clay is one thing, but makes many kinds of vessels, some called potsherds and some called pots. The potsherds are broken up and become a pot; the pot is broken up and becomes potsherds, and afterwards it returns to being clay. As a potsherd nothing is lost, and as a pot nothing is gained.[10] The difference is only in designation. Conceiving difference in name-and-form is just the same. If you seek for its real counterpart, there is only name-and-form. When, having heard this explained, one sees that in all the dharmas there is no 'I' and no 'mine,' then one becomes detached, has no more fictions *(prapañca)*, and cultivates the Dharma; some men do not err about the marks of living beings but err about the marks of dharmas in name-and-form. Because they are attached to dharmas, they have fictions about name-and-form. For these men,

[the Buddha] declared that name-and-form (p. 137a1) are delusion, that form is like a phantom, like an apparition, utterly empty and calm, and the same as living beings existing because of causes and conditions but having no fixed mark.

5. Therefore, you should know that the statement that form, etc. are real-existents while milk, etc. are cause-and-condition existents, is the idea of the Hīnayāna śāstras, and is not the doctrine of the really profound śāstras. For what reason? Because living beings, relying on this idea, obtain liberation. If one said that everything is empty, their minds would have no support, and they would conceive errors and sadness. For the sake of these people, we cause them to contemplate the three marks[11] of name-and-form—impermanence, suffering, and emptiness. When their thoughts become detached, they do not rely on other examinations,[12] just as when a herbal remedy removes distress one does not need a great medicine.[13]

6. Further, [the Buddha] brings living beings to detachment from errors about form, etc., whether duality or plurality, whether permanence or annihilation. For this reason, it is stated that form, etc. are really existent while milk, etc. are designationally existent. One who contemplates in this way understands that dharmas that arise from a set of conditions[14] are not possessed of own-being *(svabhāva)*, utterly empty and calm. This being so, though there are differences between the statements, the principles are all of one purport.

7. Further, the Buddhas have attained all-knowledge; their wisdom is inconceivable. Except for the Buddhas there is no man who can perceive and retain completely according to the real-principle. Therefore the Buddhas, accommodating to what living beings understand, explain three classes of doctrine within the one meaning *(ekārtha)*. For beings with dull faculties they declare emptiness, suffering, and impermanence. These beings, having heard that all dharmas are impermanent and suffering, become profoundly detached, succeed in cutting off craving, and attain liberation. For beings with medium faculties, they declare that everything is without self, secure, quiescent, and in nirvāṇa. When these beings hear that all dharmas are without self, only nirvāṇa, security, and quiescence, they cut off craving, and gain liberation. For those with keen faculties, they declare that all the dharmas from the very beginning are unarising, unceasing, utterly empty, and like nirvāṇa.[15]

8. Therefore, within the one meaning, according to the fetters and mental faults of beings, there are differences of profundity. Just as that which cures a small sickness is called a small medicine, and that which cures a great sickness is called a great medicine.[16] There is greatness or smallness according to the sickness. The lightness or gravity of the sickness of the three poisons in the minds of living beings is like this. If the strength of lust[17] and hostility is equal, then folly is the āsrava. For what reason? Lust, though a small sin,

is hard to detach from. Hostility, though a great sin, is easy to detach from. Folly is a great sin and is hard to detach from. Because lust is hard to detach from, it has the mark of evil, and because it is a small sin, it is not evil. Because hostility is a great sin, it has the mark of evil, and because it is easy to detach from it is not evil. Because these two are of equal strength, abandoning them is easy, by means of contemplations on impurity, friendliness, compassion, impermanence, and suffering.[18] If thoughts of folly come forth, then one produces the twenty views of real-body-view *(satkāya-dṛṣṭi)*,[19] and falls deeply into error about all the dharmas. For this malady, no-self is declared. When the conditions produce a dharma, it has no own-being *(svabhāva)*, is utterly and always empty, and from the beginning has no mark of arising (p. 137b1). Therefore, the Buddha sometimes declares that beings are empty and sometimes declares that dharmas are empty. When he says that form, etc. are real dharmas while milk, etc. are cause-and-condition existents, he commits no error.[20]

Document 2: Part IV

THE CHIEF IDEAS OF THE MAHĀYĀNA
(Ta-ch'eng-ta-i-chang) (T 1856, pp. 122a–43b)

Section 15: The Emptiness of Division into Parts[1]

Texts: T, pp. 137b3–38b14.
Shan-tao-ssŭ edition, pp. 73–78.
Eon Kenkyū, pp. 40–42.
Japanese translation: *Eon Kenkyū*, pp. 177–80.

1. *Hui-yüan asks*: The *Great Perfection of Wisdom Treatise*, analyzing the fabric, seeks for its basis until it reaches the hair-particle *(romabhāga)*. It analyzes the hair-particle and seeks its basis, which is an atom *(paramāṇu)*.[2] The atoms are form, scent, taste, and touch. If these four—form, scent, taste, and touch—exist, then form, scent, taste, and touch cannot be termed imposed names.[3] In this case, in the statements about atoms, what are we to rely on? Are they existent, or are they inexistent? If there are real-dharmas, then the principle of division into parts can rightly make the fabric empty, but still cannot make its basis empty. If the basis cannot be made empty, then it is 'the one-foot rod' problem[4] and one falls into the view of eternalism. If there are no real dharmas, then the example of the tortoise hairs [applies], and one falls into[5] the view of annihilation.[6] The two are not the Middle Way. Neither can one term [the atoms] imposed names. Supposing that the ten directions are equally divided,[7] if you take division into parts to be emptiness, how can the particles go outside of the existent? They have not even gone outside of form, because form cannot be gone outside of. The Blessed One termed it subtle form, not atoms. As for the principle of division into parts, since in investigating empty cause-and-condition existents one does not arrive at real-dharmas, analysing the fabric right down to the ultimates of hair-particles, still knowledge of emptiness is possible. If this is so, afterwards one should not consider the atoms as imposed names. If the atoms are imposed names, then it can be known that the contemplation of

emptiness does not stop at cause-and-condition existents. So then, where is the limit of existence and inexistence?[8] The principle of the not-existent-and-not-inexistent should be explained.

2. *Kumārajīva answers*: The term 'atom' does not occur at all in the Buddha's doctrine. It is only said that all form, whether gross or subtle, is impermanent.[9] It is not asserted that there is a smallest [thing] or a most subtle [thing]. If you take the subtlest to be the atom, this mark cannot be perceived. But debaters conceive many errors about this. Therefore, one does not assert it. Further, one does not lead living beings to produce bonds of clinging towards the subtlest form. If there was an occasion of bondage, then the Buddha explained the doctrine for the sake of release from bondage.[10] Further, in the Mahāyāna sūtras, accommodating to worldlings, [the Buddha] talks about the designation 'atom,' but does not say that its fixed-mark exists. Just as the grossest form cannot be perceived, even so the subtlest form cannot be perceived.[11]

3. As the disciples of Ulūka say in the *Chapter Explaining Atoms*,[12] there are four fixed-marks of the atoms—form *(rūpa)*, scent *(gandha)*, taste *(rasa)*, and touch *(sparśa)*. The water atom has form, taste, and touch. The fire atom has form and touch. The wind atom has only touch.[13] That the person exists separately apart from the four dharmas is because of the earth great element.[14] The four dharmas are attributes of earth.[15] The smallest earth is called the atom, which is the basis of all forms in heaven-and-earth and is indestructible.

4. Among the Buddha's disciples there are also places where atoms are mentioned (p. 137c1). Since the Buddha said that there is subtle form, they seek for the subtlest of the subtle. Their notions are held captive by the atoms.[16]

5. To refute the false views of the Tīrthikas and the false arguments of the Buddha's disciples, we declare that the atoms have no fixed-mark and only have designation. For what reason? Just as the five fingers in combination are designated a fist,[17] form and the others combining are designated atoms. Within the Buddha's dharma there are two constantly-used modes. The first is the mode of no-self. The second is the mode of empty dharmas. The mode of no-self is that the five skandhas, the twelve āyatanas, the eighteen dhātus,[18] and the twelve nidānas are real *(sadbhūta)* dharmas, but have no self. The mode of empty dharmas is that the five skandhas, the twelve āyatanas, the eighteen dhātus, and the twelve nidānas from the beginning have nothing existent and are utterly empty.[19] If we refute the atoms according to the mode of no-self, we state that form, scent, taste, and touch are real-dharmas,[20] and that the atoms are constructed by the combining of the four dharmas, and are named designations. For what reason? Because here we only state that the self is empty; we do not state that dharmas are empty. According to [the mode of] the emptiness of dharmas, the atoms and form, etc. all have nothing

existent. We do not distinguish further as to which are real and which are expressional.

6. Further, one cannot state that form, etc. have permanence. For what reason? Because they arise from groups of causes and conditions, and perish moment by moment. Also, because they are included in the skandhas, dhātus, and āyatanas, we cannot say that they are inexistent. Altogether, combining dharmas possess designation, but they have no real-entity. It is like the two entities of the form-āyatana and the touch-āyatana which in combination are designated fire. If when two dharmas combine there is a third, fire dharma, then there ought to be something separate that is created *(kṛta)*. But in fact there is not anything created.[21] You should know that in one fire[22] and its burning, in secondary matter and its shining, there is no separate (specific) dharma, and there are only appellations. Therefore, whether we talk about designations or about real-dharmas, there is no error.

7. Further, in the Buddha's dharma there are four kinds of holy contemplation. The first is impermanence. The second is suffering. The third is emptiness. The fourth is no-self.[23] The Buddha sometimes saves living beings with the contemplation of no-self and sometimes saves living beings with the contemplation of emptiness. When he speaks about no-self, then there are other dharmas. When he speaks about emptiness, then there are no existents. If he refutes the atoms with the doctrine of emptiness, then men do not believe and accept. For what reason? You say that there is no gross form; why alone say that there is no atom? It if is because of the doctrine of no-self that there are no atoms, then men believe easily. But it is not true that if there are no real dharmas, the example of tortoise hair [applies] and one enters views of annihilation.[24]

8. For what reason? Some say that the self is the same as the body. When the body ceases, the self ceases with it. Also, there is no one who goes to a subsequent body.[25] If there are no atoms, then [the case] does not come under this rule. Further, one does not hold views of eternality or annihilation regarding the self. For what reason? Because views of 'I' and 'mine' are termed real-body-view *(satkāyadṛṣṭi)*, and the five views are each separate.[26] Some say of the five skandhas that the cause changes into the effect (p. 138a1). This is termed eternality. Some consider that the five skandhas are conditioned dharmas and that after the cause ceases there is an effect that arises. This is termed annihilation. But the wise, analysing and seeking for the ultimate principle of the atoms, [know that] since fundamentally there are no dharmas, there is nothing to perish. If the self is fundamentally and intrinsically inexistent, then though I say it is inexistent, I do not fall into views of annihilation. Refuting the atoms in this way with the mode of no-self, one does not fall into views of annihilation.

9. Further, in the Mahāyāna doctrine, though one asserts that form, etc. are empty even within the atoms, and mind and mental dharmas are empty even within the mind,[27] one does not fall into annihilism, either. For what reason? Because it is only asserted in order to demolish misconceptions and false views. It is not the real-mark of the dharmas. If one asserts impermanence, it is in order to demolish the misconception of permanence. If one says that mind and mental dharmas cease moment by moment, it is to demolish [ideas of] the oneness of the combination of many conditions. Permanence is not real, and neither is impermanence real. As combination is not real, separation is not real, either. As existence is not real, inexistence is not real, either.[28] When all views are obliterated, how can one speak of views of annihilation? 'Views of annihilation' means 'It formerly existed and now inexists.'[29]

10. In the Hīnayāna dharma, from the first one cannot perceive the grossest form and so on down to the finest form. In the Mahāyāna dharma, [dharmas] are utterly empty, appearances seen by the eye, like a phantom, like a dream. Their mark of real-being cannot be perceived, much less their finest particles or atoms. The grossest and the finest are all only false views and fictions of the Tīrthikas.

11. As in the Tīrthika *Chapter on the Atoms*,[30] the master says, "The atoms are marked by permanence.[31] For what reason? Because these entities do not arise from causes.[32] Question: How can these be known? Answer: When atoms combine, gross form is visible.[33] You should know that gross form is the effect of subtle form. The effect is gross, therefore visible. The cause is subtle, therefore not visible. Therefore, if there is a cause, there must be an effect; if there is an effect, there must be a cause.[34] Further, since impermanence negates *(pratiṣedha)* permanence,[35] you should know that there really is the dharma of permanence.[36] For what reason? Because it is the contradictory of the impermanent. Because of non-knowledge *(avidyā)* there really are permanent dharmas. Since non-knowledge *(avidyā)* is the reason for [the existence of] knowledge *(vidyā)*, we should know that in the impermanent dharmas there is a permanent dharma.[37] Because gross things are a combination of many [subtle ones], form, being present in them, is clearly visible. Though there is form in the atoms, because there are no other [atoms] it is not visible.[38] Supposing that many winds combine, since form is not present in them, they cannot be seen.[39] Number-dharmas such as oneness and twoness; magnitude-dharmas; individuality; combination; separation; thisness; thatness; and action, because they combine in dependence on form, can be seen. If number, magnitude, etc. are in non-form, then they cannot be seen."[40]

12. In such ways the Tīrthikas figment fictions about atoms. Therefore we assert that the atoms (p. 138b1) are like the moon [reflected] in water. The adult sees it and does not seek for a real-entity.[41] Thus gross form or subtle, far or near, lovely or ugly, past or future,

are all delusion, all like the moon reflected in water, all indescribable. We only wish to bring men's minds to conceive detachment and attain nirvāṇa. Feeling, conception, dispositions and consciousness are just the same.

13. Further, because living beings have been deeply attached to fictions *(prapañca)* throughout beginningless worlds, there are few who see that there are faults and troubles amid the existent and inexistent, and who arrive directly at nirvāṇa.

14. Therefore the Buddha, because he wants to lead them out of existence and inexistence, declares the not-existent and not-inexistent, and that there is no dharma outside of these. Those that do not understand the Buddha's aim then become attached to the not-existent-and-not-inexistent. Therefore, the Buddha further demolishes the not-existent-and-not-inexistent. If 'not-existent-and-not-inexistent' is able to demolish views of existence and inexistence, then those who do not still crave the not-existent-and-not-inexistent do not need the demolition of the not-existent-and-not-inexistent.[42]

15. As for the not-existent-and-not-inexistent, if though existents and inexistents have been demolished people still figment fictions about the not-existent-and-not-inexistent, then the Buddha says "Abandoning the not-existent-and-not-inexistent is just like abandoning the existent-and-inexistent. Not apprehending and not craving the dharmas is my Buddha-dharma." It is like a man who treats a disease with a medicine. If the medicine causes trouble, then one cures it with a further remedy. If this medicine gives no trouble, then one stops. In the Buddha-dharma, the medicine of prajñā is just like this. By this medicine one demolishes the objects of addictions. If people then conceive addiction to prajñā, one must pursue a method of treatment. If there are no addictions to prajñā, then further treatment is not applied.[43]

Document 3

SPIRIT DOES NOT PERISH
(The Śramaṇa Does Not Make Obeisance to the King, Part V)
by Hui-yüan

Texts: T LII, 31b–32a.
Eon Kenkyū, pp. 88–90.
Ssŭ-pu-pei-yao.
Japanese translations: *Kokuyaku Issaikyō, Wakan Senjutsu, Gokyōbu* I, 125–27.
Eon Kenkyū, pp. 388–93.
Previous English translations: Liebenthal, "Hui-yüan," pp. 251a–52.
Hurvitz, "Render unto Caesar," pp. 106–12.

1. QUESTION: The meaning of your argument is that the termination of transformations is the Utmost Ultimate,[1] and so [you think that] one who goes to the Ultimate must go counter to the transformations to find the Ideal; finding the Ideal is not founded on conforming to the transformations. Therefore, you cite the rulers and kings throughout the ages and make them agree with the Buddha's teaching. You cause the utmost realization of the Ultimate to reside in the line of rulers as an expedient means *(upāya)*.[2] What your elegant argument is based on must be the Great Pervader.[3] When we examine the actuality that matches (corresponds), then the Reason (Principle) is not so.
2. Why? The endowment of vital ether comes to an end with one life. When the life terminates, then [the vital ether] dissipates and is the same as inexistent. The spirit, even though it is a sublime thing (though it inspirits things)[4] is certainly nothing but a transformation of *yin* and *yang*. Having transformed, it becomes [something] living. Having transformed again, it becomes something dead. When it has collected, it makes the beginning. When it disperses again, it makes the end.
3. By inference from this, we know for certain[5] that spirit and body

both transform together, that fundamentally they do not have different lineages. Psychic and physical are the one vital ether, and share the same lodging from beginning to end. When the lodging is whole, then the vital ether being collected, there is a numen *(ling)*. When the lodging disintegrates, then, the vital ether being dispersed, cognition is extinguished. When [vital ether] disperses, it returns what it had received to the Celestial Origin.[6] When [cognition] is extinguished, it reverts again to the Thingless.[7] Returning and terminating are all nothing but destinies of the self-so.[8] Who makes them?

4. If you suppose that [body and spirit] are originally different,[9] then different vital ethers combine according to destiny. When they are combined, then they transform together. Also the spirit occupies the body just as fire resides in wood.[10] While [the body] is alive, [the spirit] must have being. When [the body] disintegrates, [the spirit] must perish. When the body separates, then the spirit disperses, having nothing to depend on. When the wood falls apart, then the fire dies out, having nothing to support it. The principle is so.

5. As distinctions of sameness and difference[11] are obscure and hard to make clear, statements about 'existent and inexistent' must keep to 'collecting and dispersing.'[12] 'Collecting and dispersing' is the general term for the changes of the vital ether, the birth and cessation of the myriad transformations. Therefore Chuang-tzŭ says,[13] "The birth of a man is the collecting of vital ether. While it is collected, he is alive. While it is dispersed, he is dead. As death and life are each other's companions, how can suffering trouble me any more?"

6. The ancients who were skilled in speaking about the Way must have had the means to apprehend it. If in fact this is so, we can prove the idea that the final principle[14] comes to an end with one life, and that when the life is used up, it does not transform.

7. REPLY: What is 'spirit'? It comes to be called 'numinal' because it is the ultimate of the psychic.[15] The ultimate of the psychic is not something that the trigrams and digrams[16] can diagram. Therefore the Holy Men define it as inspiriting things.[17] Even though one possessed the highest knowledge, one still could not determine its structure and form,[18] and probe to the utmost its abstruse meaning. Yet you debaters, using your ordinary knowledge, conceive doubts and agree frequently with your own confusions.[19] The errors you have committed are already grievous. If one wishes to describe it, this is describing the indescribable. Now, in the midst of the indescribable, we merely simulate.[20]

8. As for spirit, responding perfectly, it has no lord;[21] subtly all-pervading,[22] it has no name. Inciting things, it moves;[23] borrowing destinies, it operates.[24] Though it incites things, it is not a thing, and thus when things transform, it does not perish. Though it borrows destinies, it is not a destiny, and thus when destinies are used up, it is not exhausted. Since it has feelings,[25] it can be cited through

things;[26] since it has consciousness, it can be sought through destinies Among destinies there are the psychic and the physical,[27] and thus [people's] natures are each different. Among intelligences there are the bright and the dull, and thus [people's] cognitions are not the same.

9. Reasoning by inference from this, we know that transformations are incited by feelings, and spirit is transmitted by transformations. Feelings are the mother of transformations, and spirit is the root of feelings.[28] In feelings there is the process of meeting things;[29] and in spirit there is the operation of occult migration. Only those who wake up and see clearly return to the Origin. Those who misconceive the Order *(li)* merely pursue things.[30]

10. The ancients who discussed the Way were also never in agreement [with you].[31] Allow me to explain by quotations. Chuang-tzŭ uttered speech about the metaphysical in the *Ta-tsung* [chapter],[32] saying, "The Great Lump makes me toil while I am alive and gives me rest when I am dead." He also thinks that life is man's inn,[33] and death is returning to the True (Absolute).[34] This is what is meant by "knowing that life is the great trouble and considering that no-life (no-arising) is returning to the Origin."[35] Wen-tzŭ, quoting the Yellow Emperor's words, says,[36] "When the body undergoes dissolution, the spirit does not transform. Because the non-transforming rides on the transformations, its changes are interminable." Chuang-tzŭ also says,[37] "When one merely finds shape in a human body,[38] one is still delighted at it. But the bodies such as man's never reach an end-point though they transform ten thousand times."[39] This means that we know births are not exhausted in one transformation, and that while pursuing things one does not return [to the Origin].[40]

11. Although I have not totally fathomed the truth of the two masters' discussions, yet I have come near the Ideal and have heard something about it.[41]

12. You, not enquiring into the statement, "now living, now dying,"[42] misinterpret 'gathering and dispersal in one transformation.' Not noticing that in the way of the spirit there is a numen that inspirits things,[43] you assert that the psychic and the physical are exhausted together. Is it not indeed sad!

13. The simile of the fire and the wood is originally from the texts of the Holy Ones.[44] [People] lost the thread of the tradition, and thus no one sought to revive the abstruse [meaning].[45] The subtle sayings subsequently were submerged by ordinary teachings,[46] so that debaters [like you] utilize them to create doubts. If at present there were still no expert who understands the Ideal, then you would not know that there has been the wisdom of the former sages, and no one would ever hear about the operation[47] of the occult transmission.

14. Why? Feelings and destinies incite each other, and their transformations have no termini. Causes and conditions secretly interlock

and hiddenly pass each other along. Only one with penetrating vision knows their changes. Allow me to demonstrate it for you with an actual [example]. The transmission of fire in fuel is like the transmission of spirit in the body. The transmission of fire to other fuel is like the transmission of spirit to another body. The former fuel is not the latter fuel, so we know what a mystery is the art of the fingers exhausting [their duty].[48] The former body is not the latter body, so we understand how profoundly feelings and destinies incite [each other]. The deluded, when they see the body decay after one life, think that spirit and feelings both are lost, just as when they see that a fire is exhausted after one piece of wood, they think that at the last moment both are simply consumed. This is based on talk about 'nourishing life'[49] rather than on a thoroughgoing examination of the analogy.

15. If, following the argument that you sent, we suppose that spirit and body transform together, they begin from a celestial (natural) origin.[50] Stupid and wise are furnished with life, and are endowed alike with whatever they receive. I ask whether what they receive is received from the body, or whether it is received from the spirit. If they receive it from the body, then everything in an existing body would become spirit when it transforms.[51] If they receive it from the spirit, then spirit is transmitted to spirit, and then Tan-chu [Yao's unworthy son] and Emperor Yao would be equally saintly, and Ch'ung-hua [Shun] and Ku-sou [Shun's worthless father] would be equally numinal. Can this be so? Can this be so?

16. Since it cannot, we know that the interlinking of occult conditions is manifested through the persistence of the past[52] and one's lot of intelligence or stupidity is decided before the body [is formed]. Though the numinal potter's wheel rotates well,[53] it cannot alter the self-so-ness of one's nature (character). How much less so anything inferior to this?[54] If you verify it with Reason, then the subtle saying has proof. Check it with the facts, and you can have no delusion about the Great Pervader.[55]

17. We prove it according to principles (reason), so the subtle sayings have confirmation. We verify it by means of facts, so it is possible to have no errors about the Great Way.

DOCUMENT 4

PREFACE TO THE ABRIDGED GREAT PERFECTION OF WISDOM TREATISE, BY HUI-YÜAN

Text: CST, pp. 75b–76b.
Eon Kenkyū, pp. 98–101.
Japanese translations: Hayashiya Tomojirō, *Kokuyaku Issaikyō*, Shidenbu I, 289–92.
Eon Kenkyū, pp. 433-39.
Previous English translation (Section IV only): Liebenthal, "Hui-yüan, p. 246b.

I. The Treatise and China's Destiny

1. Now, the Ultimate Ideal being established in its position as the unconditioned (actionless), the Holy Man achieves its (his) power.[1] Dim and bright, yielding to each other, open the rotations, and flourishing and decay combine their changes.[2] Thus we know that dangerous and easy displace each other, and in the Order *(li)* there is proceeding and there is lying hidden.[3] Contraction and expansion incite each other, and in the numbers there is departing and returning.[4] Looking at it from this standpoint, though the occult pivot responds hiddenly, the complete scene is inexhaustible.[5] One cannot even out the displacing and shifting of the four symbols, or unify their meeting and passing through.[6] How much more so when, though the mandate (fate) of the times is tangled in error and the courses of the age bring each other to naught, [people] do not make the roots deep, the stem firm, and the apex stable, so as to endure![7] If one understands that there is a rotation of opening and shutting,[8] and that the coming of the seasons is not through chance, then it is not in vain that Perfect Enlightenment is concentrated [on the realm] beyond things.[9] The tendencies[10] in the spread of the Teaching can indeed be known by degrees.[11]

II. Nāgārjuna's Career

2. There was a Mahāyāna bodhisattva[12] named Nāgārjuna. He was born in India, and came from the Brahman caste. Having accumulated virtue[13] in bygone ages, his mind fitted existence in this [world]. He lived during the ninth century[14] [after the Parinirvāṇa], and at a moment when [the Dharma] was decadent and weak. He was grieved at the benightedness of the multitudes, and treading the steep (dangerous) track, he did not falter.
3. Thereupon, he secluded himself in a private mode of life,[15] and roamed cloudlike in Kapilavastu.[16] He grieved that his cultural light had not issued forth,[17] and that though his thoughts might leap [in the depths], they were not put to use.[18] Then he said with a deep sigh, "When the heavy night is darkening, the firefly's light cannot illuminate it.[19] Though the white sun has put its light to rest, one can still continue by the bright moon." Accordingly, he made his vows, took the tonsure, and adopted the dark garment.[20] He dwelt in seclusion in the woods and swamps, lived as a hermit, and practiced dhyāna. He stilled his cogitations and studied the subtle. His thoughts penetrated the supra-normal.[21]
4. Consequently, he had an awakening and said, "I have heard in previous treatises (discussions) that the Great Square has no limits.[22] There may be someone who has gone beyond it." He suddenly turned his steps towards the Himālayas, opening his spirit-intelligence in order to pursue his resolve.[23] He was about to pass through a place formerly frequented by adepts *(ṛṣis)* when he suddenly met a śramaṇa beneath a cliff. He questioned him about points on which he had doubts, and learned for the first time that there were the *Vaipulya* doctrines. When he came to the Dragon Palace,[24] there was no important canon or secret text that he did not master. When the roots of his impediments had been pulled up, then his name crowned the bodhisattva stages, and his virtue fulfilled the three patiences.[25] Only then did he open up the nine fords in the mighty abyss[26] and, befriending the scaly species, roam together with them.[27] His students were like [the trees in] a forest. The talented and accomplished inevitably gathered [around him]. Consequently, the Tīrthikas esteemed his manner, and famous gentlemen submitted to his dictates. From this time, the enterprise of the Mahāyāna flourished again.

III. The Doctrinal Character of the Treatise

5. He (Nāgārjuna) considered the *Prajñā Sūtra* to be the sublime gate to the numinal treasury,[28] the way to the Ideal Unity. Because the twelve sections of the Three Vehicles came forth from it, he esteemed it even more. But this Sūtra is abstruse and recondite, and its meaning is hard to understand. Those who are not acute and learned seldom

grasp its sense. Therefore, he expounded its system (essential structure) and distinguished its deep meaning. Though his intention lies beyond words, the principles are wrapped in his phrases. He often attributes [ideas] to "guest" and "host," feigning doubts in order to set up a dialogue. He calls them "Objection" and "Author."

6. Its objective is to start the carriage at the crossroads, and clear the delusions from the gate of knowledge. It takes no-matching as its actual and no-cognition as its Ideal.[29] Since it has no matching, the spirit is concentrated on its goal.[30] Since it has no cognition, knowledge is quiescent in what it performs. Since it performs knowledge while quiescent, the various false notions are removed,[31] and affirmation and negation cease in it. Since the spirit is concentrated on its goal, the Two Truths share the same track, and the metaphysical trail is unified in it. Who but the numen of the Fully Enlightened One touching and turning the Wheel of the Dharma for the second time could restore the great enterprise when it was about to collapse and tie up the loose ends of the abandoned net, causing the subtle words, though they were coming to an end, to be handed on again, and the metaphysical sounds, though they were stopping, to be chanted again!

IV. The Leitmotif: Nirvāṇa and Saṁsāra

7. Though I have not been able to live in the same generation with such a man and to call at his ford and ask the Way,[32] yet I have gone to the limit in studying the sense [of the Treatise]. I always read each section three times and am delighted at what I find (at my good luck). With its content, one can inform the ignorant and brightly illuminate the myriad dharmas in the water-mirror.[33] It is certainly not something that ordinary knowledge can discern. Allow me to speak about it briefly.[34]

8. The path of living begins in the beginningless region; the transformations interlink through arenas of good luck and bad luck.[35] Everything exists when it arises from the not-yet-existent and inexists when it has ceased from the already-existent. Inferring the conclusion from this, we know that existent and inexistent alternate in the one entity.[36] Though they depend on each other, they are not the origin. Arising and ceasing proceed separately[37] in the one transformation. Though they shine in the void,[38] they have no lord.[39] Therefore one identifies with them in order to achieve vision[40] and reverses the mirror[41] in order to find the Ideal. When the mirror is bright, sense-dust[42] does not alight on it, and the images of the primal dichotomy[43] are visible. When the vision is profound, then understanding penetrates the subtle, and names and actuals alike are metaphysical. If you are going to find its essentials, you must put this first, before you can speak about the not-existent and the not-inexistent. I will try to discuss it.

9. To reside in the existent while existing is to make (consider) the existent existent.[44] To reside in the inexistent while inexisting is to make (consider) the inexistent inexistent. Existence of the existent is not existence; inexistence of the inexistent is not inexistence. How do we know that it is so? The nature of no-nature is termed 'dharma-nature.' Dharma-nature has no nature, yet causes and conditions arise through it. As the conditions of arising have no own-mark,[45] though existent they are forever inexistent. Though forever inexistent, they are not cut off from existence. It is like a fire which, being transmitted, does not cease.[46]
10. Consequently, the entities do not have different destinations. First and last sink into the void,[47] and are ultimately the same. How[48] can the existent and the inexistent return to each other? Therefore the minds of those who roam in the recondite do not depend on cognition. Their knowledge does not make an object of anything. Without extinguishing marks, they are still; without cultivating samādhi, they are at rest. Unless one experiences it with the spirit[49] and penetrates it, how can one know the metaphysical [truth] of the emptiness of emptiness? This is the utmost point, this is the Ultimate. No one can know anything beyond this.[50]

V. The Literary Form of the Treatise

11. Furthermore, as for the formal structure of the Treatise: its position begins in the placeless,[51] so it cannot be probed to the utmost. Though in permuting categories it rings many changes, it cannot be exhausted.[52] Sometimes it opens up the far-reaching principles in order to promulgate them. Sometimes it leads those addicted to the commonplace[53] to enter the profound. Sometimes it closes the diverse paths in the one Dharma (dharma of oneness), but it is not manifold. Sometimes it opens the hundred deliberations in the mark of sameness, but it does not divide.[54] This is cutting off talk [that resembles] piling up bricks[55] and not having a rival in the whole world. So it quotes prolixly from the Scriptures in order to enrich its style, and expands the speech about the doctrine[56] in order to amplify its fine qualities. When the fine qualities are complete, then there is nothing that knowledge does not encompass. When the style is prolix, then it is broad and grand and endowed with everything.[57] Therefore, though one climbs its banks, there is no ford; though one dips from its stream, it is inexhaustible. It is so expansive that nothing can measure its size; it is so oceanic that nothing can compare with it in volume. Even "the hundred streams flowing into the Yellow River"[58] does not suffice to describe its rhetoric. Even "wading into the ocean and seeking its source" does not suffice to exhaust its immensity.
12. This being so, only one with deep wisdom and broad judgment can "lie hidden and leap"[59] along with it. Only one who transcends names and turns away from numbers[60] can be tranquilly impassive

along with it.[61] Only one who penetrates the abstruse and enters into the occult can be vacant and calm along with it.

VI. Kumārajīva's Feat of Translation

13. There is a high-throne śramaṇa named Kumārajīva. His talent is vast and his view is broad; his knowledge embraces a multitude of books.[62] He studies and adheres to this Treatise, and has carried it at his waist (revered it) for a very long time. Though his spirit-like understanding 'pervaded his inside,'[63] he had to wait for incitement (invitation) before responding. At that time, the lord of Ch'in, the prince Yao, revering and delighting in the Great Dharma, summoned an assembly of famous scholars to glorify the Three Jewels. His prestige (virtue) permeated the foreign peoples[64] and his cultural influence flowed into the Western Regions. This caused Kumārajīva to hear his reputation and come. When he reached 'Right of the Passes' (Ch'ang-an), then [Yao Hsing] induced him to translate it.
14. Because this Treatise is deep and vast and difficult to study minutely in a short time, and because it is easy to abbreviate in the Chinese language,[65] Kumārajīva abridged the original to a hundred chüan. An estimate of what was left out is that it was perhaps more than three times [what was translated]. Even so, literary gentlemen still considered it too verbose. All were troubled by its vastness, and few arrived at its true [meaning]. It is like a large [cauldron of] stew; if it is not well blended, even though it is tasty, it will not be prized.[66] If a magic pearl shines inwardly [but not outwardly], then though it is precious, it will not be used.[67] "Trustworthy words are not fine-seeming"[68] certainly has good grounds.
15. If, then, the true text is left hidden under ornamentation, and the metaphysical substance is spoiled by trivialities,[69] then the Hundred Schools[70] will strive in debate, and the Nine Currents[71] will swirl in discord. When they are about to be darkly engulfed in the long night, turning their backs on the sun and moon, they proceed in darkness. Is it not pitiful!

VII. The Abridgment

16. If in stillness [of thought] you seek for its foundations and discover its basis, then you will know that the Holy Man sets up instruction according to particular cases,[72] and that rhetoric and substance (content) have a different structure. If [people] respond to the substance according to the rhetoric, then those who doubt it will be many. If [people] respond to the rhetoric according to the substance, then those who enjoy it will be few. Therefore, the fashion that is practiced in India is plainness of style and subtlety of ideas, small range of language and great range of import.[73] If the ideas are

subtle, then being hidden and dark they have no figures.[74] If the import is great in range, then no one seeks for the occult clue. Thus it leads those who study common teachings to cling to commonplaces, and causes those who adhere to the "doctrine of names"[75] to be bewildered by the [hitherto] unheard of. If one opens a road of easy advance, then the series of stages has a foundation. If one understands the method of gradual awakening, then there is a ford for those who begin to cross.

17. In this [Treatise, I], Hui-yüan, have abridged the verbose and corrected the faulty, thus clarifying the content. I have caused rhetoric and substance to have a formal correspondence, and have made it so that nowhere do the ideas overpass [what is fitting].[76] Thereupon, I set up the original on the basis of the Sūtra [i.e., the *Mahā-prajñā-pāramitā*], and connected it with 'Objection' and 'Author.' I rectified its positions and parts, so that each topic possesses continuity. Together with the monks who live with me, I have carefully and specially composed a collection of the essentials, which is twenty chüan altogether. Though it is not good enough to add to the lustre of the Holy Texts, I hope that there are no great errors in it. If it is imperfect,[77] I beg you to await a future wise man.[78]

Document 5

PREFACE TO THE MIDDLE TREATISE, BY SENG-JUI

Texts: T XXX, 1a–b (at beginning of *Middle Treatise*).
T LV, 76c–77a (CST, chüan 11, No. 1).
Commentary: Chi-tsang, *Chung-lun-shu*, T XLII, 1a–5b.
Japanese translations: Hatani Ryōtai, *Kokuyaku Issaikyō*, Kukanbu I, 55–56.
Hayashiya Tomojirō, *Kokuyaku Issaikyō*, Shidenbu I, 294.

1. In the *Middle Treatise* there are five hundred verses, composed by the bodhisattva Nāgārjuna. It is named 'Middle' to proclaim its actual (object). It is entitled 'Treatise' to complete the wording. The actual is not understood except through names; therefore they designate it 'Middle' in order to declare it. The wording is not completed except through explanations; therefore they adopt 'Treatise' to make it clear. When the actual is declared and the wording is clear, then in the bodhisattva's course the intuition of the bodhimaṇḍa shines brilliantly, and "the suspension-cords are untied."[1]

2. Craving and delusion[2] arise from misconceptions, and by them the three domains are submerged. One-sided understanding[3] springs from knowledge [characterized] by aversion,[4] and through it their resolve[5] errs from the goal.[6] Thus we know that great bodhi resides in vast intuition,[7] and small knowledge is bound by the constricted mind. If the intuition is not vast, then it does not suffice to raze the existent and the inexistent, to unify the religious and the profane.[8] If knowledge is not consummate, then with it one cannot traverse the Middle Path and obliterate the two limits.[9] That the religious and the profane are not unified and that the two limits are not obliterated is what grieves the bodhisattva.[10] Therefore the great man *(mahāsattva)* Nāgārjuna equalized them with the Middle Path,[11] enabling students who have erred from the goal (meaning)[12] to look at the metaphysical pointer[13] and totally change. He encompassed them with [the principle of] identity with transformations,[14] and caused the clients of metaphysical understanding to lose their plans and deliberations in the morning's clear rays.[15]

3. How vast it is![16] It may truly be said to put in order and make level the road to (along) the "hollow stairs"[17] and to open out the metaphysical gate[18] within the cosmos, to fan the wind of prajñā[19] among the dry twigs, and pour the sweet dew *(amṛta)* on the withered and downcast. When the hundred-beamed (cedar-beamed) mansion arises, it makes the tumble-down thatched cottage seem mean.[20] When you behold how grand this treatise is, then you know how inferior one-sided understanding is. How fortunate it is that this land of China has suddenly had Mount Gṛdhrakūṭa moved to it to be its chief mountain,[21] and that biased minds in outlying areas[22] receive the flowing light of its surplus of kindness.[23] From now on, for the first time[24] the worthies who discuss the Tao can converse about the reality, (the actual).[25]

4. It is said that in all the states of India there are none who venture to engage in studies who do not pore over this treatise and take it for their canon.[26] Very many of them have moistened their quills and written commentaries.[27] The one that we are now issuing[28] is the commentary by the Indian brahman named Pin-chia-lo, in the Ch'in language, 'Blue Eyes.'[29] Though he believed and understood the profound Dharma, his language is not elegant and apposite. The Dharma-master [Kumārajīva] edited and emended all the errors, deficiencies and redundancies in it, interpreting it according to the *Stanzas*, so that the principles are definitive,[30] though in some places the language is not entirely excellent.

5. The *Hundred Treatise* disciplines outsiders (Tīrthikas) and shuts out falsehoods. This text frees insiders (Buddhists) and dissolves their obstructions.[31] The *Great Perfection of Wisdom Treatise* is profound and vast. The *Twelve Topics* is concise and to the point.[32] When you examine these four, it is indeed as if the sun and moon entered your bosom. There is nothing that is not mirrored forth clearly.

6. I have handled [this book] and have pored over it and have not been able to let it out of my hand. So, forgetting my lowness and ineptness, I have expressed my insights and feelings in a preface, and have put a table of contents at the beginning. But how can I hope to explain it! It is merely to express delight at my own sentiment of agreement.

Document 6

PREFACE TO THE TWELVE TOPIC TREATISE, BY SENG-JUI

Texts: T XXX, 159b (at beginning of the *Twelve Topics*).
T LV, 77c–78a (CST, chüan 11, No. 4).
Commentary: Chi-tsang, *Shih-erh-men-shu*, T XLII, 171a–74b.
Japanese translations: Hatani Ryōtai, *Kokuyaku Issaikyō*, Kūkanbu I, 341–42.
Hayashiya Tomojirō, *Kokuyaku Issaikyō*, Shidenbu I, 297.

1. The *Twelve Topic Treatise* is the refutative Middle [that conforms to reality,[1] and the essential track to the bodhimaṇḍa.[2] 'Twelve' is the great number that comprises the many branches. 'Gates' (Topics) is the term for opening up, clearing the way, and having no obstructions. The intention in writing a treatise on them is to probe their source thoroughly and work their principle out completely. If the one principle is not completely worked out, then the many differences run riot,[3] and there are deviations that err from the goal.[4] If the one source is not thoroughly probed, then the many paths proliferate, and there are the pathways of heterodox ideas.
2. That heterodox ideas are not razed to the ground and that deviations from the goal are not obliterated is what grieves the great man *(mahāsattva)*. Therefore Nāgārjuna Bodhisattva opened up a road for those who wish an exit,[5] and wrote the *Twelve Topics* to set them right. When they are set right with the *Twelve*, then the existent and inexistent are both made clear, and no matter is not consummated.[6] When matters are consummated in the existent and the inexistent, then the work of a Creator-of-transformations is denied.[7] If principles culminate in the empty position,[8] then the self is lost with the two extremes.[9] So then, losing the self[10] lies in discarding the fishtrap.[11] Forgetting the trap consists in relinquishing supports.[12] Only when fishtrap and self are both forgotten can you approach reality.[13] When you approach reality, then empty and real are both merged,[14] and success and failure have no boundary [between them]. When they are merged and unbounded, then you can forget hazards[15]

in the doubly metaphysical,[16] drown calamities in the one destination, return your carriage evenly to the bodhimaṇḍa, and finally cause your mind to arrive at the Buddha-stage.

3. How spacious it is! Truly it may be termed 'turning the blade of emptiness around in the [place of] no interstice,'[18] 'playing the inaudible music throughout the cosmos,'[19] 'ferrying the lifelong exiles across the metaphysical ford,'[20] and 'going forth from existent and inexistent to beyond the [worldly] domain.'[21]

4. How fortunate are the students of later times! The level road is already made plain, and the dark pass[22] is already opened. Truly we can shake the carriage-bells[23] by the Northern Ocean[24] and gallop the white ox[25] on the return to the South, rouse the great awakening in the realm of dreams,[26] and arrive home in peace through identifying with the hundred transformations.[27]

5. In this case, how do we know that the radiant numen [the sun] is about to shine forth, though the dark land is not illuminated?[28] I, Seng-jui, with my lowly, shallow wit, still venture to make clear and certain the empty pass,[29] cherish longing towards the Ultimate Ideal, hope that there may be benefit in the use of days, and look for what brings welfare in the reckoning of years. How much more so might someone of fine talent! Being overcome by the utmost reverence,[30] I venture with my dull style and small thoughts to write a preface and introduce [this work]. I have added a table of chapters and contents at the front. How can it be of benefit? I only hope with these thoughts to open up the road of personal progress.

DOCUMENT 7

PREFACE TO THE HUNDRED TREATISE, BY SENG-CHAO[1]

Texts: T XXX, 167c–68a (at beginning of the *Hundred Treatise*).
T LV, 77b–c (CST, chüan 11, No. 3).
Commentary: Chi-tsang, *Pai-lun-shu*, T XLII, 232a–38a.
Japanese translations: Hatani Ryōtai, *Kokuyaku Issaikyō*, Kūkanbu I, 251–52.
Hayashiya Tomojirō, *Kokuyaku Issaikyō*, Shidenbu I, 290.

1. The *Hundred Treatise* is the ford and road that provide access to the Holy Mind,[2] the essential treatise that opens up the absolute truth.[3] Eight hundred and more years after the Buddha's nirvāṇa there was a bodhisattva monk named Deva.[4] His metaphysical mind was uniquely enlightened,[5] and his genius was outstanding. His Way illumined his time and his spirit rose to the supra-mundane.[6] Thus he was able to unlock the double bars from the Tripiṭaka and level the abstruse road of the twelve [sections of the scriptures].[7] He strode alone through Kapilavastu,[8] and became a moat to the City of the Dharma.[9]
2. At that time, the Tīrthikas ran riot, heterodoxies arose in conflict, and false debates imperilled the truth, so that the Right Way was nearly lost in confusion. Then, looking up he lamented the decline of the Holy Teaching, and looking down he grieved that the strayed multitude were given over to delusion. With the intention of rescuing far and wide those who were drowning,[10] he composed this treatise. The reason why it buttresses the right and checks the false is because it makes the Ultimate Ideal thoroughly clear. Thus the right persuasion is exalted by it, and the wrong ways are replaced by it. Who but one endowed with all sublime qualities could do such a thing?[11]
3. In the treatise there are a hundred verses, so it is called the *Hundred*. Its principles and meaning are profound and metaphysical. It comprises the essentials of many books. Rhetoric and import[12] being pleasant and concise, it is superlative among fine compositions. However, its final meaning (goal) being abstruse and tersely [expressed

few gained the gateway to it.[13] The bodhisattva Vasu,[14] wisdom and insight ripe within him, surpassing in sublime thought, from afar matched with the metaphysical footprints, and wrote an expository commentary for it. He made manifest the hidden meaning with his fine pen. His style was very popular, and so has been passed on to future generations. His rhetoric is brilliant, and that path to the Ideal is easy to discern.

4. The character of this discourse is that though it speaks it has no matching (object-counterpart) and though it refutes it grasps nothing [else].[15] Though utterly without support,[16] in [touching] affairs it does not lose the absolute [truth]. Though it is totally without point d'appui, the principles of themselves meet metaphysically. The Way of returning to the origin is revealed in this.[17]

5. There is an Indian śramaṇa, Kumārajīva, whose talent is deep and broad, whose superb spirit far surpasses [the ordinary]. Though I have studied under him for several years, still I cannot fathom him completely.[18] He always pores over and recites this treatise, and considers it the mind's essential.[19] Though he himself had translated it before, the technical terms were not well worked out,[20] so that those who sought the thought stumbled in the faulty text, and those who elicited its theses went astray from the central concepts.

6. Yao Sung, *ssŭ-li-hsiao-wei* of Great Ch'in and Marquis of An-ch'eng, is of a pure and leisurely disposition, and his 'empty mind'[21] is both straightforward and excellent. He is widely learned in both the Buddhist and the secular fields. In principles and thoughts he is universally penetrating. When young, he loved the Great Way, and as he grew up, he became even more devout. Though his body has been encumbered with temporal duties, he has continued to discuss the Dharma. Whenever he handled this text, there were very many things that grieved him. In the sixth year of *Hung-shih*, under the asterism *Shou-hsing*, he gathered the śramaṇas who relish principles, and together with Kumārajīva they edited a correct text and revised it, and then polished up the second version. They strove to preserve the sense of the treatise so that it would be "substantial but not rustic, brief but to the point."[22] The meaning of the theses is fully expressed, and there are no gaps in it.[23]

7. The Treatise consists of twenty chapters altogether, each with five verses.[24] Because [Kumārajīva] did not think that the last ten chapters were of any use to this country, he omitted and did not transmit them. I hope that gentlemen with brilliant minds will examine this [work] in detail.

DOCUMENT 8

PRAJÑĀ HAS NO KNOWING (Chao-lun, Part III), BY SENG-CHAO

Text: T XLV, 153a–54c.
Japanese translation: *Jōron Kenkyū*, pp. 22–36.
Previous English translation: Liebenthal, *Chao*, pp. 67–85.

I.1 Announcing the Theme (p. 153a8)

Prajñā, void and metaphysical, is the Ultimate Ideal of the Three Vehicles. It is indeed the Absolute One without a second *(advaya)*, without difference; yet debates on aberrant doctrines[1] have run riot for a very long time.

I.2 The Dharma-master Kumārajīva (p. 153a9)

There is an Indian śramaṇa, Kumārajīva. In his youth he walked the Great Square[2] and studied the subtleties[3] of this subject.[4] He stood alone beyond words and symbols,[5] and fitted [his mind] sublimely to the sphere of the invisible and the inaudible.[6] He confuted the heterodoxies in Kapilavastu,[7] and raised the pure wind in the fans of the East.[8] When he was about to illuminate the various regions, his light was hidden in the land of Liang.[9] This is because the Way does not respond aimlessly; there is certain to be a reason for its response.[10] In *Hung-shih* 3 (A.D. 401) the year of the cyclical sign *Hsing-chi*,[11] Ch'in, taking advantage of [Liang's] plan to enter the country,[12] mustered an army to bring him [to Ch'ang-an]. I think that the destiny of the North[13] has come true.[14]

I.3 Encomium of Yao Hsing, the King of Ch'in (p. 153a15)

The Celestial King of Great Ch'in,[15] whose policies accord with the principles of the hundred kings [of the past] and whose influence will imbue a thousand generations to come, effortlessly dispatches his myriad details [of state affairs][16] and all the day propagates the Way (Dharma). Truly, he is like Heaven to beings in the Third Period, and like a staff to the Dharma bequeathed by Śākyamuni.[17] At this time, he gathered more than five hundred śramaṇas who were doctrine-students together in the Hsiao-yao Pavilion.[18] He in person held the Ch'in text,[19] and together with Kumārajīva compared and determined [the wording of] the Vaipulya Sūtra.[20] What he pioneered is not only a benefit to the present day, but a ford and bridge for many kalpas to come.

I.4 The Purpose of the Essay (p. 153a20)

I, though a mere tyro and dull-witted, participated in the august assembly, and thus finally heard the strange and important [doctrine]. However, Holy Knowledge is abstruse and subtle, deeply concealed and hard to fathom. Being markless and nameless, it is not something that words and symbols can convey. I will merely attempt to [express] my sentiments [like] Thoughtless,[21] and apply crazy words to it.[22] I surely do not mean that the Holy Mind can be analysed! But I will attempt to discuss it.

II.1 Main Announcement of Theme (p. 153a24)

The *Fang-kuang* says,[23] "In Prajñā there are no marks at all; there are no marks of arising and ceasing." The *Tao-hsing* says,[24] "In Prajñā there is nothing that is known, and nothing that is seen." 1 ⌜This specifies [holy] knowledge's function of intuition, but why do we say that it has no marks and has no knowing?⌝ 2 ⌜It is evident that there is a markless knowing and an unknowing intuition.⌝

II.2 Explanation (p. 153a27)

For what reason?

3 ⌜If there is something that is known, then there is something that is not known.⌝ 4 ⌜Because in the holy mind there is nothing that is known, there is nothing that is not known.⌝[25] 5 ⌜The knowing of unknowing is termed all-knowing *(sarvajñatā)*.⌝ Thus the Sūtra[26] is to be believed when it says, "In the Holy Mind, there is nothing that is known and nothing that is not known."

6 ⌜Therefore the holy man empties his mind and fills (makes real) his intuition.⌝[27] Though he always knows, he never knows. Thus he can muffle his brilliance and sheathe his light.[28] 7 ⌜His empty mind mirrors the metaphysical.⌝ Shutting up his Knowledge and blocking his hearing, all alone he perceives the inscrutable.[29]

II. 3 Synthesis (p. 153b2)

Consequently, 8 ⌜In [Holy] Knowledge there is a mirroring that probes the abstruse, yet there is no knowing in it.⌝ 9 ⌜In the Spirit there is the functioning of responding to occasions,[30] yet there is no deliberation in it.⌝ 10 ⌜Because there is no deliberation in the Spirit, it is able to reign alone beyond the world.⌝ 11 ⌜Because there is no knowing in Knowledge, it is able to intuit metaphysically outside of events.⌝ 12 ⌜Knowledge, though outside of events, is never devoid of events.⌝ 13 ⌜Spirit, though beyond the world, is always within the world.⌝ Therefore, looking down [to Earth] and looking up [to Heaven],[31] he adapts himself to the transformations. 14 ⌜His intercourse [with living beings] is illimitable.⌝[32] 15 ⌜There is nothing abstruse that he does not discern, yet he has no process (results) of intuition.[33] This is what no-knowing knows, and what the Holy Spirit meets.⌝[34]

II. 4 Explaining the Essence (p. 153b8)

So then, as for its character:
16 ⌜Though real, it is not existent; though empty, it is not inexistent.⌝
17 ⌜It is only Holy Knowledge that, though it has being, cannot be discussed.⌝[35]

For what reason?
18 ⌜If you wish to say that it exists, it is formless and nameless.⌝[36]
19 ⌜If you wish to say that it inexists, the Holy One is numinal because of it.⌝[37] 20 ⌜The Holy One is numinal because of it, so though empty it does not fail to intuit.⌝ 21 ⌜It is formless and nameless, so though it intuits it does not fail to be empty.⌝ Though it intuits it does not fail to be empty, so it is manifold [together with the myriad things] but does not change.[38] Though empty it does not fail to intuit, so it moves to contact concrete things.[39]

Therefore, the function of Holy Knowledge never ceases even for a moment, yet if you seek it in shapes and marks, you can never perceive it even for a moment.

Therefore Ratnakūṭa says,[40] "Without mind or intention, you display activities." The *Fang-kuang* says,[41] "Without moving from Perfect Enlightenment, [the Tathāgata] establishes all the dharmas."

For this reason, 22 ⌜though the Holy One's footprints are multiform, their destination is the one.⌝[42]

II. 5 General Conclusion (p. 153b15)

Therefore, 23 ⌜Prajñā, though empty, can still intuit,⌝ 24 ⌜the Absolute Truth, though inexistent, can still be known.⌝[43] 25 ⌜The myriad moving things can be still while identical [with movement].⌝[44] 26 ⌜The Holy Response can act, though inexistent.⌝ This is[45] being unknowing yet knowing spontaneously, and being unacting yet acting spontaneously.[46] What more can one know? What more can one do?[47]

III. Questions and Replies.

First Question: Concerning the Agent and the Affectee.

OBJECTION: The Absolute Mind of the Holy Man, shining in solitude, intuits each and every thing; his intercourse [with things] being limitless,[48] his movements meet events. Because he intuits each and every thing, there is nothing that his knowing omits. Because his movements meet events, his meeting does not miss the crucial instant.
27 ⌈Because his meeting does not miss the crucial instant, meeting of the meetable certainly exists.⌉ Because there is nothing that his knowing omits, knowing of the knowable certainly exists. Because knowing of the knowable certainly exists, it is not in vain for the Holy One to know. Because meeting of the meetable certainly exists, it is not in vain for the Holy One to meet. Since he knows and since he meets, why do you say that he has no knowing and no meeting?

If [you mean] something like that he forgets his knowing and disregards his meeting, then [the point] is that there is no self-interest in the Holy Man's knowing and meeting, and thus he succeeds in his self-interest.[49] This could mean that he does not personally possess his knowing, but how can it be that he has no knowing?
REPLY: The Holy Man's good works are as mighty as Heaven and Earth, yet he is not humane.[50] His brightness surpasses the sun and moon, yet it is all the darker for that. How could I say that he is insentient like wood and stone, that he is merely without knowing.
28 ⌈In fact, it is simply that the difference between [the Holy Man] and human beings is his spirit-intelligence,⌉[51] and so it cannot be found through the marks of events (events and marks).[52]

You propose that the Holy Man does not personally possess his knowing and yet the Holy Man never does not possess knowing.
29 ⌈But are you not misunderstanding the Holy Mind and missing the meaning of the sūtras' text?⌉

For what reason?
30 ⌈A sūtra says,[53] "Absolute Prajñā is as pure as space, without knowing, without seeing, without arising, and without objects *(ālambana)*."⌉[54]
31 ⌈Thus knowing is in itself without knowing, and does not depend on 'reversal of intuition'[55] in order to become without knowing.⌉
32 ⌈If it has knowing and you call it pure because its nature is empty, then it is not distinguished from deluded knowledge.⌉[56] The Three Poisons[57] and the Four Misconceptions[58] are all pure, too. Why honor Prajñā alone? When you extol Prajñā because of what is known, what is known is not Prajñā.[59] What is known is in itself pure, and so Prajñā is never pure. Thus there is no reason to praise the purity of

Prajñā.[60] 33 ⌜So, when the sūtra says that Prajñā is pure, it means that[61] the essential nature ***(svabhāva)*** of Prajñā is absolutely pure, fundamentally devoid of knowing that apprehends deludedly.⌝ 34 ⌜As it is fundamentally devoid of knowing that apprehends deludedly, it cannot be called 'knowing'.⌝ 35 ⌜Not only is no-knowing called no-knowing, but knowing in itself is no-knowing.⌝
36 ⌜Therefore the holy man with knowingless prajñā intuits the markless absolute truth.⌝ In the Absolute Truth, there is no "falling short [like] the hare and the horse."[62] 37 ⌜There is nothing that the mirror of Prajñā does not search to the utmost. For this reason, when it meets [crucial instants], it does not miss anything; when it matches [the absolute truth], it does not affirm anything.[63] Calm and in repose, it has no knowing, yet there is nothing that it does not know.⌝

Second Question: Concerning Names and Essences

OBJECTION: 38 ⌜Because things have no means of signifying themselves, we establish names to signify things.⌝[64] 39 ⌜Though the thing is not the name, there really are nameable things and they match these names.⌝ Therefore if one has found[65] the name and seeks the thing, the thing cannot hide. But you say that there is no knowing in the Holy Mind, and also that there is nothing that it does not know.
40 ⌜In my opinion, no-knowing is never knowing, and knowing is never no-knowing. This is something that is generally accepted by the 'doctrine of names,' and is[66] the basic principle in using language (framing statements).⌝[67] 41 ⌜However, you wish [knowing and no-knowing] to be one in the Holy Mind, and different in the meaning of the words. When I examine the [two] words and seek out their [two] significances,[68] I do not see that they tally.⌝[69] Why is this? If 'knowing' is applicable to the Holy Mind, then in it there is nothing to be qualified by 'no-knowing.' If 'no-knowing' is applicable to the Holy Mind, then in it there is likewise nothing to be qualified by 'no-knowing.' If both are inapplicable, then there is nothing more to discuss.
REPLY: 42 A sūtra says,[70] ⌜"The meaning of Prajñā is 'nameless, indescribable, not existent, not real, and not empty.'"⌝ 43 ⌜Though empty, it does not fail to intuit; though it intuits, it does not fail to be empty.⌝[71] It is a nameless dharma, so it is not something that language can express. 44 ⌜Yet, though language cannot express it, nothing other than language can communicate it.⌝ Therefore the Holy Man "always speaks and never speaks."[72] Now I will attempt with crazy words to explain it for you.[73] 45 ⌜The Holy Mind, being ethereal and markless, cannot be considered existent; being extremely vigorous in its functioning, it cannot be considered inexistent.⌝[74] 46 ⌜Because it cannot be considered inexistent, Holy Knowledge has being in it.

Because it cannot be considered existent, the 'doctrine of names' does not concern it at all.⌉

Therefore, 47 ⌈When we call it 'knowing,' it is not that we consider it to be 'knowing,' but that we wish by this to explain its mirroring.[75] 'Not-knowing' is not 'not-knowing,' but we wish by this to specify its marks.⌉ As we specify its marks, we do not consider it inexistent; as we explain its mirroring, we do not consider it existent. 48 ⌈Because it is not existent, while knowing it has no knowing; because it is not inexistent, while having no knowing it knows.⌉

Therefore, 49 ⌈knowing is identical with no-knowing, and no-knowing is identical with knowing.⌉ 50 ⌈You should not[76] impute differences to the Holy Mind because the words ['knowing' and 'no-knowing'] are different.⌉[77]

Third Question: Concerning the Sense-spheres and Knowledge (Part I)

OBJECTION: The Absolute Truth, being profound and metaphysical, is not fathomed except through knowledge. The power of Holy Knowledge is manifest in this respect.[78] Therefore a sūtra says,[79] "If you do not obtain Prajñā, you will not see the Absolute Truth." So the Absolute Truth is the object *(ālambana)* of Prajñā. When you seek for Knowledge because of [the existence of][80] its object, [you see that] Knowledge is knowing.

REPLY: When you seek for Knowledge because of [the existence of] its object, [you see that] Knowledge is not knowing. For what reason?

The *Fang-kuang* says,[81] "Not producing consciousness with form as its object is called not seeing form." It also says,[82] "Because the five skandhas are pure, Prajñā is pure." 52 ⌈'Prajñā' is the knower and the 'five skandhas' are the known. 'The known' is the object *(ālambana)*.⌉[83] 53 ⌈The knowing and the known exist conjointly and inexist conjointly.[84] Because they inexist conjointly, no thing is existent. Because they exist conjointly, no thing is inexistent. Because no thing is inexistent, [knowing] is aroused by its object.[85] Because no thing is existent, [knowledge] is not something that objects can arouse.[86] Because [knowledge] is not something that objects can arouse, though it intuits its object[87] it is not a knowing. Because [knowing] is aroused by its object, knowing and its object arise in mutual dependence.⌉[88] 54 ⌈Therefore knowing and no-knowing arise from the known.⌉ For what reason? 55 ⌈Knowledge is called knowing because in knowing the known it grasps marks.⌉[89] 56 ⌈Absolute Truth in itself being markless, how would Absolute Knowledge know?⌉

As for the reason why it is so: 57 ⌈A known is not a known.[90] The known arises from the knowing. The known has already produced the knowing, and the knowing also produces the known.⌝ 58 ⌜The knowns have arisen conjointly [with the knowings].[91] Those that have arisen conjointly are dependent entities. Because they are dependent entities, they are not absolute. Because they are not absolute, they are not the Absolute Truth.⌝

Therefore the *Middle Treatise* says,[92] "Because things exist through causes and conditions, they are not absolute; because they do not exist through causes and conditions, they are identical with the Absolute." Now, Absolute Truth is called absolute. But if it is absolute, it is not dependent (an object).[93] Because the Absolute is not dependent, no thing arises from conditions.

Thus a Scripture says,[94] "One does not see an existent dharma that arises without conditions." Therefore, 59 ⌜Absolute Knowledge contemplates Absolute Truth and never grasps a known.⌝ 60 ⌜When Knowledge does not grasp a known, how is the Knowledge a knowing?⌝

Consequently, 61 ⌜Knowledge is not no-knowing, but Absolute Truth is not a known, and therefore Absolute Knowledge is likewise not a knowing.⌝ Yet you wanted to seek for Knowledge because of [the existence of] its object and so to think that Knowledge is a knowing. Its object being intrinsically not an object, where are you going to find a knowing?

Question Four: Concerning the Sense-spheres and Knowledge (Part II)

OBJECTION: When you say "It does not grasp," do you mean that because it is knowingless it does not grasp, or that after it has known it does not grasp? If because it is knowingless it does not grasp, then is the Holy Man as blind as a traveller in the night who cannot tell black from white? If after it has known it does not grasp, then its knowing is different from its not grasping.

REPLY: I deny that because it is knowingless it does not grasp, and I also deny that after it has known it does not grasp. 62 ⌜Its knowing is identical with its not grasping, and so while it is not grasping it is knowing.⌝

Question Five: Concerning the Sense-spheres and Knowledge (Part III)

OBJECTION: Your proposition that 'It does not grasp' is really that because the Holy Mind does not impute thingness to things, there is no deluded grasping in it.[95] When there is no grasping, there is no affirming.[96] When there is no affirming, there is no matching.[97] Who, matching the Holy Mind, says that in the Holy Mind there is nothing that is not known?

REPLY: It is so. But, as for 'There is no affirming and no matching:'

63 as ⌜[in the Holy Mind] there is no matching, there is no thing that it does not match.[98] As there is no affirming, there is no thing that it does not affirm. Because there is no thing that it does not affirm, while affirming it has no affirming. Because there is no thing that it does not match, while matching it has no matching.⌝[99]

Therefore a Sūtra says,[100] "[The Bodhisattva] sees the dharmas in their entirety, yet there is nothing that is seen."

Question Six: Concerning the Sense-spheres and Knowledge (Part IV)

OBJECTION: It is not that the Holy Mind is unable to affirm. Actually, he can affirm by affirming nothing. Though there is nothing to affirm that can be affirmed, he certainly must[101] affirm that there is nothing to affirm.[102] Therefore, the saying in the Sūtra[103] "Because the Absolute Truth is markless, Prajñā is knowingless," really means that in Prajñā there is no possessing of markful knowing (knowing of the marks of the existent).[104] If it takes the markless (nothingness) to be markless (nothingness), what trouble is there about Absolute Truth?[105]
REPLY: 64 ⌜For the Holy Man, the markless is inexistent.⌝ For what reason? 65 ⌜If he considered the markless to be markless, then being markless would become a mark.⌝ To forsake the existent and go to the inexistent is like shunning the peaks and walking into a canyon. In either case one does not escape trouble. Therefore, 66 ⌜the Perfect Man while dwelling in the existent does not consider it existent, and while residing in the inexistent does not consider it inexistent.[106] Though he does not grasp the existent and the inexistent, neither does he forsake the existent and the inexistent.⌝ For this reason, he blends his brilliance into "the dust and grief"[107] and circulates throughout the Five Destinies *(gatis)*. Though at rest, he goes; though in repose, he comes.[108] 67 ⌜Though serenely without action *(wu-wei)* there is nothing that he does not do.⌝[109]

Question Seven: Concerning Arising and Ceasing (Part I)

OBJECTION: Though the Holy Mind is knowingless, in its course of responding and meeting (responding to occasions) it does not err. Therefore, it responds to what should be responded to, and leaves alone what should not be responded to. Consequently, the Holy Mind sometimes arises and sometimes ceases. Can it be so?
REPLY: 68 ⌜'Arising and ceasing' is arising and ceasing thoughts *(citta)*.⌝[110] 69 ⌜As the Holy Man has no thoughts, how can their arising and ceasing occur?[111] Or rather, it is not that he has no thoughts, but simply that he has no considering thoughts to be thoughts.⌝
70 ⌜Also, it is not that he does not respond, but simply that he does not consider response to be response.⌝ 71 ⌜Therefore, the course of

the Holy Man's responding to occasions is as dependable as the four seasons. But as he has void-nothing as his essence, he cannot arise and cannot cease.⌝[112]

Question Eight: Concerning Arising and Ceasing (Part II)

OBJECTION: 72 ⌜The 'none' of Holy Knowledge and the 'none' of deluded knowledge are both 'no arising and ceasing.'⌝[113] What is the difference between them?

REPLY: 73 ⌜The 'none' of Holy Knowledge is 'no-knowing';⌝ 74 ⌜the 'none' of deluded knowledge is 'knowing a nothing.'⌝ Though that they 'have none' is the same, what they 'have none' of is different. For what reason?

75 ⌜The Holy Mind, being void and still, has no knowing that can be considered a nothing. It can be called 'no-knowing,' but cannot be said to 'know a nothing.'⌝ 76 ⌜Deluded knowledge, because it has knowing, has a knowing that can be considered a nothing. It can be called 'knowing a nothing,' but cannot be called 'no-knowing.'⌝

77 ⌜'No-knowing' is the 'none' of Prajñā; 'knowing a nothing' is the 'none' of Absolute Truth.⌝[114]

78 ⌜Therefore, as for Prajñā and Absolute Truth: If you speak about their function, then while being the same they are different. If you speak about their state, then while being different they are the same. Because they are the same, there are no thoughts of self and other. Because they are different, they do not fail in the process (results) of intuition.[115] Therefore, if you specify sameness, it is sameness in difference; if you specify difference, it is difference in sameness. Thus they cannot be considered as different, and they cannot be considered as the same.⌝

For what reason?

79 ⌜Inside, there is the solitary mirror's brightness; outside, there is the reality of the myriad dharmas.[116] 80 Though the myriad dharmas are realities, they are not perceived except through intuition.⌝[117]

81 ⌜Inside and outside co-operate to achieve the process (results) of intuition. These are the functions that the Holy One cannot make the same.⌝ 82 ⌜The inside, though it intuits, has no knowing; the outside, though it is real, has no marks.⌝ 83 ⌜Inside and outside, being in stillness, are conjointly inexistent. This is the stillness that the Holy One cannot make different.⌝

Therefore, when a Sūtra says,[118] "The dharmas are not different," how can it mean that one must stretch the duck's [legs] and shorten the crane's,[119] level the peaks and fill up the valleys, before there are no differences? 84 It really means that because one does not consider difference as difference (differentiate differences), though different they are not different.

Therefore, a Sūtra says,[120] "It is extremely strange, World-Honored

One! Amid the non-different dharmas, you declare that the dharmas are different." It also says,[121] "Prajñā and the dharmas are not a unity and not a plurality." This is true.

Question Nine: Concerning Arising and Ceasing (Part III)

OBJECTION: You say "In function they are different, and in stillness they are the same." It is not clear whether within Prajñā there is a differentiation between function and stillness.
REPLY: 85 ⌜Function is identical with stillness; stillness is identical with function. Function and stillness are one in essence. "They issue from the same [source], but they are named differently."[122] There certainly is no functionless stillness that rules the function.⌝

Therefore, 86 ⌜the darker the Knowledge, the brighter the intuition; the stiller the spirit, the more active the response.⌝ How can you say that the brightness and darkness, the activity and stillness, are different?

Therefore, the *Ch'eng-chü* says,[123] "[The Buddha], while he does not act, surpasses action." Ratnakūṭa says,[124] also, "[The Buddha] has no thoughts and no consciousness, but there is nothing that he does not cognize." These are pronouncements about the utmost Spirit and the consummate Knowledge, about the Ultimate that lies beyond symbols. If you apply them to this explanatory essay, then the Holy Mind can be known.[125]

Document 9

EMPTINESS OF THE NON-ABSOLUTE (Chao-lun, Part II), BY SENG-CHAO

Text: T XLV, 152a–53a.
Japanese translation: *Jōron Kenkyū*, pp. 14–22.
Previous English translation: Liebenthal, *Chao*, pp. 56–66.

I. 1 Introduction

The utterly void and birthless is the sublime goal (object) of Prajñā's metaphysical mirroring, and the Ultimate Ideal of existing things. Unless one has the special penetration of Holy Intelligence, how can one fit one's spirit to the interstice between the existent and the inexistent?[1]

Therefore, the Perfect Man makes his spirit and mind penetrate the limitless and cannot be impeded by limits, pushes to the utmost the sight and hearing of eye and ear and cannot be constrained by sounds and forms—because he identifies with the self-voidness of the myriad things. Thus things cannot hinder his spirit-intelligence.

Therefore, when the Holy Man, mounted on Absolute Mind, conforms to the principles, there is no obstacle that he does not pass through. Because he discerns the One Energy[2] and so views the transformations, he accords with what he meets. Because there is no obstacle that he does not pass through, he can merge into the multiplicity and reach simplicity.

Because he accords with what he meets, in touching things he is one [with them].

1 ⌜So, though the myriad forms are different, they cannot make themselves different. Thus we know that the forms are not absolute forms.⌝

2 ⌜Because the forms are not absolute forms, though forms they are not forms.⌝

So, things and myself have the same root; affirming and denying are the One Energy.[3] The hidden, subtle, abstruse, and secret is hardly something that common minds can know exhaustively.

I.2 Refuting Aberrant Views

Thus in recent discussions there are always disagreements about the topic of emptiness. When people approach agreement through disagreement, what thing can be agreed upon?[4] Thus, while the many disputants wrangle back and forth, none agree about the nature [of Reality].[5]

What are these [different views]?

1. 'Mentally Inexistent'[6]—"one has no mentation towards the myriad things, but the myriad things are never inexistent."

Where this is right is on stillness of spirit.

Where it misses the point is on the voidness of things.[7]

2. 'Identical with Form'[8]—states that because form does not make itself form, though called form it is not form.

Now, the word 'form' simply refers to (corresponds to) form qua form. To be form, it need not wait until form makes itself form.

This [school] only says that form does not make itself form, but does not understand that form is not-form.[9]

3. 'Primordial Inexistence'[10]—Many who feel partial to inexistence are dominated by inexistence in everything they say. Thus, 'not existent' [they take to mean] 'the existent is inexistent' and 'not inexistent' [they take to mean] 'the inexistent is also inexistent.'[11]

3. Now, the original sense of these texts is simply that 'not existent' means 'not absolutely existent' and 'not inexistent' means 'not absolutely inexistent.' Why must 'not existent' make this existent inexistent, and 'not inexistent' make that inexistent inexistent? This is nothing but inexistence-loving talk. Does it describe the temper of mind that accords with events, penetrates the actuals, and identifies with things?

I.3 Explaining the Point of the Essay

4 ⌜If with 'things' you call things 'things,' then what you call things may be called things.⌝[12]

5 ⌜If with 'things' you call non-things 'things,' then though you call them things, they are non-things.⌝

Therefore, 6 ⌜things, not being identical with names, do not arrive at their actuals (counterparts).⌝ 7 ⌜Names, not being things, do not go to the absolute.⌝[13]

8 ⌜So, Absolute Truth is lone and still, outside the [sphere of the] 'doctrine of names.'⌝ We cannot say that it is something that language can distinguish, but we cannot remain speechless, so I will just put down words to give some idea of it. Here is my attempt to discuss it.

II.1 Quoting the Teaching to Explain Emptiness

The *Mahāyāna-śāstra*[14] says, "The dharmas have neither the mark of existence nor the mark of inexistence."
9 ⌜The *Middle Treatise*[15] says, "The dharmas are not existent and not inexistent." This is the supreme, Absolute Truth.⌝ 10 ⌜But it does not mean that one must wash out the myriad things,[16] stop up sight and hearing and be soundless and formless like an empty valley[17] before one realizes absolute truth.⌝ 11 ⌜In fact, it is because one identifies with things, conforms and passes through, that no thing obstructs.⌝
12 ⌜Because one realizes the identity of the counterfeit and the absolute, no nature changes.⌝ 13 ⌜Because no nature changes, though inexistent [the dharmas] exist.⌝ 14 ⌜Because no thing obstructs, though existent they inexist.⌝ 15 ⌜That though existent they inexist is what 'not existent' means.⌝ 16 ⌜That though inexistent they exist is what 'not inexistent' means.⌝ 17 ⌜So it is not that there are no things, but that things are not absolute things.⌝ Because things are not absolute things, what can be called a thing?

Thus a sūtra says,[18] "Form is empty by nature, not by destruction" in order to explain the relation between the Holy Man and things.
18 ⌜He identifies with the self-voidness of the myriad things.⌝ 19 ⌜He does not depend on hacking and chopping to clear his way.⌝

Therefore, [Vimalakīrti] talked about the non-absolute as he lay sick,[19] and the *Chao-jih-ching*[20] says that [the four elements] are identical with voidness. So, though the texts in the Tripiṭaka are diverse, the theme on which they are strung is one.

Thus the *Fang-kuang*[21] says, 20 ⌜"The highest, Absolute Truth has no achieving and no attaining. Because of popular truth there is achievement and there is attaining."⌝
21 ⌜'Having attainment' is the counterfeit name for 'having no attainment.'⌝
22 ⌜'Having no attainment' is the absolute name for 'having attainment.'⌝
23 ⌜Because of the absolute name, though absolute it is not existent.⌝
24 ⌜Because of the counterfeit name, though counterfeit it is not inexistent.⌝

Therefore, 25 ⌜What is called 'absolute' never exists;⌝ 26 ⌜What is called 'counterfeit' never inexists.⌝ 27 ⌜The two terms are never the same; the two principles are never different.

Thus a sūtra says,[22] "[Question:] 'Is there a difference between Absolute Truth and popular truth?' He replied, 'There is no difference.'" 28 ⌜This sūtra simply asserts Absolute Truth to explain 'not existent' and popular truth to explain 'not inexistent.'⌝ 29 ⌜It does not impute twoness to things because of the twoness of the truths.⌝

II.2 Applying Reason to Explain Emptiness

So in fact there are some respects in which the myriad things are not existent, and some respects in which they are not inexistent. 30 ⌜Because there are some respects in which they are not existent, though existent they are not existent.⌝ 31 ⌜Because there are some respects in which they are not inexistent, though inexistent they are not inexistent.⌝ 32 ⌜'Inexistence' is not utter voidness. 'Existence' is not absolute existence.⌝ 33 ⌜As the existent does not coincide (is not identical) with the absolute and the inexistent does not 'obliterate the traces,' existent and inexistent differ in name but are one in their reference.⌝

Thus the young man [Ratnakūṭa][23] exclaimed, "You declare that the dharmas are neither existent nor inexistent; the dharmas arise because of cause and conditions." The *Keyūra-sūtra*[24] says, "In turning the Dharma-wheel neither is there turning nor is there no turning." This means that in turning there is nothing turned. This is the subtle language of the many sūtras. What [does it mean?]

Would you say that things are inexistent? Then annullist views would not be erroneous. Would you say that things are existent? Then eternalist views would be correct. 34 ⌜Because things are not inexistent, annullist views are erroneous.⌝ 35 ⌜Because things are not existent, eternalist views are not correct.⌝ 36 ⌜So, 'not existent and not inexistent' is indeed speech about Absolute Truth.⌝

II.3 Further Quotations Explaining Emptiness

Thus the *Tao-hsing*[25] says, "Mind is not existent and not inexistent." The *Middle Treatise*[26] says, 37 ⌜"Because things come from causes and conditions, they are not existent; because they arise through conditions, they are not inexistent."⌝

When we reason this out, we realize that it is so. The reason why it is so is as follows. If existence were absolute existence, then the existent would always exist of itself, and would not have to wait for conditions before it existed. In the case of absolute inexistence, inexistence would always inexist of itself, and would not have to wait for conditions before it inexisted. 38 ⌜Because the existent is not self-existent, but waits for conditions before it exists, we know that the existent is not absolutely existent.⌝ 39 ⌜As the existent is not absolutely existent, though it exists it cannot be termed 'existent.'⌝

As for 'not inexistent,' inexistence can be called 'inexistent' if it is profoundly motionless. If the myriad things were inexistent, then they should not arise. As they arise, they are not inexistent. 40 ⌜Thus it is clear that because they arise from conditions, they do not inexist.⌝

Thus the *Mahāyāna-śāstra* says,[27] "All the dharmas should exist, because of all the causes and conditions. All the dharmas should not exist, because of all the causes and conditions. All inexistent dharmas, because of all causes and conditions, should exist. All existent dharmas, because of all causes and conditions, should not exist." These utterances about existence and inexistence are not mere assertions of opposition.

41 ⌜What should exist is the same as the existent, and one should not say that it is inexistent.⌝ 42 ⌜What should inexist is the same as inexistent, and one should not say that it is existent.⌝ 43 ⌜This is borrowing 'existent' to explain 'not inexistent' and borrowing 'inexistent' to distinguish 'not existent.'⌝ 44 ⌜Here the fact is one and the terms are two.⌝ The words seem not to be the same, but if you understand where they are the same, then there are no differences that are not made the same.

II. 4 Again Applying Reason to Explain Emptiness

45 ⌜So, since in fact there are some respects in which the myriad dharmas do not exist, they cannot really exist.⌝ 46 ⌜Since there are some respects in which they do not inexist, they cannot really inexist.⌝

For what reason? If you would say that they exist, their existence arises non-absolutely. If you would say that they inexist, their forms have taken shape. 47 ⌜Having forms and shapes, they are not identical with the inexistent.⌝ 48 ⌜Being non-absolute, they are not real existents.⌝ So, this explains the idea of the emptiness of the non-absolute.

Thus the *Fang-kuang*[28] says, 49 ⌜"The dharmas are borrowed appellations, and not absolute.⌝ It is like a phantom man."[29] It is not that there is no phantom man, but that the phantom man is not a real (absolute) man.

II. 5 Arriving at Names and Reals to Explain Emptiness

50 ⌜If you seek a thing through a name, in the thing there is no actual that matches the name.⌝ 51 ⌜If you seek a name through a thing, the name has no efficacy to obtain the thing.⌝ 52 ⌜A thing without an actual to match its name is not a thing.⌝ 53 ⌜A name without efficacy to obtain a thing is not a name.⌝ Therefore, 54 ⌜names do not match actuals, and actuals do not match names.⌝ Since there is no matching of names and actuals, where do the myriad dharmas occur?

Thus the *Middle Treatise* says,[30] 55 ⌜"In things there is no self (this) and other (that), yet one man takes self to be self and other to be other. The other takes self to be other and other to be self."⌝[31] Neither self nor other is fixed in one name, yet the deluded cherish the idea that it is certainly so. So, other and self are not existent beforehand, and the delusion is not inexistent beforehand. 56 ⌈When you realize that other and self are not existent, what thing is there to which you can impute existence?⌉ Thus we know that the myriad things are not absolute but are forever conventional designations.

Therefore, the *Ch'eng-chü*[32] makes its statement about arbitrary names, and Chuang-tzŭ[33] relies on the similes of the finger and of the horse. So is there anywhere that deep and far-reaching statements are not found?

II. 6 Conclusion

Therefore, 57 ⌈the Holy Man mounted on the thousand changes does not change and traveling through the myriad delusions always passes through, because he identifies with the self-voidness of the myriad things and does not borrow emptiness to make things empty.⌉

Thus the sūtra[34] says, "It is exceedingly strange, World-Honored one! 58 ⌈Without moving from the Absolute Limit *(bhūtakoṭi)* you establish positions for the dharmas."⌉ 59 ⌈It is not that he leaves the Absolute to establish positions, but that establishing positions is identical with the Absolute.⌉ 60 ⌈So, is the Way far away? While touching events, it remains absolute.⌉ 61 ⌈Is the Holy One far away? When you realize him, you are identical with his Spirit.⌉[35]

Document 10

THINGS DO NOT SHIFT (Chao-lun, Part I), *BY SENG-CHAO*

Text: T XLV, 151a–c.
Japanese translation: *Jōron Kenkyū*, pp. 7–14.
Previous English translation: Liebenthal, *Chao*, pp. 46–55.

I.1 Introduction (p. 151a9)

The usual opinion of men is that when birth and death yield to each other and when cold and hot seasons alternate, there are things that flow and move. I think that it is not so.

I.2 The Theme of the Essay (p. 151a10)

For what reason? The *Fang-kuang*[1] says, 1 ⌈"The dharmas have no departing or arriving, no moving or rotating."⌉ If we examine 'the action of not moving,' it is not that [the dharmas] leave motion to find stillness, but that they must find stillness in all movements. 2 ⌈Because they must find stillness in all movements, though moving they are always still.⌉ 3 ⌈Because they do not leave motion to find stillness, though still they do not part from motion.⌉

So, though motion and stillness have never been different, the deluded do not agree. Consequently, the true words[2] are stopped up by those who wrangle in debates, and the path to the Ideal is made crooked by difference-lovers, so that it is not at all easy to speak about the end-point of stillness and motion.[3] For what reason? 4 ⌈If they talk about the absolute, then they go against the popular.⌉ 5 ⌈If they conform to the popular, then they contravene the absolute.⌉ 6 ⌈Because they contravene the absolute, they fail to find the [true] nature [of things] and do not return.⌉[4] 7 ⌈Because they go against the popular, their words are insipid and tasteless.⌉[5]

Consequently, the mediocre person does not decide whether to accept or reject, and the inferior person claps his hands and pays no attention.[6]

It is only the nature of things that is near and yet cannot be known, is it not? Yet I cannot stop myself. Let us just lodge the mind on the limit of motion and rest. Though [what I say] is not necessarily so, I will attempt to discuss the matter.

II. 1 Quoting the Sūtras (p. 151a20)

The *Tao-hsing*[7] says, "The dharmas are fundamentally without a place from which they come or a place at which they arrive."[8] The *Middle Treatise* says,[9] "When you look at a place, you know that the other [goer] is departed, but the departer does not reach the place." These [quotations] are both about seeking stillness while being identical with motion, and so we know that things do not shift.

II.2 Indicating Things to Explain Non-Shifting (p. 151a22)

8 ⌜What people mean by motion is that because past things do not reach the present they move and are not still.⌝ 9 ⌜What I mean by stillness is that because past things do not reach the present they are still and do not move.⌝ 10 ⌜[Others think that] in moving they are not still, because they do not come.⌝ 11 ⌜[I think that] being still they do not move, because they do not depart.⌝

So, what we meet (experience) is never different, and what we see never agrees. What the contravener calls a barrier, the conformer calls a passage. If you gain the Way, what then obstructs you?

II.3 Dismissing Errors (p. 151a27)

Alas! It is a long time during which men's thoughts have erred. Though their eyes face the Absolute, none perceives it. Since they know that past things do not come, they think that present things can pass. Since past things do not come, where do present things pass to?

What does this mean? 12 ⌜If you seek past things in the past, they are never inexistent in the past.⌝ 13 ⌜If you seek past things in the present, they are never existent in the present.⌝ 14 ⌜They are never existent in the present, so we understand that things do not come.⌝ 15 ⌜Because they are never inexistent in the past, we know that things do not depart.⌝ If next we examine the present, the present likewise does not pass. 16 ⌜This means that past things occupy the past of themselves, and do not reach the past from the present.⌝ 17 ⌜Present things occupy the present of themselves, and do not reach the present from the past.⌝

Therefore Confucius says, "Hui, behold the renewal [of all things]. Even while we link arms, they are not the same as before."[10] So it is clear that things do not pass and come from one to the other. Since there are no subtle signs[11] of passing and returning, what thing is there that can move?

So, is it any wonder that the cosmic cyclone while toppling the mountains is forever still, that the Yangtzŭ and the Yellow River while surging down do not flow, that the 'wild horses' (spring vapors) while billowing and beating do not move, that the sun and moon while transiting the heavens do not circle?

II.4 Reconciling the Teachings (p. 151b9)

[OBJECTION:] Oh! As the Holy Man says, "Man's life speeds past more swiftly than a flowing stream."[12] Therefore the śrāvakas achieve the Way *(bodhi)* by awakening to impermanence, and the pratyeka-buddhas identify with the Absolute by realizing isolation of (from) externals. If indeed the myriad movements do not change, then [śrāvakas and pratyeka-buddhas] surely cannot climb the stairs to the Way by examining transformations.
[REPLY:] If we examine the Holy One's saying closely, we see that it is recondite and hard to fathom. 18 ⌜Seeming to move, [dharmas] are still; seeming to depart, they remain.⌝ One can meet them with the spirit,[13] but it is hard to find them through events. Therefore, 19 ⌜When he says 'depart,' it is not necessarily 'depart'—it stops people's ideas of permanence.⌝ 20 ⌜When he says 'stay,' it is not necessarily 'stay'—it dismisses what men think of as passing.⌝ 21 ⌜He does not mean that in departing [a thing] can leave, or that in staying a thing can remain.

Thus the *Ch'eng-chü*[14] says, 22 ⌜"The bodhisattva, dwelling among those who imagine permanence, preaches the teaching of impermanence."⌝ The *Mahāyāna-śāstra*[15] says, "The dharmas do not move, and have no place of departing or coming." These [quotations] are both to edify ordinary beings. The two sayings have one meeting-point. You cannot say that, because the letters differ, they err from their meaning (goal).

Therefore, 23 ⌜though one says 'permanent' [things] do not stay. Though one says 'depart,' they do not shift.⌝ 24 ⌜Because they do not shift, though passing they are always still.⌝ 25 ⌜Because they do not abide, though still they always pass.⌝ 26 ⌜Because though still they always pass, in passing they do not shift.⌝ 27 ⌜Because though passing they are always still, though still they do not remain.⌝

So, what Chuang-tzŭ said about hiding a mountain,[16] and what Confucius said as he stood by the river[17] both express their feelings about how hard it is for that which passes to remain. They certainly do not mean that in quitting the present [things] can pass over. Therefore, when we look at the Mind of the Holy Man, we see that it does not agree with what people perceive.

In what way? People say that the child and the adult are the same in body, and that throughout a hundred years [the person] is one in substance. They only know that the years pass, but do not perceive that the form follows suit. Therefore, the brahman went forth [as a wanderer]. He returned white-haired, and when the neighbors saw him, they said, "Does the former man still survive?" 28 ⌜The brahman said, "I resemble the former man, but I am not the former man."⌝ The neighbors all were startled and disapproved of what he said. But is this not the meaning of the statement that a strong man runs away with it on his back while people in the dark (stupid people) are unaware?[18]

Therefore, according to whatever common beings are obstructed by, the Tathagata uses suitable language to expose their errors.[19] Mounted on the non-dual Absolute Mind, he utters the non-single various teachings. Is it not the Holy One's speech alone that though contrary cannot be made to impute difference? Thus, 29 ⌜when [the Buddha] talks about the Absolute there is the predication 'does not shift,' and when he gives popular guidance there are predications of 'moving' and 'flowing.'⌝ Though the thousand paths are proclaimed differently, they converge on the same goal (reference).

But when those who rely on the letters hear about not shifting they think that past things do not reach the present. When they hear about moving and flowing, they think that present things can reach the past. As they have already said that they are past and present, why do they wish to shift them?

Therefore, 30 ⌜to say that [things] pass does not necessitate their passing. In the past and in the present [things] always subsist, because they do not move.⌝ 31 ⌜To say that [things] depart does not necessitate their departing. It means that they do not reach the past from the present, because they do not come.⌝ 32 ⌜Because they do not come, they do not race between past and present.⌝ 33 ⌜Because they do not move, each nature abides in one time.⌝

So, though the many books vary in their words and the Hundred Schools have divergent statements (theories), yet if one finds their meeting-point the varying texts certainly cannot induce error.

II.5 Contradicting Permanence (p. 151c10)

Therefore, 34 ⌜what other people call abiding, I call departing. What other people call departing, I call abiding.⌝ 35 ⌜So, though departing and abiding are different, their reference is one.⌝ Thus, when the Scripture[20] says, "Right words seem contradictory. Who is going to believe them?" this saying has good grounds.

Why? 36 ⌜Other people seek the past in the present and say that it does not abide.⌝ 37 ⌜I seek the present in the past, and know that it does not depart.⌝ 38 ⌜If the present reached the past, there should be the present in the past.⌝ 39 ⌜If the past reached the present, there should be the past in the present.⌝ 40 ⌜There is no past in the present, so we know that it does not come.⌝ 41 ⌜There is no present in the past, so we know that it does not depart.⌝ 42 ⌜As the past does not reach the present and the present likewise does not reach the past, each event by nature abides in one time. What thing can depart or come?

So, the four seasons rush past like the wind and the Great Bear revolves like lightning. If you understand the subtle points of this idea, then however they speed, they do not revolve.

II. 6 Conclusion (p. 151c18)

Therefore, 43 ⌜while the Tathāgata's efficacy flows through a myriad generations, it is always intact.⌝ His Way, while passing through a hundred kalpas, stays ultra-firm. The reason why the building of a mound is as if completed with the first basketful,[21] and the journey entails arrival with the first step,[22] is that karmic efficacy really cannot decay. 44 ⌜It is clear that because karmic influence cannot decay, though it resides in the past it does not change.⌝ 45 ⌜Because it does not change, it does not shift. Because it does not shift, it remains immutable.⌝ Thus when the Sūtra says, "While the three catastrophes engulf everything, my karma stays immutable," I believe what it says.[23]

For what reason? 46 ⌜The effect does not occur with the cause; the effect depends on the cause.⌝ 47 ⌜Because the effect depends on the cause, the cause does not perish in the past.⌝ 48 ⌜Because the effect does not occur with the cause, the cause does not come to the present.⌝ Since it does not perish and does not come, the reference of 'not shifting' is clear. What further error about departing and remaining, or wavering between motion and stillness?

So, when heaven and earth turn upside down, it does not mean that they are not still. When the deluge dashes up against heaven, it does not mean that it moves. If only you can match your spirit to identity with things, then [that things do not shift] is near at hand to be known.[24]

Notes

Notes

Works listed in the Bibliography are cited in shortened form in the Notes. All other works are cited in full in the first reference to them in each chapter.

CHAPTER I

1 Burnouf, Eugène, *Introduction à l'histoire du Bouddhisme Indien* (Paris, Imprimerie Royale, 1844); La Vallée Poussin, *Prasannapadā.*

2 Stcherbatsky, *Nirvāṇa*, p. 1; Murti, *Buddhism*, p. vii; Robinson, "Logical Aspects," pp. 291–92; De Jong, *Chapitres*, pp. ix–xii; Schayer, "Absolutum," p. 401.

3 Robinson, "Logical Aspects," pp. 291 ff.

4 May, "Recherches"; "La philosophie bouddhique"; "Kant et le Mādhyamika"; *Prasannapadā*.

5 Liebenthal, *Chao*; "Hui-yüan."

6 Stcherbatsky, *Nirvāṇa*; "Die drei Richtungen in der Philosophie des Buddhismus," *Rocznik Orjentalistyczny* X (1934), 3–37; La Vallée Poussin, "Réflexions"; "Buddhica," *Harvard Journal of Asian Studies* (1937), pp. 137–60; Schayer, *Kapitel*; "Absolutum."

7 *Prasannapadā*, Avant Propos.

8 a. Yamakami Sōgen, *Systems of Buddhist Thought*, pp. 186–209 (Calcutta, University Press, 1912).
b. Dasgupta, *History*, pp. 138–45.
c. Radhakrishnan, Sarvepalli, *Indian Philosophy* I, 643–69 (London, Allen and Unwin; New York, Macmillan, 1923).
d. Keith, Arthur Berriedale, *Buddhist Philosophy in India and Ceylon*, pp. 235–41 (Oxford, Clarendon Press, 1923).
e. Walleser, Max, "Der Buddhistische Negativismus," *Zeitschrift für Buddhismus* (1924), pp. 168–82.
f. Grousset, René, *Les Philosophies Indiennes* I, 202–63 (Paris, Desclée, de Brouwer, 1931).
g. Thomas, Edward Joseph, *The History of Buddhist Thought*, pp. 212–27 (London, Paul, Trench, Trubner; New York, Knopf, 1933).
h. Chandradhar Sharma, *Indian Philosophy*, ch. 6, pp. 72–95 (Barnes and Noble, University Paperbacks, UP–40, 1962).

i. Renou, Louis et Filliozat, Jean, *L'Inde Classique*, II, 577–79 (Paris, Imprimerie Nationale; École Française d'Extrême-Orient, Hanoi, 1953).
j. Frauwallner, Erich, *Die Philosophie des Buddhismus*, pp. 170–78 (Berlin, Akademie-Verlag, 1958).

9 Schayer, *Kapitel*, Einleitung; "Absolutum"; De Jong, *Chapitres*, Introduction; "Absolu"; May, *Prasannapadā*, Introduction; cf. May, "Recherches"; "La philosophie bouddhique"; "Kant et le Mādhyamika."

10 "Kant et le Mādhyamika."

11 Extant translations attributed to Kumārajīva's main predecessors may be grouped as follows:
i. An Shih-kao (A.D. 147?–70), 53 titles: Āgamas, Meditation, Vinaya, Abhidharma (Bagchi, p. 8).
ii. Lokakṣema (A.D. 167?–86), 12 titles: Prajñā-pāramitā and other Mahāyāna sūtras (Bachi, p. 37).
iii. Chih-ch'ien (A.D. 220–53), 53 titles: Āgamas, Prajñā-pāramitā and other Mahāyāna sūtras (Bagchi, p. 283).
iv. Dharmarakṣa (A.D. 265–313), 93 titles: Āgamas, Prajñā Sūtras, Saddharma-puṇḍarīka, Daśabhūmika class sūtras, etc. (Bagchi, p. 83).
v. Dharmaratna (A.D. 381–95), 29 titles: Āgamas, sundry Mahāyāna sūtras, spells (Bagchi, p. 322).
vi. Gautama Saṅghadeva (A.D. 383–98 plus), 5 titles: Āgamas and Abhidharma (Bagchi, p. 161).

12 Beal, *Buddhism in China*, p. 41: "The Buddhism of which we speak is, in fact, not Chinese Buddhism, but the Buddhism of India in China." P. 254: "[Buddhism] did nothing, however, to promote the knowledge of the true God, nor has it supplied any substitute for the worship of Shang-ti, the Lord and maker of the world; and what it has given in lieu of this, viz., a somewhat meaningless spiritualism, will hardly compensate for the loss of the great thought of a 'supreme, personal Ruler' directing and governing the world."

Liebenthal, p. 57, n. 184: "In Indian Buddhism neither the individual nor the universe is ruled by a central agent (anātmatā). But the Chinese never gave up this idea."

Suzuki, *Zen Buddhism*, p. 50: "The inner sense of Enlightenment was not understood in China, except intellectually, in the earlier days of Buddhism. This was natural, seeing that it was in this respect that the Chinese mind was excelled by the Indian. As I said before, the boldness and subtlety of Mahāyāna philosophy must have fairly stunned the Chinese, who had, before the introduction of Buddhism, practically no system of thought worthy of the name, except moral science." PP. 57–58: "The superabundance of Indian imagination issued in supernaturalism and wonderful symbolism, and the Chinese sense of practicalness and its love for the solid everyday facts of life, resulted in Zen Buddhism." P. 58: "No, Zen had to have its own way; the Chinese mind refused blindly to follow the Indian models."

13 Summary of the ***Sampanna-prabhāsa-samādhi-sūtra (Ch'eng-chŭ-kuang-ming-ching)*** (T 630, XV, 451b–58b).

The scene opens in Kapilavastu. The first interlocutor, the kulaputra Shan-ming, with five hundred companions, offers pūjā. Ordinary dāna and Buddha-dāna. A stotra. The Buddha and assembly go to Shan-ming's house. Miracle of the feeding of the host. Shan-ming asks a question. The Buddha attains bodhi by practicing the six pāramitās. Defects in practice of the pāramitās. Shan-ming obtains the four purities. The Buddha explains the Sampanna-prabhāsa-samādhi. One must practice 135 things to enter this samādhi. These are enumerated. They include the thirty-seven bodhipakṣa dharmas.

"He regards existent and inexistent as fundamentally one. Having known the one, he gets rid of the one. He does not conceive conceptions about the one.

"The mind, being without desire, is constantly compassionate.

"The bodhisattva . . . stands in the tenth stage."

Enumeration of the attainments and rejoicing of various classes of hearers.

Shan-ming asks the Buddha what can be done about his stupidity. After a reply, he asks how not dwelling in notions of purity is the vision of emptiness. The Buddha says, "The mind does not dwell inside and does not abide outside, is not in the Absolute and not in the Popular, not in the existent, not in the inexistent, not in arising, not in ceasing, not in motion. In these dharmas there is no dharma, and thus their names are arbitrarily assigned."

The four practices. The four essentials. Gāthā on emptiness and the sampanna-prabhāsa-samādhi. Story of the former Buddha Tsun-fu-yŭ-wang and the youth Min-chien, who was Shan-ming's former person. Prediction that after 200 kalpas Shan-ming will become a Buddha. Shan-ming gains the ten masteries *(tzŭ-jan)*. Shan-ming puts forth the wish that all should quickly realize the sampanna-prabhāsa-samādhi. The Buddha smiles and lights up the ten quarters. Ānanda asks, in prose and verse, why the Buddha smiled. The Buddha predicts that Shan-ming's 500 companions will obtain the sampanna-prabhāsa-samādhi when Maitreya comes, and will all become Buddhas 360,000 kalpas after that. The 500 rejoice and gain the five non-reverting thoughts. They then (1) vow to manifest in places where there is no Buddha, show a Buddha's marks, and silence doubters who say there is no Buddha, (2) vow to correct the word-chopping of one-sided people, (3) vow to manifest themselves and confute Tīrthikas who infiltrate the Saṅgha, (4) vow to manifest as a teacher for any who recite the sūtras in the wilderness or other isolation, (5) vow to manifest as a Buddha and take blasphemers and show them through the heavens and the hells so that they see the rewards and punishments.

After the Buddha's decease, the disciples will erect temples, represent the Buddha's form, and establish lecture halls (p. 456b5).

The 500 request the Buddha's help in fulfilling these vows. The Buddha gives a sermon on avoiding pride and sloth.

Wu-hui-wang Bodhisattva asks the Buddha to manifest the might of the sampanna-prabhāsa-samādhi. The Buddha delegates the act to Ta-li-p'u-p'ing Bodhisattva, who then enters samādhi. Instantly, all mountains vanish from the three thousand great thousand worlds. Everything is made of vaiḍūrya. All Buddha-countries appear as one expanse. The Buddhas, like stars and constellations, are all balanced on one finger. The assembly is greatly edified.

The Buddha explains to Shan-ming why beings do not practice the sampanna-prabhāsa-samādhi. Shan-ming asks how this samādhi is to be cultivated by a nobleman who holds district or state office and is distracted by affairs of government. The Buddha replies that the nobleman should write out the text of this sūtra, place it in a pavilion, and offer worship to it. He should also keep fifteen observances (an expanded version of the five precepts). Shan-ming asks how the handicapped plebeian can practice this samādhi. The Buddha replies that the ordinary man should write out this sutra and offer pūjā to it, and keep ten observances (the five precepts plus reciting this text, and other duties). Shan-ming asks how a noblewoman whose karma imposes marriage and household life may train in this samādhi. The Buddha replies that she should write out this sūtra, offer worship to it, desire release from womanly form, eradicate lusts, and keep twenty observances. Shan-ming asks how the poverty-stricken plebeian woman can practice this samādhi. The Buddha says that she should keep ten observances.

The Buddha tells Shan-ming that the merit from these practices is greater than giving a whole world full of jewels. He says that after his decease the twelve Celestial Spirits will protect those who practice this samādhi. He then lists the names of the twelve Yakṣas.

The Buddha entrusts the sūtra to Ānanda. The assembly rejoices and disperses.

14 For the modern Chinese use of the *Vajracchedikā* for this purpose, see Robinson (trans.), "Modern Zen Master."

15 Suzuki, "Existentialism, Pragmatism and Zen," *Zen Buddhism*, pp. 268–69: "One may ask, Why these contradictions? The answer is, They are so because of *tathatā*. They are so just because they are so, and for no other reason. Hence, no logic, no analysis, and no contradictions. Things, including all possible forms of contradictions, are eternally of *tathatā*. 'A' cannot be itself unless it stands against what is not 'A'; 'not-A' is needed to make 'A' 'A', which means that 'not-A' is in 'A'. When 'A' wants to be itself, it is already outside itself, that is, 'not-A'. If 'A' did not contain in itself what is not itself, 'not-A' could not come out of 'A' so as to make 'A' what it is. 'A' is 'A' because of this contradiction, and this contradiction comes out only when we logicize. As long as we are in *tathatā*, there is no contradiction whatever. Zen knows no contradictions; it is the logician who encounters them, forgetting that they are of his own making."

Liebenthal, *Chao*, p. 17: "Chao's paradoxes must not be understood as sophisms or expressions of scepticism, but, as I shall try to prove in my analysis, they reflect the experience of a mystic. They were revealed to Chao in moments of ecstasy; and what takes the form of arguments, in some cases condensed to syllogisms, are in fact restatements or paraphrases of this one invaluable experience."

16 Hill, *Introduction to Linguistic Structures*, p. 9: "The entities of language are symbols, that is, they have meaning, but the connection between symbol and thing is arbitrary and socially controlled." P. 1: "Language activity can be observed, and is therefore subject to verification. Thought can be observed only by subjective introspection, and so is not subject to verification. Language activity is therefore more knowable, thought less knowable."

17 Firth, "A Synopsis of Linguistic Theory," pp. 11–12: "The habitual collocations in which words under study appear are quite simply their mere word accompaniment, the other word material in which they are most commonly or most characteristically embedded. It can safely be stated that part of the 'meaning' of cows can be indicated by such collocations as *They are milking the cows. Cows give milk.*"

18 Brough, "Some Indian Theories of Meaning," p. 168: ". . . as Jespersen himself realizes elsewhere, the 'meaning of the component words taken separately' is something which cannot be determined apart from a context; . . . The apparently objective criterion upon which Jespersen relies to diagnose a free expression, namely, substitution in sentential functions, is as we have seen explicitly rejected by Bhartṛhari as being in fact illusory."

19 *Ibid.*, p. 166: "We do not in fact express ourselves or understand what is spoken in a series of meaning-units. After a sentence has

been understood we may look back at it, analyse it into words, and maintain that we discern words in it."

20 Mitra (ed.), *Aṣṭasāhasrikā*, p. 467: "The sum total of words contained in this sūtra on perfect wisdom certainly has its limits, but not so the perfection of wisdom itself. For the sum total of the words in this sūtra is not identical with the perfection of wisdom itself."

21 Link, "Daw-an," pp. 1b-2a: "... if in the archaic period of Chinese translation—that of the Hann and the Three Kingdoms—such technical Sanskrit Buddhist terms as *Arhat*, *Bodhi*, and *Nirvāṇa* are at times rendered respectively by such time-honored and philosophically loaded Taoist expressions as *Yinq-jen*, *Daw*, and *Wu-wei*, this fact is of the utmost importance for a correct evaluation of the Chinese comprehension of Buddhist thought and, as such, it should be noted."

22 a. *Vimalakīrti-nirdeśa*(T 475, p. 538a1), ch. 1, gāthā, verses 12–15; Robinson, *Chinese Buddhist Verse*, p. 20; Lamotte, *Vimalakīrti*, pp. 109–11.
b. *Samādhirāja*, Sanskrit: *Buddhist Sanskrit Texts*, no. 2 (P. L. Vaidya, ed., Mithila Institute of Post-Graduate Studies and Research in Sanskrit Learning, Darbhanga, 1961), quoted in La Vallée Poussin, *Prasannapadā*, p. 277, l. 12; Schayer, *Kapitel*, p. 78 with n. 54.
c. *Tathāgata-guhya-sūtra*(T 312, pp. 719b21 ff.). See Lamotte, *Traité* I, 30, n. 2, and De Jong, *Chapitres*, p. 23, n. 62.

23 Liebenthal, *Chao*, p. 7: "Chao's language is largely Taoist, particularly in the earliest paper (Part III of the translation) ...." P. 44: "For the Taoist language and patterns, prevailing in the Buddhist literature of the early centuries, do not indicate a Taoist world-view."

24 Waley's review of *Jōron Kenkyū*, p. 196a: "The Japanese translation makes easy and agreeable reading. This has been achieved by inserting into brackets words, phrases and whole sentences that are lacking in the original. This expansion of what is a kind of telegraphese into ordinary language has been done in a very convincing way."

Waley, *The Way and Its Power*, p. 190: "The repeated use of nouns as verbs, not possible in English to the same extent as in Chinese, makes anything but a clumsy paraphrase of the first ten lines of the chapter impossible."

Liebenthal, *Chao*, p. viii: "My translation is fairly literal, but sometimes it seemed to be impossible to render the meaning without changing the phrasing. In one or two cases the translation is so free that it almost amounts to a mere outline of the content."

25 Allen, "Relationship in Comparative Linguistics," p. 64: "We should presumably expect that different asterisked labels, with different implications would be required according to the number and nature of the languages compared; . . ."

26 *Ibid.*, p. 54: "It should be stated in advance that any theory in this paper lays no claim to exclusiveness—it is *a* theory, not *the* theory."

Chao, "The Non-uniqueness of Phonemic Solutions," p. 363: "The main purpose of the present paper is to show that given the sounds of a language, there are usually more than one possible way of reducing them to a system of phonemes, and that these different systems or solutions are not simply correct or incorrect, but may be regarded only as being good or bad for various purposes."

CHAPTER II

1 Chi-tsang accepted the *Fu-fa-tsang-yin-yüan* as an authority. However, see Maspéro, "Sur la date et l'authenticité du Fou-fa-tsang yin yuan tchuan," p. 149: "In resumé, the present *Fu-fa-tsang-yin-yüan-chüan* is a forgery composed in China towards the middle or the end of the 6th century, by compiling fragments of previous works; no Hindu original exists for this work. The list of the twenty-four patriarchs is the work of the same forger; it is one of the numerous chronological systems of the Buddhist doctors which were widespread in China at this epoch."

2 Chi-tsang also discusses the date of Nāgārjuna in the *San-lun-hsüan-i*, T 1852, p. 6b7 ff., quoting the prophecies from the *Laṅkāvatāra* (T 671, p. 569a; T 672, p. 627c) and the *Māyā Sūtra* (T 383, p. 1013c).

3 Suzuki, *Laṅkāvatāra Sūtra*, "Sagāthakam," pp. 239–40, verses 165 and 166: "In Vedali, in the southern part, a Bhikṣu most illustrious and distinguished [will be born]; his name is Nāgāhvaya he is the destroyer of the one-sided views based on being and non-being. He will declare my Vehicle, the unsurpassed Mahāyāna, to the world; attaining the stage of Joy he will go to the Land of Bliss."

Nāgāhvaya may well be another person than Nāgārjuna.

4 Johnston, *Early Sāṁkhya*, p. 8, note: "In fact, for the period before the Gupta dynasty the *Āryamañjuśrīmūlakalpa* [*Mañjuśrī-mūla-tantra*, pp. 616-17, T. Ganapati śāstrī edition, Trivandrum Sanskrit Series, nos. 70, 76, 84, Trivandrum, 1920–22] is obviously dependent on Buddhist legendary material and affords no definite information of which we were not already in possession."

5 See also Vaidya, *Catuḥśataka*, pp. 16 ff.

6 Obermiller, "Prajñā-pāramitā," p. 4, n. 9, mentions that the *Vyavahāra-siddhi* has not been translated into Tibetan, and lists differing Tibetan opinions as to which work should replace it as sixth in the list.

7 1. Sanskrit text edited and translated by Giuseppe Tucci, *Journal of the Royal Asiatic Society*, 1934, pp. 307–25; 1936, pp. 237–52, 423–35. Tibetan text, Tib. mdo 'grel XCIV, 129a–52b.
2. See May, *Prasannapadā*, p. 26.
3. Sanskrit text edited by Gokhale. Tibetan text, Tib. mdo 'grel SVII, 165b–66a.
4. Sanskrit text edited and translated by Tucci, *Minor Buddhist Texts*. Tibetan text, Tib. mdo 'grel XVII, 156a–57a.
5. Sanskrit text reconstructed by Ayaswami Sastri, Adyar, 1938. Tibetan Text, Tib. mdo 'grel XVII, 170b–71b.
6. Tibetan text edited and translated by W. L. Campbell, Calcutta University, 1919.
7. Tibetan text, Tib. mdo 'grel XXXIII, 74a–81b. Chinese text, T 1672, 1673, 1674.

8 For a bibliography of European language translations of works attributed to Nāgārjuna and Āryadeva, and of commentaries thereon, see Constantin Régamey, *Buddhistische Philosophie* (Bern, A. Francke, 1950) 14.11 to 14.66, pp. 54–58.

Japanese translations of works extant in Chinese are to be found in the *Kokuyaku Issaikyō*, Chūkanbu, and Shakukyōronbu.

9 Translated by Guiseppe Tucci, *T'oung-Pao* 1925–26, pp. 25 ff.

10 See Vaidya, *Catuḥśataka*, pp. 50 ff; La Vallée Poussin, "L'auteur, du Joyau dans la main"; Murti, *Buddhism*, p. 95, n. 2.

11 Murti, *Buddhism*, p. 93: "*The Śata Śāstra* (trans. by Kumārajīva A.D. 404, into Chinese) and the *Śata Śāstra Vaipulya* (trans. by Hieun Tsang A.D. 650) are probably the last 8 chapters of the *Catuḥ Śataka*, the contents being reshuffled." Tucci, *Pre-Diṅnāga* p. xiv, says that chapters, in the *Catuḥ Śataka* and the *Śata Śāstra* respectively, correspond as follows: ix, x to ix; xi–xii to v, vi; and xvi to viii.

12 Page references are to the edition by La Vallée Poussin of Candrakīrti *Prasannapadā (Madhyamaka-vṛtti)*. Stanza references are to chapter and verse of the *Middle Stanzas*. I follow Hatani's numbering of the verses, which corresponds more closely with the Chinese text than does La Vallée Poussin's numbering. The vandana is reckoned as verses 1 and 2 of the first chapter by Hatani, but not by La Vallée Poussin. See footnotes to *Chūron* translation, *Kokuyaku Issaikyō*, Chūkanbu I, where the Sanskrit Stanzas are reproduced from La Vallée Poussin's edition.

13 Liebenthal, *Satkārya*, p. 54; Schayer, "Aussagenlogik," pp. 90-96.

14 See *Majjhima-nikāya* I, 133, sutta 22 (Horner, p. 172); La Vallée Poussin, "Réflexions," p. 32.

15 Russell, "On Order in Time" (*Logic and Knowledge*, p. 347): "It is generally agreed that instants are mathematical constructions, not physical entities . . . an instant is most naturally defined as a group of events having the following two properties: (1) Any two members of the group overlap in time, i.e. neither is wholly before the other. (2) No event outside the group overlaps with all of them. . . . I have shown . . . that every event *x* has a first instant if every event that begins after *x* has begun is wholly after some event which exists when *x* begins.

"The present paper investigates further the conditions for the existence of instants, and what happens when they do not exist. It is shown that the existence of instants requires hypotheses which there is no reason to suppose true—a fact which may be not without importance in physics."

16 vijñāna, sparśa, vedanā, and tṛṣṇā—the psychic links in the twelve nidānas.

17 Schayer, "Absolutum," p. 405 says: "In this connection it must be strongly emphasized that the concept of a non-spatial Being, especially the hypostasis of a psychic, non-extended reality which has been current in Occidental philosophy since Descartes, remained foreign to the Indian systems."

Johnston, *Early Sāṁkhya*, p. 38: "In India we may perhaps represent the position by saying that all classes of phenomena are looked on alike as having a material basis, the difference resting merely on the degree of subtlety attributed to the basis."

Bertrand Russell, in 1911, *Logic and Knowledge*, pp. 106–7: ". . . this is a distinction which divides entities into three classes: (a) those which are not in any place, (b) those which are in one place at one time, but never in more than one, (c) those which are in many places at once. . . . Relations, obviously, do not exist anywhere in space. Our bodies, we think, exist in one place at a time, but not in more than one. General qualities, such as whiteness, on the contrary, may be said to be in many places at once."

The modern philosopher takes the non-spatial character of relations for granted, and the ancient Indian takes it for granted that all entities are spatial.

18 For the following section, compare Robinson, "Logical Aspects" and H. Nakamura, "Kūkan no kigō-ronrigaku-teki ketsumei" (Some clarifications of the concept of voidness from the standpoint of symbolic logic), *Indogaku Bukkyōgaku Kenkyū* III, 1 (1954), 223–31.

19 See Candrakīrti on *Stanzas* 1.7 (*Prasannapadā*, p. 31, l. 9), 20.15 (*Prasannapadā*, p. 402, l. 1), and 22.6 (*Prasannapadā*, p. 438, l. 12). Also see Kumārajīva's trans. of 1.6.

20 Compare *Brahmājala-sutta, Sacred Books of the Buddhists* II, 46–47.

21 See Miyamoto, *Chūdō*, pp. 251–80.
22 Schayer, *Kapitel*, p. xxv.
23 Stcherbatsky, *Nirvāṇa*, p. 44: "Applying this method to the Hīnayānist conception of an extinct Buddha, representing nevertheless an eternal lifeless substance *(svabhāva* or *dharma)*, Nāgārjuna flatly denies the reality of the latter, notwithstanding all the reverential feelings which the idea must have evoked. . . . The real Buddha must be perceived *directly by intuition.* The reserved questions, the impossibility to answer whether the world is finite or infinite, and whether the Buddha survives after Nirvāṇa are referred just to this impossibility of whatsoever determination.

See also Schayer, *Kapitel*, pp. xxiv ff., and De Jong, "Absolu," p. 326.

CHAPTER III

1 Kumārajīva's dates: Nobel, "Kumārajīva," p. 228, n. 2, decided that the correct death date was the one in Seng-chao's *Obituary of the Dharma-master Kumārajīva* (KHMC, pp. 264b–65b), that is, the 13th day of the 4th month of A.D. 413. Tsukamoto has reopened the question and undertaken an examination of much evidence that Nobel did not consider. He has presented three versions of his theory:
1) "The Dates of Kumārajīva and Seng-chao Re-examined,"
2) "Kumarajū no katsudō nendai ni tsuite,"
3) "Kumarajū: shoshutsu-nendai no suitei" (*Jōron Kenkyū*, pp. 130–35).

According to Tsukamoto's revised dating, Kumārajīva was born in A.D. 350 and died late in 409. The evidence is as follows: (1) The *Obituary* is not in any collection of documents until early T'ang, when it first appears in the *Kuang-hung-ming-chi.* Therefore Tsukamoto disallows its testimony. However, this is an argument from silence, and is subject to several objections. The *Obituary* contains no doctrine and lends support to no putative translation. Thus it could not have been forged to lend support to any heresy. With the poor communications between Kuan-chung and Chiang-nan during the Nan-pei-ch'ao, the *Obituary* might easily have survived in a library or on a stele in Kuan-chung without the Southern historians knowing about it. As Wright says: "The relative inaccessibility of North China and the fact that Hui-chiao did not, so far as we know, travel there probably limited the amount of this type of material available to him from that area. Such monuments, for example as the Fo-t'u-teng stele of [A.D.] 322 (?) which was still to be seen in the period [A.D.] 766–780. Cf. Wright ["Fo-t'u-teng"], HJAS [No.] 11 [1948], 334." ("Biography and Hagiography," pp. 427–28 and 428, n. 1.) And again:

"Hui-chiao's heavy reliance on Seng-yu's work led him, in at least one case, to perpetuate an error in the earlier work which he might have corrected from other sources available to him. Cf. T'ang 5–6, 'On the date and place of Fa-hu's death'" (*ibid.*, p. 422, n. 5).

There would have been no incentive for anyone except the historically-minded to copy the *Obituary*, and hence it is likely that it would not have been as widely circulated as the prefaces and sundry essays.

From inspection of the *Obituary*, without making a systematic analysis, it is apparent that its phrasing and its content have a great deal of similarity to those of works acknowledged as authentically Seng-chao's. A critical study of the text itself will be necessary before its authenticity can be decided.

(2) The colophon of the *Satyasiddhi Śāstra* (CST, p. 78a7–10) states that this text was translated by Kumārajīva and completed in A.D. 412 on the fifteenth day of the ninth month. Tsukamoto admits that this contradicts the *Kao-seng-chuan* death date of 409, but notes that neither Hui-chiao nor Chi-tsang pays any attention to this document. He also refers to a statement in T'an-ying's biography (KSC, p. 364a7) that the *Satyasiddhi* was translated before the *Saddharma-puṇḍarīka*, that is, before the fifth month of 406, and to the *Li-tai-san-pao-chi* (T 2034), which says that the *Satyasiddhi* was translated in 409. There was evidently a faction quarrel over the text, with one side circulating an "unedited" version.

It is doubtful that Kumārajīva would have had time to translate the voluminous *Satyasiddhi* (16, 20, or 24 chüan, according to variant versions) between finishing the *Great Perfection of Wisdom Treatise* in 405, on the twenty-seventh day of the twelfth month, and finishing the *Saddharma-puṇḍarīka* in the fifth month of 406. Thus Hui-chiao's sequence is not credible. No objections of this sort can be raised against the 409 date, but then no strong evidence has been advanced for that date. Certainly a note in the *Li-tai-san-pao-chi* is not sufficient evidence to disallow a colophon that appears in the *Ch'u-san-tsang-chi-chi*.

(3) Tsukamoto demonstrates in an intricate fashion that Buddhabhadra left Ch'ang-an before A.D. 412 and that Hui-kuan went South with him. He then quotes Hui-kuan's biography which says that Hui-kuan went South after Kumārajīva's death. This argument, he says, is sufficient in itself to make his case certain.

It must be noted, though, that this argument rests on one phrase in the *Kao-seng-chuan* biography of Hui-kuan. As all three death dates for Kumārajīva that Hui-chiao mentions are previous to 411–12, this only proves that the author of the *Kao-seng-chuan* was self-consistent. If he thought that Kumārajīva died in 409 at the latest and also knew that Hui-kuan went South after 409, naturally he would say that he went after Kumārajīva's death. (4) Tsukamoto examines the correspondence between Yao Hsing and his brother, Yao Sung. He establishes the sequence: (a) Yao Hsing draws up a list of doctrinal points; (b) there is trouble in the royal household; (c) Kumārajīva dies; (d) Yao Hsing writes to his brother; (e) Yao Sung answers; (f) Seng-chao composes *Nirvāṇa is Nameless* and sends it up to the king. Tsukamoto says: "A process as involved as this would surely take several years." ("The Dates of Kumārajīva and Seng-chao Re-examined," p. 573). As Seng-chao died in 414, there would have been very little time for him to compose a long essay in the period between Kumārajīva's death and his own, if Kumārajīva died in 413. He also argues that the exchange of correspondence between Yao Hsing and Yao Sung would have taken a long time, and concludes that the 409 date is more congruent. He then recounts certain events in 409 which would correspond to Yao Hsing's "there was trouble in our household."

Seng-chao's biography says: "After Kumārajīva's decease, [Seng-chao], mourning his everlasting departure and suffering severe grief, then wrote the essay *Nirvāṇa is Nameless* [Chao-lun, part IV]" (KSC, p. 365b29). Thus Hui-chiao thought that Seng-chao's grief and his essay were closely connected. As for the sequence that Tsukamoto adduces: It would be difficult to show that the 409 troubles fit the king's general allusion any better than any other troubles in the strife-filled annals of such a royal household. There can have been few years in which there was no trouble there. Also, it does not take very long to write short pieces such as letters, and even the present text of *Chao-lun*, part IV is only about 7000 characters. It could easily be written in a week or so.

Another possibility to consider is that Seng-chao may not have died in 414. I know of no evidence for such a supposition, but if congruence is the sole test it would be just as simple to lengthen Seng-chao's life as to shorten Kumārajīva's.

It should be noted that the Yao Hsing—Yao Sung correspondence does not appear in any collection before the *Kuang-hung-ming-chi*. In this respect, its testimony is no stronger than that of the *Obituary*. It is just as likely that royal correspondence would be forged as that an obituary would be faked.

(5) Seng-chao wrote a letter to Liu I-min and sent it on the fifteenth day of the eighth month of some year after Chih Fa-ling arrived back from Serindia, that is, after 408. This letter states that Kumārajīva is translating the scriptures that have recently arrived. Tsukamoto dates this letter in 409 (*Jōron Kenkyū*, p. 152a).

T'ang, *History*, p. 329, dates this letter in 410. He says that

Tao-sheng, taking *Chao-lun*, part III, went South to Lu-shan at the end of the summer of 408. Liu I-min answered in the twelfth month of the next year (409). Another year later, on the fifteenth day of the eighth month (410), Seng-chao replied. (My copy of T'ang's *History* seems to have a misprint—409 instead of 410—on p. 327, line 4.) Liebenthal (*Chao*, p. 96) follows T'ang. Tao-sheng arrived in Ch'ang-an in 405 at the earliest, and probably in 406. He stayed at least two years, perhaps three. Liebenthal ("Biography of Tao-sheng," p. 71) states that Tao-sheng must have left right after the translation of the *Hsiao-p'in* (T 227) in 408. Certainly Tsukamoto's chronology leaves Tao-sheng very little time in Ch'ang-an. Seng-chao, in the letter in question, says that Tao-sheng was in Ch'ang-an several years, and Yüan-k'ang says, without stating his authority, that "several" means "two or three." (Liebenthal, *Chao*, p. 100 with n. 394.)

(6) Tsukamoto revises Kumārajīva's birth date to 450 by assuming that the legend of the arhant's prophesy is founded on a historical fact, namely that in 384 when Lü Kuang forced Kumārajīva to break the Vinaya, the latter was thirty-five years of age.

However, the meaning of such a prophesy is ambiguous, and its provenance is dubious. If documentary evidence such as the *Satyasiddhi Colophon* and the *Obituary* is not free from suspicion, then how can a mere legend command authority?

The *Ch'u-san-tsang-chi-chi* says merely that Kumārajīva died during the *I-hsi* period of Chin (A.D. 405–419; CST, p. 102a8).

Tsukamoto may be right, all these objections notwithstanding. However, until the difficulties mentioned are resolved, I will continue to prefer the date given in the *Obituary* and accepted by Nobel.

2 See Demiéville, "Pénétration," p. 23; also, Sakaino, *History*, p. 251 (re *Pañcaviṁśati*) and p. 265 (re Dharmaraksa's *Saddharma-puṇḍarīka*, T 263). Kasugai, p. 695, quotes a passage from the *Kao-seng-chuan* life of Buddhayaśas which says that Kumārajīva had been hesitating to translate the *Daśabhūmika* for over a month, when Buddhayaśas joined him in the enterprise. Kasugai thinks that Kumārajīva did not understand Khotanese, hence his hesitation. The text was apparently one sent from Khotan by Chih Fa-ling, like the original of Buddhabhadra's *Avataṁsaka*. But there are numerous other reasons why Kumārajīva may have delayed the start of actual translation. Furthermore, it is unlikely that a great scholar who had spent his early years in Serindia would not have had occasion to use Khotanese texts before.

3 T'ang, *History*, p. 283; Demiéville's review of *Jōron Kenkyū*, p. 231.

4 The following account is based on the *Kao-seng-chuan* biography of Kumārajīva. Nobel, "Kumārajīva," pp. 207–8, suggests that the

fundamental source for this may have been Seng-jui's *Erh-ch'in-lu* (catalogue of translations made under Former and Later Ch'in). This would account for the conversations between Kumārajīva and Seng-jui that the *Kao-seng-chuan* reports. Cf. *Jōron Kenkyū*, pp. 135–45.

5 The Five Sciences *(vidyā)* are given in the *Mahāvyutpatti*, 1554–59, as (1) grammar *(śabda-vidyā)*, (2) logic *(hetu-vidyā)*, (3) metaphysics *(adhyātma-vidyā)*, (4) medicine *(cikitsā-vidyā)*, and (5) the arts and crafts *(śilpa[-karma-]sthāna-vidyā)*.

6 The sentence about the two brothers becoming monks is problematical. It reads: "wei kuo ch'ing ts'ung erh wei sha men" (KSC, p. 330c13). Lévi, "Tokharien B," p. 337, paraphrases: "Deux personnages distingués vinrent alors lui demander l'autorisation de le suivre et l'ordination monastique:..." Nobel, "Kumārajīva," p. 213, translates: "Die hatten ihr Land aufgegeben und gebeten ihm (Kumārajīva) als Śramaṇas nachfolgen zu dürfen."

As Kumārajīva was then only a śrāmaṇera, he could not have taken disciples. Furthermore, the following passage shows that Sūryasoma was already well established as a teacher, and so was unlikely to have left lay life under a mere śrāmaṇera whom he shortly afterwards acquainted with Mahāyāna, Sūryasoma's own strongly-held faith.

T'ang, *History*, p. 284, says: "This sentence is very hard to interpret. The main idea seems to be that the brothers gave up the royal throne and 'went forth.'"

The Chinese text must be construed as: "Entrusting their countries [to someone else], they requested [someone] that they might follow [him] and be śrāmaṇeras." The text does not specify any of the affectees between square brackets. The problem disappears if it is recognized that Kumārajīva cannot be the antecedent of "[someone]" and "[him]."

7 Péri, "Vasubandhu," pp. 375–76, quotes a postface to the *Saddarma-puṇḍarīka* which the *Fa-hua-chuan-chi* (T 2068) presents and attributes to Seng-chao: "Kumārajīva dit:... autrefois, quand j'étais dans l'Inde, j'ai parcouru les cinq Indes en étudiant le Mahāyāna. J'ai été disciple du grand maître Sūryasoma qui me fit goûter la raison. Avec bonté il me donna un livre sanscrit en disant: 'Le soleil du Buddha s'est couché dans l'Ouest, et ce qui reste de son éclat va atteindre le Nord-Est. Le livre que voici est destiné au Nord-Est. Toi, avec respect, travaille à le répandre. Autrefois le maître en çāstra Vasubandhu (en) fit un upadeça; c'est ce livre même; il n'y a pas à choisir parmi ce qu'il a écrit.' Je l'ai reçu avec respect et l'ai apporté dans ma hotte à livres en venant (ici)."

This postface is unattested before T'ang times. It does not appear in the *Ch'u-san-tsang-chi-chi*, and is not mentioned in the *Kao-seng-chuan*. Its version of Kumārajīva's studies is vaguer and more grandiloquent than the one in the *Kao-seng-chuan*, which is earlier and better evidence.

8 *Summary of the Anavatapta-nāgarāja-paripṛccha-sūtra* (T 635, XV, 488–507): Chapter I. Anavatapta asks what the bodhisattva course is. Śākyamuni says that it is arousing the thought of enlightenment and not abandoning living beings. There are thirty-two dharmas that lead to the thought of all-knowledge. There are sixteen deeds that develop the thought of all-knowledge. There are twenty-two deeds that remove wrong ways.

Chapter II. The bodhisattva practises eight ways of purification. There are purity of body, emptiness, and fundamental purity.

Chapter III. Bodhi is not obtained by practice, so the bodhisattva should abandon notions of practice.

Chapter IV. Anavatapta invites Śākyamuni to spend three months in his great nāga-pool. Śākyamuni goes, with a great retinue and magic pageantry.

Chapter V. The bodhisattva practises non-desire by considering causes and conditions as empty. The bodhisattva's sixteen powers.

Chapter VI. Anavatapta asks how the bodhisattva can meet the Buddhas. Śākyamuni says that he can do so by cultivating faith, that is, pious practices.

Chapter VII. Anavatapta asks how the bodhisattva can turn the wheel of the Dharma. Praises of the Dharmacakra. Rhetoric on preserving the Dharma.

Chapter VIII. Subhūti asks whether the Buddha ceases, is born, etc. The answer is śūnyavādin. Anavatapta asks whether the Buddha is considered as the skandhas. The dialogue follows the usual śūnyavādin pattern.

Chapter IX. Patience is empty.

Chapter X. Absence of support *(apratiṣṭhita)*; dharmatā.

Chapter XI. The assembly worships Śākyamuni. Anavatapta receives a prediction.

Chapter XII. The Buddha entrusts the sūtra to Maitreya, Mañjuśrī and Ānanda.

9 Vimalākṣa was a North Indian Vinaya master who made his way to Kuchā. When the Chinese took Kuchā in 383, he escaped. Later, hearing that Kumārajīva was teaching successfully in Ch'ang-an, he set out to join him, and reached Ch'ang-an in 406. After Kumārajīva's death, he went South, where he finally completed the translation of the *Sarvāstivādi- vinaya* that Kumārajīva had begun. He died at the age of seventy-seven (KSC, p. 333b–c; Bagchi, pp. 338–39).

10 Mochizuki, *Bukkyō Kyōten Seiritsu Shiron*, pp. 441–71, especially

pp. 445–46. Mochizuki demolishes the attribution to Kumārajīva, and discounts the story that Tao-jung requested its translation. He concludes that the work was composed in China.

11 See Hirakawa Akira: "Jūjūbibasha-ron no chosha ni tsuite" (On the Author of *Daśabhūmika-śāstra*). Hirakawa points out some divergences between the text in question and the *Great Perfection of Wisdom Treatise*, but says that it would be dangerous to assert that they are not by the same author.

One reason why some Japanese scholars are loath to deny the attribution of the *Jūjūbibasha* to Nāgārjuna is that this text contains some Amitābhist passages which are important in Jōdo-shū- and Jōdo-shin-shū dogmatics. In November, 1958, when the Prince Patriarch of Nishi Honganji was in Toronto, I asked him what difference it would make to his sect if the *Jūjūbibasha* were proven to be not by Nāgārjuna. He stated that, in that case, Nāgārjuna would simply no longer be counted as a Jōdo-shin-shū patriarch, but that his sect would naturally not take mere conjecture for proof.

12 Concerning the dhyāna texts that Kumārajīva translated, their contents, and their connection with the state of Chinese Buddhism at the time, see Demiéville, "Yogācārabhūmi," pp. 351–63.

13 But see Tsukamoto, "The Dates of Kumārajīva and Seng-chao Re-examined," p. 576, where it is pointed out that according to T'an-ying's biography the *Satyasiddhi* was translated before the *Saddharma-Puṇḍarīka*, that is, before the fifth month of 406. Also, the *Li-tai-san-pao-chi* says that it was translated in Hung-shih 11 (A.D. 409). See KSC, p. 364a7 (Life of T'an-ying).

14 The only source for the 409 date is the two notes, one at the end of T'an-ying's *Middle Treatise Preface* (CST, p. 78a4), and the other at the end of Seng-jui's *Preface to the Twelve Topic Treatise* (CST, p. 78a4). Tsukamoto (*Jōron Kenkyū*, p. 144b) grants very small credence to these notes, though he says that Kumārajīva might have gone on from translating the *Hsiao-p'in* (T 227) in Hung-shih 11 (A.D. 409) to the two Mādhyamika treatises. He also says that Kumārajīva probably told his students about the content of the *Middle Treatise* before 409, because Seng-chao's *Prajñā Has No Knowing* (*Chao-lun*, part III), written about 406, already quotes the *Middle Treatise*.

15 See Wright, "Fo-t'u-teng."

16 See Ōchō Enichi, "Shaku Dōan no honyaku-ron"; *Chūgoku bukkyō no kenkyū*, pp. 219–55, "Chūgoku bukkyō shoki no honyaku-ron"; "Kumarajū no honyaku."

Ōchō deals for the most part with opinions about translation expressed by Chinese monks in early prefaces and biographies, expressly declaring that he is leaving to others comparison of Kumārajīva's translations with the original texts ("Kumarajū no honyaku," p. 23). As the purpose at hand is the adequacy of Kumārajīva's Mādhyamika translations, I refrain from summarizing Ōchō's historical and synoptic treatment of the subject.

17 Paraphrased by Demiéville, "Pénétration," p. 33.

18 A long tongue is one of the thirty-two marks of a Buddha. See *Lakkhana Suttanta*, Dīgha-nikāya, IV, 138 (27th mark).

19 Liebenthal, "Biography of Tao-sheng," p. 70, n. 30.

20 *Prasannapadā*, p. 84, n. 1.

21 Rahder's review of *Traité*, p. 125b, says: "Lamotte renders the key-terms *anupalabdha* , *anupalabhya* sometimes correctly by 'insaisissable' (1104), 'non-établi,' 'introuvable' (75), 'non-acquis' (1112), 'non-perçu' (1106), 'not being a predicate' (1091 n.), but very often incorrectly by 'non-existent' (724, 733–5, 750, 919, 981, 1092, 1100)."

However, since Kumārajīva's translations persistently confuse the epistemological and the existential, and since 'pu te' renders both 'anupalabhya' and 'na vidyate,' the translator is confronted with a tangle that cannot always be resolved with certainty.

22 T 310, 15 was translated by Śikṣānanda about A.D. 700. No translation done before A.D. 405 is extant.

23 Kumārajīva's lengthy quotation from this sūtra differs much from the corresponding passage in T 632, the only translation that antedates him. The passage in T 633 (listed as anonymous by Seng-yu and later assigned to Sung (A.D. 420–79) is less corrupt than T 634 but does not correspond any better to Kumārajīva's version. T 634, translated after 1053, is more verbose than the other translations, and its version of the passage in question differs radically from those of Kumārajīva and the other translations. See T XV, 463b15, 470b22, and 480b13. Kumārajīva was either quoting a different text of the sūtra, or paraphrasing.

24 T 100 may have been translated before A.D. 405, as it is classed as 'anonymous, 350–431.' T 99 was translated by Guṇabhadra after A.D. 435.

25 This simile occurs in Dharmarakṣa's *Saddharma-puṇḍarīka* (T 263), but not in Kumārajīva's own translation (T 262). See Demiéville, "Yogācārabhūmi," p. 351, n. 5.

CHAPTER IV

1 Of the 257 independent biographies in the *Kao-seng-chuan*, 35 are of translators, 101 are of exegetes, 20 are of wonder-workers, 21 are of meditators, 13 are of discipline experts, 11 are of self-immolators, 21 are of sūtra-reciters, 14 are of creators of merit, 11 are of sūtra-masters, and 10 are of chanters.

See Wright, "Biography and Hagiography," pp. 386–7, for statistics and their significance. Also, see Wright, "Hui-chiao as a Chinese Historian," p. 380.

2 See Demiéville, "Pénétration," 23, for a paraphrase and interpretation of the early years of Hui-yüan's biography. As Demiéville says, Hui-yüan's development is typical of the Chinese literatus up to the 7th century who went over to Buddhism. Zürcher has translated the whole *Kao-seng-chuan* biography of Hui-yüan (*Conquest*, pp. 240–53), and has given a thorough and discerning account of his career, his religion and his ideas (*Conquest*, pp. 204–39). The manuscript of this book was completed in 1959, shortly before *Conquest* appeared. The present chapter has not been substantially altered since then. Time has not permitted me to utilize the studies published in *Eon Kenkyū*, vol. II.

On Hui-yüan's career and teachings, see: T'ang, *History*, pp. 341–73; Liebenthal, "Hui-yüan," pp. 243–59; Hurvitz, "Render Unto Caesar," pp. 80–114.

3 *shih-hsiang* 實相 is one of the commonest terms in certain texts translated by Kumārajīva, yet its Sanskrit equivalent is difficult to identify. See Rahder's review of *Traité*, p. 125a–b, where Lamotte's rendering, 'satyalakṣaṇa,' is said to be wrong, and where 'tattvalakṣaṇa,' 'dharmatā,' and 'bhūtanaya' are given as attested by actual correspondences. I think perhaps 'hsiang' here represents the suffixes '-tva' and '-tā' in at least some cases, which would make 'tattva' and 'bhūtatā' possible equivalents.

4 See Hurvitz, "Render unto Caesar," p. 85, n. 13.

5 See Liebenthal, "Immortality," pp. 355 ff.

6 Compare Chih Tun's (Chih Tao-Lin's) exegesis on *Chuang-tzŭ*, ch. 1, KSC, p. 348b20; Demiéville, "Pénétration," p. 27.

7 "Ideology" is used here in a sense similiar to one that Wright assigns to it: "Ideology, in the sense in which I shall use it, means the sum of assertions, in words or in ritual-symbolic acts, of ideas and principles intended to sanction and justify power and elicit the consent or support of various social groups. An ideological measure means a single assertion with such an intent" ("The Formation of Sui Ideology," p. 352, n. 3).

8 Liebenthal, "Hui-yüan," p. 259b: "What is astonishing is only that a man who spent the greater part of his life under Tao-an (he left him A.D. 378 when he was forty-five years old), studying the Prajñāpāramitā Sūtras, assimilated so little of the Indian Buddhist theory." This perhaps overstates, but not with regard to Hui-yüan's *Prajñā* studies.

9 The term *tsung* 宗 means (a) Absolute Truth, (b) a proposition or thesis, (c) the goal of a quest, (d) an ideological school. Its connotations are those of the historically earlier meaning, "clan

shrine, clan." Wherever meanings (a) and/or (c) are involved, I translate by "Ideal." Frequently the term is too multivalent to be rendered by any one of the equivalents (a) to (d).

10 Liebenthal, "Hui-yüan," p, 248a: "The introduction to the Ta-chih-tu-lun ch'ao, which was written in the last years of Hui-yüan, shows more than others the influence from Ch'ang-an, perhaps even the influence of the ***Chao-lun*** Part III which had reached the Lu-shan in A.D. 408. The argument on existence and non-existence is wholly in the style of Seng-chao."

11 Liebenthal, "Hui-yüan," p. 247b: "The Indian problem was how to get out of the World which includes life and death, or a sequence of lives and deaths, into Nirvāṇa, which of course is not death.... Hui-yüan, if he speaks of non-existence which for him is identical with Truth, thinks of death."

CHAPTER V

1 Wright, "Seng-jui," establishes the identity of Seng-jui and Hui-jui, and thus determines that this person was born in A.D. 352 and died in 436. The Seng-jui biography (KSC, p. 364a–b) has been translated by Nobel, "Kumārajīva," pp. 229-33, and by Wright, "Seng-jui," pp. 273–77. Wright ("Seng-jui," pp. 278–79) also translates the Hui-jui biography. In the following, I combine the two biographies into one continuous account.

2 T'ang, ***History***, pp. 193–97 (Tao-an's itinerary); Ui, ***Dōan***, pp. 177–86 (Tao-an's chronology).

3 See KSC, p. 354b, also Wright, "Fo-t'u-teng," p. 328: "CHU Seng-lang is the first monk recorded as having founded a monastery in Shantung; in the course of a long life he built up a great center of Buddhism there. He was a man of strict piety and insisted on severe monastic discipline. His learning was considerable, and he had a strong influence on Seng-jui, Kumārajīva's most prominent Chinese associate."

Did Seng-jui go to Shantung, or did Seng-lang come to Honan?

4 Bagchi, pp. 156–57; CST, p. 64c. T'ang, ***History***, p. 196, states that Tao-an was the author of the preface to this translation. See Ui, ***Dōan***, p. 152, n. 1.

5 One of these early dhyāna manuals, the ***Yogācārabhūmi*** of Saṅgharakṣa, exists in a partial translation by An Shih-kao (***Tao-ti-ching***, T 607), and a complete translation by Dharmarakṣa (***Hsiu-hsing-tao-ti-ching***, T 606). The text has been studied and précised by Demiéville, "Yogācārabhūmi." Tao-an's preface to this work has been translated by Link ("Daw-an," pp. 4–10).

Another early work on dhyāna, the ***Ānāpāna-smṛti-sūtra*** was also translated by An Shih-kao (***Ta-An-pan-shou-i-ching***, T 602). Link has prepared an English resumé, the manuscript of which he has been kind enough to show me.

6 Liebenthal, "Biography of Tao-sheng," p. 67, n. 15.
7 *Ibid.*, p. 81, n. 67.
8 *Ibid.*, p. 72.
9 Compare T'ang, "Ko-yi," p. 278, n. 1. Demiéville, "Pénétration," p. 26, says: "The theory of 'rien spirituel' thus participates in that method which consisted of interpreting Taoism by Buddhism, and vice versa, the method which we have seen Hui-yüan practicing in 357. Very widespread at this period, this method was described as 'analysis of ideas' (*ko-i*, literally 'scrutinize the sense,' implied: beyond the letter)."

T'ang's interpretation of "ko-i" differs considerably from the one that Demiéville offers. He says: "It is evident that, in matching concepts with concepts and terms with terms, Chu Fa-Ya and his colleagues were carrying on one of the practices of Han scholarship. With the advent of the Wei-Chin era, a new philosophy, Hsüan-hsüeh, became dominant. It emphasized profound searching for first principles and regarded with contempt the matching of concepts; it is not surprising, therefore, that its proponents, who used the new method of 'the distinction of words and meanings' would discover the defects of Ko-yi" ("Ko-yi," p. 286; cf. *History*, pp. 234–38). The problem is well analyzed by Zürcher, *Conquest*, p. 184. As he says, *Ko-i* was some *particular* method of explaining dharma-lists. It was not merely the use of phrases from the Chinese classics as euphemisms for Buddhist concepts, a practice that Seng-jui continued vigorously while he condemned *Ko-i*.

CHAPTER VI

1 Among the more important modern studies on Seng-chao are: (1) T'ang, *History*, pp. 328–29, (2) Itano Chōhachi, "Eon, Sōjō no shinmeikan wo ronjite, Dōshō no shinsetsu ni oyobu," (3) Liebenthal, *Chao*, (4) *Jōron Kenkyū*. The reviews on (3) and (4) have also contributed materially to Seng-chao studies. Among Liebenthal's reviewers are: Wright, *Journal of the American Oriental Society* (1950), pp. 324a–26b; Waley, *Journal of the Royal Asiatic Society* (1950), p. 80; and D. L. Snellgrove, *Bulletin of the School of Oriental and African Studies*, XIII (1951), 1053–55. Among the reviewers of *Jōron Kenkyū* are Waley and Demiéville.
2 Tsukamoto advances good reasons to suggest that Seng-chao died in 414 at the age of forty-one, rather than at the age of thirty-one (*Jōron Kenkyū*, p. 121).
3 The biography (KSC, p. 365a15) says 及在冠年而名振關輔.
4 The rendering of this quotation is problematical. The text reads 吾解不謝子. 辭當相挹. Liebenthal, *Chao*, p. 6, translates: "My understanding equals yours, but not my phrasing."

5 The third-century Neo-Taoist.
6 On Liu I-min, see Liebenthal, *Chao*, p. 86, n. 329, and Hurvitz, "Render unto Caesar," p. 85, n. 11.
7 Since this text is probably a Chinese composition rather than a translation, the Preface is subject to suspicion.
8 This is not listed by T'ang or Liebenthal. Its authenticity has already been discussed in Chapter Two. The evidence indicates that it is spurious.
9 T'ang, *History*, p. 332, surmises that the *Pao-tsang-lun* was composed after mid-T'ang times, by someone connected with the Ch'an movement and interested in Taoist studies. Tsukamoto, *Jōron Kenkyū*, p. 149, says that the *Pao-tsang-lun* is quoted by Tsung-mi (A.D. 780–841). It may be dated about the K'ai-yüan period (A.D. 713–41), but can hardly be pre-T'ang.
10 Numbers between corners refer to the passages between corners in Document 8.
11 Compare the meaning of 'prakāśa' in Yoga, Sāṁkhya, etc.
12 Liebenthal, *Chao*, p. 71, n. 266: "I do not know where Chao found this amazing syllogism." Much of the logical material in this chapter has already appeared in my "Mysticism and Logic in Seng-chao's Thought."
13 Seng-chao quotes the *Prajñā-pāramitā-hṛdaya* in his letter to Liu I-min, *Chao-lun*, p. 156c5.
14 Suzuki, *Zen Buddhism* (Anchor Books), pp. 111–21.
15 Compare *Stanzas* 22.11.
16 "On the 'Six Houses,'" see T'ang, *History*, pp. 229–78, and Liebenthal, *Chao*, pp. 146–66.
17 Compare MT, pp. 11a25 and 18a11.
18 Compare MT, p. 1c12.
19 See Waley, *The Way and its Power*, ch. 38, p. 190.
20 But see Kumārajīva's translation of *Middle Stanzas* 17.28 and 18.10; MT, pp. 23b9 and 24a9.
21 Numbers between corners refer to the passages between corners in Document 9.
22 These terms are like Indian 'ruta—artha.'
23 Liebenthal, *Chao*, p. 9: "Reasoning is no longer meant to lead to concrete results, but is used only to place before the reader the insoluble wonder of Existence, the 'Gate to the Mystery.' His paradoxes become more and more pointed; emotion reaches its highest pitch. The Gate is open; it can be entered at any moment; the solution of the great riddle 'is not far to seek.' This is the final word which Seng-chao has to say concerning salvation."
24 This is apparently a paraphrase of T 262, p. 43c3–12, *Miao-fa-ching*, chapter 16.
25 Numbers between corners refer to the passages between corners in Document 10.

26 Whitehead, ***Process and Reality***, p. 453: "Actual occasions, ***R*** and ***S***, which are ***contemporary*** with ***M***, are those actual occasions which lie neither in ***M***'s causal past, nor in ***M***'s causal future. . . . A 'duration' is a locus of actual occasions, such that (a) any two members of the locus are contemporaries, and (b) that any actual occasion, not belonging to the duration, is the causal past or causal future of some members of the duration."

27 Liebenthal, ***Chao***, p. 32: "Chao's syllogisms are not genuine ***prasaṅga***. For Nāgārjuna merely refutes mundane entities, but Chao wishes to establish the existence of supramundane ones; . . ."

28 Ingalls, "Comparison," p. 4: "The Indian example contains a grammatical error concerning the nature of negation. The existence of the past is not grammatically denied by saying the past does not exist, but by saying the past did not exist. Underneath this grammatical error, lies a mathematical problem in the doctrine of the infinite divisibility of time. This to Nāgārjuna destroyed the concept of time just as the Greek example seems to destroy the concept of space. But neither Nāgārjuna nor his antagonists ever recognized this as a mathematical problem."

CHAPTER VIII

1 The same tradition is given by Mochizuki, ***Bukkyō Daijiten*** II, 1702–3.

2 See T'ang, ***History***, p. 737, and the ***Nan-ch'i-shu***, Chou Yung Chuan, Chapter 41 (Lieh-chuan, 22).

3 ***Kuan-shih-yin-ching*** probably means Chapter 23 of Dharmarakṣa's ***Cheng-fa-hua-ching***, T 263.

4 The present Shou district in Anhuei.

5 This would normally mean Ceylon, but I find it strange that a ***brahman*** should come from Ceylon, and even stranger that he should come on a camel by way of Central Asia rather than by ship along the southern sea route.

6 See chapter 3, n. 1, for the problem of when the ***Satyasiddhi*** was actually translated.

7 Liebenthal, "World-conception of Tao-sheng," pp. 73–100, especially pp. 77–78 ("The Middle Path"). Also see Demiéville, "Pénétration," pp. 32–35, regarding the place of Tao-sheng's sudden appearance in the history of Chinese thought.

8 See Yūki, "Sanron-genryū-kō" (A Study on the Lineage of Chinese San-lun Masters).

9 Liebenthal, "Biography of Tao-sheng," p. 75, n. 51 and p. 76, n. 52.

DOCUMENT 2, PART I

1 This is an inexact quotation from the ***Abhidharmasāra*** (T 1550), in the translation of which Hui-yüan collaborated with Saṅghadeva.

It deals with the objection that if arising has an arising there will be an infinite regress. The whole argument (T XXVIII, 811b18–28) runs: "All conditioned dharmas have, each one, four characteristics—arising, abiding, alteration, and disintegration. . . .
OBJECTION: If all conditioned dharmas have, each one, four characteristics, then these four characteristics will in turn have characteristics.
REPLY: These, too, have four characteristics. Within those characteristics, the remaining four characteristics arise together. Arising effects arising, abiding effects abiding, alteration effects alteration, and disintegration effects disintegration.
OBJECTION: If that is so, then there is an infinite regress.
REPLY: As they develop, they in turn effect each other. These characteristics, each by each, effect each other. Thus arising and arising produce each other, abiding and abiding produce (retain) each other, alteration and alteration alter each other, and disintegration and disintegration disintegrate each other. Therefore, it is not an infinite regress. The latter four characteristics each act on one dharma. The former four characteristics each act on eight dharmas. Arising produces eight dharmas—the [other] three former [characteristics], the four latter [characteristics], and that [main] dharma. The other [three primary characteristics] do likewise."

This is the theory of the secondary characteristics *(anulakṣaṇa)* that is expounded in the *Abhidharmakośa* (La Vallée Poussin, pp. 224–26; T XXIX, 27b8 ff.), where it serves the same purpose of refuting the charge of regressus ad infinitum. The first primary characteristic (arising) produces (1) the main dharma *(mūladharma)*, then the other three primary characteristics, namely (2) abiding, (3) alteration, and (4) disintegration, and the four secondary characteristics, namely (5) arising of arising, (6) abiding of abiding, (7) alteration of alteration, and (8) disintegration of disintegration. But arising of arising only produces one dharma, namely the primary arising. Similarly, abiding of abiding makes the primary abiding abide, and the primary abiding causes eight dharmas to abide—the main dharma, the three other primary characteristics, and the four secondary characteristics.

Former 前 and latter 後 unfortunately suggest temporal succession, whereas the originals, *mūlakaṣaṇa* and *anulakṣaṇa*, mean only 'primary characteristics' and 'secondary characteristics.'

Compare the thesis of the opponent in *Middle Treatise*, ch. 7, p. 9b10:
"QUESTION: You state that the three marks constitute an infinite regression. This is not right. Although arising, abiding, and ceasing are conditioned, they are not infinitely regressive. For what reason? [*Stanzas* 7.4]: 'The product of the arising of arising is the arising of the primary arising. The product of the primary

arising is in turn the arising of the arising of arising.' At the time when a dharma arises, including its own entity seven dharmas arise together: (1) the dharma, (2) arising, (3) abiding, (4) ceasing, (5) arising of arising, (6) abiding of abiding, (7) ceasing of ceasing. The primary arising, exclusive of its own entity, is the producer of six dharmas. Arising of arising is the producer of the primary arising, and the primary arising is the producer of the arising of arising. Therefore, although arising, abiding, and ceasing are conditioned, they are not infinitely regressive."

2 Taisho 人法 should be emended to 八法 (eight dharmas) on the basis of the *Abhidharmasāra* prototype of this passage. See n. 13, below.

3 GPWT, p. 439b1: "If arising [produces] arising, then the dharma of arising has already arisen and should not arise again. If non-arising [produces] arising, then because the dharma of arising does not exist yet, it should not arise."

GPWT, p. 287c12: "Further, because [the dharmas] are conditioned, there is ceasing at the moment of arising, and arising at the moment of ceasing. If the already-arisen arises, then [its arising] is useless. If the unarisen arises, then there is nothing produced. Indeed, there should not be any difference between dharma and arising. For what reason? If arising produces a dharma, there should be an arising of arising. In this case, there should be still further arising, and this would be an infinite regression. If in the arising of arising there is no further arising, then in arising there should not be any arising. If there is no arising in arising, then likewise there should not be any arising in a dharma. In this case, arising cannot be found. Likewise for ceasing."

Also see GPWT, T XXV, p. 60b22, Lamotte, *Traité* I, 37, *Eon Kenkyū*, p. 248, n. 243.

4 Delete the second occurrence of 若不免无窮之難.

5 Either delete 沒 or change it to 設. *Eon Kenkyū*, p. 36, n. 10.

6 Change 同 to 因 with *Eon Kenkyū*.

7 GPWT, p. 110a15; Lamotte, *Traité* I, 423.

8 See Doc. 4, n. 36.

9 GPWT, p. 200b1: "Further, because all the dharmas are marked by impermanence, they do not have a time of abiding. If thought abode for one moment, it should also abide for a second moment. This would be constant abiding and there would be no mark of ceasing. As the Buddha stated, all conditioned dharmas abide in the three marks, and also have the mark of ceasing. If they had no ceasing, they should not be marked as conditioned. Further, if after a dharma there is [its] cessation, we must know that before it there was cessation already. It is like a man who is wearing a new garment. If on the first day that he wears it it is not

old, then on the second day also it should not be old. In this way, right up to ten years it should always be new and should not be old. But really it has become old. We must know that it exists together with the new. Because it is subtle, it is not perceived. Only after the oldness is completed is it recognized. For this reason, we know that all the dharmas have no time of abiding."

Compare GPWT, pp. 222c10, 286c20, and HT, ch. 6, p. 177a13, for a similar example concerning a new sabot.

Eon Kenkyū, p. 248, n. 244 says that the source is not identified.

10 GPWT, p. 62a8, Lamotte, *Traité* I, 50, *Eon Kenkyū*, p. 248, n. 245; Cf. GPWT, pp. 200c19, 170a.

11 The Abhidharma-master Kātyāyana, author of the *Jñānaprasthāna*. He is mentioned frequently in the *Great Perfection of Wisdom Treatise*. See GPWT, p. 70a10, Lamotte, *Traité* I, 109, n. 2.

12 See GPWT, p. 439a7. "Śāriputra had this thought: The Buddha's sūtras state that two dharmas include all the dharmas. They are either conditioned or unconditioned. The arising ones are conditioned. The non-arising ones are unconditioned." *Eon Kenkyū* quotes the *Pañcaviṁśati*, T 223, VIII, 242c7ff., which does not seem to merit being singled out.

13 See GPWT, p. 65c17, Lamotte, *Traité* I, 78: "The expressions 'location,' 'time,' 'separation,' 'combination,' 'unity,' 'plurality,' 'long,' and 'short' come forth from conventional designations *(nāmasaṁketa)*. The thoughts of worldlings adhere to them, and they say that they are real *(sadbhūta)* dharmas. For this reason, one must get rid of dharmas that are worldly, conventional designations, and verbalisms."

14 See *Middle Stanzas* 15.11. *Eon Kenkyū*, n. 247 quotes GPWT, p. 78c7.

15 HT, ch. 7, p. 178a14: "Do you not know? Because the sprout, etc. continue from the seed, there is no annihilation, and because the causes—the seed, etc.—are destroyed, there is no permanence In this way, the Buddhas declared that the causes and conditions in twelve sections produce the dharmas."

HT, ch. 8, p. 179a16: "If [you assert that] a thing produces a thing just as the mother produces the child, then this is not true. For what reason? The mother really does not produce the child, because the child exists previously and comes forth from the mother."

Both these examples occur widely in discussions of pratītya-samutpāda.

16 See n. 1, above.

17 Emend 或 to 惑. *Eon Kenkyū* has 惑 and notes no variant.

18 Source not yet identified. No note in *Eon Kenkyū*.

19 *Middle Stanzas* 1.14.

20 GPWT, p. 104c26, Lamotte, *Traité* I, 380; *Middle Stanzas* 13.6; HT, ch. 8, p. 179a8. Read 同 with *Eon Kenkyū* rather than 因 with Taishō.

21 HT, ch. 8, p. 178a23.

22 HT, ch. 8, pp. 178a27–28.

23 HT, ch. 8, p. 178b6.

24 HT, ch. 8, p. 178b10. Add 然 after 不. This passage seems corrupt.

25 HT, ch. 8, p. 178b12. Emend 妄 to 成 following HT. *Eon Kenkyū* fails to emend.

26 Beginning, middle, and last. HT, ch. 8, p. 178b17: "[INSIDER]: Beginning, middle, and last do not arise in succession. 'Beginning' means having nothing before but having something afterwards. 'Middle' means having something before and having something afterwards. 'Last' means having something before but having nothing afterwards. Thus beginning, middle, and last are interdependent. If they are separated, how can they exist? Therefore, the beginning, middle, and last must not arise in succession. Arising at one time is likewise not admissible. If they arise at one time, you should not say, 'this is the beginning, this is the middle, this is the last.' They would not be interdependent, and therefore it is not admissible."

27 The *Abhidharmasāra*, which Hui-yüan referred to as a *ching* at the beginning of this section.

28 *Stanzas* 18.7. See De Jong, *Chapitres*, p. 22, and La Vallée Poussin, "Madhyamaka," pp. 236–37. Also see GPWT, p. 96c13, Lamotte, *Traité* I, 323.

29 GPWT, p. 99a3, Lamotte, *Traité* I, 337: "Sūtra: They have traversed the patience towards profound dharmas."

GPWT, p. 99a13, Lamotte, *Traité* I, 338: "Again, explanation that the marks of all the dharmas are real *(satya)*, indestructible *(akṣaya)*, and immovable, is the profound dharma."

GPWT, p. 106c18, Lamotte, *Traité* I, 394: "Further, the patience of sameness can endure everything with regard to living beings. The patience that accommodates to the Dharma endures [everything] with regard to the profound Dharmas. The augmentation of these two patiences brings about the realization of patience with regard to non-arising."

GPWT, p. 107a4, Lamotte, *Traité* I, 396: "Further, as for the profound Dharmas, in the twelve nidānas there is a progression *(pravṛtti)*, and effects are produced. The effect is neither existent nor inexistent in the cause, yet it comes forth from it. This is termed a profound Dharma."

GPWT, p. 107a7, Lamotte, *Traité* I, 396: "Further, it is termed a profound Dharma to view all the dharmas as not empty and not non-empty, not endowed with marks and not markless, not active and not inactive, and not to attach the mind to this sort of view."

DOCUMENT 2, PART II

1 GPWT, p. 521a27–28: "Because the suchness, dharma-nature, and reality-limit which the prajñā-pāramitā depends on (takes as an object) are unconditioned dharmas, it is permanent."

Also see GPWT, p. 513a20, 22; p. 563a7 (sūtra); p. 297b22 (sūtra).

2 GPWT, p. 370a21: "The prajñā-pāramitā is the real-mark of all the dharmas, indestructible and imperishable. Whether there is a Buddha or is not a Buddha, it abides constantly in the marks of the dharmas, in the dharma-position."

Fang-kuang, T 221, p. 135c23: "Subhūti said, 'Blessed One, Whether there exists a Buddha or there does not exist a Buddha, does dharma-nature always abide?' The Buddha said, 'It is so. Whether there exists a Buddha or does not exist a Buddha, dharma-nature always abides.'" *Eon Kenkyū*, p. 250, n. 251.

Also GPWT, p. 75a11, Lamotte, *Traité* I, 157; p. 515c15 (sūtra); p. 516c6 (sūtra); p. 703c20 (sūtra).

3 Perhaps this refers to the etymological explanation of 'tathāgata' at GPWT, p. 71b, Lamotte, *Traité* I, 126.

Fang-kuang, p. 77b1: "The Tathāgata's true and perfect enlightenment knows the suchness of all the dharmas. It is so and not non-so, and nothing can make it non-so. He knows all the suchnesses and all the so-nesses. For this reason the Buddhas, the Blessed Ones, are called Tathāgatas." *Eon Kenkyū*, p. 250, n. 251.

4 "Because the bodhisattva enters the dharma-nature, he does not realize the reality-limit. Therefore, he is able to bestow fortune (merit) with pure recompense" (GPWT, p. 303c6).

Fang-kuang, p. 84b22: "The bodhisattva, even though he has attained the way of emptiness, signlessness, and wishlessness, if he is parted from prajñā-pāramitā and does not hold to upāya-kauśalya, then he realizes the reality-limit and attains the śrāvaka vehicle." *Eon Kenkyū*, p. 250, n. 251.

5 This may mean that understanding of dependent co-arising will solve the dilemma about dharma-nature.

6 See GPWT, pp. 297b22 ff. for a lengthy explanation of dharmatā, tathatā, and bhūtakoṭi. This, though, cannot be the "Non-Arising Patience' section to which Kumārajīva refers.

7 Read 其 rather than 丑. *Eon Kenkyū*, p. 38, n. 6.

8 GPWT, p. 96c13; *Stanzas* 18.7. See Doc. 2, Part I, n. 25.

9 GPWT, p. 697a14: "It means that the real-mark of the dharmas is termed reality-limit."

10 The marks—arising, abiding, altering, and ceasing—are moments. On time, see the discussion of kālavāda, GPWT, p. 65b, Lamotte, *Traité* I, 76 ff.

11 Suchness is not created by any of the great elements. GPWT, p. 299c5: "For this reason, the Buddha states that the power of mind is greatest. Because of practicing the prajñā-pāramitā [a bodhisattva can] disperse the great earth into atoms. Because earth has form, scent, taste, and is heavy, there is nothing that it can do by itself. Because water lacks scent, it moves, and its action surpasses that of earth. Because fire lacks scent and taste, its force surpasses that of water. Because wind lacks form, scent, and taste, it moves and its action surpasses that of fire. Mind has none of the four qualities, and so its power is greatest."

For the last sentence, compare GPWT, p. 223a26: "These three seals are something that none of the master dialecticians can destroy."

12 GPWT, p. 301a27: "The bodhisattva mahāsattva knows that in the real-mark of the dharmas there is nothing to take, nothing to reject and nothing to be destroyed."

13 GPWT, pp. 298a6; 299a16.

14 GPWT, p. 297b26. The number of the great elements differs elsewhere in the *Great Perfection of Wisdom Treatise*. P. 298c19–20 gives five elements: "For example, the earth-dharma is solid and heavy; the water-dharma is cold and wet; the fire-dharma is hot and light-giving; the wind-dharma is light and mobile; the mind-dharma is conscious and understanding."

See also GPWT, p. 194b23, Lamotte, *Traité* II, 1096–97.

The *Abhidharmasāra*, T XXVIII, 809a13, lists six great elements and their characteristics: (1) earth—solidness, (2) water—wetness, (3) fire—hotness, (4) wind—motion, (5) space—unimpededness, and (6) consciousness—formlessness.

15 GPWT, p. 113c1, Lamotte, *Traité* I, 446. See *Vaiśeṣika Sūtras*, V, 2, 13, Faddegon, p. 13.

16 GPWT, p. 298c29: "If one knows that dharma-nature is measureless and boundless, that it is the most subtle and sublime, that there is no further dharma that surpasses dharma-nature or transcends dharma-nature, then the mind is satisfied and does not seek anything else, and then achieves realization. It is like traveling on a road. Day after day one presses on unceasingly. When one reaches the destination, one has no thought of departing again. Even so is the traveler who abides in the reality-limit. When the arhants and pratyeka-buddhas abide in the reality-limit, even though Buddhas [more numerous than] the sands of the Ganges were to preach the doctrine for them, they still would not advance any farther, and also would not be born again in the three planes *(traidhātuka)*. When the bodhisattva enters this dharma-nature, he knows the reality-limit from afar [Mano, p. 838, 'haruka ni']. While he has not yet become fully endowed with the six pāramitās,

he instructs living beings. If at that time he attains realization, he foregoes [read 放 for 妨] achievement of Buddhahood. At this time the bodhisattva, through great compassion and power of zeal *(vīrya)*, returns and cultivates all the practices."

17 GPWT, p. 297c14:
"QUESTION: Suchness, dharma-nature, and reality-limit—are these three items one, or are they different? If they are one, why do you speak of three? If they are three, then now you should distinguish and explain them.
REPLY: These three are all synonyms for the real-mark of the dharmas."

18 GPWT, p. 567b5:
"[SŪTRA]: Subhūti said to Śāriputra, 'Do you wish to have it that in the suchness of the dharmas there are three kinds of men—those of the śrāvaka-yāna, the pratyekabuddha-yāna, and the Buddha-yāna?'"

GPWT, p. 567c28: "If you enter the gate of final emptiness, all the dharmas are utterly of one mark. If you come out from final emptiness, then there is a difference between the Three Vehicles. Because the Buddha is now distinguishing the dharmas, he states that there are superior, middle, and inferior vehicles. He is not speaking for the sake of final emptiness."

19 The *Great Perfection of Wisdom Treatise* gives various gradations of suchness. The lower grades pertain to the nature of mundane, particular entities, which perhaps accounts for suchness being placed at the bottom of the triad.

GPWT, p. 297b24: "In the suchness of the dharmas there are two kinds. The first is individual-mark [suchness]. The second is real-mark. As for individual-mark—the solidness of earth, the wetness of water, the hotness of fire, the movingness of wind—in this way one distinguishes that each of the dharmas has its own mark. As for real-mark, when one analyses and seeks for the real in the individual-marks, it cannot be found and cannot be demolished."

GPWT, p. 298c14: "To know that each of these dharmas has entity and is complete, is called the mundane, inferior suchness. To know that these nine dharmas eventually revert to mutation and extinction, is called the middle suchness. For example, this body comes forth from impurity, and though one bathes and adorns it, it eventually reverts to impurity. [To know that] this dharma is not existent and not inexistent, not arising and not ceasing, and to extinguish all contemplations and be utterly pure, is called the highest suchness."

GPWT, p. 298a28: "In the śrāvaka-dharma, contemplating the marks of arising and ceasing of the dharmas is considered suchness. Extinguishing all contemplations, one obtains the real-mark

of the dharmas. In this place, [the Buddha] speaks about dharma-nature.
QUESTION: In this place, he only speaks about suchness and dharma-nature. Where does he speak about reality-limit?
REPLY: Because these two have causes and conditions, he speaks about them. Because reality-limit has no cause and conditions, he does not speak about reality-limit."

See La Vallée Poussin, *Siddhi*, pp. 750–51.

20 GPWT, p. 465c12: "By reason of this suchness the Buddha is called 'tathāgata.'"

GPWT, p. 71b16, Lamotte, *Traité* I, 126: "Why is he called 'tathāgata'? As *(yathā)* he understands the dharma-marks, so *(tathā)* he preaches the dharma-marks. As *(yathā)* the [previous] Buddhas came *(āgata)* along the road of security *(yogakṣema-mārga)*, so *(tathā)* the [present] Buddha came, and did not depart *(agata)* again to further existences *(punarbhava)*. Therefore, he is called 'tathāgata.'"

For the literature on this question, see Lamotte's long note, *Traité* I, 126, n. 1.

21 GPWT, p. 71c1, Lamotte, *Traité* I, 127: "He is also called 'samyaksambuddha.' Why is he called samyaksambuddha'? 'Samyak' means 'correctly,' 'sam' means 'comprehensively,' and 'budh' means 'to know.' This expression means 'one who correctly and comprehensively knows all dharmas.'"

GPWT, p. 73a2, Lamotte, *Traité* I, 137: "He is also called 'buddha.' What dharmas does he know? He knows all the dharmas, past, future, and present, belonging to the animate and belonging to the inanimate, permanent and impermanent. Because under the bodhi-tree he comprehended them definitively, he is called 'buddha.

22 Saṁyuktāgama, No. 299, T, II, 85b23 ff. This sūtra is quoted several times in the *Great Perfection of Wisdom Treatise*. See p. 75a9, Lamotte, *Traité* I, 157, n. 1 (partial quotation); p. 298a11–20 (whole sūtra); p. 722c25 (catch-phrase only). Kumārajīva quotes the whole sūtra, though his wording here differs considerably from his wording in the *Great Perfection of Wisdom Treatise* translation, as well as from the version in the Chinese Saṁyuktāgama. In the Pali canon, compare the *Naḷakalāpī*. *Saṁyutta-nikāya* II, 112 (5 vols., L. Féer, ed., London, Pali Text Society, 1844–98; cited by Lamotte, *Traité* I, 1080, footnote). Also see La Vallée Poussin, *Siddhi*, pp. 743 ff. Compare *Aṅguttara-nikāya* 3.134 (5 vols., R. Morris and E. Hardy, eds., London, Pali Text Society, 1885–1900).

23 Version 3. 位 = niyāma. 住 would be sthiti. Both are in the Indic original.

24 GPWT, p. 75a7, Lamotte, *Traité* I, 156: "Just as the sun, though it did not create the heights (mountains) and low places (valleys)

and did not create the level land, equally illuminates them, even so the Buddha does not render the existent inexistent and does not render the inexistent existent. He constantly preaches the truth, and the light of his prajñā illumines all the dharmas."

25 GPWT, p. 298a8:
"QUESTION: Why does [the Buddha] not speak about this suchness, dharma-nature, and reality-limit in the śrāvaka-dharma, while he speaks about them in many places in the Mahāyāna-dharma?
REPLY: In the śrāvaka-dharma there are also places where he speaks about them, but they are few." Then follows the quotation of Saṁyukta No. 299, which mentions suchness and dharma-nature, but not reality-limit. See end of n. 19, above.

26 GPWT, p. 297c9: "As the Viśeṣacintābrahma-paripṛcchā-sūtra [T 585] states, 'Dharma-nature is limitless. Even though the śrāvakas attain dharma-nature, because their wisdom has limits they cannot speak about it in a limitless manner. It is like a man who, though he reaches the great ocean, because his vessel is small, cannot take an unlimited amount of water.' This is dharma-nature."

27 This passage is a paraphrase of GPWT, pp. 298c29ff., translated in n. 16, above. I have not yet identified the source of the simile of the ocean-drinkers.

GPWT, p. 566b15: "Though [the arhants] hear the *Prajñā*, they do not hear as well as the bodhisattvas, and so they achieve realization in the reality-limit."

Eon Kenkyū, p. 251, n. 258, proposes 'hoshii mama,' 'itaru,' and 'itasu' as *kun* readings for 放.

GPWT, p. 264b7:
"QUESTION: The arhants' passions are already quenched and their vestiges are also not yet quenched. Why are they not born [again]?
REPLY: The arhant has no great compassion and has no original vows to save all living beings. Also, because he has achieved realization in the reality-limit and is already separate from saṁsāra."

28 GPWT, p. 106c17, Lamotte, *Traité* I, 394. See Doc. 2, Part 1, n. 26.

GPWT, p. 303c19:
"QUESTION: If the bodhisattva has no fetters, how can he receive birth in the world?
REPLY: This has been answered already. The bodhisattva gains no-arising-dharma-patience, attains a body born through dharma-nature, and transforms magically in many places in order to save living beings and embellish the world. Through cause and condition of these virtues, even though he has not yet attained Buddhahood, he can bestow fortune (merit) with pure recompense."

GPWT, p. 235a12: "Relying on this faculty *(indriya)*, he enters the bodhisattva-predestination *(bodhisattva-avasthā)* [See La Vallée Poussin, ***Siddhi***, p. 778, also GPWT, p. 342c8]. So long as he has not obtained the fruit of no-arising-dharma-patience, this is called the 'faculty of what I do not yet know I will know.' In this [stage], he knows the real-mark of the dharmas conclusively, so it is called the 'faculty of knowledge.' Following this, he obtains the fruit of no-arising-dharma-patience, abides in the non-reverting stage, and receives a prediction. In the interval from this until he fulfils the tenth stage, sits on the bodhimaṇḍa, and attains the vajra-samādhi, it is called 'the faculty of knowing.' Because he cuts off all vestiges of the passions, attains anuttara-samyak-sambodhi and with his prajñā pervades all knowable dharmas, it is called 'the faculty of having already known.'"

For the Vaibhāṣika three anāsravendriyāṇi, see La Vallée Poussin, ***Kośa***, pp. 116 ff.

29 GPWT, p. 299a16: "Just as within all rūpa-dharmas there is an element of space *(ākāśa)*, even so within all dharmas there is a nirvāṇa-nature. This is called dharma-nature [Probably 'dharmadhātu.' See La Vallée Poussin, ***Siddhi***, p. 753]. Within all the manifold upāya-dharmas through which nirvāṇa is attained, there is a nirvāṇa-nature. At the time when one attains realization, then suchness and dharma-nature are the reality-limit. Furthermore, dharma-nature is measureless and boundless. It is not anything that mind or mental dharmas can measure. This is called dharma-nature. The sublime end-point of this is called reality-limit."

30 Emend 論 (discuss) to 證 (realize).

DOCUMENT 2, PART III

1 GPWT, p. 59c9, Lamotte, ***Traité*** I, 31:
"QUESTION: The supreme (first) siddhānta is absolutely true, and because it is true it is called supreme. The others should not be true.
REPLY: That is not right. Each of these four siddhāntas possesses truth. Suchness, dharma-nature, and reality-limit are inexistent because of the mundane siddhāntas but existent because of the supreme siddhānta. For what reason? Because the person's five skandhas which are his causes and conditions exist, the person exists, just as because the milk's form, scent, taste, and touch which are its causes and conditions exist, the milk exists. If the milk were really inexistent, the milk's causes and conditions should also be inexistent. But because the milk's causes and conditions are really existent, the milk should also be existent. It it is not like the second head or the third hand of one person,

which have no causes and conditions but have a designation."

GPWT, p. 147c5, Lamotte, *Traité* II, 727: "Furthermore, there are three kinds of existent—first, interdependent existents; second, designational existents; and third, dharma-existents. Interdependent are the long and the short, that and this, etc. . . . In these, there is no real dharma, and they are not like form, scent, taste, and touch, etc. Designational existence is like cream, which has four factors—form, scent, taste, and touch. Because the causes and conditions combine, it is designated as cream. Though it is existent, it does not exist in the same way as cause-and-condition dharmas. Though it is inexistent, it does not in-exist like rabbit horns or turtle hair. Only because the causes and conditions combine is it designated that the cream exists. Likewise for the fabric.

2 Secondary matter—bhautika. See La Vallée Poussin, *Siddhi*, ch. 1, p. 64 and Stcherbatsky, *Central Conception*, p. 12. *Eon Kenkyū*, n. 262 says that the *ching* is unidentified. The distinction between *bhūta* and *bhautika* is an Abhidharma one, so *ching* ought to refer to the *Abhidharmasāra*, Hui-yüan's main source for Abhidharma. The idea in question does not appear in T, 1550, the abridged version, but may have occurred in the now-lost longer version which Saṅghadeva translated in A.D. 384 (CST, p. 10c10), as it does appear in the *Tsa-a-p'i-t'an-hsin-lun* of Dharmatrāta translated by Saṅghavarman, T 1552, XXVI, 877a4 ff. Compare *Abhidharmakośa*, 1.35, T 1558, XXIX, 8c1 ff.

3 GPWT, p. 264b15: "The bodhisattva, quitting the five lusts, obtains all the dhyānas, and because he has kindness and compassion, for the sake of living beings he takes the six magic powers and displays all the seldom and marvelous deeds and renders living beings' minds pure . . . (p. 264b22). Secondly, he can also transform all things, change earth into water, change water into earth, change wind into fire, and change fire into wind. In this way, he transmutes all the great elements."

GPWT, p. 264c15: "For this reason, we know that all the dharmas are without fixed-mark. Thus when [the bodhisattva] exercises his magic power and transforms [things], it is genuine and not spurious. If the basis were individual fixed-marks, then they could not be transmuted."

4 According to the Āgamas, there are three marks. According to the Vaibhāṣikas, there are four. See La Vallée Poussin, *Kośa*, ch. 2, p. 223. Hui-yüan refers to four in other passages. The *Great Perfection of Wisdom Treatise* refers usually to four, but sometimes to three. *Middle Stanzas*, ch. 7 deals with a list of three rather than four marks. See Lamotte, *Traité* I, 36, n. 3.

GPWT, p. 296a28: "Further, there are people who say: unconditioned dharmas have no arising, abiding, or ceasing. These are called inexistent dharmas. Conditioned dharmas arise, abide, and cease. These are called existent dharmas."

Middle Stanzas 7.1: "If arising is conditioned, then the three marks are possible in it. If arising is unconditioned, how can it be a mark of the conditioned?"

5 *Middle Stanzas* 24.19: "No dharma exists that is not dependently co-arisen; hence no non-empty dharma exists." Compare *Chao-lun*, part III, p. 154a22.

6 GPWT, ch. 43, pp. 264a ff.

7 Emend 空者 to 二者 with *Eon Kenkyu* and Shan-tao-ssŭ edition.

GPWT, p. 287b10:

"QUESTION: Demolishing the body and demolishing the house is in order to demolish unity and demolish multiplicity. Demolishing unity and demolishing multiplicity is a demolition of the Tīrthika scriptures. In the Buddha's sūtras it is stated that there really are internal and external dharmas. That is to say, the internal are the six senses *(indriya)* and the external are the six spheres *(viṣaya)*. Why are these inexistent?

REPLY: These internal and external dharmas are a designation for combining provisional existence, just like the body, just like the house. Furthermore, to speak concisely, there are two kinds of emptiness, emptiness of living beings, and emptiness of dharmas. The disciples of the Hīnayāna have dull faculties, so for them [the Buddha] speaks about the emptiness of living beings. Because there is no 'I' or 'mine' they do not cling to other dharmas. The disciples of the Mahāyāna have keen faculties, so for them he speaks about the emptiness of dharmas."

GPWT, p. 319b18: "This is the emptiness of living beings. It is often declared in the śrāvaka-dharma. All the Buddha's disciples knew that in the dharmas there is no self *(ātman)*. Five hundred years after the Buddha's decease, [Buddhists] divided into two sections. Some believed in the emptiness of dharmas, and some only believed in the emptiness of living beings."

8 GPWT, p. 59b24, Lamotte, *Traité* I, 28: "What is the mundane siddhānta? Existent dharmas, because they come from the combination of causes and conditions, are existent, but there is no separate nature in them, just as the chariot exists because of the combination of the shafts, the axles, the spokes, and the rim but there is no separate chariot, even so a person exists because of the combination of the five skandhas, but there is no separate person."

9 The four formless skandhas—feeling, conception, dispositions and consciousness—are termed 'name.' Hence 'name and form' is synonymous with the five skandhas. See Lamotte, *Traité* II, 737, n. 2, also GPWT, p. 150a4, Lamotte, *Traité* II, 749: "Further, the combination of name and form is designated a person." Also

GPWT, p. 518c29: "Two dharmas comprehend all the dharmas, namely name and form. The four great elements and secondary matter are comprehended in 'form.' The [other] four skandhas—feeling, etc.—are comprehended in 'name.'

10 GPWT, p. 546c26: "Just as within the lump of clay the natures of pots and potsherds both exist. With the clay one makes a pot. One breaks up the pot and makes potsherds. In this way, it is transformed, but nothing at all is lost."

See also HT, ch. 7, p. 177c7.

11 Emend 二 (two) to 三 (three).

12 GPWT, p. 297c23: "For this reason, the Buddha declared three dharmas, which are the three dharma-seals *(dharma-mudrā)*, namely the seal of impermanence of all conditioned dharmas, the seal of the no-self of all dharmas, and the seal of cessation in nirvāṇa."

GPWT, p. 298a1: "Because a certain man is attached to the misconception of permanence, he is made to abandon views of permanence, but does not become attached to marks of impermanence. This is the dharma-seal. It is not meant that abandoning permanence and becoming attached to impermanence is the dharma-seal... (p. 298a5). After one has attained this suchness of the dharmas, one enters dharma-nature, extinguishes all examinations *(vipaśyanā? parīkṣa?)* and does not conceive different beliefs, because the nature is self-so."

For *kuan* (examination), see Demiéville, *Lhasa*, p. 73, n. 3 and p. 78, n. 3.

13 GPWT, p. 60a16, Lamotte, *Traité* I, 33; GPWT, p. 81a13, Lamotte, *Traité* I, 210. For other medical similes, see MT, p. 18c20; GPWT, pp. 107a23, 180b21, 198a23, 245c6, 285b22, 288a8, 294c15, 478c20, 559a16, 696c7.

14 Emend 衆生緣法 to 衆緣生法 with *Eon Kenkyū*, p. 41, n. 10.

15 This schema is based on the three dharma-seals, ranked in ascending order:

first seal	impermanence	lowest class
second seal	no-self	middle class
third seal	cessation	highest class

GPWT, p. 222b17: "In the first seal, [the Buddha] is speaking about the five skandhas. In the second seal, he states that all the dharmas are without self. In the third seal, he speaks about the fruit of the [first] two seals. This is called the seal of cessation. As all factitious dharmas [*kṛtaka-dharma*. See Stcherbatsky, *Central Conception*, p. 17, n. 63] are impermanent, he demolishes the 'mine,' the external five lusts. When he declares no-self, he demolishes internal dharmas of self. Because 'I' and 'mine' are demolished, it is called 'cessation is nirvāṇa.' When the practicer contemplates the impermanence of factitious dharmas, he conceives aversion, and is averse to the sufferings of the world. Though he already knows how to be averse to suffering, he retains attachment to the lord [i.e., the self] of contemplation. He says, 'I am able to perform this contemplation.' Because of this there is the second dharma-seal. He knows that everything is without self. In the five skandhas, the twelve āyatanas, the eighteen dhātus and the twelve nidānas, internally and externally though one distinguishes and analyses, the lord of contemplation cannot be found. Because he cannot be found, all the dharmas are without self. When he has performed this knowing, he does not have fictions, has no place of support, and only betakes himself to cessation. For this reason, the seal 'cessation is nirvāṇa' is declared."

16 GPWT, p. 81a13, Lamotte, *Traité* I, 210: "It is like a small physician who uses one kind of medicine or two kinds of medicine but is not fully equipped and so cannot cure a serious illness. The great physician is fully equipped with many medicines and can cure all illnesses."

17 Version 2.

18 In its main features this pathology of the psyche is identical with those of the meditation manuals. See ***Bodhisattva-dhyāna***, T 614, XVI, 270c27 ff., parts translated by Waley in Conze (ed.), ***Buddhist Texts throughout the Ages***, p. 276. See also GPWT, p. 60a15, Lamotte, *Traité* I, 33, where the medical analogy is carried through elaborately.

19 Emend 十二 (twelve) to 二十 (twenty). See GPWT, p. 148b20, Lamotte, *Traité* II, 737: "Further, the five skandhas, because they arise from causes and conditions, are empty and without self. But by reason of ignorance *(avidyā)* [people] produce the twenty real-body-views *(satkāyadṛṣṭi)*. These views of self arise from the serial continuity of the five skandhas. Because they arise from the conditions of these five skandhas, they figure that these five skandhas are a self."

The twenty satkāyadṛṣṭis are: (1) form is the self (like a lord), (2) there is form in the self (like an ornament), (3) the self possesses form (like a slave boy), (4) the self is inside form (like a vessel), (5) feeling is the self, (6) there is feeling in the self, (7) the self possesses feeling, (8) the self is inside feeling, (9) conception is the self, (10) there is conception in the self, (11) the self possesses conception, (12) the self is inside conception, (13) dispositions are the self, (14) there are dispositions in the self, (15) the self possesses dispositions, (16) the self is inside dispositions, (17) consciousness is the self, (18) there is consciousness in the self, (19) the self possesses consciousness, (20) the self is inside consciousness.

See Lamotte, *Traité* II, 737, n. 3, and Mano, p. 317, n. 14. *Eon Kenkyū*, p. 42, n. 1 suggests 六十二 instead of 十二.

20 GPWT, p. 222c29: "The Buddha's discourse conforms to the supreme truth *(paramārtha)*. Even though he speaks about mundane dharmas, he commits no error, because he does not contradict the Two Truths."

MT, ch. 18, p. 24c10: "Because the Buddhas with their all-knowledge examine living beings, they speak to them in various ways. They both state that there is a self, and state that there is no self. For the sake of those whose minds are not ripe, who do not yet have the prerequisites of nirvāṇa [*nirvedhabhagīya?* La Vallée Poussin, *Kośa*, part VI, p. 177 ff.] and who do not know to fear sin, he states that there is a self. Also, for the sake of those who have attained the way and who know that all the dharmas are empty and that a self exists only as a designation, he states that there is a self and commits no error. Also, there are some who have merit through charity, morality, etc., who have aversion to the woes of saṁsāra but fear the everlasting extinction of nirvāṇa. For their sake, the Buddha states that there is no self. The dharmas are only combinations of causes and conditions. At the time of arising, they arise empty. At the time of cessation, they cease empty. Therefore, he states that there is no self. Only as a designation does he state that there is a self."

DOCUMENT 2, PART IV

1 GPWT, p. 147c29, Lamotte, *Traité* II, 730: "Further, if there are atoms, in them there are form, scent, taste, and touch, which constitute parts. But that in which form, scent, taste, and touch constitute parts is not called an atom. If we thus analyse and seek the atom, it cannot be found. As the sūtra says, 'Form, whether gross or subtle, whether internal or external, when contemplated in general, is impermanent and without self.' But it does not say that atoms exist. This is called the emptiness of division into parts."

2 GPWT, p. 147c15, Lamotte, *Traité* II, 728: "Further, because there are form, scent, taste, and touch of the atoms, there are hair-particles. Because of the hair-particles, there are hairs. Because of hairs, there is down. Because of the down, there are threads. Because of the threads, there is a fabric. Because of the fabric, there is a garment."

3 Add 色 (form) and 香 (scent) to the Taishō text. *Eon Kenkyū*, n. 273 deletes 味 and 觸. GPWT, p. 147c24, Lamotte, *Traité* II, 729: "The most subtle has no reality (actual). It is arbitrarily named."

4 Read 尺捶之論 with *Eon Kenkyū*, p. 42, n. 10. *Chuang-tzŭ*, "T'ien-hsia": 一尺之捶．日取其半．万世不竭. Legge, *The Texts of Taoism* II, 230: "If from a stick a foot long you every day take the half of it, in a myriad ages it will not be exhausted."

5 Version 6.

6 GPWT, p. 147b22, Lamotte, ***Traité*** II, 726: "Also, rabbit horns and tortoise hairs have only a name and have no reality (actual). Although the fabric is not inexistent like rabbit horns and tortoise hairs, it exists because causes and conditions meet, and inexists because causes and conditions disperse."

7 GPWT, p. 147c26, Lamotte, ***Traité*** II, 729: "Further, if there is atomic form, then it has parts in the ten directions [east, south-east, south, south-west, west, north-west, north, north-east, zenith, and nadir.] If it has parts in the ten directions, then it cannot be called an atom. If it does not have parts in the ten directions, it cannot be called form."

同分 (equally divided) is perhaps a corruption of 分齊 (divide) in GPWT, p. 147c28.

詘 is probably an error for 出. *Eon Kenkyū* offers no emendation, but paraphrases with 'hitei-shi saru koto' (negating and quitting).

8 See ***Chao-lun***, part II, p. 152a3: "Unless one has the special penetration of Holy Intelligence, how can one fit one's spirit to the interstice between the existent and the inexistent?"

9 See the quotation in n. 1, above.

10 Compare MT, ch. 16, pp. 21a11 ff.

11 *Saddharma-puṇḍarīka*, ch. 7, T 262, IX, 22a5: 乃下一點．大如微塵 ekaṃ paramāṇuraja upanikṣipet, "he would drop a dust-particle [the size of] an atom." *Eon Kenkyū*, n. 278.

GPWT, p. 194c28, Lamotte, ***Traité*** II, 1100: "If you say that because [heat] is subtle it cannot be known, then it would not be different from the inexistent. If there is something gross that can be perceived, then one may know that there is something. If there is nothing gross, then there is also nothing subtle. For such reasons of many kinds, the mark of earth cannot be perceived. As the mark of earth cannot be perceived, the marks of all the dharmas likewise cannot be perceived."

12 Ulūka is Kaṇāda, the reputed author of the Vaiśeṣika Sūtras. See Dasgupta, ***History***, pp. 71 and 305; Faddegon, pp. 10–15; Ui, ***Vaiśeṣika Philosophy***, pp. 3–7.

13 ***Vaiśeṣika Sūtras*** II, 1–4, Faddegon, p. 153; ***Daśapadārthi***, Ui, ***Vaiśeṣika Philosophy***, p. 93.

14 This is the Vaiśeṣika doctrine that the human body possesses only the nature of earth, but that it is not an organized aggregate of the elements (earth, water, fire, air, and space). See Faddegon, pp. 180 ff.

15 屈 (yield) is a corruption of 屬 (belong to).

16 捊 *p'ou* "attirer et prendre" (Couvreur, Séraphin, ***Dictionnaire classique de la langue chinoise***, réimpression, Peiping, H. Vetch, 1947).

17 GPWT, pp. 295c9, 746b28; MT, p. 19b19–20.

18 性 (nature) in Kumārajīva's translation often does duty for 'dhātu' in 'dharmadhātu.' See La Vallée Poussin, *Siddhi*, p. 753. 'Dhātu' in the eighteen dhātus is more generally rendered by 界 (domain). See, for example, GPWT, p. 288c22.

19 GPWT, p. 288c23: "Now, conditioned dharmas are empty for two reasons. First, they are empty because they have no 'I' and no 'mine,' and their permanency and non-alteration cannot be found. Second, the conditioned-dharmaness of conditioned dharmas is empty because it does not arise and does not cease and has nothing existent."

20 GPWT, p. 206b3: "All the dharmas arise from causes and conditions and have no real-dharma." Also, *Laṅkāvatāra Sūtra* (Bunyiu Nanjio, ed., Kyoto, Otani University Press, 1956), p. 153, l. 11 (Suzuki, *Laṅkā Studies*, p. 454), "Skandhānāṁ skandhatā tadvat prajñaptyā na tu dravyataḥ." (The skandhahood of the skandhas is likewise because of designation and not because of real-entity.) The T'ang translator in this passage renders 'dravya' by 實事 (real entity). 實法 (real-dharma) in Kumārajīva's terminology probably stands for 'dravya' in most cases.

21 GPWT, p. 292c28: "Further, the specific nature of all the dharmas is likewise not so. For what reason? It is like fire which burns and secondary matter which shines. Because the two dharmas [form and touch] combine, it is called fire. If there were fire apart from these two dharmas, then there should be a separate (specific) function of fire. But there is no separate function. Therefore, we know that fire is a designation and has nothing real. If there is really no dharma of fire, how can you say that heat is the nature of fire? Further, hot-nature arises from several conditions. Internally there is the body-organ *(kāyendriya)* and externally there are form and touch. When they combine, body-consciousness arises and one cognizes that there is heat. At the time when they have not combined, there is no hot-nature. For this reason, we know that there is no determinate heat that constitutes the nature of fire."

The secondary matter which shines constitutes the sense-organs. Stcherbatsky, *Central Conception*, p. 10: "Sense-organs *(indriya)* conceived as a kind of translucent subtle matter which covers the body while living."

22 Perhaps this should read 一切 (all) rather than 一 (one).

23 GPWT, p. 287a6:
"QUESTION: As for the emptiness of the four abodes of recollection *(smṛtyupasthāna)*, one should contemplate all dharmas as impermanent, suffering, empty, and without self. For what reason? One contemplates the body as impure, one contemplates feeling as suffering, one contemplates mind as impermanent, and one contemplates dharmas as without self."

24 Reference to Hui-yüan's thesis in the first paragraph.

25 GPWT, p. 547a27: "The spirit is identical with the body: certain people say that the body is identical with the spirit. For what reason? Because when one analyses this body and seeks for the spirit, it cannot be found. Further, feelings of beauty and ugliness, pleasure and pain are all bodily. Therefore, they say that the body is identical with the spirit. The body and the spirit are different: certain people say that the spirit is subtle and not perceptible to the five senses. Also, it is not something that worldlings can see, but the man who concentrates his thoughts, becomes pure, and attains dhyāna and samādhi is able to see it. Therefore, they say that body and spirit are different. Further, if the body is identical with the spirit, then when the body perishes, the spirit also perishes. This is a false view. If one asserts that body and spirit are different, then when the body perishes the spirit abides permanently. This is an extremist view."

GPWT, p. 547b10: "Certain people say that [the spirit] does not come from anywhere in a previous life and does not pass on to anywhere when it perishes. Certain people say that body and spirit combine to make a man. After death, the spirit passes on, but the body does not pass on."

Compare Hui-yüan's essay, *Spirit Does Not Perish* (Document 3).

26 The five views are: (1) real-body-view *(satkāyadṛṣṭi)*, which consists of belief in 'I' and 'mine,' (2) extremist-view *(antagrahadṛṣṭi)*, which consists of belief in the eternality or annihilation of the self, (3) false-view *(mithyādṛṣṭi)*, which consists of denial of verities such as the Four Truths, (4) approval-of-views-view *(dṛṣṭiparāmarśadṛṣṭi)*, which consists of highly esteeming false views, and (5) approval-of-asceticism-view *(śīlavrataparāmarśadṛṣṭi)*, which consists of considering deities as cause of the world, considering suicide as cause of birth in heaven, and considering the precepts and vows of the ascetics as well as the doctrines of Sāṁkhya and Yoga as the path to liberation. Each view from No. 2 to No. 5 depends on the previous one, and the whole series constitutes a 'ladder of imperfection.' When Kumārajīva says that the five views are each separate, he probably means that they are successive rather than concomitant. See La Vallée Poussin, *Kośa*, part V, p. 15, and Oda, p. 523c.

27 Form, etc. constitute the form-skandha. Mind equals consciousness, the fifth skandha. The mental dharmas comprise feeling, conception, and the dispositions. Thus this is another way of saying that the five skandhas are empty. For a disquisition on the boundlessness and inapprehensibility of mind, mental dharmas and form, see GPWT, pp. 433a20 ff.

28 *Stanzas* 15.5; MT, p. 35a29 (*sub* 25.7). Compare MT, p. 12a15 (*sub* 7.34): "Because there is the conditioned, there is the unconditioned."

29 *Stanzas* 15.11; MT, ch. 1, p. 2a1.

30 This passage reads like an anthology from the adhyāyas one, two, four, and seven of the *Vaiśeṣika Sūtras*. Most of the doctrines stated here are also found in the *Daśapadārthi* (translation in Ui, *Vaiśeṣika Philosophy*, pp. 93–119).

31 *Vaiśeṣika Sūtras* IV, 2, 5; Faddegon, p. 154: "[It is] an error [to suppose that the ultimate atom is not eternal]."

32 *Vaiśeṣika Sūtras* IV, 1, 1; Faddegon, p. 154: "The eternal is that which is existent and uncaused."

Daśapadārthi (Ui, *Vaiśeṣika Philosophy*), p. 103, explains that when earth, water, fire, and wind do not inhere in another substance, do not consist of parts, are not destroyed by their causes, are ultimate particulars, and are spherical, then they are eternal. That is, the atoms of these elements are eternal.

33 *Vaiśeṣika Sūtras* IV, 1,8; Faddegon, p. 284: "Perception of colour [arises] from its combination with a compound of substances more than two, and from [its possession of] some special characteristic of colour."

Daśapadārthi (Ui, *Vaiśeṣika Philosophy*), p. 105: "Colour, taste, smell, and touch are either perceptible or imperceptible. . . . They are perceptible when they abide in large substances and more than one substance. . . . They are imperceptible when they abide in atoms and binary atomic compounds."

34 *Vaiśeṣika Sūtras* I, 2, 1–2, Faddegon, p. 131: "Non-existence of effect [follows] from the non-existence of the cause. But non-existence of cause [does] not [follow] from the non-existence of the effect."

Logically, the *Vaiśeṣika Sūtras* propositions are: "not-A implies not-B; but not-B does not imply not-A." Kumārajīva's version is: "B implies A; A implies B." He makes the existence of the cause equivalent to the existence of the effect, whereas the *Vaiśeṣika Sūtras* specifies that the implication is not an equivalence.

35 *Vaiśeṣika Sūtras* IV, 1, 4; Faddegon, p. 154: "'Non-eternal'—such [intuition and expression] can be accounted for only as the negation of the eternal."

36 Emend 空 to 定. *Eon Kenkyū*, p. 44, n. 3.

37 The text seems to be out of order here. Tentatively emend by interchanging the two characters 明 (knowledge) and 常 (permanence), that is, emend 令无常明故．當知无明中有常法． to | | 明 | | . | | | 常 | | | | .

See Ui, *Vaiśeṣika Philosophy*, p. 127: "The transitoriness of substances must presuppose their eternity and the concept of transitoriness depends on that of eternity, just as imperfect cognition is possible by presupposing perfect cognition."

38 This means that form *(rūpa)* is not visible in the atomic state, since the atoms are imperceptible *(atīndriya)*. It is only in combination that it becomes visible. *Vaiśeṣika Sūtras* IV, 1, 8; Faddegon, p. 284: "Perception of colour [arises] from its combination with a compound of substances more than two, and from [its possession of] some special characteristic of colour."

39 *Vaiśeṣika Sūtras* IV, 1, 7; Faddegon, p. 284: "The non-perception of air, in spite of there being substance-ness and magnitude, is due to the non-existence of the evolution of colour."

40 *Vaiśeṣika Sūtras* IV, 1, 11—12; Faddegon, p. 284: "Numbers, magnitudes, separateness, conjunction and disjunction, priority and posteriority, and action become objects of visual perception, through their combination with substances possessing colour. In substances not possessing colour they are not objects of visual perception."

This list includes nos. 5 to no. 11 of the twenty-four qualities *(guṇa)*. See *Daśapadārthi* (Ui, *Vaiśeṣika Philosophy*), p. 94. They are explained in the *Vaiśeṣika Sūtras*—number (VII, 2, 1–8, Faddegon, p. 198); magnitude (VII, 1, 8–21, Faddegon, p. 215); individuality (VII, 2, 1–8, Faddegon, p. 198, p. 199); conjunction (VII, 2, 9, Faddegon, p. 226); disjunction (VII, 2, 10–13, Faddegon, p. 226); priority and posteriority (VII, 2, 21–25, Faddegon, p. 214).

Action is the third category *(padārtha)*. See *Vaiśeṣika Sūtras* I, 1, 7, Faddegon, p. 105: "Throwing upwards, throwing downwards, contraction, expansion, and motion are actions." Compare *Daśapadārthi* (Ui, *Vaiśeṣika Philosophy*), pp. 98–99.

As it stands, 一二寸 is not intelligible. 寸 (inch) is a scribal error for 等 (plural; etc.) Shan-tao-ssŭ edition so emends. *Eon Kenkyū* keeps 寸 and notes no variants.

41 GPWT, p. 102b14, Lamotte, *Traité* I, 364: "Further, it is like a small child who sees the moon in the water, is delighted, and wants to take hold of it. When an adult sees him, he laughs."

42 The use of the tetralemma as an upāya is explained in MT, ch. 18, p. 25a14 ff., commenting on *Stanzas* 18.8. See Chapter Two, above.

MT, ch. 25, p. 26b12: "Since the *Chapter on Causes and Conditions* [MT, ch. 1], we have analysed and examined all the dharmas. There is nothing existent; there is nothing inexistent; there is nothing existent-and-inexistent; and there is nothing neither-existent-nor-inexistent. This is the real-mark of all the dharmas. It is also called suchness, dharma-nature, reality-limit, and nirvāṇa."

Stanzas 25.17–18, T XXX, 35c23: "It is not said that after his final decease the Tathāgata exists, nor that he does not exist, nor that he both exists and does not exist, nor that he neither exists nor does not exist. It is not said that while he is alive the Tathāgata exists, [etc.]"

MT, ch. 25, p. 35a4: "Further, the sūtra says that nirvāṇa is not existent, nor inexistent, not both-existent-and-inexistent, and not neither-existent-nor-inexistent."

Compare MT, ch. 22, p. 30b24, and MT, ch. 27, p. 39b6.

43 Compare MT, p. 18c18, *sub Stanzas* 13.9 (equals Sanskrit 13.8): "The Great Saint declared emptiness in order to demolish the sixty-two views and all the passions such as ignorance and craving. If a man again conceives views about emptiness, this man cannot be reformed. It is like someone who has an illness which can be cured if a medicine is taken. But if the medicine in turn causes illness, then this cannot be cured."

Kumārajīva's example, unlike the one from the *Middle Treatise*, does not pronounce incurable those who become addicted to emptiness. For other medical similes, see Document 2, part III, n. 13.

DOCUMENT 3

1 至極 (Utmost Ultimate). Compare Hui-yüan biography, KSC, p. 360a18, 仏是至極 (the Buddha is the Utmost Ultimate), and 至極以不變為性．得性以体極為宗． (The Utmost Ultimate has non-changing for its nature. Attaining (its) nature has realizing the Ultimate as its Ideal.)

2 Hurvitz, "Render unto Caesar," p. 107: "appear to reside temporarily in the line of rulers." 權—see Oda, p. 579, 3: "opposite of 'real'; synonym of 方便 *(upāya)*; something used for a while and ultimately discarded."

3 大通 (Great Pervader)—*Chuang-tzŭ* 6, 3A.32b, 離形去知．同於大通．此為坐忘 Legge, *The Texts of Taoism* I, 257: "Thus leaving my material form and bidding farewell to my knowledge, I am become one with the Great Pervader. This I call sitting and forgetting all things." The sub-commentary says 大通猶大道也. (The Great Pervader is like the Great Way.) This passage describes the ekstasis of a Taoist adept in trance. The opponent may mean that Hui-yüan is appealing to mystic experience to prove transmigration. This tallies with Hui-yüan's statement later on that only those with paranormal vision can observe the operations of the "occult transmission." This is the fourth *abhijñā*—purvanivāsānusmṛti (memory of former lives).

4 妙物 (inspirits things). See n. 16, below.

5 Ssŭ-pu-pei-yao version, 固.

6 天本 (celestial origin). Cf. *Huai-nan-tzŭ*, chüan 7, 夫精神者．所受於天也．而形体者．所稟於地也．

(The psychic spirit is something received from Heaven; the

bodily form is something furnished by Earth.) For Heaven as the source of all autogenous things, see n. 8, below.

7 *Tao-te-ching*, ch. 14.

8 All things are 自然 (autogenous, self-so) and thus their fates are self-determined rather than imposed from outside. Kuo Hsiang, 1B.4a–6, says 无既无矣．则不能生有．有之未生．又不能為生．然则生生者誰…以天言之．所以明其自然也．…夫天且不能自有．況能有物哉．…故物各自生． (Since the inexistent is inexistent, it cannot produce the existent. When the existent has not yet arisen, it also cannot produce. This being so, who is it that produces the producer?... We call it 'Heaven' in order to explain its self-so-ness.... Now, Heaven cannot even make itself existent; how much less can it make things existent!... Therefore, each thing produces itself.)

9 Version 21.

10 The example of fire and fuel occurs frequently in Buddhist and non-Buddhist literature alike. Buddhist instances:
1. *Majjhima* I, 487–88 (the Tathāgata is like the fire that has gone out).
2. *Majjhima*, sutta 38 (viññāna is like a fire).
3. *Majjhima*, sutta 72 (fire and fuel, and where is the arhant reborn?).
4. *Milindapañha* (V. Trenckner, ed., London, Pali Text Society, 1880), p. 71, l. 16 (rebirth is like lamp and light).
5. *Milindapañha*, p. 40, l. 1 (identity and non-identity of lamp flames).
6. *Middle Treatise*, p. 13c7 ("If it follows the body, then when the body inexists, the spirit inexists; as when the lamp is extinguished, the light is extinguished").
7. *Abhidharmasāra*, p. 818b6 ("The fire can burn all the saṁskāras' fuel").
8. *Abhidharmasāra*, p. 818b13 ("It eliminates the fire of all the passions, so it is stopping; it surpasses all dharmas, so it is sublime").
9. *Āryatathāgataguhyasūtra*, T XI, 732c27 ff. (Thought *(citta)* is like fire and the object is like fuel. When fuel is used up, the fire goes out.) Quoted in the *Prasannapadā*, ch. 18. See De Jong, *Chapitres*, p. 21.

The chief classical Chinese instance of this simile is in *Chuang-tzŭ* 3, 2A.8a, Legge, *The Texts of Taoism* I, 202. See n. 44, below.

11 同異 (sameness and difference)—whether at death body and spirit share the same course, or go different ways.

12 That is, 有 (existent) equals 生 (alive), and 无 (inexistent) equals 死 (dead). Liebenthal, "Hui-yüan," p. 247b, imputes this view to Hui-yüan himself. See n. 35, below.

13 *Chuang-tzŭ* 22, 7B.16a, Legge, *The Texts of Taoism* II, 59.

14 至理 (final principle). This is the title of *Pao-p'u-tzŭ*, chüan 6. The supreme goal for the seekers of longevity was indefinite prolongation of the one life that is man's natural endowment. See also Kuo Hsiang, *Chuang-tzŭ* 2, 1B.35a.

15 Liebenthal, "Hui-yüan," p. 251b, translates this sentence, "Extremely subtile, it is the Spiritual Light (of the universe)." Hurvitz, "Render unto Caesar," p. 108, translates, "It is subtlety that has reached an extreme and become immaterial." 精 is not subtlety, but psychic force. 靈 is a numen, or something numinous or numinal. It is the defining property of 神. See *Tao-te-ching*, p. 39, 神得一以靈. (Through attainment of the One, the spirits are numinal.) Hurvitz's translation introduces the concept of becoming, which is incompatible with the celestial, supernatural character of Spirit. Things do not *become* supernatural. This sentence is patterned on the *I-ching* sentence quoted in n. 17, below. That may be translated, "As for spirit, it is so-called because it inspirits (subtly pervades) the myriad things."

精極 (ultimate of the psychic)—see *I-ching* 7.8a, Legge, "Yi-King," p. 369, "the most exquisite thing under heaven," and Wilhelm, p. 239, "das allergeistigste auf Erden." *Chuang-tzŭ* 19, 精而又精．反以相天. Legge, *The Texts of Taoism* II, 13, "From the vital force there comes another more vital, and man returns to be the assistant of Heaven."

16 The eight trigrams *(kua)* and the four diagrams (hsiang) of the *I Ching*. See Legge, "Yi-King," p. 12. This is the same as saying that it transcends mundane destinies (numbers).

17 *I-ching*, "Shuo-kua" 9.2a–b 神也者．妙万物而為言者也. Wilhelm, p. 205, "Der Geist ist geheimnisvoll in allen Wesen und wirkt durch sie." Compare Legge, "Yi-King," p. 427, "When we speak of Spirit, we mean the subtle (presence and operation of God) with all things."

18 体状 (structure and form)—Hurvitz, "Render unto Caesar," p. 108, "its subtantial form." Liebenthal, "Hui-yüan," p. 251b, "the kind of its existence."

Compare *I-ching*, "Hsi-tz'ŭ Shang" 7.3b, 故神无方而易无体. Wilhelm p. 224, "Darum ist der Geist an keinen Ort gebunden und das Buch der Wandlungen an keine Gestalt."

19 多同自乱 The translation is tentative. Hurvitz, "Render unto Caesar," p. 108, "and much you seem to be confused." *Eon Kenkyū*, p. 394, n. 22, clarifies nothing.

20 依俙 — the *Tz'ŭ-hai* ("A Comprehensive Dictionary," comp. by Shu Hsin-chieng, Shanghai, Chung-hua Shu-chü, 1936–37), p. 104, 1, defines this phrase as 彷彿[稀亦作俙] "resemble, simulate, etc." Perhaps in this context one should read 依希 "rely on the inaudible." Compare *Tao-te-ching*, p. 14, 視之不見名曰夷．聽之不聞名為希. (What sight cannot see is called 'invisible';

what hearing cannot hear is called 'inaudible.') Compare *Chao-lun*, part IV, p. 157c, 斯乃希夷之境．太玄之鄉． (This is the sphere of the inaudible and invisible, the region of the Great Metaphysical.)

21 See *Preface to the GPWT Abridgment*, CST, p. 76a1, Document 4, notes 37 & 38.

22 妙盡 (marvelous consummation)—see *Chao-lun*, *Reply to Liu I-min*, pp. 156a25 ff. 窮靈極數．乃曰妙盡．妙盡之道本乎无寄． (Totally fulfilling the numinal and reaching the ultimate of numbers (destinies) is called the marvelous consummation. The way of the marvelous consummation is founded on the supportless *(apratiṣṭhita)*.

23 It is an unmoving mover; it activates but is not active.

24 It acts through living beings, manifesting as a Buddha or as a less exalted agent of the Dharma. See n. 2, above.

25 情 (feelings) is used in two senses: (a) propensities, innate tendencies (usual in the *I-ching*), and (b) emotions, volitions, feelings. The two senses are often blended together in Hui-yüan's discussions of rebirth.

26 The question whether the Holy Man had feelings was topical among the Neo-Taoists in the third century. Wang Pi said, "The respect in which the Holy Man surpasses men is his spirit-intelligence. That in which he is the same as men is the five feelings. . . . This being so, the feelings of the Holy Man, though they respond to things, have no attachment to things. It is a great mistake to say that he does not respond to things because he has no attachment [to them]" (*P'ei-chu* on *San-kuo-chih* 28, *Wang Pi Chuan*. Quoted by Jung Chao-tsu in *Wei-chin ti Tzŭ-jan-chu-i*, p. 26).

27 精粗 (psychic and physical)—Liebenthal, "Hui-yüan," p. 251b, "fine and coarse (elements, i.e. souls and bodies)." It cannot be said, however, that the psychic was considered immaterial.

28 Compare *Tao-te-ching*, p. 1, 有名．万物之母． (The named is the mother of the myriad things.)

29 Version 26.

30 *Chuang-tzŭ* 33, 10B.24a, Legge, *The Texts of Taoism* II, 251.

31 Hurvitz, "Render unto Caesar," p. 109, "They who in antiquity discussed the Way did not necessarily agree among themselves." Since this introduces Hui-yüan's attempt to prove that Chuang-tzŭ and Wen-tzŭ unanimously support Hui-yüan, it is to be assumed that they disagreed with the opponent.

32 *Chuang-tzŭ* 6, 3A.10b, Legge, *The Texts of Taoism* I, 242; *Chuang-tzŭ* 6, 3A.21a, Legge, *The Texts of Taoism* I, 249.

33 Taishō, 人犄, *I-ch'ieh-ching-yin-i*, p. 904c, 人犄…與羇同義也. Ssŭ-pu-pei-yao text, 5.10a, has 人羇. Compare Waley *The Way and its Power*, p. 35: "The *shen* (soul) is like a grandee on his travels (*Kuan-tzŭ*, P'ien 36, beginning). If the inn is not well managed and tidy, he will not stay there."

Hurvitz translates "man's harness." However, the conceit of the body as a dwelling-place is common in Chinese literature on the spirit, while the harness figure is not. Compare *Pao-p'u-tzŭ*, chüan 5, 有者无之宫也．形者神之宅也． (The existent is the palace of the inexistent; the body is the lodging of the spirit.)

The corresponding text in *Chuang-tzŭ* has 猗, a final particle.

34 *Chuang-tzŭ* 6, 3A.23a, Legge, *The Texts of Taoism* I, 251.

35 Liebenthal, "Hui-yüan," p. 252a, n. 57: "Anutpatti, Wu sheng 无生 is not death but Nirvāṇa. Hui-yüan does not distinguish." Actually, it is Chuang-tzŭ, not Hui-yüan, who considers death as returning to the True. Hui-yüan considers that ordinary death is merely the prelude to further birth. In substituting 'no-birth' for 'death' he is forcing the interpretation of Chuang-tzŭ to support his Buddhist exegesis. One of the points at issue is whether man's supreme goal (至理) is achieved in the ordinary modes of human life. Death and Nirvāṇa-without-remainder are alike in not being ordinary biological life. This is in keeping with Hui-yüan's devaluation of the world and worldly affairs, and his emphasis on transcendance at the expense of immanence, which contrasts with Seng-chao's strong emphasis on immanence and repudiation of any duality between saṁsāra and nirvāṇa.

36 Liebenthal, "Immortality," p. 357, n. 80, refers to "Wen-tzŭ Tsuan-i, Shou-p'u" chapter, (The Twenty-two Philosophers, p. 10b). See also *Huai-nan-tzŭ*, chüan 7 (*Chu-tzŭ chi-ch'eng* [Complete Works of the Masters], vol. 7, Peking, Chung-hua Shu-chü, 1954; reprinted 1959, p. 105). 形有靡而神未嘗化者．以不化應化．千變万抮．而未始有極． (The body undergoes dissolution, the spirit never transforms. Because the non-transforming responds to transformations, in a thousand changes and ten thousand revolutions, it never comes to an end-point.)

37 *Chuang-tzŭ* 6, 3A.12a; Legge, *The Texts of Taoism* I, 243.

38 Liu Wen-tien, 3A.12a, quotes a parallel passage from *Huai-nan-tzŭ* which has 範. Legge adopted this reading.

39 This rendering is preferable to Hurvitz's "would not begin to possess the Ultimate." ("Render unto Caesar," p. 109). The next sentence, 其為變可勝計邪, Kuo Hsiang paraphrases, 變豈有極乎.

The idea is that the Great Metal-caster keeps pouring the material endlessly into the finite number of archetypal molds of things. Consequently, if finding a body is an occasion for rejoicing, there are countless occasions for joy.

40 *Chuang-tzŭ* 33, Legge, *The Texts of Taoism* II, 231–32: "Alas! Hui Shih, with all his talents, vast as they were, made nothing out, he pursued all subjects and never came back (with success).'

41 Alternative translation, "Although the arguments of the two masters do not totally fathom the truth (actuality), yet they had come near the Ideal and had heard something about it." Liebenthal,

"Hui-yüan," p. 252a, adopts this alternative. Hurvitz, "Render unto Caesar," p. 109, adopts the first alternative.

42 *Chuang-tzŭ* 2, 1B.12b, Legge, *The Texts of Taoism* I, 182. Kuo Hsiang, 1B.12b, commenting on this section, likens the alternation of life and death to the rotation of the four seasons.

43 See n. 17, above.

44 Specifically, *Chuang-tzŭ* 3, 2A.8a, Legge, *The Texts of Taoism* I, 202.

45 Hurvitz, "Render unto Caesar," p. 110: "You have run afoul of their track. Therefore the mysterious ecstasy has remained unsought by you." I think that Hui-yüan meant that though the simile occurs in *Chuang-tzŭ*, later generations had forgotten its "esoteric meaning," namely transmigration. He claimed to revive the true interpretation of the passage.

46 Hui-yüan means superficial interpretations—the "doctrine of names" practiced by "ordinary minds"—in contrast to "metaphysical (occult) meanings" *(hsüan-i)*.

47 Version 33 and Ssŭ-pu-pei-yao.

48 *Chuang-tzŭ* 3, 2A.8a, Legge, *The Texts of Taoism* I, 202. See Hurvitz, "Render unto Caesar," p. 110, n. 84. The passage is obscure. I translate, "The fingers exhaust [their duty] in providing fuel. The fire is transmitted, and we do not know whether it is extinguished." Kuo Hsiang, 2A.8b, says "The former fire is not the latter fire. Thus when one provides fuel, fire is transmitted. When fire is transmitted, the life continues, yet still its fodder reaches its end-point. Does the world not know that when it has been quenched it is born again?" Hui-yüan's interpretation is obviously based on Kuo Hsiang's. 更生 (is born again) for Kuo Hsiang means 'daily renewal.' Hui-yüan interprets it as metempsychosis rather than palingenesis. Compare *Chuang-tzŭ* 19, 7A.2a.

One plausible explanation of the passages in both *Chuang-tzŭ* and Hui-yüan is that the art of the fingers is exhausted in igniting the fire by a fire-drill. The action of the hands evokes fire from the fuel. When it consumes the fuel, it is not destroyed, as there is fire latent in any other piece of fuel. In this case, the "fingers" stand for the mechanism of rebirth, which effectuates continuity in spite of impermanence.

49 Title of *Chuang-tzŭ*, chapter 3.

50 See n. 6, above.

51 The physical attributes as well as the moral onés would transmigrate.

52 See *Correspondence*, p. 133a28, 大慈大悲積劫之所習．純誠著於在昔． (The purity and truthfulness cultivated through cumulative kalpas by Great Kindness and Great Compassion are manifested through the persistence of the past.) Hui-yüan is asserting that the

inequalities of inborn attributes cannot be explained by the Neo-Taoist theory of autogenesis *(tzŭ-jan)*, since in the Celestial Origin there is no differential cause. Hence, by elimination, it is proved that such differences are caused by karma persisting from previous lives.

53 靈鈞 (numinal potter's wheel) equals 天鈞 (celestial potter's wheel), for which see *Chuang-tzŭ* 2, 1B.17a, Legge, *The Texts of Taoism* I, 185, n. 1. This is the principle of self-so-ness according to which everything is equally affirmable or deniable because it is equally self-identical. Hui-yüan means that no amount of making differences the same can alter the fact that the self-so character of Yao is different from that of Tan-chu. Metaphysical uniformity does not obliterate empirical diversity, which must be explained in terms of karma.

54 已還=以還=以前，以下. *Ta-ch'eng-ch'i-hsin-lun-i-shu*, T 1843, XLIV, pp. 189c29, 190a5.

55 Version 7 and Ssŭ-pu-pei-yao.

DOCUMENT 4

1 *I-ching*, "Hsi-tz'ŭ Hsia" 8.9b, 天地設位．聖人成能. Legge, "Yi King," p. 405: "The places of heaven and earth (in the diagrams) having been determined, the sages were able (by means of the Yi) to carry out and complete their ability."

2 *I-ching*, "Hsi-tz'ŭ Shang" 7.1a, 日月運行．一寒一暑. Legge, "Yi King," p. 349: "and the revolutions of the sun and moon, which give rise to cold and warmth."

3 *I-ching*, "Hsi-tz'ŭ Shang" 7.1b, 剛柔相推．而生變化. Legge, "Yi King," p. 350: "The strong and the weak (lines) displace each other, and produce the changes and transformations (in the figures)." "Hsi-tz'ŭ Shang" 7.2b, 辭有險易. Legge, "Yi King," p. 353: "and the explanations of some are startling, and of some are unexciting." Hexagram 1, 1.4a, 陽氣潛藏. Legge, "Yi King," p. 414: "The energy denoted by the undivided line is laid up and hidden away in the deep." Hexagram 1, 1.4a, 與時偕行. Legge, "Yi King," p. 414: "Continually, as the time passes and requires, does he act."

Analects 7.10.1, 用之則行．舍之則藏．惟我與爾有是夫. Waley, p. 124: "The maxim

When wanted, then go;
When set aside, then hide.

is one that you and I could certainly fulfil." *Eon Kenkyū*, p. 376, n. 4.

In this passage, 理 has the meaning of cosmic law that it has in the *I-ching*, "Shuo-kua" 9.1a, 窮理盡性以至於命.

Liebenthal, "World Conception of Tao-sheng," p. 66: "(The

sages), in perfect harmony with Cosmic Order, in realization of their own nature, fulfilled the will of Heaven." For the range and history of this term, see Liebenthal, "World Conception of Tao-sheng," pp. 65–67, and Demiéville, "Pénétration," pp. 28–31.

4 *I-ching*, "Hsi-tz'ŭ Hsia" 8.4a, 屈信相感而利生焉. Legge, "Yi King," p. 389: "It is by the influence on each other of this contraction and expansion that the advantages (of the different conditions) are produced."

5 See *Chao-lun*, *Reply to Liu I-min*, p. 156a7, *Jōron Kenkyū*, p. 46: 冥機潛運. 其用不勤. "The occult pivot turns hiddenly, and its function is indefatigable."

Compare *Chuang-tzŭ* 2, 1B.13b, 樞始得其環中. 以應无窮. Legge, *The Texts of Taoism* I, 183: "As soon as one finds this pivot, he stands in the centre of the ring (of thought), where he can respond without end to the changing views."

Chuang-tzŭ 24. 盡有天. 循有照. 冥有樞. 始有彼. Legge, *The Texts of Taoism* II, 112: "Thus Heaven is to him all; accordance with it is the brightest intelligence. Obscurity has in this its pivot; in this is the beginning." *Eon Kenkyū*, p. 439, n. 6.

6 *I-ching*, "Hsi-tz'ŭ Shang" 7.9a–b, 往来不窮. 謂之通. Legge, "Yi King," p. 372: "and the passing from one of these states to the other may be called the constant course (of things)." *I-ching*, "Hsi-tz'ŭ Shang" 7.10b, 聖人有以見天下之動. 而觀其會通. Legge, "Yi King," p. 378: "A (later) sage was able to survey the motive influences working all under the sky. He contemplated them in their common action and special nature."

7 *Chuang-tzŭ* 16: 世命大謬也. Legge, 419: "The conditions laid upon them by the times were very much awry."

Chuang-tzŭ 16: 世與道交相喪也. 道之人何由興乎世. Legge, 419: "The world and the Way, when they came together, being (thus) lost to each other, how could the men of the Way make themselves conspicuous in the world?" *Eon Kenkyū*, p. 440, n. 9.

Chuang-tzŭ 6A.11b, 不當時命. 而大窮於天下. 則深根寧極而待. Legge, 372: "When those conditions shut them up entirely from such action, they struck their roots deeper (in themselves), were perfectly still, and waited."

Compare *Tao-te-ching*, p. 59, Waley, *The Way and its Power*, p. 213: "This is called the art of making the roots strike deep by fencing the trunk, of making life long by fixed staring."

Hayashiya translates: "Shikamo shinkon kotei naki ni oite wa, nanzo kiwamete motte matan ya." (However, when there is no deep root and firm stem, how may one reach the ultimate and so await!)

I interpret 寧極 as the third part of the tree metaphor—root, trunk, and top branches. This is supported by the use of 極 in *Tao-te-ching*, ch. 59, 莫知其極, and the *Han Fei Tzŭ* passage to which it alludes, 其述遠則衆人莫見其端末．是以莫知其極． (Quoted in the Hsüeh-sheng Kuo-hsüeh edition of the *Tao-te-ching*, p. 59, n. 5.)

A fairly literal translation is: "...stabilize the extremity, and so be supported."

8 *I-ching*, "Hsi-tz'ŭ Shang" 7.9a, 閤户謂之坤．闢户謂之乾．一閤一闢謂之變． Legge, "Yi King," p. 372: "Thus, a door shut may be pronounced (analogous to) Khwăn (or the inactive condition), and the opening of the door (analogous to) Khien (or the active condition). The opening succeeding the being shut may be pronounced (analogous to what we call) a change."

9 *Chuang-tzŭ* 1, 1A.14b, 其神凝．使物不疵癘． Legge, *The Texts of Taoism* I, 171: "that by the concentration of his spirit-like powers he could save men from disease and pestilence." *Chuang-tzŭ* 19, 7A.6a, 用志不分．乃凝於神． Legge, *The Texts of Taoism* II, 15: "Where the will is not diverted from its object, the spirit is concentrated." *Lieh-tzŭ* (Chu-tzŭ Chi-ch'eng edition, Peking, Chung-hua Shu-chü, 1954; reprinted 1959), p. 15, 心凝形釋．骨肉都融． Lionel Giles, *A Gallery of Chinese Immortals* (Wisdom of the East Series), London, J. Murray, 1948, p. 42: "My mind was frozen, my body in dissolution, my flesh and bones all melted together."

Compare *Preface to the Poems on Buddha-recollection*, KHMC, p. 351b15, 此假修以凝神．積功以移性．

In the sentence to which this note refers, 正覺之道 replaces 神 in the collocation 神凝. 正覺 equals 'sambodhi.' 道 equals 'bodhi' and is added as a translation-gloss like those of An Shih-kao, e.g. 袈裟法服 (kaṣāya dharma-garb), 薩云若智 (sarvajñatā knowledge), 沙門道人 (śramaṇa cleric) and 鉢器 (pātra vessel).

For 不虛 (it is not in vain that), see *Chao-lun*, part III, p. 153b23 (First Question) 聖不虛知 and 聖不虛會. Yüan-k'ang, T 1859, p. 174c27, asserts that the questioner in *Chao-lun*, part III is Liu I-min. If so, maybe 不虛 was a common phrase in the discussions on Lu-shan. See *Dharmatrāta Preface*, CST, p. 65c8, 理有行藏．道不虛授． "In the Order there is proceeding and storing. The Tao does not bestow in vain."

The sentence here annotated echoes the first sentence of the *Preface* and refers to the Holy Man who sits in the transmundane control-room of the universe, absorbed in the contemplation of Cosmic Order *(li)*, yet responding in conformity to the receptivity of living beings, embodying as the Duke of Chou and Confucius in accommodation to the needs of an immature age, and bringing the Dharma to China by stages when the Chinese were ready for it.

10 情 are the inner stirrings of a thing before it begins an overt action. *I-ching*, "Hsi-tz'ŭ Hsia" 8.2a, 類万物之情.

Legge, "Yi King," p. 383: "and to classify the qualities of the myriad things."

Liebenthal, translating T'ang's "Wang Pi," p. 144, renders *ch'ing* as "innate tendencies," and defines it (n. 45) as "the natural tendency that determines a life."

11 漸 (by degrees) is the antonym of 頓 (sudden, suddenly). Hui-yüan uses both terms frequently. Apparently at this time the gradual-sudden controversy was in full swing in his community on Lu-shan. In addition to the several references in this *Preface*, the following instances occur in Hui-yüan's other writings:
(a) *Dharmatrāta Preface*, CST, p. 65b23, 雖精數有異分．而階籍有方． "Though there are different lots among the determinations of vital essence, yet there are [corresponding] stations in the series of stages."
(b) *On the Śramaṇa Baring his Right Shoulder*, HMC, p. 33a9, 遠求其實則階差有分． "If you seek its reality (truth) a long distance, then there are divisions in the series of stages."
(c) *Explaining Karmic Response*, HMC, p. 34a23, 而訓必有漸．知久習不可頓廢． Liebenthal, "Immortality," p. 362, "But teaching can proceed only gradually because inveterate habits cannot be changed in an instant."
(d) *The Śramaṇa Does Not Offer Obeisance to the King*, Part 4, HMC, p. 31a10, 此但方內之階差．而猶不可頓設． "These are just worldly graded stages, yet even so they cannot be set up suddenly."
(e) *Correspondence*, p. 133b5, 羽翮復何由頓生 若可頓生．則諸菩薩无復積劫之功． "By what means could feathers suddenly grow again? If they could grow suddenly, then there would no longer be the bodhisattva's good works through accumulating kalpas."
(f) *Correspondence*, p. 140a12, 若菩薩遍學．為從方便始為頓入无漏一道也． "If the bodhisattva trains in all ways, then through skilful means *(upāya)* he would first suddenly enter the anāsrava unique bodhi."
(g) *Correspondence*, p. 140b10, 其中應不俄爾之頃頓至法忍者． "Those present [in the Assembly] should not in an instant suddenly reach dharma-patience."
(h) *Correspondence*, p. 141c10, 若果不住住遍學．則其中无復諸住階之名． "If their studies are not in fact all-sided in each of the stages, then there should no longer be the names of the graded series of bhūmis."
(i) *The Three Recompenses*, HMC, p. 34c20, 則知有方外之賓．服膺妙法．洗心玄門．一詣之感超登上位． "So we know that there are clients of the trans-mundane who wear the sublime Dharma on their bosoms [like a pendant], who bathe their minds at the metaphysical gate [i.e., Buddhism], who in one act of initiative transcend [the stages] and mount the supreme position." Liebenthal, "Immortality," p. 365, n. 96, says that this refers to Tao-sheng and his circle, who believed in Instantaneous Illumination.

Demiéville, "Pénétration," p. 32, says: "The words *tun* and *chien* do not figure in the several fragments of the work of Chih Tun which have come down to us. But certain of these fragments seem to me to indicate definitely that from the middle of the fourth century A.D. they were discussing suddenism and gradualism in China and that Chih Tun (314–366) took part in these discussions, just as did other Buddhists of his time, for example Tao-an (314–385)."

12 高士 (eminent gentlemen) is an archaic translation of 'bodhisattva.' See Oda, p. 176,3. Apparently such archaic technical terms had acquired a classical flavor by about A.D. 400, because they are frequently used in the prefaces in preference to the new terms.

13 The Taishō text has 積誠 (accumulated sincerity). Perhaps this should be 積成, for 積德成智 or something of the sort. Compare *Chuang-tzŭ* 12, 5B.1a, 无所積．故万物成． This sentence is a piece of gradualism that Hui-yüan inserted into Nāgārjuna's biography.

14 接九百之運． I take 運 to mean a transit or cycle, hence a period of time rather than a point in time, so that the phrase equals 九百中 or 九百内, both of which mean "in the ninth century." See Ui, *Vaiśeṣika Philosophy*, pp. 42–43. Seng-chao, *Preface to the Hundred Treatise*, CST, p. 77b12, says that Āryadeva lived "eight hundred and more years after the Buddha's Nirvāṇa." If Hui-yüan's phrase means "during the ninth century," then it is compatible with Seng-chao's.

15 衡門 1208, 4—a gate with a horizontal beam; connotation of humble status; figurative for dwelling in retirement, doing as one pleases, and having no ambitions.

See also *The Three Recompenses*, HMC, p. 34b27.

16 赤澤 (the Red Swamp) is given in the *Shan-hai-ching* as the name of a stream "South of the Bamboos." Yüan-k'ang, p. 175c20, gives it as a gloss for the transliteration of 'Kapilavastu,' which he says is a synecdoche for India. The *Shan-hai-ching* phrase is not strictly a translation of 'Kapilavastu,' but no doubt it was adopted because of its classical flavor, and because it favored the propaganda claim that Buddhism was known in China at an early date. See *Abhidharmasāra Preface*, CST, p. 72c3, 龍潛赤澤．獨有其明． "He lay hidden like a dragon in the Red Swamp (*Kapilavastu*), and kept his brilliance to himself." Also see Chi-tsang, *Pai-lun-shu*, T XLII, 234a4, 迦夷羅者云赤澤國也．

17 文明—see Liebenthal's translation of T'ang, "Wang Pi," p. 150: "With a humble, cultured character, . . ." Also, *I-ching*, 4, 7a, Wang Pi on Hexagram 35, 夫以柔順文明之質．

18 *I-ching*, Hexgagram 1, 1.1a, 潛龍勿用． Legge, "Yi King," p. 57: "The dragon lying hid (in the deep). It is not the time for active doing." 1.1b, 或躍在淵． Legge, "Yi King," p. 57: "as if he were leaping up, but still in the deep."

For 忽 the Taishō version 19 gives 惑. This should be emended to 或 on the basis of the *I-ching* prototype.

19 See *Vimalakīrti-nirdeśa*, T 475, p. 541a2: "Do not take the light of the sun to be the same as a firefly's glimmer."

20 玄衣 (dark garment) equals 染衣 (dyed garment)—the monk's robes, in contrast to 白衣 (white garment), the layman's garb. Vows, tonsure, and robe is the biographer's formula for ordination. Compare T LI, 983a21, 剃染。五戒. Waley, "New Light on Buddhism," p. 361: "I shaved my head, dyed my clothes, and received the five vows." Other instances of the formula or parts of it occur in Hui-yüan's writings at HMC, pp. 30a29 and 30b11.

落簪 (discarded his hairpins) is figurative for tonsure. See *I' ch'ieh-ching-yin-i*, T LIV, 903c, also Link, "Shih Tao-an," p. 46, n. 1.

21 *I-ching*, "Hsi-tz'ŭ Hsia" 8.8a, 知者觀其彖辭。則思過半矣. Legge, "Yi King," p. 400: "But if the wise will look at the explanations of the entire diagrams, their thoughts will embrace more than half of this knowledge."

22 *Tao-te-ching*, p. 41, Waley, *The Way and its Power*, p. 193: "The largest square has no corners."

23 神明 (spirit-intelligence) is here a synonym for 'prajñā.' The classic instance of the term is in the *Book of Rites (Li-chi)* (Shih-san-ching edition, p. 92), 其氣發揚于上爲昭明。…此百物之精也。神之著也. "The ether (breath) rises upwards and becomes a shining brightness.... This (odor) is the creature's vital essence; it is a manifestation of the spirit." See Liebenthal, "Immortality," pp. 333 ff. For the meaning of *shen-ming* in the *Chao-lun*, see Chapter 6.

24 See Nāgārjuna's biography, T 2047, pp. 184c8 ff., also Walleser, "Life of Nāgārjuna," p. 447.

25 See *Dharmatrāta Preface*, CST, p. 66a27, 非夫道冠三乘。智通十地。孰 "Who except one whose Tao crowns the Three Vehicles, whose knowledge has passed through the Ten Stages, . . ."

Chi-tsang, *Chung-lun-shu*, T XLII, 1c9, quotes Hui-yüan with variant 貫 for 冠. He says, p. 1c24, that 道位 means the ten bhūmis.

Authorities differ as to the items in the Three Patiences. See Edgerton, *Buddhist Hybrid Sanskrit Dictionary*, p. 199b; Har Dayal, *The Bodhisattva Doctrine in Buddhist Sanskrit Literature*, London, K. Paul, Trench, Trubner, 1932, pp. 209–12; Oda, p. 1362,3 and *Eon Kenkyū*, pp. 440–41, n. 30.

26 See *Dharmatrāta Preface*, CST, p. 66a8, 爾乃闢九關於龍津. "Only then did he open the Nine Passes in the Dragon Ford."

Seng-jui, *Pañcaviṁśati Preface*, CST, p. 152c28, 登十階之龍津 "[the *Mahāprajñāpāramitā*] ascends the ten-stage Dragon Ford."

The number nine refers, I think, to the nine crossing-points between the ten bhūmis. It also suggests a parallel with the subterranean 九泉 (Nine Springs). This theme of the submarine journey suggests intriguing if not actually consequential analogies with Persephone, Dante, and Urashima Tarō.

27 T 2047, p. 184c16, 龍還送出於南天竺. "The dragon escorted him back, and he came out in South India."

28 *Chuang-tzŭ* 5: 故不足以滑和．不可入於靈府.

Legge, *The Texts of Taoism* I, 232: "They are not sufficient therefore to disturb the harmony (of the nature), and are not allowed to enter into the treasury of intelligence." Kuo Hsiang says that 靈府．精神之宅. "The numinal treasury is the mansion of the psyche-spirit." *Eon Kenkyū*, p. 318, n. 54.

29 无照 (no cognition) here corresponds to 无知 (no knowing) in *Chao-lun*, part III. Whereas 照 means 'intuition' in the *Chao-lun*, it here means normal cognition. For the history of this term, see Demiéville, *Lhasa*, p. 78, n. 2.

无當 (no matching) here means that there is no counterpart relation between consciousness and its object. In the *Chao-lun*, 當 generally signifies the relation between a term 名 and its actual 實. In this passage, Hui-yüan seems to be confusing cognitive relations with symbolic relations, since he pairs 'actual' 實 with 'spirit' 神 rather than with 'term' 名.

30 趣 (goal) here means something like an entelechy, as well as an epistemological object and a semantic referent.

31 Metathesis of 華 and 慮. Emend following Hayashiya, p. 290.

32 Taishō version 24.

33 水鏡 (water-mirror). For a historical and comparative account of the mirror metaphor, see Demiéville, "Le miroir spirituel."

Compare *Chuang-tzŭ* 13, 5B.1b, 聖人之心靜乎天地之鑑也．万物之鏡也. Demiéville, "Le miroir spirituel," p. 118: "Quiet est l'esprit du Saint, miroir du Ciel et de la Terre, qui reflète toute la multiplicité des choses."

The figure of the mirror in Mādhyamika treatises illustrates śūnyatā, whereas Hui-yüan here means ādarśa-jñāna (mirror-knowledge). See GPWT, p. 104b18, Lamotte, *Traité* I, 378: "Just as the image in the mirror is not made by the mirror, is not made by the face, it not made by the one who holds the mirror, and is not self-made, and yet is not without cause and conditions."

HT, ch. 8, p. 179a22: "If in order to maintain that thing gives birth to thing, you say that it is like an image in the mirror—this also is not right. And why? Because there is nothing from which the image in the mirror comes. And again, as the image in the mirror is similar to the face, in the same way, the effect must be similar to the cause—but this is not so" (Tucci's translation, *Pre-Diṅnāga*).

The *Pratyutpanna-samādhi-sūtra*, T 418, which was basic to the Amitābha cult on Lu-shan (T'ang, *History*, p. 372), contains an elaborate mirror simile (T XIII, pp. 905c18 ff.) about a youngster looking at his image in various kinds of reflectors, which illustrates that mental images likewise do not come out from within and do not come in from outside. This principle is then used to solve the problem whether the Buddha that is seen in samādhi is real or fancied. The passage concludes (p. 906a1): "Mind makes the Buddha; mind sees itself; mind is the Buddha; mind is the Tathāgata. . . . Mind having marks is ignorance; mind having no marks is Nirvāṇa."

The mirror example occurs frequently in the writings of Hui-yüan and his contemporaries:

(a) *Preface to the Poems on Buddha-recollection*, KHMC, p. 351b23, 即所緣以成鑒. "One identifies with the object in order to achieve the mirroring (become the mirror)."

(b) The same, KHMC, p. 351b25, 於是覩夫淵凝虛鏡之体．则悟靈根. "Then, when one sees the essence of that profound, concentrated (fixed) and void mirror, one awakens to the numinal basis."

(c) *Abhidharmasāra Preface*, CST, p. 72c21, 水鏡六府. "to water-mirror the six viscera." (See Liebenthal, "Hui-yüan," p. 256a, n. 108.

(d) *Correspondence*, p. 131b21, 如其不能．則水月鏡像復何因而有. "If [rūpa] cannot [make rūpa], then in dependence on what do the moon in the water and the image in the mirror exist?"

(e) Wang Ch'i-chih, *Ode on Buddha-recollection Samādhi*, KHMC p. 351c14, 寂爾淵鏡．金水塵紛. Liebenthal, *Chao*, p. 195: "Motionless sleep the Deep Lake and the Mirror, but their surfaces teem with moving forms."

(f) Seng-jui, *Pañcaviṁśati Preface*, CST, p. 53a1, 水鏡未可以喻其澄朗．故假慧以稱之. "The water-mirror could never serve as a figure for its limpid lucidity, so they apply the designation 'prajñā to it."

I wonder whether in their meditation Hui-yüan's brotherhood used mirrors and vessels of water as kasinas.

34 Compare *Dharmatrāta Preface*, CST, p. 65b26, where the same deferential transition-formula occurs.

35 *Tao-te-ching*, p, 58, Waley, *The Way and its Power*, p. 212: "It is upon bad fortune that good fortune leans, upon good fortune that bad fortune rests." Hui-yüan twisted this passage to enlist Lao-tzŭ's authority for transmigration.

36 法 may render either 'bhāva' (existent, entity) or 'dharma.' In *Middle Stanzas* 10.16, 12.8, and 13.3 it renders 'bhāva.'

37 兩行 (proceed separately)—all my translations of this term are tentative. Two certain components of its meaning are that it is a predicate of a pair of opposites, and that the two opposites remain separate. The classic instance is in *Chuang-tzŭ* 2, 1B.17a, 是以聖人和之以是非．而休乎天鈞．是之謂兩行. Legge, *The Texts of Taoism* I, 185, "Therefore, the sagely man brings together a

dispute in its affirmations and denials, and rests in the equal fashioning of Heaven. Both sides of the question are admissible."

Kuo Hsiang, on *Chuang-tzŭ* 2, 1B.13b, says 一是一非兩行无窮.

The term occurs elsewhere in Hui-yüan:

(a) *On the Śramaṇa Baring his Right Shoulder*, HMC, p. 32c3, 而邪正兩行. "...then wrong and right follow each other around."

(b) *The Three Recompenses*, HMC, p. 34c7, 善惡之報殊錯而兩行. "Good and evil recompenses, being differently allocated, follow each other in turn." (Liebenthal, "Hui-yüan," p. 257a: "We... are rewarded and punished in turn, in various ways but never without reason." See n. 109, p. 257a.)

(c) *Correspondence*, p. 135a26, 有无即分.則斷常兩行矣. "Since existence and inexistence are parted, annulling and permanence proceed separately."

(d) *Correspondence*, p. 138b18, 前念非後念.雖同而兩行. "The former thought is not the latter thought. Though they are the same, they occur separately."

38 Hayashiya: kū ni ei-jite (shining in the void). Liebenthal, "Hui-yüan," p. 247a, "A play fascinating...."

39 无主 (without a lord)—see Kuo Hsiang on *Chuang-tzŭ* 2, 1B.14a, 今是非无主.紛然淆亂. "Now, affirmation and negation have no lord, and [things] are all mixed up." Han K'ang-po, on *I-ching*, "Hsi-tz'ŭ Shang" 7.4a, 理自玄應.化之无主.數自冥運. "The Order itself responds metaphysically; transformations have no lord; numbers (fates) occultly rotate themselves."

40 觀 (vision)—see Demiéville, *Lhasa*, p. 78, n. 3. Of the Sanskrit equivalents that Demiéville gives, 'vipaśyanā' is the most likely in this context. In Eastern Chin texts, *kuan* also renders 'pratyavekṣā,' as in the *Kāśyapaparivarta*, Stael-Holstein, section 63, p. 94. Actually, Hui-yüan need not have had any translation-term in mind.

41 反鑑 (reverse the mirror) is equivalent to 反照 (introvert and intuit). See Demiéville, *Lhasa*, p. 78, n. 2, on 返照心源. (Retourner la vision vers la source de l'esprit.)

42 Taken almost verbatim from *Chuang-tzŭ* 5, 2C.6b, Demiéville, "Le miroir spirituel," p. 119: "Lorsqu'un miroir est clair, c'est qu'il ne s'y trouve point de poussière."

43 儀像 (images of the primal dichotomy)—Liebenthal, "Hui-yüan," p. 247a: "it pictures the universe in all its details." The primal dichotomy is *ch'ien*—heaven, male, yang, etc.—and *k'un*—earth, female, yin, etc. Perhaps this phrase might also mean "the primal dichotomy and the [four] figures." See Legge, "Yi King," p. 12.

44 Hayashiya: u ni shite u ni aru mono wa u yori mo u nari (Something that while existing resides in the existent is even more existent than the existent.) Compare *Eon Kenkyū*, p. 442, n. 54.

45 Hayashiya: en wo shōzuru mo, josō nakereba, . . . (As, though it produces the conditions, it has no mark, . . .)

46 Compare the fire simile in ***Spirit Does Not Perish*** (Document 3).

47 淪虛 (sink into the void)—compare *Chao-lun*, part IV, 158a15, 永淪太虛. *Jōron Kenkyū*, p. 63: tokoshie ni michi sono mono no naka ni chinsen shiyō (to submerge forever in the Tao itself).

48 爭 (how)—Hayashiya reads 'ikadeka' (how). *Eon Kenkyū*, p. 422, n. 56, is wrong.

49 神遇 (experience with the spirit)—*Chuang-tzŭ* 3, 2A.3a, 方今之時．臣以神遇．而不以目視. Legge, *The Texts of Taoism* I, 199: "Now I deal with it in a spirit-like manner and do not look at it with my eyes." Kuo Hsiang's commentary, 闇與理會. "He darkly meets (conforms to) the archetype [of the ox]."

50 *I-ching*, "Hsi-tz'ŭ Hsia" 8.4a, 過此以往．未之或知也. Legge, "Yi King," p. 390: "Going on beyond this, we reach a point which it is hardly possible to know."

51 Compare *I-ching*, Hsi-tz'ŭ Shang" 7.3b, 故神无方而易无体. Legge, "Yi King," p. 354: "It is thus that his operation is spirit-like, unconditioned by place, while the changes which he produces are not restricted to any form."

52 觸類 (permuting categories)—*I-ching*, "Hsi-tz'ŭ Shang" 7.7b 觸類而長之. Legge, "Yi King," p. 366: "If we prolonged each by the addition of the proper lines." Wilhelm, p. 238: "Wenn man . . . die Zustände durch die Uebergänge in die entsprechenden andern vermehrt, . . ." Comment: Jedes der 64 Zeichen kann durch entsprechende Bewegung von einem oder mehreren Strichen in ein anderes übergehen." I think Hui-yüan is referring to passages in the *Great Perfection of Wisdom Treatise* where a list of predicates is matched off with each of the five skandhas, etc., in turn.

53 近習 (addiction to the commonplace)—compare *Explaining Karmic Response*, HMC, p. 34a23, 知久習不可頓廢. "We know that inveterate addictions cannot be discontinued suddenly."

54 *I-ching*, "Hsi-tz'ŭ Hsia" 8.3b, 天下同歸而殊塗．一致而百慮 Legge, "Yi King," p. 389: "They all come to the same (successful) issue, though by different paths; there is one result, though there might be a hundred anxious schemes."

55 *Chuang-tzŭ* 8, 駢於辯者．纍瓦結繩．竄句遊心於堅白同異之間. Legge, *The Texts of Taoism* I, 269: "An extraordinary faculty in debating leads to the piling up of arguments like a builder with his bricks, or a net-maker with his string. (Its possessor) cunningly contrives his sentences and enjoys himself in discussing what hardness is and what whiteness is, where views agree and where they differ, . . ." Chuang-tzŭ was criticizing Yang Chu and Mo Ti for their dialectics and semantics. Hui-yüan is saying that the *Great Perfection of Wisdom Treatise* demolishes all sophistries. *Eon Kenkyū*, p. 442, n. 66.

56 義音 (speech about the doctrine)——attributive compound analogous to 義學 (doctrinal studies).

57 *I-ching*, "Hsi-tz'ŭ Hsia": 易之為書也．廣大悉備. Legge, "Yi King," p. 402: "The Yi is a book of wide comprehension and great scope, embracing everything." *Eon Kenkyū*, n. 67.

58 *Chuang-tzŭ* 17: 秋水時至．百川灌河. Legge, *The Texts of Taoism* I, 374: "The time of the autumnal floods was come, and the hundred streams were all discharging themselves into the Ho." *Eon Kenkyū*, p. 442, n. 69.

59 This sentence imitates the structure of certain sentences in the *I-ching*, "Hsi-tz'ŭ Shang," for example, 7.8a, 非天下之至精．其孰能與於此. Legge, "Yi King," p. 369: "(If the Yi) were not the most exquisite thing under heaven, would it be concerned in such an operation as this?" This form is a cliché in Buddhist prefaces of the late fourth and early fifth centuries. 潛躍 (lie hidden and leap)—see the two *I-ching* passages on Hexagram 1, quoted in n. 18. The dragon is a common metaphor for the bodhisattva. (See notes 16, 18, and 26.) In this case, it is applied to Kumārajīva. The deep lake is the *Great Perfection of Wisdom Treatise.* Perhaps 'lying hid' refers to Kumārajīva's period of waiting in detention in Ku-tsang, and 'leaping' to his period of activity in Ch'ang-an.

60 數 (numbers) may stand for 事數 (technical terms) here, in view of the parallel with *ming* (names).

61 *Chuang-tzŭ* 16: 古之人在混芒之中．與一世而得澹漠焉. Legge, *The Texts of Taoism* I, 369: "The men of old, while the chaotic condition was yet undeveloped, shared the placid tranquillity which belonged to the whole world." *Eon Kenkyū*, p. 442, n. 72.

62 See *I-ching*, "Hsi-tz'ŭ Shang" 7.3a, 智周乎万物. Legge, "Yi King," p. 354: "His knowledge embraces all things."

高座 (high-throne)—see Lamotte, *Traité* I, p. 490, n. 1. Note that Dharmarakṣa's teacher was Chu Kao-tso (KSC, p. 326c3; Bagchi, p. 83, n. 2). Also see KSC, p. 327c12, biography of the Kuchean, Śrīmitra: "The men of the times called him Kao-tso" (Bagchi, p. 319).

63 *I-ching*, "K'un-Kua, Wen-yen": 美在其中，而暢於四支．發於事業．美之至也. Legge, "Yi King," p. 421: "His excellence is in the centre (of this being), but it diffuses a complacency over his four limbs, and is manifested in his (conduct of) affairs:—this is the perfection of excellence."

The expression also occurs in the *Abhidharmasāra Preface*, CST, pp. 72c15 ff. *Eon Kenkyū*, p. 282, n. 19.

64 殊俗 (foreign peoples)—the allusion goes back to the *Shih-chi*, *Ch'in Shih-huang pen-chi* (Ssŭ-pu-pei-yao, case 32, chüan 6, 33b), 秦王既沒．餘威振於殊俗. Chavannes, *Les Memoires Historiques*, II, 229, "Même après la mort du roi de *Ts'in*, le prestige qu'il

avait laissé fut encore redoutable aux yeux des peuples étrangers." As Yao Hsing styled himself 'King of Ch'in,' the allusion is flattering if one only considers the sentence just quoted, but rather barbed if one considers its wider context in Ssŭ-ma Ch'ien's "Judgment."

65 方言 can mean either 'technical terms' or 'local language.' Seng-jui, *GPWT Preface*, CST, p. 75a28, 法師以秦人好簡．故裁而略之． Translated by Demiéville in his review of *Traité*, p. 388: "le maître de la Loi l'abrégea en y pratiquant des coupures, parce que les Chinois aiment la concision." Seng-jui goes on to say (p. 75b1), "The Dharmācārya recounted the main framework in Chinese. He only translated [any sentence] once into the ***local language.*** He omitted and did not transmit the sundry embellishments.

See Demiéville's review of *Traité*, regarding the whole question of the *Great Perfection of Wisdom Treatise* translation.

66 *Tso-chuan*, *Chao Kung*, 20th year, Legge, *Chinese Classics*, text, p. 679, translation, p. 684: "Harmony may be illustrated by soup. You have the water and fire, vinegar, pickle, salt, and plums, with which to cook fish. It is made to boil by the firewood, and then the cook mixes the ingredients, harmoniously equalizing the several flavors, so as to supply whatever is deficient and carry off what is in excess."

67 See *Saddharma-puṇḍarīka*, ch. 8, T IX, 29a6 ff., and SBE, 21, 201. The parable of the gem tied in the man's garment.

68 *Tao-te-ching*, p. 81.

69 *Chuang-tzŭ* 2, 1B.11a, 道隱於小成．言隱於榮華． Legge, *The Texts of Taoism* I, 182, "Tao becomes obscured through the small comprehension (of the mind), and speech comes to be obscure through the vaingloriousness (of the speaker)." The *shu* of Ch'eng Hsüan-ying says that 小成 (trivialities) means humaneness, justice and the five virtues, and that 榮華 (ornamentation) means sophistry (1B.11a and 1B.11b).

70 百家 (the Hundred Schools)—the Late Chou philosophers, here cast in a bad light as signifying dissension. Hui-yüan was not prepared to let the hundred flowers bloom.

71 The nine major groups of the pre-Ch'in and early Han schools: (1) the Confucians, (2) the Taoists, (3) the Yin-Yang School, (4) the Legalists, (5) the School of Names, (6) the Mohists, (7) the Tsung-heng School, (8) Sundry schools, and (9) the Agriculturalists.

72 This is the principle of upāya, which the ensuing passage connects with the accommodation of rhetoric to the hearer's disposition.

73 *Mencius* 7B32, 1 言近而指遠者．善言也． Legge, *Four Books*, p. 1001: "Words which are simple, while their meaning is farreaching, are good words." *Eon Kenkyū*, p. 443, n. 90.

74 象 (figures)—the four digrams. See note 42. Hui-yüan may also mean 'images in a mirror.' Compare *The Three Recompenses*, HMC, p. 34c25, 鏡万像於无像者也. "who mirrors the myriad images in the imageless."

75 名教 (doctrine of names) is mundane and literalist learning, and contrasts with 'metaphysical studies' *(hsüan-hsüeh)*. Hui-yüan also uses the term at HMC, pp. 31a18, 33a1, 33b6, and 34c23.

76 *I-ching*, "Hsi-tz'ŭ Hsia" 8.6a, 其称名也，雜而不越. Legge, "Yi King," p. 395: "The appellations and the names (of the diagrams and lines) are various, but do not go beyond (what is to be ascribed to the nature of these two conditions)." Compare *Lun-yü*, 6.16 (see Doc. 7, n. 22).

77 Adopt Hayashiya's reading, 充, rather than the Taiṣhō 允.

78 Compare the deferential formula at the end of the *Abhidharmasāra Preface*, CST, p. 72c28.

DOCUMENT 5

1 *Chuang-tzŭ* 3, 2A.7b, Legge, *The Texts of Taoism* I, 201–2. The expression indicates the immortality of the sage who has transcended the bonds of life and death, and so conforms to the changes.

2 Chi-tsang, p. 2c13, says that attachment produces lust, while delusion produces [false] views. Hatani, however, interprets the phrase as attributive rather than co-ordinate—"the attachment of the deluded."

3 The viewpoint of śrāvakas and pratyeka-buddhas who adhere to doctrines of the reality of Śākyamuni's mundane birth and parinirvāṇa, or of mere emptiness, and who do not walk in the Middle Path (Chi-tsang, p. 3a10–14).

4 The Hīnayānist conceives aversion for saṁsāra and delight in nirvāṇa, and so falls into one-sided views (Chi-tsang, p. 3a15–18).

5 耿介 (resolve) is glossed by 志節 (Chi-tsang, p. 3a21).

6 Their resolve is set on Hīnayāna nirodha as the summum bonum, and so they err from the Great Way of the Mahāyāna (Chi-tsang, pp. 3a23 ff.). Hatani renders 'kai wo itasu' (induces error). But Chi-tsang paraphrases 與大道相乖 (is at variance with the Great Way).

7 The realization that all the dharmas are non-arising and utterly empty is called 'vast intuition' (Chi-tsang, p. 3b5).

8 'Existent' and 'inexistent' are the two extreme views. The Hīnayānists do not recognize that nirvāṇa is identical with saṁsāra, and that living beings are identical with the Buddhas. Consequently, they cannot unify the religious *(nirvāṇa)* and the profane *(saṁsāra)* (Chi-tsang, p. 3b14–18).

9 Seng-jui probably intends an allusion to *Stanzas* 25.20, "Between

the limit of nirvāṇa and the limit of saṁsāra not even the slightest [difference] exists" (Chi-tsang, pp. 3b23 ff.).

10 Compassion was Nāgārjuna's motive for writing the *Middle Treatise* (Chi-tsang, p. 3b29–c1).

11 'Equalized' means abolished all dualities between opposites such as existent and inexistent, nirvāṇa and saṁsāra, Buddha and living beings, etc. (Chi-tsang, p. 3c18).

12 He enables Hīnayānists to become Mahāyāna bodhisattvas (Chi-tsang, p. 3c21).

13 玄指 (metaphysical pointer) means the *Middle Treatise* (Chi-tsang, p. 3c22). Compare Seng-jui, *Vimalakīrti Commentary Preface*, CST, p. 58c24, "I received the metaphysical pointer [i.e., *Vimalakīrti-nirdeśa*] from my former master." 'Pointer'—literally, 'finger.' Chi-tsang adduces the example of the finger pointing at the moon.

14 The *Middle Treatise* text has 括, which Hatani renders 'kukuru' (fasten, tie up). The CST text has 恬, which Hayashiya renders lyasunzuru' (satisfy, content). Chi-tsang (p. 3c27–28) glosses with 撿括 (gather together and embrace). 即化 (identifying or coalescing with transformations)—see *Chao-lun*, part IV, p. 161a13, 至人戢玄機於未兆. 藏冥運於即化. (The Perfect Man sheathes his metaphysical device [i.e., his mind] in the unmanifested, and conceals his occult rotations in identity with the transformations.)

15 'Clients of metaphysical understanding' means the Taoists, who are Chinese Tīrthikas, and by transference it means the Indian Tīrthikas. 朝徹 (morning's clear rays)—*Chuang-tzŭ* 6, 3A.16b, Legge, *The Texts of Taoism* I, 246, where it is used as a term for mystic illumination in an account of the stages of Taoist dhyāna. By using this term for the Mādhyamika truth, Seng-jui is asserting that Nāgārjuna's teaching is the solution to the Neo-Taoist problems, just as in India it is the solution to the Tīrthika's problems (Chi-tsang, pp. 4a2 ff.).

16 Reference to *Shu-ching*, "Hung-fan," "The king's road is vast, vast! It is not one-sided and not partisan." The implication is that the *Middle Treatise* and the Middle Way that it expounds are like the broad, level thoroughfare of the ancient kings (Chi-tsang, 4a16 ff.). Note the metaphor of the road in the next sentence.

17 沖階 (hollow stairs)—the bodhisattva-bhūmis (Chi-tsang, p. 4a21–22). The sentence means that Nāgārjuna facilitated the ascent of the bodhisattva stages. Seng-jui seems to have mixed his metaphors, as roads do not usually ascend stairways.

18 玄門 (metaphysical gate)—see *Tao-te-ching* 1: "The metaphysical beyond the metaphysical, the gate of all mysteries." In the *Tao-te-ching*, it is the sameness of the named and the nameless that is the 'metaphysical gate.'

19 CST, p. 76c27 and MT, p. 1a19 have both 慧風 (wind of prajñā). Chi-tsang, p. 4a26, gives 惠風 (wind of kindness), explained as the spring winds. But at p. 4a29, he says, "to fan this treatise's wind of prajñā (智慧)." Elsewhere, in the *Vimalakīrti Commentary Preface*, CST, p. 59a1, Seng-jui uses 'wind of prajñā.' Hatani, p. 56, n. 14, prefers 'wind of kindness.'

20 CST, p. 76c28 and MT, p. 1a20 both read 百 (hundred). Chi-tsang, p. 4b3, reads 柏 (cedar, cypress). The edifice in question is an elevated hall *(t'ai)* of Emperor Wu of the Han dynasty. It is said to have been famous for its fragrant cedar beams. Others say that it was named 'Hundred' because it had a hundred beams (Chi-tsang, pp. 4b5 ff.).

21 Hitherto China had only had the Five Peaks (see *Tz'ŭ-hai* [A Comprehensive Dictionary], comp. by Shu Hsin-ch'eng, Shanghai, Chung-hua Shu-chü, 1936–37, p. 69, 2, 五嶽) for its great mountains. Now it was as if Gṛdhrakūṭa had been moved to China. The *Middle Treatise* is metaphorically represented as a sacred mountain, destined to preside over the intellectual landscape of the country (Chi-tsang, p. 4b21–23).

22 China was a peripheral country and India was the central country (Chi-tsang, pp. 4b28 ff.). See also Hui-yüan's biography, KSC, p. 360a21, where Kumārajīva says, 邊國人未有經 (the people of outlying areas have not yet got the sūtras). Also, Tao-an, *Preface to the Yin-ch'ih-ju-ching*, CST, p. 45a10, 世不值佛．又處邊國. (In my generation, I have not met a Buddha, and further, I live in an outlying country.) Also see Seng-jui, *Vimalakīrti Commentary Preface*, CST, pp. 58c29–59a1.

GPWT, p. 76c29, Lamotte, *Traité* I, 174: "Though the great friendliness of the Buddha extends equally [to all places], the great cities such as Ujjayinī are in outlying countries, and so [the Buddha] did not dwell there."

23 Nāgārjuna wrote the *Middle Treatise* primarily to benefit India, and only secondarily to benefit other countries. Hence, the 'light' that was left over from India was passed on to China (Chi-tsang, p. 4c7–8).

24 Before Kumārajīva, 'matching concepts' *(ko-i)* prevailed among those who expounded the sūtras, and caused them to err from the original meaning. The Six Houses were all one-sided. Before the *Middle Treatise* and *Hundred Treatise* arrived, there was no 'comprehensive mirror.' Thus Seng-jui's former master, Tao-an, was thwarted by corrupt texts yet lacked a doctrinal standard to decide the issues (Chi-tsang, p. 4c10–13, quoting Seng-jui's *Vimalakīrti Commentary Preface*, CST, p. 59a1–8).

25 Dharma-masters can determine what the true doctrine is, and distinguish true interpretations from false ones (Chi-tsang, p. 4c15–16).

26 喉衿 (throat and collar-piece)—Chi-tsang, p. 5a5, glosses as 要宗之事 (the matter of cardinal importance).

27 According to T'an-ying, several tens of authors had written commentaries on the *Stanzas*. According to Ho-hsi (Tao-lang? See Chapter 9), seventy authors (Chi-tsang, p. 5a7).

28 MT, p. 1a26 has 今, which is lacking in CST.

出 (issue)—Hatani reads 'idasu' (put out, issue). Waley's review of *Jōron Kenkyū*, p. 196, suggests that this means an oral translation as opposed to a written one. Link, "Review of Wei Shou," p. 67b, says, "*Ch'u* as a technical term is an abbreviation for *i-ch'u* (譯出) 'to put out in translation, to translate.'"

Some other instances of the term are:

(a) *Chao-lun, Reply to Liu-I-min*, T XLV, p. 155c17, 毘婆沙法師於石羊出舍利弗阿毘曇胡本．雖未及譯．時問中事． "In the Stone Sheep Monastery the vibhāṣa dharma-masters are *issuing* the Indic text of the *Śāriputra-abhidharma* [cf. T 1548]. Though they have not yet *completed a translation*, from time to time we ask about its contents." Yüan-k'ang, T 1859, pp. 185b28 ff., quotes Tao-piao's preface to the text in question, which says that Dharmagupta and Dharmayaśas were ordered to *write down* the Sanskrit text. In the tenth year (A.D. 408) they were supposed to *issue* it jointly. But because the two did not agree with each other, it was feared that [the translation?] would not be entirely excellent. Up to the 16th year (A.D. 414), they gradually became proficient in Chinese. They were ordered to *recite and translate* (宣譯) it themselves, and only afterwards was it *received with the writing-brush*.

(b) *Chao-lun, Reply to Liu I-min*, p. 155c27, 什法師以午年出維摩經．貧道時預聽次． "When the dharma-master Kumārajīva was *issuing* the *Vimalakīrti-sūtra* in the year *wu* (A.D. 406), I attended the lectures."

(c) *Chao-lun, Reply to Liu I-min*, p. 155c13, 什法師於大石寺出新至諸經． "In the Great Stone Monastery, Kumārajīva is *issuing* the newly arrived sūtras."

(d) Hui-yüan's biography, KSC, p. 360a8, 後有弗若多羅．來適關中．誦出十誦梵本．羅什譯為晉文． "Afterwards, Puṇyatrāta came to Kuan-chung. He recited and issued the Sanskrit text of the *Shih-sung* [cf. T 1435], and Kumārajīva translated it into the language of Chin." Here 'issue' is connected with the recitation of the Indic text rather than its translation into Chinese. Perhaps it was connected with writing down the text, which the reciter had been carrying in his head. If so, the text had not been fully written down, as according to the subsequent account the translation had to stop when Puṇyatrāta died, and was not resumed until the arrival of Dharmaruci, who was also able to recite the *Shih-sung*. Example (c), however, is definitely concerned with an operation performed from already-written manuscripts.

29 Chi-tsang, p. 5a9 ff., argues that Blue Eyes is not Vasubandhu, because Vasubandhu was said to have thoroughly understood the meaning of the sūtras, while Blue Eyes committed numerous errors in his commentary—deviating from the meaning of the *Stanzas*, giving inadequate explanations of the *Stanzas*, undue prolixity, and repetitions of what has already been explained.

30 MT, p. 1a29 and CST, p. 77a8, 經通; Chi-tsang, p. 5a22; 通經.
Hatani, p. 56: kyō ni oite kore wo tsūjite, ri wa tsuku (interpreted it with regard to the *Stanzas*, and the principles are finalized).
經 here means the *Middle Stanzas* (Chi-tsang, p. 5a23).

31 Insiders block up the Buddha's teaching. The *Middle Treatise* clears away their obstructions and enables the Buddha's teaching to flow freely (Chi-tsang, pp. 5b1 ff.).

32 CST, version 5, MT, p. 1b3, and Chi-tsang, p. 5b9, 精詣.

DOCUMENT 6

1 折中 (refutative Middle)—this treatise shows that saṁsāra, nirvāṇa, and the myriad transformations are identical with reality *(bhūtalakṣana, tattva)*. There are four views of reality that are non-middle and hence to be refuted: 1. The common worldly view, concerned with preserving the family and the state. These impure things are not reality. 2. The 96 schools, each considering its own doctrine as absolute. These false notions are not reality. 3. The 500 Hīnayāna śāstra-masters who all maintain that the dharmas possess determinate marks and do not accept the doctrine of utter emptiness. 4. The Mahāyānists who misconceive emptiness and are injured in the same way as one who recites a spell wrongly or grasps a serpent wrongly (see *Stanzas* 24.11) (Chi-tsang, p. 171a15).

2 Reality is the object-sphere of vision, and the bodhimaṇḍa is the prajñā that intuits it. 'Essential' means both 'necessary' and 'pruned of inessentials, concise' (Chi-tsang, pp. 1b2 ff.).

3 From the one source (the *Ekayāna*) proceed three streams (the Three Vehicles). The followers of the Three Vehicles have not thoroughly fathomed the Source, so they think that the three are different (Chi-tsang, pp. 171c20 ff.). It is because the Hīnayānists have not worked through to the One Principle that they maintain their heterodoxies (Chi-tsang, p. 172a1 ff.).

4 Because they misconceive the goal and err from the One Way, living beings continue to transmigrate in the Six Paths (Chi-tsang, pp. 172a6 ff.).

5 The Treatise is a road of exit from the Six Paths of transmigration which the *Saddharma-puṇḍarīka* figuratively represents as a burning house from which exit must be effected (Chi-tsang, pp. 172a27 ff.).

6 The existent and the inexistent are the basis of all maladies, and the primary obstructions to the Middle Path. Hīnayānists are attached to the existent, and Mahāyānists are attached to the inexistent. Worldlings cling to the existent, and the Two Vehicles cling to the inexistent. Those who are lustful incline to the existent. Those who have false views incline to emptiness (Chi-tsang, pp. 172b21 ff.).

'Made clear'—(a) the maladies of existent and inexistent are eliminated, (b) the doctrine of the Two Truths is clarified, and (c) the thought (mind) of the Buddhas and bodhisattvas is revealed (Chi-tsang, pp. 172c4 ff.).

7 造化者 (creator of transformations)—*Chuang-tzŭ* 2, 1B.36b, Kuo Hsiang: 故造物者无主．而物各自造． "Thus the Creator of things has no lord, and each thing creates itself." Chi-tsang paraphrases a passage from this same section of Kuo Hsiang, but attributes it to *Chuang-tzŭ*. Also see *Chuang-tzŭ* 6, paragraphs 9 and 10, *Chuang-tzŭ* 2, paragraph 11, and *Chuang-tzŭ* 27, paragraph 5. Chi-tsang says that this criticism of the Taoist term, 'Creator,' is meant as a censure of the Indian Tīrthikas who asserted that Īśvara created all things. In the tenth chapter of the *Twelve Topics*, T XXX, 165c–66c, there is a refutation of the concept of a Creator God (Chi-tsang, pp. 172c8 ff.).

On the concept of a creator in *Chuang-tzŭ*, see Demiéville, "Enigmes taoistes," pp. 59–60.

8 'Empty position' means 'reality.' It is a synonym for suchness and dharmatā (Chi-tsang, p. 172c29).

Note the antithesis between *shih* (matters, i.e. phenomena) and *li* (principles, i.e. noumena). This is later developed in the parts of the *Vajrasamādhi* that were written in China (see Liebenthal, "Vajrasamādhi"), and becomes a cornerstone of Hua-yen (Kegon) metaphysics.

9 The two extremes—(a) the Buddhist anātmavāda and the Tīrthika ātmavāda, (b) saṁskṛta ātman and asaṁskṛta ātman, (c) ātman with skandhas and ātman apart from skandhas, and (d) ātman and ātmīya (Chi-tsang, pp. 173a2 ff.), also (e) pūrvakoṭi and aparakoṭi (Hatani, p. 342, n. 8).

10 喪我 (losing the atman)—*Chuang-tzŭ* 2, 1B.2a, 今者吾喪我, Legge, *The Texts of Taoism* I, 176, "I had just now lost myself." In this story, Tzŭ-chi had just come out of a trance. Seng-jui uses the expression to adduce Taoist authority for the nairātmya doctrine.

11 *Chuang-tzŭ* 26, 9A.13b, 荃者所以在魚．得魚而忘荃． Legge, *The Texts of Taoism* II, 141, "Fishing-stakes (baskets) are employed to catch fish; but when the fish are got, the men forget the stakes." 'Fishtrap' is a metaphor for verbally expressed teaching of emptiness, which serves to refute the concept of ātman, and which must in turn be discarded (Chi-tsang, pp. 173a10 ff.).

12 Supports—the reasons on which the doctrine of emptiness is based (Hatani, p. 342, n. 11).

13 Only when refuting and establishing are both forgotten, when object and vision are both stilled, can one approach the reality of the dharmas (Chi-tsang, p. 173a22).

14 Seng-jui has just dismissed the emptiness of refuter and refuted. Now he coalesces the reality of not-refuter and not-refuted (Chi-tsang, p. 173a24).

15 "In these sections, Seng-jui uses Confucian and Neo-Taoist expressions to expound Buddhism" (Chi-tsang, p. 173b7).

造次 (hazards)—*Analects* 4.5. See n. 17, below. Here, it stands for transmigration in the Six Paths, turning away from the Ideal (Chi-tsang, p. 173b9–10). My translation follows Chi-tsang's interpretation, which differs somewhat from the apparent meaning of the passage in *Analects*.

16 兩玄 (doubly metaphysical)—*Tao-te-ching* 1: "the metaphysical beyond the metaphysical, the gate of all mysteries." Here it refers to the ultimate goal, the emptiness of emptiness (Chi-tsang, pp. 173b11 ff.).

17 一致 (one destination)—the One whose cardinal position is described in *Tao-te-ching* 39.

顛沛 (calamities)—*Analects* 4.5, Legge, *Four Books*, p. 40: "In moments of haste, he cleaves to it. In seasons of danger, he cleaves to it." Here it stands for misconceptions *(viparyāsa)* (Chi-tsang, p. 173b16).

18 *Chuang-tzŭ* 3, 2A.4b, 恢恢乎其於遊刃必有餘地矣. Legge, *The Texts of Taoism* I, 199–200: "How easily it moves along! The blade has more than room enough." The ox is the worldly truth and the spaces within the ox are the absolute truth. The blade is prajñā (Chi-tsang, p. 173c11).

19 *Tao-te-ching* 14. Seng-jui is referring to the statement that from the night when he attained enlightenment until his parinirvāṇa, the Buddha did not speak a single sentence. The speaker has nothing to say and nothing to teach; the listener has nothing to hear and nothing to understand. This is in praise of the worldly truth, which is in reality not other than absolute truth (Chi-tsang, pp. 172c13 ff.). The Great Teaching pervades the ten quarters (Chi-tsang, p. 173c22).

20 弱喪 (lifelong exiles)—version 25—those who lost their native district when very young. All in the Six Paths and Three Vehicles, and especially those in the Two Vehicles, are people who have lost their native district, the Middle Path. This recalls the parable of the lost son, *Saddharma-puṇḍarīka*, ch. 8. The 'metaphysical ford' is the *Twelve Topic Treatise*, which leads one home again to the Middle Path (Chi-tsang, p. 173c24).

Chuang-tzŭ 2, 1B.32a: 予惡乎知惡死之非弱喪. 而不知歸者邪. Kuo Hsiang, commenting on this, gives the definition, 'lifelong exiles.'

21 The Neo-Taoist and Confucian books all maintain existence or inexistence, and liken those who deny existence and inexistence to robbers. But existent and inexistent are the basis of all false views, the origin of obstructions on the Way (Chi-tsang, pp. 174a2 ff.).

22 *Twelve Topic Treatise*, T 1568, version 14, and Chi-tsang, p. 174a10, 幽關 (obscure pass/barrier). TT, p. 159b20 and CST, p. 77c26 and Hatani, p. 341, 幽塗 (obscure road).

The obscure, hidden pass of the Two Vehicles is opened up so that beings may escape (Chi-tsang, p. 174a17). Alternatively, this expression might mean "the pass to hidden mysteries."

23 That is, drive the Great Vehicle (Mahāyāna), which Seng-jui here likens to the great carriage of the Son of Heaven (Chi-tsang, pp. 174a19 ff.).

24 北冥 (Northern Ocean)—*Chuang-tzŭ* 1, 1A.1a. Here the Buddhist allusion is to the prophecy in the *Pañcaviṁśati* that the *Prajñā-pāramitā-sūtra* will start from the East, go South, then West, and finally arrive at the North (Chi-tsang, pp. 174a21 ff.). Compare *Chao-lun*, part III, p. 153a14.

25 The white ox cart of the One Vehicle in *Saddharma-puṇḍarīka*, ch. 3, T IX, 12c (Chi-tsang, p. 174a24).

26 The dream is the long night of saṁsāra, and bodhi is the awakening (Chi-tsang, p. 174a28).

27 One discerns that the hundred transformations, the myriad things, are identical with Reality, and Reality is the way of peace (Chi-tsang, p. 174b2).

28 Just as when the sun comes out, there is no longer any dark land, so when one has seen this Treatise, doubts and impediments are eliminated forever (Chi-tsang, pp. 174b6 ff.).

29 Version 3 and Hatani.

30 Hatani: keigō no itari ni taezu (as I cannot endure the extreme of reverence). Seng-jui means that he is impelled by overwhelming sentiments of reverence so that he cannot keep silent, though he knows that his mind and eloquence are unworthy of the subject. This is a conventional expression of deference, and is quite similar to the deferential paragraphs that conclude other prefaces of this period.

DOCUMENT 7

1 Chi-tsang says that there are two prefaces to the *Hundred Treatise*, one by Seng-jui to the translation done in *Hung-shih* 4 (A.D. 402), and one by Seng-chao to the translation done in *Hung-shih* 6 (A.D. 404). As the latter was attached to the final redaction of the *Treatise*, Chi-tsang himself always read it. Chi-tsang first studied this preface when he was fourteen years old

(Chi-tsang, pp. 232a13 ff.). In *Ta-yeh* 4 (A.D. 608), when he gave the lectures on which the *Hundred Treatise* Commentary is based, he was about sixty *sui*.

2 There are three senses to 'provide access to the Holy Mind.' Firstly, causing living beings to awaken Right Vision *(cheng-chien)*, which is called 'providing access to the Holy Mind of living beings.' Secondly, when false teachings have been eliminated and the correct scriptures have been made manifest, this delights the Buddha-mind, which is called 'providing access to the Holy Mind of the Buddhas.' Thirdly, when the maladies of living beings cease, then the troubles of the bodhisattva are removed, which is called 'providing access to the Holy Mind of the bodhisattvas.' Views of annihilation and eternality obstruct access, and it is Right Vision that is obstructed. It is the *Hundred Treatise* that opens access, and it is to the Holy Mind that access is opened (Chi-tsang, pp. 232b26 ff.). The *Hundred Treatise* is the metaphysical ford to the Holy Mind and the abstruse road to Right Vision (Chi-tsang, pp. 233a5 ff.).

3 The false teachings cover over the correct teaching, and the *Hundred Treatise*, by removing the false teachings, opens up and uncovers the correct teaching. The Two Truths are the grandfather and grandmother of the Buddhas of past, present, and future. The Two Knowledges are the father and mother of the Buddhas of past, present, and future (Chi-tsang, pp. 232c3 ff.).

4 See Chapter 2.

5 玄心 (metaphysical mind) is a synonym for Right Vision (Chi-tsang, p. 233c4).

獨悟 (was uniquely enlightened) is ambivalent, meaning firstly that around 800 A.N. ordinary beings were all gone astray, and only Deva really understood, and secondly that though Nāgārjuna had many disciples, Deva was paramount among them (Chi-tsang, p. 233c5).

6 Chi-tsang, p. 233c13, paraphrases 獨出物外 "went forth alone to [the realm] beyond things."

7 'Tripiṭaka' means the Hīnayāna canon, and 'the Twelve Sections' means the complete canon. The Twelve Sections are: (1) sūtra, (2) geya, (3) gāthā, (4) nidāna, (5) itivṛttaka, (6) jātaka, (7) adbhuta-dharma, (8) avadāna, (9) upadeśa, (10) udāna, (11) vaipulya, and (12) vyākaraṇa (Oda, p. 936, 2; GPWT, pp. 306c ff.; Chi-tsang, p. 233c15). The double bars are: (1) the false words of the Tīrthikas, and (2) the Hīnayānist grasping onto svabhāva. Āryadeva removed these two modes of impediment to understanding the true, Mahāyānist meaning of the Tripiṭaka. Again the Hīnayānist bars the Tripiṭaka in two ways: (1) he gets the words but misses the meaning, and (2) he misses both words and meaning (Chi-tsang, pp. 233c21 ff.).

8 Version 8 and Chi-tsang, 檀. Chi-tsang glosses 獨也. Hatani has 擅, and reads 'hoshii mama ni' (as he pleased). 'Kapilavastu' is a common synecdoche for India, because it was the Buddha's birthplace. 'Strode alone through' means 'was undisputed master of.'

9 This refers to Deva's role as a defender of the Dharma. The sentence may also be rendered 'became a city-wall and a moat for the Dharma.' He shut out the infidels, and the Great Dharma was made manifest like a walled and moated fortress. He warded off external dangers, and gave peace to the king and people (Chi-tsang, pp. 234a6 ff.).

10 He rescued the Tīrthikas who were submerged in the ocean of suffering and carried around in the current of the evil destinies (Chi-tsang, pp. 234a27 ff.).

11 衆妙 (all the sublime qualities)—allusion to *Tao-te-ching* 1.

12 Read 旨 with version 16 and Chi-tsang.

13 Because its principles were extremely profound and its text was extremely brief, few gained entrance (Chi-tsang, p. 234b23).

14 According to Chi-tsang, p. 234b24, an old commentary states that more than ten authors compiled commentaries on the *Hundred Treatise*. The two that circulated most widely were (1) by Vasu, and (2) by Saṅghasena (僧佉斯那). Chi-tsang, p. 234b26, maintains that Vasu is Vasubandhu.

15 Chi-tsang, p. 234c20, says that 无當 (no matching) is 无住 (no abiding) and is synonymous with 无著 (no attachment). The śāstrakāra has no siddhānta (宗) of his own. The Hīnayānists, though, maintain that the dharmas have determinate marks, and thus affirm these marks as object-counterparts.

16 Chi-tsang, p. 235b23, glosses with 著 (attachment).

17 Having no matching and no grasping causes those in the six paths to return to the Source and those in the Three Vehicles to return to the Origin (Chi-tsang, p. 235b27).

18 See *Analects* 9.10, 仰之彌高. 鑽之彌堅. Waley, p. 140: "The more I strain my gaze towards it (Goodness), the higher it soars. The deeper I bore into it, the harder it becomes." Seng-chao is likening Kumārajīva to Confucius.

19 Chi-tsang, pp. 235c27 ff., tells how a prince of Kuchā named 沙車 [Yarkand] converted Kumārajīva to Mahāyāna by reciting the *Anavatapta-nāgarāja-paripṛcchā-sūtra* outside his room, then arguing with him about the theory of the atoms. Chi-tsang, p. 236a11, says that the prince then gave Kumārajīva the *Middle Treatise* and the *Hundred Treatise*.

For 心要 (essential of/for the mind) Hatani has 必要 (the necessary thing).

20 The previous translation was in *Hung-shih* 4 (A.D. 402), with Yao Hsing as dānapati (Chi-tsang, p. 236a16).

Chi-tsang, p. 236a19, says that during his 18 years in Kutsang, Kumārajīva had only learned everyday language (一往之言) and had not mastered the language completely. Presumably this means that he was not familiar with the literary and technical vocabulary. *Fang-yen* means both 'local language' and 'technical language.' See Document 4, n. 61.

21 沖心 (empty mind)—a mind that is not filled with mundane attachments. See *Tao-te-ching* 4: "The Way is like an empty vessel (沖) that yet may be drawn from without ever needing to be filled" (Waley, *The Way and its Power*, p. 146).

22 *Analects* 6.16, Waley, p. 119: "When natural substance prevails over ornamentation, you get the boorishness of the rustic. When ornamentation prevails over natural substance, you get the pedantry of the scribe. Only when ornament and substance are duly blended do you get the true gentleman."

23 无間然 (there are no gaps in it)—*Analects* 8.21, Waley, p. 137: "The Master said, In Yü I can find no semblance of a flaw."

24 Version 21 and Chi-tsang, p. 236b14.

DOCUMENT 8

1 *Analects* 2.16, 子曰．攻乎異端．斯害也已． Waley, p. 91. "The Master said, He who sets to work upon a different strand destroys the whole fabric." Legge, *The Four Books*, p. 19: "The Master said, 'The study of strange doctrines is injurious indeed.'"

2 *Tao-te-ching* 41, Yüan-k'ang, p. 175b7, says that it stands for the Mahāyāna, and, at p. 175b17, that it stands for India, where Kumārajīva went in his youth.

3 *I-ching* 7.8a.

4 That is, of Prajñā. According to Yüan-k'ang, p. 175b, this refers to Kumārajīva's study of the *Prajñā-pāramitā* text that he found in Kuchā.

5 *I-ching* 7.10a, "Hsi-tz'ŭ Shang." Yüan-k'ang, pp. 175b28 ff., quotes Wang Pi's commentary on this *I-ching* passage.

6 *Tao-te-ching* 14

7 Yüan-k'ang, p. 175c20, explains this as referring to Kumārajīva's victory over the heretic in Akṣu. But it more probably refers to his childhood victory over Tīrthikas in North India.

8 The wind is Prajñā. The East is China (Yüan-k'ang, p. 175c25).

9 Yüan-k'ang, p. 176a17, glosses "concealed and hid his talent and wisdom." Kumārajīva did not propagate Buddhism during his years in Liang.

10 When Fu Chien had died, there was no reason. When Yao Hsing emerged, there was a reason (Yüan-k'ang, p. 175c25).

11 The cyclical sign of the month stands for that of the year *ch'ou*. Yüan-kang, pp. 176b5 ff., and Liebenthal, *Chao*, n. 248.

12 Lü Kuang, fearing invasion from Northern and Southern Liang, petitioned Yao Hsing to accept his surrender (Yüan-k'ang, p. 176b19).

13 北天 for 北方? Yüan-k'ang, p. 176c3, refers to the *Pañcaviṁśati* prophecy and the *Great Perfection of Wisdom Treatise* commentary on it.

14 Perhaps this should read "yün ch'i shu jan" rather than "yün shu ch'i jan."

15 Yao Hsing.

16 *Chuang-tzŭ* 3, 2A.4b, Legge, *The Texts of Taoism* I, 199–200. See Doc. 6, n. 18.

17 Yüan-k'ang, p. 176c29.

18 This was a *kuan* in the Hsiao-yao Garden (Yüan-k'ang, p. 177a7).

19 The text of the old Chinese translation(s) (Yüan-k'ang, p. 177a11).

20 The *Pañcaviṁśati* (Yüan-k'ang, p. 177a11).

21 *Chuang-tzŭ* 12, 5A.6a, Legge, *The Texts of Taoism* I, 311–12. See Liebenthal, *Chao* , n. 257 and Demiéville's review of *Jōron Kenkyū*, p. 229.

22 *Chuang-tzŭ* 22, 7B.26b, Legge, *The Texts of Taoism* II, 68; Demiéville's review of *Jōron Kenkyū*, p. 299.

23 Liebenthal, *Chao*, n. 258, and *Jōron Kenkyū*, n. 88. T VIII, 97c and 354a.

24 T VIII, 428a20.

25 See *Vimalakīrti Commentary*, p. 265a8.

26 T XV, 39b11.

27 *Tao-te-ching* 3.

28 *Tao-te-ching* 7

29 *Chuang-tzŭ* 12, 5A.5b, Legge, *The Texts of Taoism* I, 311. *Jōron Kenkyū*, n. 92; Demiéville's review of *Jōron Kenkyū*, p. 229.

30 Yüan-k'ang, p. 177c8: "The Holy One's Spirit responds and meets critical connections (objects) but does not move thoughts." Liebenthal, *Chao*, p. 71: "Without planning, Shen responds to the necessities of a given moment." *Jōron Kenkyū*, p. 24: "responding to [the myriad things] and agreeing."

31 Liebenthal, *Chao*, n. 271, cites *I-ching* 8.2a, "Hsi-tz'ŭ Hsiah," where Fu-hsi, looking up, contemplates the symbols *(hsiang)* in Heaven, and looking down, contemplates the patterns *(fa)* on Earth. Yüan-k'ang, p. 177c16, says that [the Buddha or Bodhisattva] manifesting an infinite body is "looking up," while manifesting a three-foot body is "looking down." Perhaps Seng-chao intended this ambivalently classical and buddhological interpretation of the allusion.

32 Compare *Chuang-tzŭ* 2, 1B.13b, Legge, *The Texts of Taoism* I, 183.

33 *Kung*, like 'karman,' indicates both a process and the affectee or results of a process. In *Stanzas* 10,2, *wu kung* translates 'vaiyārthyam.'

34 *Jōron Kenkyū*, p. 25, translates *hui* by 'tekigō' (conform, adapt to).

35 Liebenthal, *Chao*, n. 272. *Jōron Kenkyū*, n. 104. See *Tao-te-ching* 6.

36 Liebenthal, *Chao*, n. 273, quotes a similar passage from Wang Pi's commentary on *Tao-te-ching* 14.

37 *Tao-te-ching* 39: "The spirits, because of obtaining the One, are numinal." See Waley, *The Way and its Power*, p. 191, n. 1, on *ling*.

38 Yüan-k'ang, p. 178a9.

39 See Document 3, n. 26.

40 T XIV, 519c21. Compare T XIV, 537c18.

41 T VIII, 140c and 401a.

42 Compare Document 4, n. 53.

43 To exist is to have marks. Yüan-k'ang, p. 178a: "Though the principle of Absolute Truth has no marks, it can be perceived."

44 Yüan-k'ang, p. 178a24: "He makes motion and non-motion identical." Note the factitive use of *chi*.

45 Yüan-k'ang, p. 178a25, has 即 instead of 則. The variant is not noted in *Jōron Kenkyū*, p. 25.

46 *Chuang-tzŭ* 6, 3A.1a, Legge, *The Texts of Taoism* I, 236. Kuo Hsiang's commentary: "He who knows the part which the Heavenly plays (knows) that it is naturally born with him."

47 *Jōron Kenkyū*, p. 26: "mata nani wo ka shiri, nani wo ka nasō ka? Yüan-k'ang, p. 178a27: "Knowing while not knowing is not having a determinate knowing. Therefore what further does one know?"

48 Yüan-k'ang, p. 178b13: "It has no limits, so it is called *wu fang*."

49 *Tao-te-ching* 7

50 *Tao-te-ching* 5. Liebenthal's suggestion, *Chao*, n. 282, that 仁 is a pun is not admissible, because 一 and 儀 were not homophones in Seng-chao's time. Karlgren, "Grammata Serica," no. 394: 一 i̯ĕt/i̯ĕt/yi; no. 211: 儀 ngia/ngjię/yi.

51 *shen-ming*. Yüan-k'ang, p. 178c2: "For the spirit-intelligence of [other] human beings, dharmas have marks to be apprehended, which is 'knowing.' The spirit-intelligence of the Holy Man does not apprehend dharma-marks. Therefore it is called 'having no knowing.'"

Seng-chao is here paraphrasing and re-interpreting Wang Pi. See Document 3, n. 25.

52 Oda, p. 892, 2, explains *shih-hsiang* as 'saṁskṛta-dharmas.'

53 T VIII, 262c24.

54 Yüan-k'ang, p. 179a, glosses *tso* by *ch'i-tso* (arise) and *yüan* by *p'an-yüan (ālambana)*. *Jōron Kenkyū*, p. 27, translates: "hataraki mo naku, en mo nai" (without operation and without *yüan*) ('object' or 'condition').

55 *fan-chao* (reversal of intuition)—see Document 4, n. 28.

56 Yüan-k'ang, p. 170a8: "If the case is that the Holy Man really has the knowing of Prajñā but that it is called no-knowing because its essential nature is empty, then both Prajñā and deluded knowledge are empty. The two are both empty and are alike without knowing. Thus there is no distinction." Compare Liebenthal, *Chao*, p. 75, third paragraph.

57 Rāga or lobha (lust); dveṣa (hostility); and moha (folly).

58 Mistaking the impermanent for something permanent, suffering for bliss, the selfless for self, and the empty for something substantial.

59 Yüan-k'ang, p. 179a14, says that 'what is known' is the markless sphere of absolute truth.

60 Meng An, p. 33a *Jōron Kenkyū* , says: "The author's idea is that because its object-sphere *(viṣaya)* has no marks, Knowledge has no knowing. In the teaching there is also no ground for setting up the predicate 'pure' to praise Prajñā. Why not just praise Absolute Truth?"

61 Yüan-k'ang, p. 179a20, explains *chiang wu i* (does it not mean?) as *i* (it means). *Jōron Kenkyū* , translates with a rhetorical question.

62 T XXIV, 1038b8 ff. *(Upāsaka-śīla-sūtra)*; T XXI, 523c *(Mahāparinirvāṇa-sūtra* ; T III, 488b20 *(Lalitavistara)*. See Liebenthal, *Chao*, n. 292, and *Jōron Kenkyū*, n. 100.

63 *Jōron Kenkyū*, p. 28: "(hannya ga nanigoto ni mo) tekigō shite tagawazu, datō shite kore to (gentei) sezu." ([Prajñā] conforms without fail (to everything) but while being appropriate to it, does not (delimit) it as "this.") See Demiéville's review of *Jōron Kenkyū*, p. 227, for a criticism of this translation. See also Liebenthal, *Chao*, n. 293, and Yüan-k'ang, p. 179b3.

64 Yüan-k'ang, p. 179b8: "Things cannot summon themselves, so it is necessary to establish names in order to designate things. Names can summon the substances of things, so names signify them."

65 *Jōron Kenkyū*, p. 28: "na ni tsuite (sore to sōtō suru) mono wo motomeru naraba," (if, having arrived at the name, one seeks the thing) (that corresponds to it).

66 See Document 4, n. 71. Liebenthal, *Chao*, n. 294.

67 *Jōron Kenkyū*, p. 28: "setsu wo tateru baai no genri de aru." (It is the fundamental principle concerning the establishment of propositions.)

68 Literally, "actuals" *(shih)*.

69 Yüan-k'ang, p. 179b17.

70 Quotes the general sense of the *Prajna Sutras*. See Liebenthal, *Chao*, n. 296, and *Jōron Kenkyū*, n. 101.

71 Liebenthal (*Chao* , n. 299) and *Jōron Kenkyū*, both make no. 43 part of the sūtra quotation, but it is simply a repetition of Seng-chao's own earlier statement.

72 *Chuang-tzŭ* 27, 9A.15b, Legge, *The Texts of Taoism* II, 143. Also *Tathāgataguhya-sūtra*, T XI, 719b21–24. See De Jong, *Chapitres*, p. 23, n. 62.

73 *Jōron Kenkyū*, n. 103. *Chuang-tzŭ* 22, 7B.26b, Legge, *The Texts of Taoism* II, 68. See n. 22, above, where *Jōron Kenkyū*, did not note the source. Demiéville's review of *Jōron Kenkyū*, p. 229: "As for the term *k'uang-yen*. . . . neither the Japanese nor Dr. Liebenthal indicate that it, too, is taken from *Chuang-tzŭ*." Demiéville overlooked n. 103 of *Jōron Kenkyū*.

74 *Tao-te-ching* 6.

75 *t'ung* and *pien* are synonyms here, despite their antonymic appearance. See Yüan-k'ang, p. 179b29–c1.

76 無 equals 勿 ?

77 Yüan-k'ang, p. 179c6.

78 This is another attempt by the opponent to prove that Prajñā has knowing because it knows Absolute Truth.

79 Liebenthal, *Chao*, n. 299; *Jōron Kenkyu*, n. 105. Compare GPWT, p. 190c20.

80 Yüan-k'ang, p. 180b7.

81 T VIII, 67a7 and 78a27.

82 T VIII, 67a7.

83 *Jōron Kenkyū*, p. 30, renders *neng chih* as 'shirumono' and 'jñāna,' and *so chih* as 'shirarerumono' and 'jñeya.'

84 Yüan-k'ang, p. 179c27, says that because popular truth has marks which deluded knowledge cognizes, the object and knowledge exist jointly. Because Absolute Truth has no marks, Absolute Knowledge has no knowing. Therefore marks and knowing inexist jointly.

85 Yüan-k'ang, p. 180a4.

86 Yüan-k'ang, p. 180a6.

87 Yüan-k'ang, p. 180a7.

88 Yüan-k'ang, p. 180a9.

89 Yüan-k'ang, p. 180a12.

90 Yüan-k'ang, p. 180a16.

91 Yüan-k'ang, p. 180a18, reads 知所知. The other texts have 所知. *Jōron Kenkyū*, p. 31, fails to note Yüan-k'ang's variant.

92 Liebenthal, *Chao*, n. 305: "Cf. MK hetu-pratyaya parīkṣā, the first *p'o yin yüan p'in*." *Jōron Kenkyū*, n. 108.

93 Seng-chao is playing on the double meaning of *yüan*—'ālambana' and 'pratyaya.'

94 Liebenthal, *Chao*, n. 306: "Quotes the general content of the Sūtras. YK (Yüan-k'ang)." But see *Stanzas* 24.19: "There has never been one dharma that did not arise from causes and conditions." (Sanskrit: apratītya-samutpanno dharmaḥ kaścin na vidyate.) Seng-chao's version renders 'na vidyate' by *pu chien* (is not seen) while the *Chung-lun* translation (T 1564) renders it

by *wei yu* (there never exists). Seng-chao may well have used an earlier version of Kumārajīva's *Middle Treatise*.

Neither Yüan-k'ang nor Liebenthal nor *Jōron Kenkyū*, identified this quotation.

95 Yüan-k'ang, p. 180b17: "It does not take things as things."

96 See Demiéville's review of *Jōron Kenkyū*, pp. 226–27, on *shih* and *tang*.

97 *Jōron Kenkyū*, p. 32: "kore da to suru koto ga nakereba, (dono na ga dono jitsu ni) ataru to iu koto mo naku naru." (If there is no considering that "it is this," then there is no matching (of any name with any actual).) Demiéville, in his review of *Jōron Kenkyū*, pp. 226–28, does not notice that this parenthetic gloss partly answers his question about the meaning of *tang*.

98 Yüan-k'ang, p. 180b23: "Having nothing to match, it matches the Absolute Principle; having nothing to affirm, it affirms the Absolute Principle."

99 Yüan-k'ang, p. 180b24: "When it affirms the Absolute Principle, though it affirms there is nothing affirmed. When it matches the Absolute Principle, though it matches there is nothing matched."

100 T, VIII, 12c4.

101 *Jōron Kenkyū*, p. 33, glosses 故 as motoyori.'

102 Yüan-k'ang, p. 180c1: "A thing is not affirmed as existent, and so it ought to be affirmed as inexistent. If you do not consider a thing to be an existent thing, then you should consider it to be an inexistent thing."

103 No one has yet found the source of this quotation.

104 *yu hsiang* may stand for either 'salakṣaṇa' (MT, p. 7b22) or 'astitva.'

105 Yüan-k'ang, p. 180c5, glosses *huan-lei* (trouble). *Jōron Kenkyū*, p. 33, renders 'kakawari' (connection), which seems less appropriate than 'trouble.'

106 Yüan-k'ang, p. 180c12: "Dwelling in the existent, he does not grasp marks of existence; residing in the inexistent, he does not grasp marks of inexistence."

107 Oda, p. 1231, 3.

108 Liebenthal, *Chao*, p. 82, translates *chi-jan* as 'noiselessly,' and *p'a-erh* as 'unnoticed.' *Jōron Kenkyū*, p. 33, translates with 'otomonaku' (soundlessly) and 'kagemonaku' (without shadow).

109 *Tao-te-ching* 37. Also see *Tao-te-ching* 48. On *wu-hsin* (no thoughts, no mind) see Demiéville's review of *Jōron Kenkyū*, p. 234.

110 Yüan-k'ang, p. 180c28: "[Chao] means that everything called 'arising' arises in the mind, and everything called 'ceasing' ceases in the mind."

111 Yüan-k'ang, p. 181a2: "It is not absence of thought as in wood and stone, but only absence of thought as in no-knowing."

112 Liebenthal, *Chao*, and *Jōron Kenkyū*, have full stop after *wei t'i*. I interpret *ssŭ* as introducing an apodosis, and put a full stop after *chih chih*. This follows Yüan-k'ang, p. 181a14.

113 Yüan-k'ang, p. 181a14; "Prajñā has no knowing—this is the 'has no' of Holy Knowledge. Deluded knowledge is empty of (by) nature—this is the 'has no' of deluded knowledge."

114 Yüan-k'ang, p. 181a25: "Prajñā has no apprehending of marks, so [Seng-chao] says that it has no knowing. Deluded knowledge in its essence is empty of (by) nature, so [Seng-chao] says it is knowing nothing. Knowing nothing is identical with the real-mark of Absolute Truth."

115 Contrast 'yet he has no process (results) of intuition' in *Chao-lun*, part II.3.

116 *Jōron Kenkyū*, p. 35, translates *shih* as 'jissai' (reality). Meng An, p. 41a (*Jōron Kenkyū*), says: "*Shih* is *li*. It is the essence *(t'i)* of the myriad things."

117 Yüan-k'ang, p. 181b: "Even though there is (are) the real principle(s), it (they) only appear(s) when illumined (intuited) by Prajñā."

118 Liebenthal, n. 321; T VIII, 382c23.

119 *Chuang-tzŭ* 8, 4A.5a, Legge, *The Texts of Taoism* I, 270.

120 T VIII, 390a4.

121 T VIII, 382c23.

122 *Tao-te-ching* 1, Waley, *The Way and its Power*, p. 141. Wang Pi says: "They issue alike—they issue alike from the Inexistent."

123 *Ch'eng-chü-kuang-ming-ting-i-ching*, T XV, 452b29.

124 *Vimalakīrti-nirdeśa*, T XIV, 537c14. Note that the Tibetan *Vimalakīrti* indicates 'Ratnākara' rather than 'Ratnakūṭa' as the original name. See Lamotte, *Vimalakīrti*, p. 111.

125 Yüan-k'ang, p. 181c10: "*T'ung* means this essay, *Prajñā Has No Knowing*. It may also indicate the above two sūtras."

Meng An, p. 42b (*Jōron Kenkyū*), says: "The 'explanatory text' is the above confirmatory quotation from the two sūtras. It also refers to all the confirmatory quotations from 'Announcement of Theme' onwards."

Wen-ts'ai, T 1860, p. 220c7: "It means exhausting the metaphysical principle of the two knowledges and consummating the 'pure talk' about [what is] beyond things. *Ming wen* (explanatory text) means the previously quoted holy teachings. Relying on the teachings to bring out the principles, one can know and awaken to the Tao of Prajñā."

DOCUMENT 9

1 'Holy Intelligence' means prajñā. Without the special penetrating insight of prajñā, how can one conform the spirit to the principle of the Middle Path, the not existent and not inexistent, the interstice between existent and inexistent (Yüan-k'ang, p. 171a3)?

2 一氣 (One Energy)—see *Chuang-tzŭ* 6, 3A.24b, Legge, *The Texts of Taoism* I, 251–52, also *Chuang-tzŭ* 22, 7B.16b, Legge, *The Texts of Taoism* II, 60.

3 See n. 2.

4 Yüan-k'ang, p. 171b18: "If by means of attitudes that disagree they approach and apprehend the principles that agree, then by what means can they achieve agreement?"

5 性 (nature) is glossed 理性 (principle-nature) by Yüan-k'ang, p. 171b20. *Jōron Kenkyū*, p. 15, renders it by 'shinri' (truth).

6 This theory was maintained by Chih Min-tu and Tao-heng. See Liebenthal, *Chao* , pp. 149–52; T'ang, *History*, pp. 266–72; and *Jōron Kenkyū*, p. 95, n. 57.

7 This theory maintains correctly that the mind should be stilled and should be emptied of imaginations and fantasies about external things. But it fails to see that all things are empty in their own-being, whether a mind has notions about them or not.

8 This theory was maintained by Chih Tao-lin (A.D. 314–66). See Liebenthal, *Chao*, pp. 152–57; T'ang, *History*, pp. 177–81 and 254–63; and *Jōron Kenkyū*, p. 96, n. 58.

9 Chih Tao-lin's view interprets śūnyatā according to Kuo Hsiang's theory of self-so-ness. See *Chuang-tzŭ* 2, 1B.4. Chih Tao-lin asserted that emptiness is identical with form. He seems to have understood that own-being is not dependent on another (*Stanzas* 18.9, "aparapratyayam . . . etat tattvasya lakṣaṇam") and hence form has no own-being and is empty. Seng-chao agrees with this, but adds that this theory neglects the principle that form is intrinsically devoid of the nature of form, and not merely composite and contingent. From the standpoint of conventional, verbal truth, form is just form. From the standpoint of absolute truth, form is not form, because it has no own-being.

10 This view was maintained by Tao-an. See Liebenthal, *Chao* , pp. 157–62; T'ang, *History* , pp. 238–54; and *Jōron Kenkyū* , p. 96, n. 59.

11 In the Taoist system, inexistence precedes existence and is its source. In Śūnyavāda, existent and inexistent are alike empty and neither precedes the other, though they are logically related as term and negation. Seng-chao objects to the view that emptiness is the primordial nothingness from which the myriad entities arose.

12 *Jōron Kenkyū*, p. 16: "ittai butsu wa (sore jitai de seiritsu-sezu, ta) (butsu ni taishite) [sōtaiteki ni] butsu to naru no de aru

kara, (butsu wa tabutsu kara) butsu to sarete (hajimete) butsu da to ieru." (In general, a thing (it not being established through own-being), being set over against (another) thing, [in a relative way] becomes a thing, and consequently (a thing, from another thing) being made a thing, (for the first time) can be said to be a thing.)

See *Chuang-tzŭ* 11, 4C.16a, Legge, *The Texts of Taoism* I, 304; and *Chuang-tzŭ* 22, 7B.31a, Legge, *The Texts of Taoism* II, 72. In *Chuang-tzŭ*, 22, 物物 is factitive, "to cause things to be things." The problem in question is the genesis of the myriad things. In *Chuang-tzŭ* 11, 物 is likewise factitive, but the voice of the verb is ambivalent and it must be construed sometimes as "to be made a thing [i.e., dominated] by things" and sometimes as "to treat things as things" (i.e., to control them).

Yüan-k'ang, p. 172a11, paraphrases: "to name an existing thing with the name 'thing.'" He thus interprets *wu* as putative rather than factitive. This is supported by the context, as the topic is the relation between things and actuals, names and absolutes.

13 Compare *Chao-lun*, *Reply to Liu I-min*, p. 156b9, *Jōron Kenkyū*, p. 49, and Liebenthal, *Chao*, p. 105, third paragraph.

14 GPWT, p. 105a7, Lamotte, *Traité* I, 381; also GPWT, pp. 259c19 ff.

15 Yüan-k'ang, p. 172b, refers to *Stanzas* 5.6, MT, p. 7c16. *Jōron Kenkyū*, p. 96, n. 63, also cites *Stanzas* 15.5, MT, p. 20a18. It is more likely that the quotation is actually *Stanzas* 5.7, MT, p. 7c24, 是故知虛空．非有亦非无． "Therefore we know that ākāśa is neither existent nor inexistent."

16 *Tao-te-ching* 10, "In *washing and purging* your mystic vision, can you be without blemish?"

17 *Tao-te-ching* 25, Waley, *The Way and its Power*, p. 174: "There was something formlessly fashioned, That existed before heaven and earth; without sound, without substance, Dependent on nothing, unchanging, All pervading, unfailing."

18 *Vimalakīrti-nirdeśa*, T XIV, 551a19. Lamotte, *Vimalakīrti*, p. 308, section 17.

19 *Vimalakīrti-nirdeśa*, T XIV, 545a26, Lamotte, *Vimalakīrti*, p. 232, section 15.

20 T XV, 532b28.

21 T VIII, 36c19.

22 *Pañcaviṁśati*, T VIII, 378c11.

23 *Vimalakīrti-nirdeśa*, T XIV, 537c15; Lamotte, *Vimalakīrti*, p. 106, verse 4. For Seng-chao's commentary on this quotation, see *Vimalakīrti Commentary*, T XXXVIII, 332c27 ff.

24 T XVI, 109a1.

25 T VIII, 425c27.

26 Liebenthal, *Chao*, p. 64, n. 221: "Cf. MK XXIV, 18–19, p. 33b16." MT, p. 33b16, *sub Stanzas* 18–19: "This thing belongs to the causes and conditions; thus it has no own-being. Because it has no own-being, it is empty. Emptiness in turn is empty." Yüan-k'ang, p. 173b9, cites *Stanzas* 24.18, MT, p. 33b11: "The entity that is produced by the causes and conditions, I declare to be the same as emptiness. It is also a conventional name *(prajñapti)*; it is also the idea of the Middle Path." This citation is not apposite.

Closer parallels are afforded by:
(a) MT, p. 8a9, *sub Stanzas* 5.8: "The wise, when they see that all dharmas arise, extinguish views of inexistence. When they see that all dharmas cease, they extinguish views of existence."
(b) MT, p. 13a14, *sub Stanzas* 8.9: "This deed arises from the causes and conditions. It is conventionally designated existent, but has nothing real. . . . (P. 13a29): Only in conformity to worldlings' notions and imaginings is it declared that a deed exists and a doer exists. In the supreme [truth] there is no deed and is no doer."

27 GPWT, p. 623a2.

28 T VIII, 128c29.

29 I place the quotation marks here following *Jōron Kenkyū*. Liebenthal takes the whole paragraph as a quotation.

30 Liebenthal, *Chao*, p. 65, n. 230: "An allusion to the pac̆askandha-parīkṣā in general, or the duḥkha-parīkṣā XII, 7? Cf. MK, p. 17a2. YK. . ." MT, p. 17a2, *Stanzas* 12.7: "If self-created suffering is not established, how can there be other-created suffering? If another man created suffering, it also would be called self-created."

But compare also *Stanzas* 15.3, MT, pp. 20a5 ff.: "If an entity has no own-being, how can it have other-being? The own-being in other-being is called other-being."

Also see MT, p. 2b22, *sub Stanzas* 1.4: "Within the conditions, there is no own-being. Because own-being is inexistent, it does not produce itself. Because own-being is inexistent, other-being also is inexistent. For what reason? Other-being exists in dependence on own-being. The other-being in the other is also own-being."

Also see, MT, p. 17a5, *sub Stanzas* 12.7: "Because self and other (this and that) are mutually dependent, if the other creates suffering, in the other it is called self-created suffering."

Also see, MT, p. 20a2, *sub Stanzas* 15.1: "Further, if a nature *(svabhāva)* is real *(sadbhūta)*, it should not come forth dependent on another. It is not like long and short or this and that, which because they have no determinate nature exist in dependence on another."

31 I end the quotation following Liebenthal, *Chao*, pp. 65–66. *Jōron Kenkyū*, p. 21, takes the quotation to be only "In things there is no self (this) and other (that)." Seng-chao's quotation is so free that the question is hard to decide, but I think that the quotations in n. 30 support Liebenthal's punctuation rather than that in *Jōron Kenkyū*.

32 T XV, 454c1.

33 *Chuang-tzŭ* 2, 1B.13b, Legge, *The Texts of Taoism* I, 183.

34 *Pañcaviṁśati*, T VIII, 140c15, or T VIII, 401a1.

35 体 is to know by assuming the structure of the object and so becoming one with it. As saṁsāra and nirvāṇa are identical, there is no part of saṁsāra that is remote from nirvāṇa, and the mere act of realization dispels all notions that nirvāṇa is remote. Here *shen* (spirit) corresponds more or less to buddhatā (buddha-nature).

DOCUMENT 10

1 T VIII, 32c19, and T VIII, 203b8.

2 The teaching of the Buddhas (Yüan-k'ang, p. 167a27).

3 Stillness and motion are not-two. This non-duality is their end-point (Yüan-k'ang, p. 167b1).

4 Yüan-k'ang, p. 167b9, glosses 'nature' with 'dharma-nature.' This is too specific. *Hsing* may stand for *tzŭ-hsing (svabhāva, prakṛti)*, *fa-hsing (dharmatā)*, *fo-hsing* (*buddhatā*, which is unlikely in the *Chao-lun*), or any of the pre-Buddhist meanings of *hsing*.

Yüan-k'ang, p. 167b9, glosses 返 (return) with 自返 (return to oneself), and 自返悟 (return to oneself and awaken). It may also be elliptical for 返本 (return to the Origin), or 返照 (introspect and intuit).

5 *Tao-te-ching* 35, Waley, *The Way and its Power*, p. 186: "How different the words that the Tao gives forth! So thin, so flavourless!"

6 *Tao-te-ching* 41, Waley, *The Way and its Power*, p. 193: "When the man of highest capacities hears the Tao, He does his best to put it into practice. When the man of middling capacity hears Tao, He is in two minds about it. When the man of low capacity hears Tao, He laughs loudly at it."

7 T VIII, 473c9 and 475a19.

8 Emend 語 to 諸, following Yüan-k'ang, p. 167c9.

9 Corresponds more or less to *Stanzas* 2.1, MT, p, 3c8. See *Jōron Kenkyū*, p. 223.

10 *Chuang-tzŭ* 21, 7B.4b, Legge, *The Texts of Taoism* II, 46: "I am in this way daily passing on, but all day long I am communicating my views to you; and now, as we are shoulder to shoulder, you fail [to understand me];—is it not matter for lamentation?"

Jōron Kenkyū, p. 9: Kai yo, (banbutsu ga nichi ni nichi ni) atarashiku natte iru no wo miyo, (omae to tagai ni) hiji wo tori atte ite mo moto no mama de wa nai. (Hui! Behold how (day by day the myriad things) become new. Even while I link elbows (with you), they are not the same as before.)

11 朕 is an omen, a sign, or a trace. There are no indications, even the subtlest, of any thing moving away from its proper time-point.

12 *Analects* 9.16, Waley, p. 142: "Once when the Master was standing by a stream, he said, Could one but go on and on like this, never ceasing night and day." William Edward Soothill, (*The Analects of Confucius*, London, Oxford University Press, 1937), p. 86: "All is transient, like this! Unceasing day and night."

13 *Chuang-tzŭ* 3, 2A.3a, Legge, *The Texts of Taoism* I, 199. See Doc. 4, n. 49.

14 T XV, 451c25.

15 T XXV, 427b4 and 428a12.

16 *Chuang-tzŭ* 6, 3A.11a, Legge, *The Texts of Taoism* I, 242.

17 *Analects* 9.16. See n. 12.

18 *Chuang-tzŭ* 6, 3A.11a, Legge, *The Texts of Taoism* I, 242 (see n. 16): "The strong man is change, which incessantly renews all things. The mountain is changed daily, yet people regard it as it was before. The former 'I' is not the present 'I.' 'I' and the present go away together. How can one preserve the past forever? Yet none in the world is aware of it. They perversely maintain that what is met in the present can continue in existence. Are they not indeed in the dark?" (periphrastic resumé of Kuo Hsiang's commentary on this passage)

19 For those whose notions are fixed on the existent, the Buddha declares the teaching of motion. For those whose notions are fixed on inexistence, he declares the doctrine of stillness (Yüan-k'ang, p. 169c8). Yüan-k'ang seems to have these two statements crossed. Motion should be the counteragent for notions of inexistence, and stillness for notions of existence.

20 *Lalitavistara*, T 186, III, 527c22. The first half of the quotation is a phrase from the *Tao-te-ching* 78, dubbed in by the translators. It is not found in the T'ang translation of the *Lalitavistara*, T 187, III, 604a24. Liebenthal, *Chao*, p. 53, n. 168, gives the *Tao-te-ching* as the source of the first four characters. *Jōron Kenkyū*, p. 95, n. 48, correctly identifies the whole quotation. See Demiéville's review of *Jōron Kenkyū*, p. 229.

Yüan-k'ang, p. 170a10, refers to the *Chung-pen-ch'i-ching*, T 196, where a similar passage is to be found. See T IV, 160a11–13.

21 *Tao-te-ching* 64.

22 *Analects* 9.18.

23 This is probably an allusion to *Saddharma-puṇḍarīka*, ch. 16, T 262, IX, 43c3–12. *Jōron Kenkyū*, p. 95, n. 53, refers to sections on the 'three catastrophes' in the *Dīrgha-āgama*, T I, 137b, and the *Ta-lou-t'an-ching*, T 23, I, 305a. The 'three catastrophes' are fire, flood, and hurricane.

24 Compare the concluding sentence of *Emptiness of the Non-Absolute* (*Chao-lun*, part II, Doc. 9).

Bibliography

Index

Bibliography

Allen, W. S. "Relationship in Comparative Linguistics," *Transactions of the Philological Society* (1953), pp. 52–108.

Bagchi, Prabodh Chandra. *Le canon bouddhique en Chine*, vol. I. Paris: Geuthner, 1927.

Bareau, André. *Les sectes bouddhiques du Petit Véhicule*, Bulletin de l'École Française d'Extrême Orient. Saigon, 1955.

Beal, Samuel. *Buddhism in China.* London: Society for Promoting Christian Knowledge, 1884.

Bhattacharya, Vidhushekhara. *The Catuḥśataka of Āryadeva.* Calcutta: Visva-Bharati Bookshop, 1931.

Brough, John. "Some Indian Theories of Meaning," *Transactions of the Philological Society* (1953), pp. 161–76.

Buston, Rin-chen-grub-pa. *History of Buddhism* (E. Obermiller, trans.). Heidelberg: Harrassowitz, 1931–32.

Butler, Cuthbert. *Western Mysticism.* London: Constable, 1927.

Chao, Yuen-ren. "The Non-Uniqueness of Phonemic Solutions of Phonetic Systems," *Bulletin of the Institute of History and Philology*, vol. IV, no. 4 (Academia Sinica, 1934); reprinted in *Readings in Linguistics*, pp. 38-54, Washington: American Council of Learned Societies, 1957.

Chavannes, Édouard. *Les Mémoires Historiques*, tome II. Paris: Leroux, 1897.

Ch'en, Kenneth. "Anti-Buddhist Propaganda during the Nan-ch'ao," *Harvard Journal of Asian Studies* (1952), pp. 166–96.

———. "On Some Factors Responsible for the Anti-Buddhist Persecution under the Pei-ch'ao," *Harvard Journal of Asian Studies* (1954), pp. 261–73.

Conze, Edward (ed.). *Buddhist Texts through the Ages.* Oxford: Cassirer, 1954.

Dasgupta, Surendranath. *A History of Indian Philosophy*, vol. I. London: Cambridge University Press, 1922.

De Jong, Jan W. *Cinq chapitres de la Prasannapadā.* Paris: Geuthner, 1949.

———. "Le problème de l'absolu dans l'école mādhyamika," *Revue philosophique* CXL (1950), 322–27.

Demiéville, Paul. "Le miroir spirituel," *Sinologica* I (Basel, 1947), ii.

———. Review of Lamotte's *Traité*, tome II, *Journal Asiatique* (1950), pp. 375–95.

———. *Le concile de Lhasa.* Paris: Presses Universitaires de France, 1952.

———. *La Yogācārabhūmi de Saṅgharakṣa*, Bulletin de l'École Française d'Extrême Orient, XLIV, no. 2 (Saigon, 1954), 339–436.

———. "Enigmes Taoistes," *Jinbun Kagaku Kenkyusyo* (Kyoto University), Silver Jubilee vol. (1954), 54–60.

———. "La pénétration du bouddhisme dans la tradition philosophique chinoise," *Cahiers d'histoire mondiale,* III, no. 1 (1956), 1–38.

———. Review of *Jōron Kenkyū*, *T'oung-pao* XLV, nos. 1–3 (1957), 220–235.

Edgerton, Franklin. *Buddhist Hybrid Sanskrit Dictionary.* New Haven: Yale University Press, 1953.

Eon Kenkyū. See Kimura, Eiichi.

Faddegon, B. "The Vaiçeṣika System," *Verhandelingen der Koninklijke Akademie van Wetenschappen te Amsterdam*, Afdeling Letterkunde, Nieuwe Reeks, XVIII, no. 2 (1918), 1–614.

Firth, J. R. "A Synopsis of Linguistic Theory, 1930–1955," *Studies in Linguistic Analysis*, *Transactions of the Philological Society*, special vol. (1957).

Frauwallner, Erich. *On the Date of the Buddhist Master of the Law Vasubandhu.* Rome: Istituto Italiano per il Medio ed Estremo Oriente, 1951.

Gard, R. A. "On the Authenticity of the Pai-lun and the Shih-erh-men-lun," *Indogaku Bukkyōgaku Kenkyū,* II, no. 2 (1954), 751–742.

———. "On the Authenticity of the Chung-lun," *Indogaku Bukkyōgaku Kenkyū,* III, no. 1 (1954), 376–370.

Gernet, Jacques. *Les aspects économiques du bouddhisme dans la société chinoise du Ve au Xe siècle,* Bulletin de l'École Française d'Extrême Orient. Saigon, 1956.

Gokhale, V. V. "Der Sanskrit-Text von Nāgārjuna's Pratītyasamutpādahṛdayakārikā," *Festschrift für W. Kirfel* (Bonn, 1955), pp. 101–6.

Hastings. *See* La Vallée Poussin, "Madhyamaka."

Hatani Ryōtai. *Kokuyaku Issaikyō.* Chūkanbu, I.

Hayashiya Tomojirō. "Shutsu-sanzō-kishū," *Kokuyaku Issaikyō*, Shidenbu, I.

Hikata Ryūshō. *Suvikrāntavikrāmi-paripṛcchā Prajñāpāramitā-sūtra.* Fukuoka: Kyushu University, 1958.

Hilbert D. and W. Ackermann. *Principles of Mathematical Logic.* New York: Chelsea, 1950.

Hill, Archibald A. *Introduction to Linguistic Structures.* New York: Harcourt, Brace, 1957.

Hirakawa, Akira. "Jūjūbibasha-ron no chosha ni tsuite," *Indogaku Bukkyōgaku Kenkyū,* V, no. 2 (1957), 504–9.

Hōbōgirin, fascicule annexe, Tables du Taishō Issaikyō. Rédacteur en chef, Paul Demiéville. Tokyo: Maison Franco-Japonaise, 1931.

Horner, Isaline Blew. The collection of the middle length sayings *(Majjhima-nikāya)*, vol. I, The first fifty discourses. London, Luzac (for Pali Text Society), 1954.

Huang Ch'an-hua. *Chung-kuo Fo-chiao-shih* (History of Chinese Buddhism). Shanghai: Commercial Press, 1940.

Hurvitz, Leon. "'Render unto Caesar' in Early Chinese Buddhism," *Liebenthal Festschrift* (Santiniketan, 1957), pp. 80–114.

Hu Shih. "The Indianization of China: A Case Study in Cultural Borrowing," *Independence, Convergence and Borrowing*, pp. 219–47. Cambridge: Harvard University Press, 1937.

I-ching, Wang-han-chu. Ssŭ-pu-pei-yao, case 1.

Idzumi, Hōkei. "Vimalakīrti's Discourse on Emancipation (Vimalakīrti-Sūtra)," *Eastern Buddhist* (1922–28), II, 358–66; III, 55–69, 138–53, 224–42, 336–49; IV, 48–55, 177–90, 348–66.

Ingalls, Daniel H. H. "The Comparison of Indian and Western Philosophy," *Journal of Oriental Research*, XXII, nos. 1–4 (Madras, 1954), 1–11.

———. "Śaṁkara on the Question: Whose is avidyā?" *Philosophy East and West*, III, no. 1 (1953), 69–72.

Itano Chōhachi. "Eon, Sōjō no shinmeikan wo ronjite, Dōshō no shinsetsu ni oyobu," *Tōyō Gakuhō*, XXX, no. 4 (1944), 1–59.

Johnston, E. H. *Early Sāṁkhya*. London: Royal Asiatic Society, 1937.

Johnston, E. H. and Arnold Kunst. "The Vigrahavyāvartanī of Nāgārjuna," *Mélanges chinois et bouddhiques*, IX (1951), 1–54.

Jōron Kenkyū. *See* Tsukamoto Zenryū.

Jung Chao-tsu. *Wei-Chin ti Tzŭ-jan-chu-i*. Shanghai: Commercial Press, 1935.

Karlgren, Bernhard. "Grammata Serica," *Bulletin of the Museum of Far Eastern Antiquities*, no. 12 (Stockholm, 1940).

Kasugai, Shinya. "Rajū sanzō no *abidaruma*-gaku" (The *Abhidharma*-Study of Kumārajīva), *Indogaku Bukkyōgaku Kenkyū*, II, no. 2 (1954), 687–99.

Keith, Arthur Berridale. *Indian Logic and Atomism*. London: Oxford University Press, 1921.

Kern, H. "The Saddharma-puṇḍarīka," *Sacred Books of the East*, vol. XXI.

Kern, H., Hendrik, and Nanjio Bunyiu (eds.). "The Saddharmapuṇḍarīka, Sanskrit Text," *Bibliotheca Buddhica* (St. Petersburg, 1908–12).

Kimura, Eiichi (ed.). *Eon Kenkyū* (Studies on Hui-yüan, Texts and Translations). Ibunhen: Sōbunsha, 1960.

Kokuyaku Issaikyō. Iwano Masao (ed.). Tokyo: Daitō Shuppan, indo senjutsubu, 156 vols., 1928–36; wakan senjutsubu, 66 vols., 1936–45.

Kuo Hsiang. *See* Liu Wen-tien.

Lamotte, Étienne. *Le traité de la grande vertu de sagesse*, vol. I, 1944; vol. II, 1949. Louvain: Bureaux du Muséon.

———. *L'enseignement de Vimalakīrti.* Louvain: Bibliothèque du Muséon, 1962.

La Vallée Poussin, Louis de. *Mūlamadhyamakakārikās de Nāgārjuna avec la Prasannapadā de Candrakīrti* (*Bibliotheca Buddhica*, vol. IV). St. Petersberg: Imperial Academy of Sciences, 1913.

———. *L'Abhidharmakośa de Vasubandhu.* Paris: Geuthner, 1923–31.

———. "Madhyamaka," *Encyclopaedia of Religion and Ethics*, James Hastings (ed.), vol. VIII. Edinburgh: T. & T. Clark; New York: C. Scribner's Sons, 1916.

———. "Réflexions sur le Madhyamaka," *Mélanges chinois et bouddhiques*, II (1932–33), 4–59.

———. "L'auteur du Joyau dans la main," *Mélanges chinois et bouddhiques*, II (1932–33), 60–67.

———. *La Siddhi de Hiuen-tsang.* Paris: Geuthner, 1928–48.

———. *Nirvāṇa.* Paris: G. Beauchesne, 1925.

Legge, James. "The Yi King," *Sacred Books of the East*, vol. XVI.

———. *The Sacred Books of China: The Texts of Taoism*, I: "Kwang-tsze," books I–XVII; II: "Kwang-tsze," books XVIII–XXXIII.

———. *The Four Books* (re *Analects*), pirate edition (no date).

———. *The Chinese Classics*, vol. V, part 2 (translation of Tso-chuan). New York: Hurd and Houghton, 5 vols., 1893–95.

Lévi, Sylvain. "Le 'Tokharien B,' langue de Koutcha," *Journal Asiatique* no. 2 (1913), pp. 311–80.

———. "Kaniṣka et Śātavāhana," *Journal Asiatique*, no. 1 (1936), pp. 61–121.

Liebenthal, Walter. *Satkārya in der Darstellung seiner Buddhistischen Gegner.* Stuttgart: Kohlhammer, 1934.

———. *The Book of Chao.* Peking: Catholic University Press, 1948.

———. "Shih Hui-yüan's Buddhism," *Journal of the American Oriental Society* (1950), pp. 243–59.

———. "The Immortality of the Soul in Chinese Thought," *Monumenta Nipponica*, VIII (1952), 327–97.

———. "A Biography of Chu Tao-sheng," *Monumenta Nipponica*, XI, no. 3 (1955), 64–96.

———. "The World Conception of Chu Tao-sheng," *Monumenta Nipponica*, XII, nos. 3–4 (1956), 65–103, 241–68.

———. "Note on the Vajrasamādhi," *T'oung-pao*, vol. LXIV (1956).

Link, Arthur E. "Shyh Daw-an's Preface to Saṅgharakṣa's Yōgācārabhūmisūtra," *Journal of the American Oriental Society* (1957), pp. 1–14.

———. "Biography of Shih Tao-an," *T'oung-pao* XLVI, no. 1 (1958), 1–48.

———. Review of Hurvitz's *Wei Shou*, *Journal of the American Oriental Society* (1958), pp. 60–70.

———. "Shih Seng-yu and his Writings," *Journal of the American Oriental Society*, LXXX, no. 1 (1960), 17–43.

Liu Wen-tien. *Chuang-tzŭ-pu-cheng*. Shanghai: Commercial Press, 1947.

Lukasiewicz, Jan. *Aristotle's Syllogistic*. London: Oxford University Press, 1951.

Mahāvyutpatti, 2 vols. (R. Sakaki, ed.). Kyoto, 1916–25; reprint, Tokyo: Suzuki Gakujutsu Zaidan, 1962.

Majjhima-nikāya, vol. I (V. Trenckner, ed.). London: Oxford University Press; first published, 1888; reprinted, 1948.

Mano Shōjun. *Daichidoron*, *Kokuyaku Issaikyō*, Shakukyōronbu, I–V (1934).

Maspéro, H. "Sur la date et l'authenticité du Fou fa tsang yin yuan tchouan," *Mélanges Sylvain Lévi* (Paris, 1911), pp. 129–49.

Matsumoto, Tokumyō. *Die Prajñā-paramitā-Literatur*. Stuttgart: Kohlhammer, 1932.

May, Jacques. "Recherches sur un système de philosophie bouddhique," *Bulletin annuel de la Fondation suisse*, III (Paris, 1954), 21–43.

———. "La philosophie bouddhique de la vacuité," *Studia Philosophica*, XVIII (1958), 123–37.

———. "Kant et le Mādhyamika," *Indo-Iranian Journal*, III (1959), 102–11.

———. *Prasannapadā Madhyamakavṛtti, douze chapitres traduits du sanscrit et du tibétain*. Paris: Adrien-Maisonneuve, 1959.

Mitra, Rajendralal (ed.). *Ashtasāhasrikā*. Calcutta: The Asiatic Society, 1888.

Miyaji Kakue. "A Viewpoint on the Textual Criticism of the Ta-chih-tu-lun," *Ryūkoku Daigaku Ronsō*, no. 304 (October, 1932), pp. 514–42. (This article is known to me only from the reference on p. 385, n. 4, of Demiéville's review of *Traité*.)

Miyamoto Shōson. *Chūdō Shisō oyobi sono Hattatsu*. Kyoto: Hōzōkan, 1944.

Mochizuki Shinkō. *Bukkyō Dainempyō*. Tokyo: Sekai-seiten-kankō-kyōkai, first ed., 1909; revised ed., 1956.

———. *Bukkyō Daijiten*. Kyoto: Hōzōkan, 1931–32.

———. *Bukkyō Kyōten Seiritsu Shiron*. Kyoto: Hōzōkan, 1946.

Murti, T. R. V. *The Central Philosophy of Buddhism*. London: Allen and Unwin, 1955.

Nagao, Gadjin. "An Interpretation of the Term 'Saṁvṛti' (Convention) in Buddhism," *Jinbun Kagaku Kenkyusyo* (Kyoto University), Silver Jubilee vol. (1954), 550–61.

Nobel, Johannes. "Kumārajīva," *Sitzungsberichte der Preussischen Akademie der Wissenschaften*, Philosophisch-Historische klasse (Berlin, 1927), pp. 206–33.

Obermiller, E. "The Doctrine of Prajñā-pāramitā as Exposed in the Abhisamayālaṁkāra of Maitreya," *Acta Orientalia,* XI (1933), 1–33.
Ōchō Enichi. "Shaku Dōan no Honyakuron" (On Dōan's Understanding for Translations of Buddhist Texts), *Indogaku Bukkyōgaku Kenkyū,* V, no. 2 (1957), 448–58.
———. *Chūgoku Bukkyō no Kenkyū.* Kyoto: Hōzōkan, 1958.
———. "Kumarajū no honyaku" (Kumārajīva's translation), *Ōtani Daigaku Gakuhō,* XXXVII, no. 4 (1958), 1–25.
Oda Tokunō. *Bukkyō Daijiten,* twelfth ed. Tokyo: Ōkura Shoten, 1929.
Otto, Rudolf. *The Idea of the Holy* (John W. Harvey, trans.). London: Oxford University Press, 1924.
———. *Mysticism East and West* (Bertha L. Bracey and Richenda C. Payne, trans.). New York: Macmillan, 1932.
Péri, Noel. *À propos de la date de Vasubandhu,* Bulletin de l'École Française d'Extrême Orient, XI (1911), 339–90.
Rahder, Johannes. Review of Lamotte's *Traité* , tome II, *Journal of the American Oriental Society* (1950), pp. 124–26.
Régamey, Constantin. "Le problème du bouddhisme primitif et les derniers travaux de Stanislaw Schayer," *Rocznik Orjentalistyczny,* XXI (Kraków, Lwów, Warszawa 1957), 37–58.
Robinson, Richard H. "Life of a Modern Zen Master," *Middle Way* (London, Winter, 1951), pp. 98–101.
———. *Chinese Buddhist Verse.* London: John Murray, 1954.
———. "Some Logical Aspects of Nāgārjuna's System," *Philosophy East and West* (January 1957), pp. 291–308.
———. "Mysticism and Logic in Seng-chao's Thought," *Philosophy East and West,* VIII, nos. 3 and 4 (1958–59), 99–120.
Russell, Bertrand. *Mysticism and Logic.* Harmondsworth: Penguin Books, 1953.
———. *Logic and Knowledge.* London: Allen and Unwin, 1956.
Sacred Books of the Buddhists, vol. IV, Dialogues of the Buddha (T. W. and C. A. F. Rhys Davids, eds.). London: Oxford University Press, 1921.
Sakaino Kōyō. *Shina Bukkyō Seishi (History).* Tokyo: Sakaino Ikō Kankai, 1935.
Sapir, Edward. *Culture, Language and Personality.* Berkeley: University of California Press, 1957.
Schayer, Stanislaw. *Ausgewählte Kapitel aus der Prasannapadā.* Krakow: Naktadem Polskiej Akademji Umiętetności, 1931.
———. "Altindische Antizipationen der Aussagenlogik," *Bulletin de l'Académie Polonaise, classe de philologie* (1933), pp. 90–96.
———. "Das mahāyānistische Absolutum nach der Lehre der Mādhyamikas," *Orientalische Literaturzeitung* (1935), pp. 401–15.
Shan-tao-ssŭ. *See Yüan-shih* . . . .
Ssŭ-ma Ch'ien. *Shih-chi,* Ssŭ-pu-pei-yao, case 32.
Stael-Holstein, A. von. *The Kāçyapa-parivarta.* Shanghai: Commercial Press, 1926.

Stcherbatsky, Theodore. *The Central Conception of Busshism*. London: Royal Asiatic Society, 1923.

———. *The Conception of Buddhist Nirvāṇa*. Leningrad: Office of the Academy of Sciences of the U.S.S.R., 1927.

Suzuki, D. T. *Studies in the Laṅkāvatāra Sūtra*. London: Routledge, 1930.

———. *The Laṅkāvatāra Sūtra*. London: Routledge, 1932.

———. "Reason and Intuition in Buddhist Philosophy," *Essays in East-West Philosophy* (Charles A. Moore, ed.). Honolulu: University of Hawaii Press, 1951.

———. *Zen Buddhism* (includes "Existentialism, Pragmatism and Zen"). New York: Doubleday (Anchor Books), 1956.

Taishō Shinshū Daizōkyō. Takakusu Junjirō and Watanabe Kaikyoku (eds.), 100 vols. Tokyo, Daizō Shuppan Company, 1924–34.

T'ang Yung-t'ung. *Han-wei-liang-chin-nan-pei-ch'ao-fo-chiao-shih* (History of Buddhism in Han, Wei, the Two Chins, and Northern and Southern Dynasties). Shanghai: Commercial Press, 1938.

———. "On 'Ko-Yi,' the Earliest Method by which Indian Buddhism and Chinese Thought were Synthesized" (M. C. Rogers, trans.), *Radhakrishnan Festschrift: Comparative Studies in Philosophy Presented in Honour of his Sixtieth Birthday*, pp. 276–86. London: Allen and Unwin, 1951.

———. "Wang Pi's New Interpretation of the I Ching and Lun-yü" (Walter Liebenthal, trans.), *Harvard Journal of Asian Studies* (1947), pp. 124–61.

Trenckner. *See Majjhima-nikāya.*

Tsukamoto Zenryū. "The Dates of Kumarajīva and Seng-chao Reexamined," *Jinbun Kagaku Kenkyusyo* (Kyoto University), Silver Jubilee vol. (1954), 568–84.

———. "Kumarajū no katsudō nendai ni tsuite," *Indogaku Bukkyōgaku Kenkyū* III, no. 2 (1955), 606–8.

———. *Jōron Kenkyū*. Kyoto: Hōzōkan, 1955.

Tucci, Giuseppe. *Pre-Diṅnāga Buddhist Texts on Logic from Chinese Sources*. Baroda: Gaekwad's Oriental Series, no. 49, 1929.

———. *Minor Buddhist Texts*, part 1. Rome: Istituto Italiano per il Medio ed Estremo Oriente, 1956.

Ui, Hakuju. *The Vaiśesika Philosophy*. London: Royal Asiatic Society, 1917.

———. *Shaku Dōan no Kenkyū*. Tokyo: Iwanami, 1956.

Vaidya, P. L. *Études sur Āryadeva et son Catuḥśataka*. Paris: Geuthner, 1923.

Vidyabhusana, Satischandra. *The Nyāya Sūtras of Gotama*. Allahabad: Lalit Mohan Basu, 1930.

Waley, Arthur. "New Light on Buddhism in Medieval India," *Mélanges chinois et bouddhiques*, I (1931–32), 335–76.

———. *The Way and Its Power (Tao Te Ching)*. London: Allen and Unwin, 1934.

———. *The Analects of Confucius.* London: Allen and Unwin, 1938.
———. *The Real Tripitaka.* London: Allen and Unwin, 1952.
———. Review of *Jōron Kenkyū*, *Bulletin of the School of Oriental and African Studies*, XIX (London, 1957), pp. 194–96.
Walleser, Max. *Die Mittlere Lehre Nāgārjuna's.* Heidelberg: Carl Winters, Universitätsbuchhandel, 1911 and 1912.
———. "The Life of Nāgārjuna from Tibetan and Chinese Sources," *Asia Major*, Hirth Anniversary vol. (London, 1922), 421–55.
Watters, Thomas. *On Yuan-Chwang's Travels in India.* London: Royal Asiatic Society, 1904.
Whitehead, A. N. *Process and Reality.* New York: Macmillan, 1929.
Wilhelm, Richard. *I Ging, Das Buch der Wandlungen.* Jena: Eugen Diederich, 1923.
Winternitz, Moriz. *A History of Indian Literature* (S. Ketkar, trans.). University of Calcutta, 1927.
Wright, Arthur F. "Fo-t'u-teng: A Biography," *Harvard Journal of Asian Studies* (1948), pp. 321–71.
———. "Hui-chiao as a Chinese Historian," *Indogaku Bukkyōgaku Kenkyū*, III, no. 1 (1954), 382–377.
———. "Biography and Hagiography, Hui-chiao's Lives of Eminent Monks," *Jinbun Kagaku Kenkyusyo* (Kyoto University), Silver Jubilee vol. (1954), 383–434.
———. "The Formation of Sui Ideology," *Chinese Thought and Institutions* (J. K. Fairbank, ed.). Chicago University Press, 1957.
———. "Seng-jui alias Hui-jui: A Biographical Bisection in the Kao-seng-chuan," *Liebenthal Festschrift* (Santiniketan, 1957), pp. 272–92.
Yamaguchi Susumu. "Pour écarter les vaines discussions" (translation of the *Vigraha-vyāvartanī*), *Journal Asiatique* (1929), pp. 1–86.
Yüan-shih Ta-ch'eng Yao-i Wen-ta [Hui-yüan's Questions and Kumārajīva's Answers about the Essential Ideas of the Mahāyāna] (Edition of *Ta-ch'eng-ta-i-chang*). Taipei, Formosa: Ching-t'u-tsung Shan-tao-ssŭ Press, 1955.
Yūki Reimon. "Sanron-genryū-kō," *Indogaku Bukkyōgaku Kenkyū* I, no. 2 (1953), 396–97.
Zürcher, E. *The Buddhist Conquest of China.* Leiden: E. J. Brill, 1959.

INDEX